SPONSORED BY

Katie Shu Sui Pui Charitable Trust

（本系列丛书由舒小佩慈善基金赞助）

|酒店及旅游业管理系列教材|

主编 邱汉琴

THE HONG KONG
POLYTECHNIC UNIVERSITY
香港理工大学

Hospitality and Tourism Marketing Management

酒店及旅游业市场营销

李咪咪（Mimi Li）徐惠群（Cathy Hsu）/著

ZHEJIANG UNIVERSITY PRESS
浙江大学出版社

图书在版编目(CIP)数据

酒店及旅游业市场营销 = Hospitality and Tourism Marketing Management：英汉对照 / 李咪咪，徐惠群著．—杭州：浙江大学出版社，2019.5(2022.10重印)

ISBN 978-7-308-18454-0

Ⅰ．①酒… Ⅱ．①李…②徐… Ⅲ．①饭店—市场营销学—双语教学—高等学校—教材—英、汉②旅游市场—市场营销学—双语教学—高等学校—教材—英、汉 Ⅳ．①F719.2②F590.82

中国版本图书馆 CIP 数据核字（2018）第 170482 号

酒店及旅游业市场营销

Hospitality and Tourism Marketing Management

李咪咪（Mimi Li）　著　徐惠群（Cathy Hsu）

责任编辑	曾　熙
责任校对	袁菁鸿
封面设计	春天书装
出版发行	浙江大学出版社
	（杭州市天目山路 148 号　邮政编码 310007）
	（网址：http://www.zjupress.com）
排　　版	杭州林智广告有限公司
印　　刷	杭州杭新印务有限公司
开　　本	787mm×1092mm　1/16
印　　张	27.75
字　　数	539 千
版 印 次	2019 年 5 月第 1 版　2022 年 10 月第 3 次印刷
书　　号	ISBN 978-7-308-18454-0
定　　价	73.00 元

浙江大学出版社市场运营中心邮购电话：(0571) 88925591；http://zjdxcbs.tmall.com

总　序

　　香港理工大学酒店及旅游业管理学院已经有40多年的历史。学院致力于引领全球酒店及旅游教育的发展，无论在科研还是教学等方面，都在全球享有较高知名度，尤其是在发表学术研究文献方面，在全球位列第二，在教与学方面，亦处于国际领先地位。学院65位教职人员来自22个国家和地区，着重教学创新与研究。学员能够在多元文化环境下追随国际知名的学者学习有着良好职业前景的学科。2011年，香港理工大学的教学及研究酒店——唯港荟正式启用，强化了学院的人才培育工作，以满足香港地区内以至全球酒店及旅游业界对专业人才的殷切需求。

　　"酒店及旅游业管理硕士学位课程"是引进了国际、国内最前沿的教育理念，为从事旅游业研究与实践的业界人士而开设的学历教育课程。该课程自2000年与浙江大学合办以来，依托世界一流的香港理工大学和浙江大学的教学资源，已经培养了600多位政府各级官员、业界管理人才以及学术界科研精英。课程通过综合的、先进的知识为学生提供了宏观的视野，让学生在具有扎实的工作经验的基础上，提高经营管理的深度，建立超前的意识，发展系统地解决问题的能力。

　　虽然香港理工大学酒店及旅游业管理学院的酒店及旅游业管理硕士学位课程取得了一定的成功，为业界培养了优秀人才，但是在办学的过程中，我们深刻地意识到教材资源的缺乏。因此，香港理工大学具有优秀双语能力的教授等师资人员专门为"酒店及旅游业管理硕士学位课程"设计

Prelude

With more than 40 years' history, the School of Hotel and Tourism Management (SHTM) at The Hong Kong Polytechnic University (PolyU) is positioned to lead the world's hospitality and tourism education in the years to come. It has high reputation in both academic research and teaching. Especially, the School is ranked No. 2 in the world among academic institutions in hospitality and tourism based on research and scholarly activities. In terms of teaching and learning, it is also in a leading position. With a faculty of 65 academic staff members from 22 countries and regions, the School offers innovative teaching and research in a creative learning environment. Students are able to study in a multicultural context and to learn from an internationally renowned faculty whose programmes provide outstanding career opportunities. The official opening of the teaching and research hotel—Hotel ICON in 2011 has further strengthened the School's efforts in nurturing hospitality graduates to address the growing demands of the hospitality and tourism industry in Hong Kong, the region, and around the world.

The MSc in Hotel and Tourism Management is a programme designed for hotel and tourism practitioners, with the aim of introducing latest education concept in Hong Kong and internationally. Since 2000, the programme has been offered collaboratively by the Hong Kong Polytechnic University and Zhejiang University, which has cultivated more than 600 government officials, industry managers, and academic talents. The programme provides students with a macro perspective from the comprehensive and advanced knowledge, improves the ability of management, and establishes advanced awareness, as well as develops systematic problem-solving skills based on solid work experience.

Although the programme of MSc in Hotel and Tourism Management offered by SHTM-PolyU has been highly successful and has cultivated many talents for the industry, we are fully aware of the lack of bilingual teaching and learning resources during the process of delivering these courses. Therefore, professors, who have excellent bilingual competencies from The Hong Kong Polytechnic

了一套中英文对照双语教材——"酒店及旅游业管理系列教材"。本系列教材包括《中国内地酒店及旅游业》《酒店及旅游业人力资源管理》《酒店及旅游业财务管理》《酒店及旅游业研究方法》以及《酒店及旅游业市场营销》。这种双语式的硕士学位课程教材在酒店及旅游业管理专业的研究生教育历史上是具有开创性的，充分体现了我们开办该课程的特色与进一步构建更好的教学交流平台的愿望。该系列教材的开发和推出，将有力地促进香港理工大学与浙江大学的双语课程的持续发展。同时，我们也期待该系列教材可以有助于中国内地日益成熟的旅游管理学硕士（MTA）市场的发展。中国的各行各业已逐渐趋向于国际化，旅游教育更是如此，我们希望这套双语教材的问世将会对内地的旅游教育起到促进作用。

最后，作者要特别感谢舒小佩慈善基金的全力资助，该基金的慷慨资助使得本系列教材得以面世。舒小佩女士寄语并祝福每位读者都能在书中找到自己的"黄金屋"，并为响应国家的"一带一路"倡议做出最好的准备。

丛书总编

邱汉琴教授

香港理工大学酒店及旅游业管理学院

University, have designed and developed this bilingual book series for this programme, including *Hospitality and Tourism in Chinese Mainland*, *Hospitality and Tourism Human Resource Management*, *Hospitality and Tourism Financial Management*, *Hospitality and Tourism Research Methods*, and *Hospitality and Tourism Marketing Management*. The uniqueness of this bilingual book series is that it is the first time that such book series were created for a bilingual master degree in hotel and tourism education history, which fully represents the characteristics of this programme and also acts as an interaction platform for students and teachers to interact in order to enhance the teaching and learning experiences. The development and introduction of the bilingual book series is not only to promote the sustainable development of bilingual programme offered by The Hong Kong Polytechnic University and Zhejiang University, but also to look forward to facilitating the development of the increasingly mature market of Master of Tourism Administration (MTA) in Chinese Mainland. Nowadays, various industries in China have been gradually internationalized and we hope that the introduction of the bilingual book series will play a significant role in enhancing tourism education in the Mainland.

Last but not least, the authors wish to express their sincere gratitude to the Katie Shu Sui Pui Charitable Trust for its financial support in making the project of publishing of the Bilingual Hotel and Tourism Management Book Series a reality. They also hereby acknowledge Ms. Shu's wish for each reader to find his/her own dream career by making the best use of the material in the book series in preparation for China's Belt and Road Initiative as a result.

Managing Editor
Hanqin Qiu
Professor
School of Hotel and Tourism Management
The Hong Kong Polytechnic University

C ONTENTS
目　录

第1章　酒店与旅游业营销管理概述 ………………………… 1

1.1　营销及营销管理 ………………………………………… 1

1.2　酒店与旅游业的服务特征与营销管理 ………………… 7

1.3　一些基本概念 …………………………………………… 11

第2章　营销管理战略的制定与实施 ………………………… 15

2.1　营销及顾客价值 ………………………………………… 15

2.2　服务企业管理战略 ……………………………………… 23

2.3　企业层级营销战略 ……………………………………… 27

2.4　业务单元层级营销战略 ………………………………… 37

第3章　市场营销信息与调研 ………………………………… 47

3.1　营销信息系统 …………………………………………… 47

3.2　营销研究 ………………………………………………… 51

3.3　营销调研过程 …………………………………………… 59

3.4　营销生产力评估 ………………………………………… 71

3.5　市场需求预测 …………………………………………… 73

第4章　消费者市场 …………………………………………… 85

4.1　消费者行为及其影响因素 ……………………………… 85

4.2　消费者主要心理过程 …………………………………… 105

C ONTENTS
目 录

Chapter 1　Overview of Hotel and Tourism Marketing Management ·················· 2

　1.1　Marketing and Marketing Management ··························· 2

　1.2　Hospitality and Tourism Service Features and Marketing Management ······ 8

　1.3　Basic Concepts ························· 12

Chapter 2　Formulation and Implementation of Marketing Management Strategy ··· 16

　2.1　Marketing and Customer Value ····················· 16

　2.2　Service Business Management Strategy ··················· 24

　2.3　Organizational Levels of Marketing Strategy ··············· 28

　2.4　Business Unit Level Marketing Strategy ················· 38

Chapter 3　Marketing Information and Research ················· 48

　3.1　Marketing Information System ··················· 48

　3.2　Marketing Research ······················ 52

　3.3　Marketing Research Process ··················· 60

　3.4　Measuring Marketing Productivity ················· 72

　3.5　Forecasting Market Demand ··················· 74

Chapter 4　Consumer Markets ······················ 86

　4.1　Consumer Behavior and Its Influencing Factors ··············· 86

　4.2　Major Psychological Processes of Consumers ················ 106

第5章　企业市场 ……………………………………………… 115

　　5.1　企业市场特征 ………………………………………… 115

　　5.2　企业购买过程 ………………………………………… 121

　　5.3　旅游企业的主要企业市场 …………………………… 125

　　5.4　企业顾客关系维护 …………………………………… 133

第6章　市场差异化及定位 …………………………………… 141

　　6.1　市场细分的原则和类型 ……………………………… 143

　　6.2　市场细分的层级 ……………………………………… 153

　　6.3　目标市场选择 ………………………………………… 157

第7章　品牌战略管理 ………………………………………… 167

　　7.1　品牌及品牌化 ………………………………………… 167

　　7.2　目的地的品牌化 ……………………………………… 173

　　7.3　品牌资产管理 ………………………………………… 179

　　7.4　品牌塑造策略 ………………………………………… 185

第8章　产品开发及管理 ……………………………………… 195

　　8.1　旅游产品的组成 ……………………………………… 195

　　8.2　产品生命周期 ………………………………………… 205

　　8.3　旅游目的地生命周期 ………………………………… 213

　　8.4　新产品开发 …………………………………………… 217

第9章　价格与定价 …………………………………………… 229

　　9.1　旅游产品定价概论 …………………………………… 229

　　9.2　价格制定的影响因素 ………………………………… 233

　　9.3　旅游产品定价方法 …………………………………… 253

第10章　分销渠道 …………………………………………… 271

　　10.1　分销渠道的基本概念 ……………………………… 271

Chapter 5   Business markets ·· 116

   5.1   Characteristics of Business Markets ·· 116

   5.2   Business Buying Process ··· 122

   5.3   Major Business Markets for Tourism Enterprises ························ 126

   5.4   Business-to-Business Customer Relationship Maintenance ·········· 134

Chapter 6   Market Differentiation and Positioning ·································· 142

   6.1   Bases and Types for Market Segmentation ·································· 142

   6.2   Levels of Market Segmentation ··· 154

   6.3   Target Market Selection ··· 158

Chapter 7   Strategic Brand Management ··· 168

   7.1   Brand and Branding ··· 168

   7.2   Destination Branding ··· 174

   7.3   Managing and Measuring Brand Equity ······································· 180

   7.4   Branding Strategies ··· 186

Chapter 8   Product Development and Management ·································· 196

   8.1   Components of Tourism Products ·· 196

   8.2   Product Life Cycle ··· 206

   8.3   Tourism Destination Life Cycle ··· 214

   8.4   New Product Development ··· 218

Chapter 9   Price and Pricing ··· 230

   9.1   Introduction to Tourism Product Pricing ····································· 230

   9.2   Factors Affecting Pricing ·· 234

   9.3   Pricing Methods for Tourism Products ··· 254

Chapter 10   Distribution Channels ·· 272

   10.1   Basic Concepts of Distribution Channels ···································· 272

10.2　旅游企业分销渠道 ··· 279

10.3　酒店分销体系 ··· 287

10.4　旅行社分销体系 ··· 303

10.5　分销渠道的选择和管理 ·· 307

第 11 章　营销传播 ··· 313

11.1　营销传播：概述 ··· 313

11.2　营销传播：战略 ··· 321

11.3　营销传播：广告 ··· 335

11.4　营销传播：公共关系和公众宣传 ···································· 351

11.5　营销传播：销售推广 ·· 357

11.6　营销传播：人员推销 ·· 363

11.7　营销传播：网络传播 ·· 377

第 12 章　营销规划及营销绩效评估 ·· 391

12.1　战略营销规划 ·· 391

12.2　战术营销规划 ·· 401

12.3　营销绩效评估 ·· 405

参考文献 ·· 415

10.2　Main Distribution Channels of Tourism Enterprises ·············· 280

10.3　Hotel Distribution System ···························· 288

10.4　Distribution system of travel agencies ·················· 304

10.5　Distribution Channel Selection and Management ············ 308

Chapter 11　Marketing Communications ···················· 314

11.1　Marketing Communications：Overview ················ 314

11.2　Marketing Communications：Strategy ················ 322

11.3　Marketing Communications：Advertising ·············· 336

11.4　Marketing Communications：Public Relations and Publicity ·········· 352

11.5　Marketing Communications：Sales Promotion ············ 358

11.6　Marketing Communications：Personnel Marketing ········· 364

11.7　Marketing Communications：Online Communication ········ 378

Chapter 12　Marketing Planning and Marketing Performance Evaluation ·········· 392

12.1　Strategic Marketing Planning ···················· 392

12.2　Tactical Marketing Planning ···················· 402

12.3　Marketing Performance Evaluation ················ 406

References ···································· 415

第1章　酒店与旅游业营销管理概述

 **本章要点**

- ■ 营销及营销管理的定义
- ■ 营销哲学的演变过程
- ■ 全面营销观念的要点
- ■ 酒店与旅游业服务特征
- ■ 构建营销管理框架的一些基本概念

营销在 20 世纪 50 年代逐渐成为企业中重要的职能部门及经营理念，营销学也从经济学中独立出来而成为一门独立的学科(Bartels，1983)。毋庸置疑，营销对于企业的成功发展至关重要。一个好的营销方案可以帮助企业树立品牌，维护客户关系，创造并维护企业的无形资产，而酒店与旅游行业所提供的产品的特殊性使得创造客户价值及满意度成为该行业营销的核心。本章将重点阐述营销及营销管理的概念、营销理念发展的历程、服务业的特点以及本书中将涉及的基本概念。

1.1　营销及营销管理

1.1.1　营销及营销管理的定义

美国市场营销协会(American Marketing Association，2013)对营销给出的官方定义是"营销是在创造、沟通、传播和交换产品的过程中，为顾客、客户、合作伙伴以及整个社会带来价值的一系列活动、过程和体系"。营销的概念可以从社会及管理两个层面理解(Kotler 和 Keller，2016)。从管理角度，著名管理理论家 Peter Drucker(1974)指出，大多数人认为需要对产品进行销

Chapter 1　Overview of Hotel and Tourism Marketing Management

 Key points of the chapter

- Definition of marketing and marketing management
- Evolution of marketing philosophy
- Essence of the holistic marketing concept
- Hospitality and tourism service features
- Basic concepts building the framework of marketing management

In the 1950s, marketing gradually became an important functional department and business idea in companies. Marketing became independent of economics and was regarded as a separate discipline (Bartels, 1983). Marketing is now essential to the successful development of a business. An effective marketing plan helps an enterprise to establish its brand, maintain customer relationships, and create and maintain intangible assets of the enterprise. The specific characteristics of hotel and tourism products makes the creation of customer value and satisfaction the core of marketing. This chapter focuses on the concepts of marketing and marketing management, the development of the marketing concept, and the characteristics of the service industry as well as the fundamental concepts covered in this book.

1.1　Marketing and Marketing Management

1.1.1　Definition of marketing and marketing management

The American Marketing Association (2013) defines marketing as "the activity, set of institutions, and processes for creating, communicating, delivering, and exchanging offerings that have value for customers, clients, partners, and society at large". The concept of marketing can be understood from social and management aspects (Kotler & Keller, 2016). From a management perspective, famous management theorist Peter Drucker (1974) indicates that most people believe that marketing is hinged on selling products, but the aim of marketing is to make selling superfluous. Marketing entails to fully understand customers so that companies can provide products and services that fit the exact needs of customers. Ideal marketing results in customers willing to buy.

售,但事实上营销的目的恰恰是让销售变得多余。营销是为了充分了解顾客,使得企业提供的产品和服务完全契合顾客的需求。最理想的营销是产生愿意购买的顾客,而企业所需要做的仅仅是提供相应的产品和服务。而从社会层面,Lusch 和 Webster(2013)认为,营销是一个个体和群体通过创造、提供以及自由交换产品和有价值的服务来满足其需求和欲求的社会过程。也就是说,若从社会层面来理解营销,个体之间、个人与企业共同创造并且分享价值是现代营销的核心所在。

从上述概念可以看出,营销的核心是交换,也即两个实体通过协商获得有利于自身的价值。也就是说,交换是一个产生价值的过程,而当双方达成一致时,才会产生交易。对整个交换及交易过程的管理即为营销管理。Kotler 和 Keller(2016)指出,营销管理是"选择目标市场,通过创造、传播以及沟通出众的客户价值以获取、维护以及扩大顾客群的艺术和科学"。

营销的主体和目标多种多样,交换和交易的内容也不尽相同。一般来讲,营销的对象有 10 种,包括物品、服务、体验、节事、人、地方、所有权、组织、信息/数据以及想法(Kotler 和 Keller,2016)。

(1)物品:实体产品或有形产品。绝大多数企业生产及营销的对象都是物品,如汽车、电器、罐装食物等。

(2)服务:伴随着社会经济的发展,一部分生产从有形产品转换为无形的服务。在经济发达地区,服务业对国民生产总值的贡献已超过第一产业和第二产业,成为经济发展的主要动力。服务范围广泛,包括航空公司、医院、银行、咨询公司、酒店等企业的服务。

(3)体验:通过将服务和物品精心组合而产生的体验也可以是营销的对象。如华特·迪士尼公司通过主题公园、零售商品、电影为消费者营造了一个梦幻王国的体验。

(4)节事:一次性或者循环举办的节事也可以成为营销的对象,如展销会、艺术表演、大型体育赛事以及地方性的节事等。

(5)人:艺术家、企业家、运动员等专业人士也可以是营销的对象,他们往往会寻求专业营销人员的帮助来树立自己的形象。

(6)地方:城市、地区、国家通过营销来吸引旅游者、居住者、投资者以及大企业的总部。对地方进行营销的专业人士包括经济发展专家、房地产中间商、地方商业协会以及旅游局等。

(7)所有权:所有权是指拥有有形的(如房产)或无形的(如股票)财产的权利。促进所有权的交换需要营销。

Companies only have to provide appropriate products and services. From a social perspective, Lusch and Webster (2013) believe that marketing is a social process by which individuals and communities satisfy their needs and desires by creating, offering, and freely exchanging products and services. From a social perspective, the core of modern marketing lies in co-creating and sharing values among individuals as well as between individuals and enterprises.

The core of marketing is the exchange, which implies that two entities both obtain benefits through negotiation. The exchange creates value. When two parties reach an agreement, transaction occurs. The management of exchange and transaction is referred to as marketing management. Kotler and Keller (2016) state that marketing management is "the art and science of choosing target markets and getting, keeping, and growing customers through creating, delivering, and communicating superior customer value".

The subject and target of marketing vary. The contents of exchange and transaction also differ. Marketing objects can be classified into 10 common types, namely, goods, services, experiences, events, persons, places, properties, organizations, information/ data, and ideas (Kotler & Keller, 2016).

(1) Goods: Physical or tangible products are considered goods. Majority of enterprises produce and market goods, such as cars, electrical appliances, and canned foods.

(2) Services: With economic development, production not only include tangible goods but also intangible services. In developed regions, the contribution of the service industry to gross domestic product has exceeded those of the primary and secondary industries, and the service industry has become a major force of economic development. Services provided range extensively, including airlines, hospitals, banks, consulting companies, and hotels.

(3) Experiences: As the result of orchestrating services and goods, experiences can be classified as marketing object. For example, the Walt Disney Company creates a magic kingdom experience for consumers with theme parks, retails, and movies.

(4) Events: One-off or time-based events can also be marketing object. These events include trade fairs, art shows, major sporting events, and local festivals.

(5) Persons: Artists, entrepreneurs, athletes, and other professionals also require marketing. They often seek the help of marketing professionals to establish a distinct image.

(6) Places: Cities, regions, and countries attract tourists, residents, investors, and corporate headquarters through marketing. Professionals who market places include economic development specialists, real estate agents, local business associations, and tourism bureaus.

(7) Properties: Properties refer to the ownership of tangible (e.g., real estate) and intangible (e.g., stocks) properties. The promotion of property exchange needs marketing.

（8）组织：营利性组织和非营利性组织都需要通过营销来提升其组织形象，以获得更多的资源。

（9）信息/数据：信息和数据是知识产生和商业决策的基础。例如许多酒店集团利用史密斯旅游研究公司（Smith Travel Research，STR）提供的信息进行商业决策，正如 STR 在其网站（STR，2016）上描述的："STR 和 STR Global 追踪酒店业供需数据，并为国际、区域连锁酒店和独立酒店提供有价值的市场份额分析。"

（10）想法：许多产品都有一个基本的想法或是理念，产品和服务是传递想法的平台。例如联邦快递传递的理念是"使命必达"，Airbnb 传递的理念是"欢迎回家"。

1.1.2　营销哲学的演变

营销通常会涉及多个利益相关者，各利益相关者有不同的甚至相互冲突的诉求。在这个过程中，如何平衡各利益相关者之间的关系是营销人员应该思考的基本问题，也即指导营销行动的哲学思想。营销哲学的演变经历了从生产、产品、销售、营销，到全面营销几个阶段。

（1）生产观念是一种最古老的指导哲学，这种观念认为市场会对易于获得的低价产品产生需求。在这种观念指导下的企业追逐的是生产效率最高化、成本最低化以及市场占有率最大化。发展中国家的制造业企业通常会充分利用本国的低价劳动力及地价，以生产为导向指导企业的发展。

（2）产品观念认为消费者会因为产品的质量、性能或是创新性特点而产生购买行为。持这种观点的营销人员认为"好酒不怕巷子深"，好的产品自然会吸引消费者的注意力。这一观点忽视了一个事实，也即一个新的或者改良的产品仍需通过定价、分销以及广告才能获得市场的注意并最终导致购买行为。

（3）销售观念认为营销人员必须积极主动地推销产品。尤其当营销的产品不是消费者真正需要的时候或是企业出现生产能力过剩的情况时，营销人员会对市场进行强行推销。而这种做法往往会造成顾客流失，或是产生负面的评价。

（4）营销观念出现在 20 世纪 50 年代中期，是一种以消费者为导向的哲学。在这种哲学的指导下，营销人员的工作视角发生了改变：不再是为产品寻找顾客，而是为顾客寻找合适的产品，创造顾客价值。营销观念包括被动市场导向、主动市场导向以及全面市场导向三种（Kotler 和 Keller，2016）。

（8）Organization：Both for-profit and non-profit organizations need marketing to enhance their organizational image for obtaining additional resources.

（9）Information/Data：Information and data are the bases of knowledge production and business decisions. Many hotel groups refer to the information provided by Smith Travel Research（STR）to make business decisions. STR（2016）states on its website that "STR is the source for premium global data benchmarking，analytics and marketplace insights. Our data is confidential，reliable，accurate and actionable. Our comprehensive solutions，analytics and unrivalled marketplace insights are built to fuel growth and help our clients make better business decisions."

（10）Ideas：Many companies follow a basic idea or philosophy. Products and services are platforms to convey these ideas. For example，the philosophy of FedEx Corporation is "We live to deliver，" and the idea that Airbnb capitalizes on is "Welcome home."

1.1.2 Evolution of marketing philosophy

Marketing usually involves multiple stakeholders，and these various stakeholders have different or even conflicting demands. Marketers should consider how to manage the relationship among various stakeholders during marketing. This issue also serves as the guiding philosophy of marketing. The marketing philosophy has evolved to holistic marketing through several stages，namely，production，product，selling，and marketing.

（1）The production concept is the oldest guiding philosophy. The market needs low-priced products that are easy to obtain. Companies guided by this concept strive for the highest productivity，lowest cost，and maximum market share. Manufacturing firms in developing countries often take advantage of low-cost labor and land prices to achieve production-oriented development.

（2）The product concept conveys that consumers purchase a product for its quality，performance，or innovative characteristics. Marketers holding this view believe that "good wine needs no bush"，and quality products surely attract the attention of consumers. This view ignores the fact that a new or improved product needs to be priced，distributed，and advertised properly to capture the attention of the market and ultimately lead to buying behaviors.

（3）The selling concept holds that the marketer must be proactive in selling products. Salesmen should give a hard sell especially when the marketing object is unnecessary to consumers or when companies have overcapacity. This practice often results in losing customers or producing negative comments.

（4）The marketing concept emerged in the mid-1950s as a consumer-oriented philosophy. Guided by this philosophy，marketing staff change their work perspective from finding customers for a product to searching for the right product and creating customer value. The marketing concept includes responsive，proactive，and comprehensive market orientations （Kotler & Keller，2016）. Responsive market orientation means understanding and meeting

被动市场导向是指了解并满足消费者表面需求,主动市场导向是指找出消费者的潜在需求,而全面市场导向是指同时满足表面及潜在的需求。

(5)全面营销观念产生于 21 世纪初期。这一观念认为,营销是一系列项目、过程、活动的设计和实施,涉及企业活动的方方面面,因此需要一种全局的系统的视角。Kotler 和 Keller(2016)指出全面营销包含四个部分:关系营销、整合营销、内部营销以及绩效营销。

营销的最终目的是与其目标市场建立一种长期稳定互惠的关系。关系营销即通过平衡各利益相关者之间的关系,最终建立起包含消费者、员工、分销商以及供应商的营销网络,从而产生利润。整合营销是指通过聚集各种营销计划来创造、沟通以及传递顾客价值。整合营销包含两个层面的含义:一方面是多种营销活动的整合,如广告、公共关系、直销、促销等;另一方面是营销活动与企业的其他活动的配合。内部营销作为全面营销的一部分,侧重于对员工的招聘、培训以及激励。只有当全体员工认可企业的愿景以及企业文化时,营销活动才能达到其最佳的效果。绩效营销关注营销活动的商业和非商业影响,除市场份额、顾客满意度、产品质量外,还关注营销活动的社会影响以及环境影响等。越来越多的顾客要求企业在营销时要体现其社会责任感。

1.2　酒店与旅游业的服务特征与营销管理

营销的最初的目的是销售有形产品,如汽车、牙膏、家具等。随着社会的不断发展,服务业已成为许多发达国家国民生产总值的主要来源,即使在发展中国家,服务业对国民经济的贡献也日渐显著,而酒店与旅游业已成为服务业中的重要组成部分。例如 2013 年中国的第三产业对国民生产总值的贡献首次超过第二产业(中国国家统计局统计科学研究所,2014),服务业成为国民经济的重要组成部分,旅游业的发展被纳入国家"十三五"重点专项规划中。

酒店与旅游业非常重要的任务是在企业内部自上而下地创立服务文化(Kotler、Bowen 和 Makens,2009),也即以服务及满足顾客为重心的企业文

consumer demands, whereas proactive market orientation is identifying the potential demands of consumers. Comprehensive market orientation is meeting both existing and potential demands.

(5) The holistic marketing concept originated in the early 21st century. The concept regards marketing as the design and implementation of a series of projects, processes, and activities involving all aspects of business activities. Marketing requires an overall and systematic perspective. Kotler and Keller (2016) point out that holistic marketing comprises four parts, namely, relationship marketing, integrated marketing, internal marketing, and performance marketing.

The ultimate goal of marketing is to establish a long-term, stable, and mutually beneficial relationship with the target market. Relationship marketing involves establishing a marketing network that includes consumers, employees, distributors, and suppliers by balancing the relationships among stakeholders, thereby generating profits. Integrated marketing refers to the creation, communication, and delivery of customer value by aggregating various marketing programs. Integrated marketing contains two meanings: one refers to the integration of a variety of marketing activities, such as advertising, public relations, direct marketing, and promotion, and the other is the coordination of marketing campaigns with other business activities. Internal marketing, as a part of the holistic marketing, focuses on the recruitment, training, and motivation of staff. The optimal results of marketing activities can only be achieved when all employees recognize the corporate vision and culture. Performance marketing concentrates on the commercial and non-commercial effects of marketing activities that include social and environmental effects in addition to market share, customer satisfaction, and product quality. A growing number of customers require enterprises to show their social responsibility in marketing campaigns.

1.2 Hospitality and Tourism Service Features and Marketing Management

The initial purpose of marketing is to sell tangible products, such as cars, toothpaste, and furniture, among others. With the continuous development of society, the service industry has become the main source of Gross National Product (GNP) of many developed countries. Even in developing countries, the contribution of service industry to the national economy is increasingly becoming prominent. The hotel and tourism sectors have also become an important part of the service industry. The contribution of the tertiary industry to the GNP of China exceeded that of secondary industry for the first time in 2013 (Institute of Statistical Science, National Bureau of Statistics of the People's Republic of China, 2014). The service industry has become an integral part of the national economy, and the development of tourism has been incorporated in the 13th Five-year Plan for focus areas and key industries.

The mission of the hospitality and tourism industry is to create a service culture

化。例如,丽思卡尔顿酒店的每一位员工都要熟记黄金标准,并且以黄金标准作为服务客人的行动指引。服务是指以无形的方式,在顾客与服务人员、商品的有形资源或服务系统的相互作用中发生的、可以满足顾客需要的一种或一系列行为(Gronroos,1990)。旅游服务是指满足旅游者在旅游活动中所需要的产品和服务的总和,其与有形商品存在很多方面的差别,主要体现在无形性、不可分割性、变动性和易逝性。

(1) 无形性:消费者在购买前无法看到、品尝、听到或者闻到将接受的服务。酒店及旅游行业销售的很多产品都是无形的体验,这种无形性使得酒店及旅游业的产品的消费具有很大的不确定性,而消费者通常需要通过有形的证据来消除不确定性,例如酒店大堂的装潢、工作人员的制服等。香港半岛酒店购入劳斯莱斯幻影系列轿车作为酒店礼宾用车,车上配备迷你冰箱和苹果设备连接器,为入住客人提供尊贵而舒适的体验。

(2) 不可分割性:对于酒店及旅游业的大多数产品和服务来讲,生产和消费是同时进行的,生产的瞬间即是消费,消费者也是生产的一部分。这意味着企业需要对消费者进行选择、培训和管理。瑞吉酒店在创始时只接待由阿斯特夫人精心挑选的"精英 400"成员,即当时美国上流社会的代表。如今,瑞吉酒店依旧保留这一传统,并发展为"瑞吉鉴赏家"项目——酒店挑选社会各界有品位的人士担任"瑞吉鉴赏家",并定期发布"瑞吉鉴赏家"对瑞吉酒店、时代潮流、艺术等方面的意见。

(3) 变动性:由于服务提供者、服务提供的时间和场所的不同,每一笔交易的服务品质都有所不同。服务的不可分割性导致服务传递过程的质量很难把控,它在很大程度上取决于服务产生时服务提供者的技巧和表现。旅游与酒店业服务的不一致性或变动性是影响消费者满意度的主要原因,鉴于此,丽思卡尔顿酒店制订了服务黄金标准,以保证员工服务质量的稳定。黄金标准包括服务信条、座右铭、优质服务三步骤、服务准则、"第六颗钻石"(即服务理念)以及员工承诺。

(4) 易逝性:服务是无法被储藏的,为了利益最大化,旅游与酒店业企业必须有效地管理其容量和需求。例如飞机、火车等交通工具的座位,酒店的客房,餐厅的餐位如果无法在一定时间内完成销售,将永久失去其创造收入的

which is the organizational culture focusing on serving and satisfying customers from top to bottom of an organization (Kotler, Bowen & Makens, 2009). For example, every member of the Ritz-Carlton Hotel is required to remember Gold Standards as a guide to serving guests. Service refers to one or a series of actions that occur invisibly during a customer's interaction with a service staff, a tangible resource of a commodity, or a service system, to satisfy customer needs (Gronroos, 1990). Tourism service is the sum of products and services that meet the tourist needs in tourism activities. Many aspects of tourism service differ from tangible goods, and these include intangibility, inseparability, variability, and perishability.

(1) Intangibility: Consumers cannot see, taste, hear, or smell the services they will receive before purchasing. Many products sold in the hospitality and tourism industries are intangible experiences, making the consumption of hotel and tourism products highly uncertain. To eliminate uncertainty, consumers often demand for tangible evidence, such as the interior decoration of the hotel lobby and uniforms of the service staff. The Hong Kong Peninsula Hotel introduces the Rolls-Royce Phantom sedan as the concierge car equipped with in-car mini-fridge and Apple device connectors to provide guests with distinguished and comfortable experience.

(2) Inseparability: For most hotel and tourism products and services, production and consumption are carried out simultaneously, because the moment of production is when consumption happens, and consumers are an integral part of production. Companies must select, train, and manage their consumers. The St. Regis Hotel started by entertaining only the members of the "400" which were hand-selected by Mrs. Astor as the representatives of the American upper class. At present, the St. Regis Hotel retains this tradition; the hotel has developed the "St. Regis Connoisseurs" campaign—the hotel selects people with distinct tastes from different sectors of the society to be "St. Regis Connoisseurs" and regularly publishes the opinions of these connoisseurs regarding St. Regis Hotel's trends, art, and other aspects.

(3) Variability: The quality of service varies from one transaction to another due to the different provider, time, and location of service. The inseparability of services leads to the difficulty of controlling the quality of service delivery, which largely depends on the skills and performance of the service provider when generating the service. The inconsistency or variability in hospitality and tourism services is the main factor influencing consumer satisfaction. In view of this aspect, the Ritz-Carlton Hotel has developed the Gold Standards to ensure the stable quality of the service provided by the staff. Gold Standards include the credo, motto, three service steps, service values, "The 6th Diamond" (i.e., service concepts), and employee promise.

(4) Perishability: Services cannot be stored. Hotel and tourism enterprises must effectively manage their capacity and demands to maximize profits. Supplies, such as vehicle seats of aircraft and trains, hotel rooms, and restaurant tables, permanently lose

机会。为此,美国航空公司在20世纪70年代采取收益管理策略,对市场需求和航班容量进行预测,并通过价格杠杆对需求进行有效管理,实现企业收益最大化。

服务业的特性使得服务营销不同于货物的营销。而供给的丰富、市场竞争的加剧使得服务业营销人员面临前所未有的压力。Kotler、Bowen和Makens(2013)指出,营销人员可以通过管理差异、管理服务质量、使服务产品有形化、管理实体环境、加强非占有性的优势、管理员工、管理感知风险、管理资金和需求、管理顾客关系等来加强营销的效果。

1.3 一些基本概念

在对营销管理做进一步了解之前,首先要熟悉以下一些基本概念,这些基本的概念构建了营销管理的基础和方向。

1. 市场

传统意义上的市场指的是一个具体存在的供人们进行交换活动的场所。而在营销概念中,营销人员将产业定义为各种卖方的集合,将市场定义为以不同标准区分的消费者类型的集合,如以需求划分的市场、区位划分的市场,或是以年龄划分的市场等。买方和卖方在市场上交换产品和信息。市场可以区分为市场地点和市场空间,前者是有形的如超市,后者是数字化的如亚马逊。

2. 需要、欲求和需求

需要是指人类的基本要求,如温饱、安全;欲求是用于满足需要的方式,当指定目标以满足需要时,需要就转换为欲求;而当拥有足够的购买力时,欲求就转换为需求,需求是对特定产品有欲求且有能力购买。企业不仅需要衡量有多少人想要生产的产品,更需要了解有多少人真正有能力购买这些产品。营销从某种意义上来讲是一种需求管理,营销并非制造需要,因为需要是客观存在的。营销的作用更多的是影响欲求,例如,营销者传递钻石戒指可以满足人们对永恒爱情的期望的信息,而营销者并没有制造对永恒爱情的需要。

了解消费者的需要和欲求是营销的基础,也是最困难的部分,因为在很多情况下消费者对自己的需要并不清晰,或是无法表达出来。随着市场竞争的日益激烈,营销者不能仅仅满足于满足消费者的需要和欲求,更需要帮助消费者发现自己的需要和欲求。

the opportunity to generate income if they are not sold within a certain period. Therefore, American Airlines adopted revenue management strategies in the 1970s to predict market demands and flight capacity and maximized corporate profits by effectively managing demands with price leverage.

The characteristics of service distinguish service marketing from product marketing. The rich supply and intensified competition in the market confront the service marketer with unprecedented pressure. Kotler, Bowen, and Makens (2013) highlight that marketers can enhance the effectiveness of marketing by dealing with differences, managing service quality, making service products tangible, controlling physical environments, enhancing non-possessory advantages, managing employees, controlling perceived risk, managing capacity and demand, and maintaining customer relationship.

1.3 Basic Concepts

To further understand marketing management, we must consider the following basic concepts constituting the foundation and direction of marketing management.

1. Market

The traditional definition of market refers to a tangible place for people to exchange. In marketing, marketers define the industry as a collection of sellers, and the market as the combination of different consumer types segmented by different criteria, such as need markets, geographic markets, and age markets. Buyers and sellers exchange products and information in the market. Markets can be divided into marketplace and marketspace with the former being tangible, such as supermarkets, and the latter being digital, such as the Amazon.

2. Needs, wants, and demands

Needs refer to the basic requirements of mankind, such as food, clothing, and security. Wants are ways to meet needs. When a target to meet the needs is specified, needs are converted to wants. When sufficient purchasing power exists, wants are converted to demands, which are wants for specific products with the ability to purchase them. Enterprises need to measure not only how many people want a product but also how many people can purchase the product. In this sense, marketing is demand management. Marketing does not produce needs because they exist. The effect of marketing is inclined toward wants. For example, marketers deliver the message that diamond rings can meet people's expectations of eternal love, but they do not create the needs for eternal love.

Understanding the needs and wants of consumers is the foundation of marketing as well as the most difficult part. In many cases, consumers are unaware of or unable to express their own needs. With the increasingly fierce market competition, marketers should not only aim to meet the needs and wants of consumers, they should also help

3. 目标市场和市场定位

营销人员不可能满足市场上每一个消费者的需要和欲求,因此需要采用某种标准对市场进行区分,并找出可能对产品感兴趣的人群。最有可能对产品感兴趣并产生购买欲望的人群被称为目标市场。市场定位是指企业针对消费者对某类产品的某些特征或属性的重视程度,为本企业产品塑造与众不同的、给人印象鲜明的形象,并将这种形象生动地传递给顾客,从而使该产品在市场上处于适当的位置(Ries 和 Trout,1972)。

4. 市场供给品和品牌

企业通过提供一系列的价值主张及预期利益来满足消费者的需要。价值主张可以体现在一系列的产品、服务、信息以及体验等市场供给品上。品牌是销售者向购买者长期提供的一系列特定的特点、利益和服务,是给使用者带来增值溢价的一种无形资产(Kotler 和 Keller,2016)。

5. 营销渠道

营销渠道是某种货物或劳务从生产者向消费者移动时,取得这种货物或劳务所有权或帮助转移其所有权的所有企业或个人(Kotler 和 Keller,2016)。营销渠道通常包括三种:沟通渠道、服务渠道以及分销渠道。

6. 价值和满意度

价值指的是消费者通过消费某种产品体验到的有形的和无形的成本和收益。价值通常包含质量、服务和价格的组合,也即顾客价值三合一。价值是营销学中的核心概念。营销可以看作是一个识别、创造、沟通、传递、监控顾客价值的过程。满意度是指个体通过对一个产品的可感知效果与他的期望值相比较后所形成的愉悦或失望的感觉状态(Kotler 和 Keller,2007)。当产品的实际消费效果达到或超出消费者预期时,就会使顾客满意,否则,就会导致顾客不满意。

7. 供应链

供应链是指产品生产和流通过程中涉及的所有环节,包括原材料供应商、生产商、分销商、零售商以及最终消费者。供应链是一个由多个环节构成的价值让渡系统,系统中每个成员贡献一部分价值。

consumers to find their own needs and wants.

3. Target markets and positioning

Marketers cannot meet the needs and wants of every consumer. The market should be segmented following certain standards so that marketers can identify the group that may be interested in a product. Those who are the most likely to be interested in the product are called the target market. Positioning is a two-part process. First, an enterprise builds distinctive and impressive image for its product according to customers' attention on certain attributes or features of the product. Then, the enterprise effectively passes this image to the customer, so that the product is appropriately positioned in the market (Ries & Trout, 1972).

4. Offerings and brands

Enterprises provide a range of value propositions and expected benefits to meet the needs of consumers. Value propositions can be embodied in a series of offerings, such as products, services, information, and experience. A brand is a set of specific characteristics, benefits, and services that sellers provide to buyers in the long term and is an invisible asset that brings value-adding premium to users (Kotler & Keller, 2016).

5. Marketing channels

A marketing channel is a business or individual that obtains or transfers ownership of goods or services from a producer to a consumer (Kotler & Keller, 2016). The three types of marketing channels are communication, service, and distribution channels.

6. Value and satisfaction

Value refers to the tangible and intangible costs and benefits that consumers experience through product consumption. Value typically contains quality, service, and price, which represent the customer value triad. Value is a core concept in marketing. Marketing can be viewed as a process of identifying, creating, communicating, delivering, and monitoring customer value. Satisfaction is the sense of pleasure or despair that results from an individual's perception of a product compared to his expectations (Kotler & Keller, 2007). When actual product consumption meets or exceeds consumer expectations, it leads to customer satisfaction; otherwise, it results in customer dissatisfaction.

7. Supply chain

Supply chain refers to all aspects involved in production and distribution, including raw material suppliers, manufacturers, distributors, retailers, and final consumers. The supply chain is a value delivery system composed of several elements. Each member of the system contributes a part of the value.

第 2 章 营销管理战略的制定与实施

 本章要点

- 顾客价值及价值链理论
- 不同层面营销战略的区别
- 企业层面营销战略
- 业务单元层面营销战略
- 一般性战略和拓展型战略模式

日益激烈的竞争环境使得企业必须积极应对由卖方市场转变为买方市场所带来的挑战,这赋予了营销更重要的使命。营销已不再是企业创造和传递顾客价值的最后一个环节,而是贯穿在整个商业流程中。营销部门无法控制产品和服务的质量,也无法单独完成企业的营销任务。本章从顾客价值、价值传递、价值链等核心概念出发,首先阐述服务企业的管理战略,然后分别从企业和业务单元两个层级介绍服务企业及企业内各个业务单元营销战略的制定过程,以及旅游及酒店企业内部营销管理及营销组织。

2.1 营销及顾客价值

企业的目的是在创造及传递顾客价值的同时获利。而营销则包括满足消费者需求的含义。根据 Kotler 和 Keller(2009)的定义,顾客感知价值是指消费者预期评估利益、产品成本及潜在替代品三者之间的差异。日益激烈的市场竞争要求企业必须细化顾客价值传递过程,并提供更优的价值。在以往的卖方市场中,企业力求尽可能提高产品或服务的销量,同时降低成本。然而,这种战略在买方市场中并不成功。企业可以通过市场调查发掘顾客的需求,然后尽可能有效地利用企业的资源满足顾客。有敏锐的市场嗅觉的市场

Chapter 2　Formulation and Implementation of Marketing Management Strategy

 Key points of the chapter

- Customer value and value chain theory
- Variations in marketing strategy at different levels
- Corporate marketing strategy
- Business unit marketing strategy
- General and expansion strategies

The increasingly competitive environment drives companies to respond actively to challenges posed by the transition from seller's market to buyer's market. This situation magnifies the importance of marketing. Marketing is no longer the last step in the creation and delivery of customer value; rather, it accompanies all stages of the entire business process. The marketing department cannot control the quality of products and services or complete corporate marketing alone. This chapter begins with discussing core concepts, such as customer value, value transmission, and value chain. First, this chapter introduces the management strategy of service enterprises. Second, it presents the development of marketing strategy in service enterprises and their business units from two different levels. This chapter also explains the internal marketing management and marketing organizations in tourism and hotel companies.

2.1　Marketing and Customer Value

The purpose of an enterprise is to create and transmit customer value while profiting. Marketing encompasses meeting the needs of consumers. Kotler and Keller (2009) claim that customer perceived value refers to the difference among consumers' prospective evaluation of the benefits, product cost, and potential substitutes. The increasingly fierce competition in the market requires companies to refine the customer value delivery process and provide enhanced value. In seller's market, companies strive to maximize the sales of products or services while reducing costs. However, this strategy is unsuccessful in buyer's market. Companies can explore customer needs through market research and then meet these needs as much as possible by effectively using corporate resources.

营销者认识到这一过程是企业向顾客传递感知价值的过程。这种认知产生了一种新的商业流程,即将营销置于企业计划的开端,企业将其自身视为传递定制化市场产品的流程的一部分,使得全面营销的概念贯穿企业的整个商业流程中。整体营销是指"将价值探索、价值创造和价值传递的活动通过与顾客建立长期、互动、满意的关系进行整合,并与关键的利益相关者达到双赢"(Kotler、Jain 和 Maesincee,2002)。整体营销概念能够帮助企业理解顾客感知价值。成功的整体营销者管理着一条快速传递高质量的产品和服务的高级价值链,帮助整体营销者扩大市场份额、建立顾客忠诚并获取顾客的终身价值。

企业在与顾客的价值交换过程中涉及三个阶段,即发现顾客感知价值、创造顾客感知价值、传递顾客感知价值。Porter(1985)提出的价值链理论是发现并创造顾客感知价值的工具。根据此理论,产品涉及设计、生产、营销、分销和支持五大部分,而企业则是这些活动的综合。价值链模型(图 2-1)指出,在一个专门的行业中有九个战略相关活动(五个主要活动和四个支持活动)与产品的价值和成本有关。这九个战略相关的活动包括内部物流、外部物流、运营、市场营销、销售及售后支持服务、采购、技术发展、人力资源和企业资源。企业资源涵盖了管理成本、计划、财务、会计、法律和政府关系。

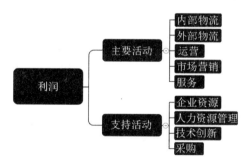

图 2-1　价值链模型

来源:根据 Porter,M. E.(1985). *Competitive Advantage*:*Creating and Sustaining Superior Performance*. New York,London:Free Press.

企业的成功除了依靠所有部门各司其职外,还取决于企业如何整合所有的部门活动,形成企业的核心商业流程。核心商业流程包括以下几步。

- 市场监测流程:获取市场信息,在企业内部传递,并根据这些信息采取

Marketers with a keen sense of the market recognize that this process allows companies to deliver perceived value to their customers. This recognition creates a new business process in which marketing is placed at the beginning of a business plan and the enterprise sees itself as part of delivering a product customized for the market. This strategy allows the concept of holistic marketing to permeate in the entire business process of the company. Holistic marketing "integrates the value exploration, value creation, and value delivery activities with the purpose of building long-term, mutually satisfying relationships and co-prosperity among these key stakeholders" (Kotler, Jain & Maesincee, 2002). Holistic marketing helps companies to understand customer perceived value. Successful marketers manage an advanced value chain that delivers high-quality products and services quickly, helps holistic marketers to enlarge market share, establishes customer loyalty, and captures customer lifetime value.

Enterprises are involved in three stages of value exchange with customers, namely, discovering, creating, and delivering customer perceived value. Porter (1985) proposes value chain theory which is a tool to discover and create customer perceived value. According to this theory, product involves design, production, marketing, distribution, and support, whereas business is a combination of these activities. The value chain model (Figure 2 – 1) indicates that nine strategy-related activities (five main activities and four support activities) relate to the value and cost of products in a specific sector. These nine strategy-related activities are inbound logistics, outbound logistics, operations, marketing, sales and after-sales support service, procurement, technology development, human resource (HR) management, and firm infrastructure. Firm infrastructure includes management costs, planning, finance, accounting, legal, and government relations.

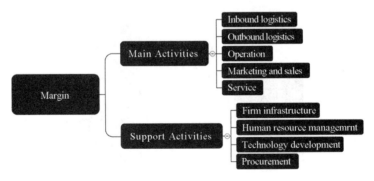

Figure 2 – 1   Value chain model

Source: Porter, M. E. (1985). *Competitive Advantage: Creating and Sustaining Superior Performance*. New York, London: Free Press.

Apart from relying on all departments to perform their duties, the success of a business depends on the integration of all departmental activities and formation of the following core business processes:

- Market monitoring: capturing market information, communicating within the

适当行动。

● 新产品实现流程：在预算范围内进行市场调查，开发并快速发布新的高质量产品。

● 获取顾客流程：确定目标市场和新客户群。

● 顾客关系管理流程：与个体顾客建立深层次的理解和关系，并提供相应的定制化产品。

● 实施过程管理流程：获取并核准订单，及时运输产品并收取货款。

顾客感知价值传递流程共有四个步骤（Kotler 和 Keller，2009）。第一步，在生产具有市场价值的产品或服务前，企业需要通过市场调查发掘市场需求的价值。市场营销者进行市场细分，选择合适的目标市场，并对产品进行顾客感知价值的定位。"市场细分、目标市场和定位"是战略营销的本质。第二步，针对目标市场顾客的感知价值，市场营销者将特定的产品、服务进行打包，并确定合适的价格。第三步，确定如何分销产品。第四步，设法将产品的价值信息传递给目标顾客。在买方市场中，企业想要获得市场优势，就需要不断重复价值传递流程。

对企业而言，拥有并培育企业资源和能力，使之成为企业的核心竞争力，是非常重要的。核心竞争力有三大特征：（1）它是一种能够为顾客感知价值提供卓越贡献的竞争优势；（2）能够应用于大部分的市场；（3）竞争对手难以模仿。竞争优势可以通过企业所拥有的独特能力来积累，而核心竞争力则反映在企业是某一方面有特殊技术或产品的专家。

酒店及旅游业企业进入壁垒较低，缺乏特殊技术，产品极易被模仿，因而其面临的最大的危机之一是产品的趋同化。在这种情况之下，企业就会因为顾客只考虑旅游产品的一般质量和产品价格而受到边际利润降低的威胁。在这种情况之下，企业只有比竞争对手更恒久地提供更高质量的服务才能保持竞争优势。

提高旅游目的地总体竞争力已成为旅游政策制定者和目的地营销部门的主要任务。目的地竞争力是一个相对的概念（Crouch 和 Ritchie，1999；Diebold、Scott 和 Lodge，1985；Enright 和 Newton，2004），是目的地各要素绩效表现的总和。Crouch 和 Ritchie（1999）基于波特（Porter，1990）的钻石模型提出的目的地竞争模型是目前学术界广泛接受的对目的地竞争力的分

company, and taking appropriate action in light of the information.

- New product realization: conducting market research within the budget to develop and quickly release new high-quality products.

- Customer acquisition: identifying the target market and new customer segments.

- Customer relationship management: establishing deep understanding and relationships with individual customers and providing customized product accordingly.

- Implementation management: capturing and approving orders, shipping products in a timely manner and collecting payment for goods.

The delivery of customer perceived value comprises four steps (Kotler & Keller, 2009). First, companies should identify the value of the market demand through market research before producing products or services containing the market value. Marketers segment the market, select the right target market, and position the product according to customer perceived value. "Segmentation, targeting, positioning" (STP) is the essence of strategic marketing. Second, marketers should package specific products and services at appropriate price based on the value perceived by the target market. Third, product distribution should be determined. Fourth, marketers need to come up with ways to communicate the value of the product to target customers. In buyer's market, companies must constantly repeat value delivery to gain market advantage.

For companies, owning and nurturing enterprise resources and capabilities and making these features the core competencies of the business are important. Core competencies feature three major characteristics, which are (1) competitive advantage that contribute to customer perceived value, (2) application to most of the market, and (3) difficulty for competitors to imitate. Competitive advantage can be accumulated with the unique capability of a company, whereas core competencies are reflected in the enterprise as an expert with special technology or product in a certain aspect.

The hospitality and tourism industry possesses a comparatively low entry barrier to enterprises due to the lack of special technology, and products can easily be imitated. As a result, one of the biggest crises facing the industry is the convergence of products. In this case, enterprises are threatened by reduced marginal profit because customers only consider the general quality of tourism products and prices. Hence, companies can only maintain competitive advantage by offering higher quality services more consistently than their competitors.

Tourism destination competitiveness (TDC) has become a major task of tourism policy makers and destination marketing organizations (DMO) at tourism destinations. Destination competitiveness is a relative concept (Crouch & Ritchie, 1999; Diebold, Scott & Lodge, 1985; Enright & Newton, 2004) referring to the sum of the performance elements of a destination. The destination competitiveness model proposed by Crouch and Ritchie's (1999), which is based on the Porter's (1990) diamond model, is a widely accepted analysis framework of destination competitiveness. The model demonstrates that

析框架。该模型认为,目的地的竞争力取决于四个主要方面,即核心资源及吸引物、支持要素及资源、目的地管理以及资格要素。在 Crouch 和 Ritchie 的目的地竞争力模型的基础上,Ji、Li 和 King(2016)基于上海自贸区政策的实施对香港旅游竞争力影响的分析,指出,在讨论目的地竞争力时应当将重大事件(influential event)纳入分析框架。

在世界经济论坛发布的《2015 年全球旅游业竞争力报告》中,旅游目的地竞争力的计算指标包括 4 个一级指标、14 个二级指标以及 90 个三级指标。4 个一级指标分别为可行环境、旅游业政策及可行条件、基础设施和自然与文化资源。14 个二级指标如表 2-1 所示。

表 2-1　旅游目的地竞争力的二级计算指标

编号	二级指标	所属一级指标	包含三级指标数量
1	商业环境	可行环境	12
2	安全与保安	可行环境	5
3	健康与卫生	可行环境	6
4	人力资源与劳动力市场	可行环境	9
5	通信技术水平	可行环境	8
6	旅游业优先级	旅游业政策及可行条件	6
7	国家开放程度	旅游业政策及可行条件	3
8	价格竞争力	旅游业政策及可行条件	4
9	环境可持续性	旅游业政策及可行条件	10
10	航空交通基础设施	基础设施	6
11	地面交通与航运基础设施	基础设施	7
12	旅游者服务基础设施	基础设施	4
13	自然资源	自然与文化资源	5
14	文化资源与商务旅行	自然与文化资源	5

来源:世界经济论坛发布的《2015 年全球旅游业竞争力报告》。

根据以上指标,世界经济论坛发布了 2015 年全球旅游目的地竞争力排名(见表 2-2)。

destination competitiveness depends on four main aspects, namely, core resources and attractions, supporting factors and resources, destination management, and qualifying dominants. Using Crouch and Ritchie's destination competitiveness model as basis, Ji, Li, and King (2016) analyze the effect of Shanghai Free Trade Area policy on Hong Kong's tourism competitiveness, and they point out that influential events should be included in the analysis framework when destination competitiveness is discussed.

The Travel and Tourism (T&T) Competitiveness Report 2015 published by the World Economic Forum (2015) includes 4 primary, 14 secondary, and 90 tertiary indicators for TDC. The four primary indicators are enabling environment, T&T policy and enabling conditions, infrastructure, and nature and culture resources. Table 2 – 1 lists the 14 secondary indicators.

Table 2 – 1   Tourism destination competitiveness indicators

No.	secondary indicators	belong to which primary indicators	No. of tertiary indicators included
1	business environment	enabling environment	12
2	safety and security	enabling environment	5
3	health and hygiene	enabling environment	6
4	HR and labor market	enabling environment	9
5	ICT readiness	enabling environment	8
6	prioritization of travel and tourism	T&T policy and enabling conditions	6
7	international openness	T&T policy and enabling conditions	3
8	price competitiveness	T&T policy and enabling conditions	4
9	environmental sustainability	T&T policy and enabling conditions	10
10	air transport infrastructure	infrastructure	6
11	ground and port infrastructure	infrastructure	7
12	tourist service infrastructure	infrastructure	4
13	natural resources	natural and cultural resources	5
14	cultural resources and business travel	natural and cultural resources	5

Source: *The Travel & Tourism Competitiveness Report 2015*. published by the World Economic Forum (2015).

Based on the above indicators, the World Economic Forum (2015) released the global TDC ranking in 2015 (Table 2 – 2).

表 2 - 2　2015 年全球旅游目的地竞争力排名

排名	国家
1	西班牙
2	法国
3	德国
4	美国
5	英国
6	瑞士
7	澳大利亚
8	意大利
9	日本
10	加拿大

来源：世界经济论坛发布的《2015 年全球旅游业竞争力报告》。

2.2　服务企业管理战略

旅游行业作为服务性行业，需要同时关注客人与员工，因为客人和员工的满意度是服务业利润链中的重要因素。服务业利润链包括以下五个方面：

（1）良好的利润与增长：服务型企业具有优于竞争对手的表现。

（2）满意度高且忠诚的客人：满意度高且忠诚的客人会重复购买，并将企业的产品或服务介绍给其他客人。

（3）优越的服务价值：企业能够创造更多有效的顾客价值并将其传递给顾客。

（4）满意度高并具有高劳动率的员工：企业需要忠诚、满意度高并努力工作的员工。

（5）内部服务质量：企业有良好的员工招聘流程及培训，高质量的工作环境，并能够为服务客人的员工提供强有力的支持。

相比于生产型企业偏重传统营销方法，服务型企业的营销方法更强调内部营销与互动营销。内部营销是指企业对员工进行有效的培训并给予适当激励，培养所有员工树立团队精神，以顾客为先，向顾客提供优质的服务，从而提高顾客的满意度。同时，企业内的所有员工都应该学习营销方法，而非

Table 2 - 2　2015 global tourism destination competitiveness ranking

Rank	Country
1	Spain
2	France
3	Germany
4	United States
5	United Kingdom
6	Switzerland
7	Australia
8	Italy
9	Japan
10	Canada

Source：*The Travel & Tourism Competitiveness Report 2015*. published by World Economic Forum (2015).

2.2　Service Business Management Strategy

As a service industry, the tourism industry needs to focus on guests and employees simultaneously because the guest satisfaction and employee satisfaction are important factors in the profit chain of the service industry. The service profit chain includes the five following aspects：

(1) Good profit and growth：The service company performs better than its competitors.

(2) Highly satisfied and loyal guests：High satisfaction and loyalty of the guests result in repeat purchase from the company and introduction of the company's products or services to other guests.

(3) Superior service value：The company can create effective customer value and deliver it to the customer.

(4) Highly satisfied and very efficient employees：Companies must have loyal, satisfied, and hard-working employees.

(5) Internal service quality：The company features good staff recruitment and training and quality working environment and can provide strong support to the staff who serve guests.

Compared with production-oriented enterprises, which focus on traditional marketing methods, service-oriented enterprises use marketing methods with emphasis on internal and interactive marketing.Internal marketing refers to the effective training of employees and appropriate incentives to encourage all staff to build team spirit, prioritize customers, and provide customers with quality service, thereby enhancing customer

单靠市场营销部门进行传统的市场营销。生产与消费同时发生是服务性行业的一个特点,因此,顾客对产品(服务)质量的感知取决于服务发生时服务人员与顾客之间的互动。顾客对服务质量的判断取决于技术性质量(如食物的质量)和功能性质量(如餐厅提供的个性化服务)。服务性行业的员工需要同时掌握互动营销技巧和服务技巧(Gronroos,1984)。外部营销、内部营销和互动营销之间的关系如图 2-2 所示(Kotler、Bowen 和 Makens,2009)。

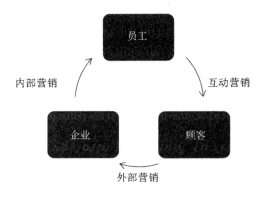

图 2-2　外部营销、内部营销和互动营销之间的关系

来源:Kotler,Bowen & Makens.(2009). *Marketing for Hospitality and Tourism* (5th ed.). Upper Saddle River,NJ:Pearson Prentice Hall.

随着企业运营成本的提高和市场竞争日趋激烈,服务型企业需要从三个方面提升自身的营销与管理能力:差异化竞争能力、服务质量和生产率。

差异化是应对价格战的方法之一,企业可以通过对自身产品(服务)进行改进或创新来形成差异化。然而,服务性行业的差异化容易被复制,企业必须不断地创新或形成差异化以获得短暂的竞争优势。同时,不断创新或形成差异化能够帮助企业在顾客中形成"创新"的企业形象,进而吸引更多希望获得更好的服务体验的顾客。

企业可以通过人才、物质环境和服务流程三方面来实现差异化战略。可靠和有能力的服务人才能够让企业将自身与竞争对手区分开来(如香格里拉酒店集团专门成立了香格里拉学院,以培养自身人才)。另一方面,企业为顾客提供更有特色的物质环境也能体现差异化(如香港 Ovolo 品牌旗下酒店大

satisfaction. All employees within the enterprise should learn marketing methods rather than relying solely on the marketing department for traditional marketing. The co-occurrence of production and consumption is a characteristic of the service industry. Therefore, the customer perception of the product (service) quality depends on the interaction between service personnel and customers when service occurs. The quality of customer service depends on technical (e.g., food quality) and functional qualities (e.g., personalized service provided in the restaurant). Employees in the service industry must possess interactive marketing and service skills (Gronroos, 1984). Figure 2 – 2 illustrates the relationship among external, internal and interactive marketing (Kotler, Bowen & Makens, 2009).

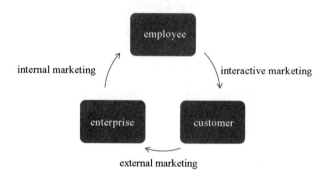

Figure 2 – 2　Relationship between external, internal, and interactive marketing

Source: Kotler, Bowen & Makens. (2009). *Marketing for Hospitality and Tourism* (5th ed.). Upper Saddle River, NJ: Pearson Prentice Hall.

With the rise in business operation cost and increasingly fierce market competition, service companies need to enhance their marketing and management capability through three aspects, that is, competitive differentiation, service quality, and productivity.

Differentiation is one of the means to respond to price wars. Companies can improve or innovate their own products (services) to differentiate. However, differentiation in the service industry is easily to replicate. Enterprises need to be constantly innovative or differentiated to obtain short-term competitive advantages. At the same time, continuous innovation or differentiation can help enterprises to form an "innovative" corporate image among customers, thus attracting more customers who want enhanced service experience.

Enterprises achieve differentiation with talented people, tangible environment, and service process. Reliable and competent service personnel differentiate companies from their competitors (e.g., Shangri-La Hotel Group establishes its own Shangri-La school to train skilled staff for the company). Companies can also provide customers with distinctive tangible environment to show differentiation (e.g., most hotels under Hong Kong Ovolo hotel brand are converted from old industrial buildings). In addition, companies can choose to design effective service processes to achieve differentiation (e.

部分都是由旧的工业大厦改建而来）。同时，企业也可以选择设计更好的服务流程来实现差异化（如喜达屋集团推出无钥匙（key-less）入住系统，客人可以利用 SPG App 开启房门）。最后，品牌与标志也是企业实现差异化的一种工具，如万豪、希尔顿、香格里拉等就采用了这种工具。

服务性行业产品质量（服务质量）的判断来自于顾客的期望在何种程度上被满足。顾客保留率可以作为衡量服务质量的一种方法：企业保留顾客的能力取决于其持续传递并满足顾客价值的能力。

业绩良好的服务型企业在服务质量方面有共同的优点：（1）顶级的服务型企业能够让顾客"着迷"，它们通过持续满足顾客的需求来赢得顾客的忠诚。（2）业绩良好的服务型企业能够在相当长的时间里维持服务承诺，这些企业不仅关注自身的财务表现，同时也关注服务方面的表现，如万豪、迪士尼等。（3）顶级的服务型企业会设定高标准以维持良好的服务质量，高标准不仅仅是"好"的服务，而且是百分百让顾客满意的服务。（4）顶级的服务型企业会密切关注自身和竞争对手的服务质量。它们会利用对比消费、顾客调查、建议和投诉表格等方法来了解服务质量。此外，顶级的服务型企业还会与员工沟通关于服务质量方面的问题，并向员工提供有关服务质量方面的反馈。

在酒店行业中，员工是产品（服务）和营销组合中的重要一环。因此，人力资源和营销部门需要密切合作。人力资源部主要负责招聘合适的员工，并进行有效的培训。而营销部门则需要培养员工以顾客为中心的思维方式，推广内部营销。两者结合才能真正提高员工的生产率。

2.3　企业层级营销战略

对于经营多种业务的企业来说，一般在四个层级进行顾客价值选择、创造、传递及沟通。这四个层级是：第一，公司层级，指整个企业/集团的生存和发展战略。它基于企业集团的价值理念和企业的使命形成，所要解决的问题是确定经营范围和企业资源在不同业务单元之间的分配事项。这一个层级的决策由企业的最高管理层决定，决定周期相对较长。第二，部门层级，指各职能部门的具体战略，如运营战略、人力资源战略、营销战略、财务战略等；第三，业务单元层级，指公司所从事的各个业务模块的经营战略，集中于在某一既定的经营业务内确定如何竞争的问题。第四，产品层级。

在公司层级，总部负责制定企业发展的整体战略，包括资源的调配以及

g., Starwood Group introduced the key-less check-in system that enables guests to open the door using the SPG application). Moreover, the brand and logo serve as a tool for companies to achieve differentiation. Marriott, Hilton, and Shangri-La adopt this tool.

The judgment of product quality in service industry (i.e., service quality) originates from the extent to which customer expectation is met. Customer retention rate can be used as a measure of service quality in which the ability of the company to retain customers depends on its continuous delivering and meeting customer value.

Service enterprises with good performance enjoy common advantages in terms of service quality, which are as follows: (1) Top service companies make customers "fascinated" because they continuously meet customer needs to win customer loyalty. (2) Service providers with good performance maintain their service commitments for a long period. These companies focus on financial performance as much as service performance. Examples of these companies are Marriott and Disney. (3) Top service companies set high standards to maintain superior service quality. High standards do not refer to "good" service but to service that achieves 100% customer satisfaction. (4) Top service companies pay close attention to their service quality and those of competitors. They use comparison shopping, customer survey, suggestions, and complaint forms to look into service quality. Top-tier service companies also communicate with employees regarding service quality issues and provide employees with feedback on service quality.

In the hospitality industry, employees are important in the product (service) and marketing mix. Therefore, the HR and marketing departments need to work closely together. The HR department is responsible for recruiting the right staff and conducting effective training. The marketing department needs to train the staff with customer-oriented thinking and promote internal marketing. Only through the integration of these two processes can companies strongly improve employee productivity.

2.3 Organizational Levels of Marketing Strategy

Enterprises managing various business undergo four levels to select, create, deliver, and communicate customer values. First, the corporate level refers to the entire enterprise/group survival and development strategies. This level is formed on the basis of the corporate values and corporate mission to determine the business scope and distribution of company resources in different business units. Decisions at this level are made by the top management of the enterprise, and, thus, the decision cycle is relatively long. Second, the division level refers to specific strategies of various functional departments. These strategies include operational, HR, marketing, and financial strategies. The third level is the business unit level, which refers to the business strategy of various business modles the company is engaged in, with a focus on determining how to compete within a given business scope. The fourth level is the product level.

At the corporate level, the headquarters is responsible for developing the overall

业务单元的选择。各部门负责将所获得的资源分配到不同的业务单元。业务单元层级的主要目的是盈利,而产品层级则以完成其市场目标为目的。图2-3所示为一个完整的战略规划、实施、控制的流程。

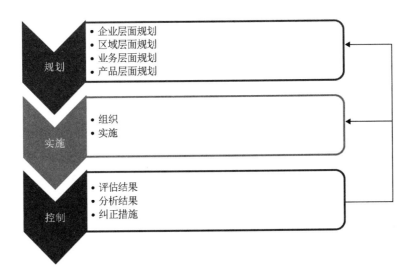

图 2 - 3 战略规划、实施、控制的流程

来源:Kotler,Keller.(2009). *Marketing Management*(13th ed.). Upper Saddle River,NJ:Pearson Prentice Hall.

在企业这一层级,高层管理者在制定企业层面的营销战略时需要考虑以下方面:企业使命、企业业务、战略业务单元资源分配、评估增长机会、企业组织结构、创新。

首先,企业要有一个明确的使命。在确定企业使命时,管理者需要明确回答以下问题:企业的业务是什么? 谁是企业的顾客? 顾客所需求的价值是什么? 企业的业务未来会怎么样? 企业的业务现在应该是什么样? 为什么顾客会从竞争对手那儿购买商品或服务? 一般而言,愿景是关于未来企业发展方向的描述。当愿景被实现后,企业需要重新制定愿景。使命则是关于企业目的的描述,着重表达企业的性质及其行为准则。一个清晰的、经过深思熟虑的使命陈述能够为员工提供方向、机会以及使命感。最好的使命陈述能够反映企业愿景。表 2 - 3 列出了部分国内外知名企业的愿景与使命陈述。

strategy for company development, including the deployment of resources and business unit selection. Each division is responsible for allocating resources to different business units. The main target of the business unit level is to profit, whereas the product level aims to achieve its market objectives. Figure 2 – 3 shows the complete process of strategic planning, implementation, and control.

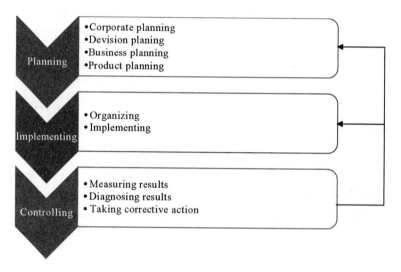

Figure 2 – 3   Strategic planning, implementation, and control
Source: Kotler, Keller. (2009). *Marketing Management* (13th ed.). Upper Saddle River, NJ: Pearson Prentice Hall.

At the corporate level, senior managers need to consider the following aspects when formulating corporate-level marketing strategies: corporate mission, company business, resource allocation to each strategic business unit, growth opportunity assessment, business organizational structure, and innovation.

First, enterprises should have a clear mission. When determining the corporate mission, managers need to answer clearly the following questions: What is the business of the enterprise? Who is the customer? What is the value that the customer demands? What happens to the business in the future? What should the business of the enterprise be like at this moment? Why would customers buy goods or services from a competitor? The vision is a description of the future direction of business development. When the vision is fulfilled, companies need to redefine their vision. The mission is a description of the purpose of the enterprise, focusing on describing the nature of the enterprise and its code of conduct. A clear and carefully considered mission statement can provide direction, opportunity, and a sense of mission to employees. The best mission statements reflect the corporate vision. Table 2 – 3 lists the vision and mission statements of well-known enterprises at home and abroad.

表 2 - 3　知名企业的愿景与使命陈述

企业	愿景	使命
首旅酒店集团	打造中国最具影响力的、富有民族特色的国际化酒店集团。	不断探索和把握酒店品牌连锁经营的规律,以多元化品牌满足消费者的个性化需求;实施连锁经营提升酒店经营效益;创造良好的业绩,实现公司的可持续发展。
华侨城集团	成为中国最具创新文化和影响力的企业。	通过独特的创新文化,致力提升中国人的生活品质。
港中旅集团	中国第一,亚洲第一,世界前五。	港中旅集团作为大型国有企业、旅游行业的排头兵,做大、做强、做优企业既是国有企业服务大众、造福社会应承担的社会责任,更是向世界展示中国实力和改革开放成果应承担的政治责任。
开元旅业	持续追求价值领先的旅游产业投资与运营集团。	营造中国品质,创造快乐生活。
洲际酒店集团（IHG）	使洲际酒店集团旗下品牌成为客人和业主的首选。	成为客人所喜爱的优秀酒店。
雅高酒店集团（Accor）	雅高酒店,世界酒店行业经营者的标杆。	管理雅高酒店集团旗下所有酒店,并为酒店业主提供最好的服务选择。
香格里拉酒店集团（Shangri-La）	成为客人、同事、股东和经营伙伴的首选。	以发自内心的待客之道,创造难以忘怀的美好经历,时刻令客人喜出望外。

　　其次,确定企业的业务范畴。企业在三个维度上能够定义业务:顾客群体、顾客需求和技术。业务应该被视为一个满足顾客需求的过程,而不是生产货物的过程。明确企业战略业务单元的目的是发展业务单元独立的战略,以及分配合适的财务资源。当企业以消费者的角度审视自身业务时,企业能够发现额外的市场增长机会。另外,企业在制定营销战略时,在考虑现有市场的同时,应该发掘潜在市场的业务增长机会。一般而言,企业可以通过三个方面确定其业务——消费者群体、消费者需求以及技术(Gruen、Osmonbekov 和 Czaplewski,2006)

Table 2 - 3   Vision and mission statements of well-known enterprises

Enterprises	Vision	Mission
Beijing Tourism Group (BTG) Hotels	To build the most influential and ethnically rich international hotel group in China.	To continue to explore and grasp effective methods for hotel chain operations, meet the individual needs of consumers with diversified brands, implement chain operations to improve the operating efficiency of our hotels and produce healthy results, thereby achieving the sustainable development of BTG Hotels.
Overseas Chinese Town (OCT) Group	Become the most imaginative and influential enterprise in China.	We strive to enhance the quality of living for Chinese people through our uniquely imaginative and creative culture.
China Travel Service (CTS)	No. 1 in China, No. 1 in Asia, top five in the world.	CTS, as a large state-owned enterprise and the vanguard of the tourism industry, has the social responsibility as well as the political responsibility to be bigger, stronger, and better in order to serve the public for the benefit of the community and to show the world the strength of China and the results of reform and opening.
New Century Tourism Group	A tourist industry investment and operation organization that continuously pursues advanced value.	Building Chinese Quality, Creating a Happy Life.
InterContinental Hotels Group (IHG)	Grow by making IHG brands as the first choice for guests and hotel owners.	To create great hotels guests love.
AccorHotels Group	AccorHotels, the world's benchmark hotelier.	Manage operations at Accor hotels and provide the best choice of services for partner hotel owners.
Shangri-La Group	To be the first choice for guests, colleagues, shareholders and business partners.	To delight our guests every time by creating engaging experiences straight from our heart.

Second, the business scope of the enterprise should be determined. Companies can define their business in three dimensions, namely, customer groups, customer needs, and technology. A business should be viewed as satisfying customer needs rather than producing goods. The purposes of clarifying strategic business units are to develop a specific strategy for each business unit independently and assign appropriate financial resources. When companies look at their own businesses from a consumer perspective, they can find additional market growth opportunities. Companies should explore the growth opportunities of potential market in addition to considering the existing market when developing marketing strategies. Generally, enterprises can determine their business through customer groups, customer needs, and technology (Gruen, Osmonbekov & Czaplewski, 2006).

　　当战略业务单元被确定后,管理层必须决定如何分配企业资源到各个单元。自 20 世纪 70 年代以来,不同的咨询公司提出了不同的模型以帮助管理层做出投资决策。"美国通用电气/麦肯锡矩阵"根据战略业务单元的竞争优势和所在行业的吸引力确定每个单元应该获得的资源;波士顿咨询集团的"增长—市场份额矩阵"将每个单元各自的市场份额以及市场的年增长率作为投资决策的条件。如今,更为广泛使用的决策工具是股东价值分析法,即分析如果企业拥有或失去某个战略业务单元,企业在股票市场的价值将会提高还是下降。每个战略业务单位都需要对企业的优势有积极的贡献。

　　评估业务单元的增长机会包括计划新业务、缩小业务规模或终止旧业务。计划新业务有三种模式,即集中增长(在现有业务基础上)、整合增长(与现有业务相关)以及多元化增长(与现有业务不相关)。对于集中增长模式,企业管理层首先考虑现有产品或服务是否能够获得更多的市场份额。其次考虑在市场发展战略中,企业是否能够为现有的产品找到或发展新的市场。最后判断在产品发展战略中,企业能否根据现有市场的潜在需求,生产新的产品。整合增长是指通过在行业中对业务进行前置整合、后置整合或横向整合,来提高收益和利润。当其他行业有足够吸引力并且拥有业务优势时,企业才能从多元化增长战略中获得成功。而当企业有降低成本或将现有资源集中到其他业务单元的需求时,企业需要谨慎地从已经失去竞争力的业务中退出。

　　企业组织结构也是公司层面战略规划中的重要一环。组织结构包括架构、政策和企业文化。图 2-4 所示为首旅集团公司(总部)的组织架构图。

　　管理层能够改变企业的架构和政策,但很难改变企业文化。然而,适应企业文化通常是成功实施新战略的关键。Kotler 和 Keller(2009)认为,企业文化的定义为"组织成员所共同拥有的经验、故事、信念和规范等特征"。在一些情境下,企业文化由企业内部发展起来,直接从企业领导层(性格、习惯)传递至员工。

When strategic business units are identified, managers must decide the allocation of business resources to each unit. Since the 1970s, different consulting firms have devised different models to help the management to make investment decisions. The "GE/McKinsey Matrix" identifies the resources that each unit should acquire based on the competitive advantage of the strategic business unit and the attractiveness of its industry. The Boston Consulting Group's "Growth-Share Matrix" uses the market shares of each business unit and the annual growth rate of the market as criteria for making investment decisions. Nowadays, the widely used decision-making tool is shareholder value analysis, that is, if the business owns or loses a strategic business unit, will the firm's value in the stock market rise or fall? Each strategic business unit should contribute to the strengths of the company.

Assessing growth opportunities of business units includes planning new business, downsizing, or terminating old business. The three modes of planning new business are intensive growth (based on existing business), integrative growth (related to existing business), and diversification growth (unrelated to existing business). For intensive growth, the management should first consider whether existing products or services can grow market share. Second, the management should consider whether companies can find or develop new markets for existing products in the market development strategy. Finally, the management should determine whether the company can produce new products according to the potential demand of existing markets in the product development strategy. Integrative growth refers to the situation in which businesses can increase revenue and profit through backward, forward, or horizontal integration in the industry. Only when other industries are adequately attractive and possess business advantages can the company succeed in integrative growth strategy. When the company demands to reduce costs or allocate existing resources to other business units, the company needs to be careful in withdrawing from the business that lost its competitiveness.

Corporate organizational structure is an important part of corporate level strategic planning. The organizational structure includes structures, policies, and corporate culture. Figure 2-4 shows the organization chart of BTG (headquarters).

Management can change the structures and policies of the enterprise, but changing corporate culture is difficult. Adapting to corporate culture, however, is often the key to the successful implementation of the new strategy. Kotler and Keller (2009) argue that corporate culture is defined as "the shared experiences, stories, beliefs and norms that characterise an organisation." In some situations, corporate culture is developed within the enterprise and communicated directly from the business leadership (character, habits) to the staff.

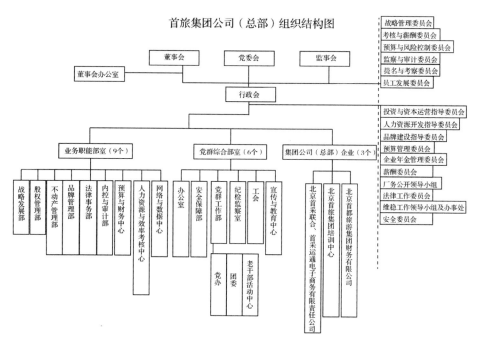

图 2-4　首旅集团组织架构

来源：首旅集团(http://www.btg.com.cn/about/about.asp? tid=8)

创新通常被认为是制定营销战略最困难的部分。传统的观点是管理层提出战略后交由员工执行。Prahalad 和 Hamel(1990)认为，企业内部的各个群体都能够对战略提出创新性的意见。Kotler 和 Keller(2009)认为，高级管理层应该从三个在战略决策方面被低估的群体中识别和鼓励新的意见：年轻的员工、远离总部的员工和新进入行业的员工。每个群体的意见都能够打破企业中固有的认知，带来新的想法。

基于熊彼得创新理论的基本观点及相关过往研究，Hjalager(2009)指出，在旅游及酒店业中的创新类别主要包括产品或服务创新、过程创新、组织创新、管理创新以及制度创新。产品或服务创新指的是市场可以直接感知到的以前从未见过的，或是对于某一企业或目的地来讲从未出现过的产品或服务。新的产品或服务会成为顾客做出购买决策的影响因素。例如产生于分享经济背景下的 Airbnb 可以被看作是住宿业产品创新。

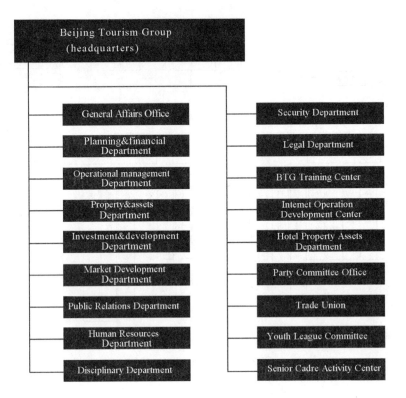

Figure 2－4　Organizational structure of Beijing Tourism Group
Source：BTG（http：//www.btg.com.cn/EN/about/about.asp？tid＝8）

Innovation is often considered the most difficult part of developing a marketing strategy. Traditionally， the management proposes a strategy and leaves the implementation to the staff. Prahalad and Hamel（1990）argue that each group within the organization can put forward innovative ideas for strategy. Kotler and Keller（2009）believe that senior management should identify and encourage new ideas from three groups that are undervalued in strategic decision making， namely， young employees， employees away from headquarters， and new entrants. The opinions of each group break the inherent awareness among the enterprise and bring new ideas.

Using the fundamental viewpoints of Schumpeter's innovation theory and relevant research as basis， Hjalager（2009）points out that innovation in the tourism and hospitality industry mainly consists of product or service， process， managerial/ organizational， management， and institution innovations. Product or service innovation refers to a product or service that the market can directly perceive as never been seen before or never been seen for a certain enterprise or destination. A new product or service can be an influencing factor to the purchase decision of customers. For example， Airbnb，which was born in the context of shared economy，can be viewed as product innovation in the hospitality industry.

过程创新一般是指后台的以提高生产效率为目标的创新，这类创新一般都是企业对科技投入资金的结果。如机场通过使用不同的技术手段提高货物、信息以及人的流动速度，从而提升机场使用效率。

组织创新指的是内部协作、员工管理和授权、工作补偿等方面的创新。对于许多旅游及酒店业的企业来说，降低员工流失率是一个非常大的挑战，因而组织创新的目标就在于提高员工满意度。

管理创新是指企业把新的管理要素或其组合引入管理系统以更有效地实现组织目标的创新活动。忠诚计划被广泛认为是酒店与旅游业企业的管理创新。

制度创新是指随着生产力的发展对企业制度进行变革，包括对企业的生产方式、经营方式、分配方式、经营观念的改变。特许经营制度和计算机预订系统都是制度创新的例子。

企业的创新是一个复杂的过程，受到一系列内部和外部因素的影响，一般认为企业创新行为的主要影响因素包括企业家、科技进步以及产业的集聚。

2.4　业务单元层级营销战略

业务单元层级的发展方向和目标必须与整个集团的目标和营销战略保持一致。目标是任务的数字成果和完成时间的客观描述。业务单元可以设定多个任务，并通过管理任务来完成目标。如果企业希望通过管理任务获得成功，则其业务单元的任务需要满足下列四个条件：

（1）对任务进行重要性排列，重要的任务必须优先完成。

（2）任务成果尽可能通过数字体现。

（3）目标具有可行性。

（4）任务之间有一致性。

目标是业务单元要达到的成果，战略则是如何实现目标的规划。在同一目标市场实施相同战略的企业被视为同一战略集团。在这个集团中，战略执行最好的企业将获得最多的利润。业务单元层级的战略包括一般性战略和拓展性战略。

2.4.1　一般性战略

一般性战略可分为三种：成本领先战略、差异化战略和聚焦战略（Porter，1985）。

Process innovation refers to the backend innovation aiming to improve production efficiency. This type of innovation usually results from business investment in science and technology. For instance, an airport enhances airport efficiency using different technological means to improve goods, information, and staff mobility.

Managerial/organizational innovation refers to innovation in terms of internal collaboration, employee management and empowerment, and compensation. For many tourism and hospitality companies, reducing employee turnover is a big challenge. Hence, the goal of organizational innovation is to improve employee satisfaction.

Management innovation refers to instances when companies introduce new management elements or combination thereof into the management system to effectively achieve organizational goals. The loyalty program is widely recognized as a management innovation in the hospitality and tourism industry.

Institution innovation refers to the change in the enterprise system with productivity development, including the change of production mode, operation mode, distribution mode, and management concept. Franchise and computer reservation systems are examples of institution innovations.

Business innovation is a complex process subject to a series of internal and external factors. Generally, the main influencing factors of enterprise innovation activities include entrepreneurs, scientific and technological progress, and industrial agglomeration.

2.4 Business Unit Level Marketing Strategy

The direction and goals at business unit level must be aligned with the organizational goals and marketing strategy. A goal is a description of the numerical outcome and the completion time of the task. Business units can set multiple tasks and achieve the goals through managing tasks. If an organization wants to achieve success through managing tasks, then the tasks of the business unit should meet the four following criteria:

(1) Tasks are arranged according to their importance. Important tasks should be prioritized.

(2) Results of the task should be reflected in numbers as far as possible.

(3) The goal should be feasible.

(4) Tasks should have consistency.

The goal is the result the business unit strives to achieve, whereas the strategy is the planning related to achieving the goal. Firms that implement the same strategy in the same target market form a strategic group. In this group, the company that implements the best strategy make the most profit. Business unit level strategies are categorized into generic and growth strategies.

2.4.1　Generic strategy model

Generic strategies can be divided into three categories, which are cost leadership, differentiation, and focus strategies (Porter, 1985).

1. 成本领先战略

成本领先战略也称为低成本战略,指企业通过有效途径降低成本,使产品成本低于竞争对手,甚至是同行业中的最低成本,从而获得竞争优势。企业在提供功能、质量相似的产品和服务的条件下,通过尽可能降低成本来取得竞争优势。简化服务内容、改进服务程序、节约消费品提供、降低人工费用或设备自动化常常作为旅游企业实施成本领先战略的手段(徐惠群,2009)。喜达屋酒店及度假村集团旗下酒店品牌雅乐轩于 2015 年 8 月宣布引入机器人提供服务。机器人取代了部分酒店岗位所需的人力资源,直接降低了酒店行业的人力资源成本,是喜达屋酒店集团实施成本领先战略的体现(酒店内参,2016)。

2. 差异化战略

差异化战略是指企业通过提供在整个行业内都被认为是独特的、具有竞争对手所不具备的特点或属性的产品,从而占有更大市场份额并获取利润的一种战略(Porter,1985)。这种差异是消费者所希望或乐意接受,并具有价值的。当差异化产品成功地被顾客接受时,企业能够获得价格溢价的优势,或者在一定的价格下出售更多的产品,又或者能建立顾客忠诚度。越是难以模仿或复制的属性和特点越能让企业受益,并能更长久地占有竞争优势。然而,旅游服务产品容易被复制,在产品创新或变革方面具有相当的难度。新产品在投入市场后会快速地被大量复制(徐惠群,2009)。携程旅行网在 2013 年与香港永安旅游、台湾易游网共同成立了鸿鹄旅游。与普通旅行社的大众旅行团不同,鸿鹄旅游专注于高端客户群体定制旅游,主打环游世界 80 天高端定制游。此旅游产品每年参加名额有限,每年推出后都在极短时间内被抢购一空(鸿鹄旅游,2016)。根据胡润百富(2015)中国奢华旅游白皮书,鸿鹄旅游在中国大陆出境游奢华旅行社中排名前十。

3. 聚焦战略

企业在同时取得成本领先和差异领先的竞争优势下,能够实现企业利益最大化,因为成本领先意味着成本的降低,与此同时差异领先会带来价格溢价,从而实现收益的累加。但由于各种条件的限制,全面、长期地同时取得成

1. Cost leadership strategy

Cost leadership strategy, also known as low-cost strategy, refers to the decision of enterprises to reduce costs by lowering product cost compared with those of competitors or even offering the lowest cost in the industry, thereby gaining competitive advantage. Companies obtain competitive advantage by minimizing costs while providing products and services of comparable functionality and quality. Simplifying service content, improving service procedures, saving consumer goods, and reducing labor costs or equipment automation are often used as means of implementing cost leadership strategy in tourism enterprises (Hsu, 2009). Starwood Hotels and Resorts implemented cost leadership strategy. In August 2015, Starwood Hotels and Resorts, specifically, Aloft hotels, announced the introduction of robotic services. The emerging robots replace part of the human resources that hotels require, directly reducing the labor cost of the hotel industry (Hotel Internal Reference, 2016).

2. Differentiation strategy

Differentiation strategy is implemented when the enterprise obtains a large share of the market and makes profit by offering products that are unique across the industry and characterized by features or attributes that those of competitors do not have (Porter, 1985). This difference is what consumers want or willingly accept, and it is valuable. When customers successfully accept differentiated products, companies accordingly benefit from obtaining the advantage of price premium, selling more products at a certain price, or establishing customer loyalty. The more difficult to imitate or copy the attributes and features, the more benefits the enterprise can obtain, and the longer the possession of competitive advantage is. However, tourism service products are easy to duplicate, making innovation or transformation of the product difficult. New products can be quickly replicated once they are released in the market (Hsu, 2009). Ctrip co-founded HHtravel with Hong Kong Wingon Travel and Taiwan ezTravel in 2013. Different from the public tours of ordinary travel agencies, HHtravel focuses on customized tours for high-end customer groups, featuring 80 days of traveling around the world in a high-end customized tour. This annual travel product is offered limitedly, and thus, it is sold out within a very short period after launch each year (HHtravel, 2016). According to The Chinese Luxury Traveler by Hurun Report (2015), HHtravel ranks among the top 10 Chinese Mainland luxury outbound travel agencies.

3. Focus strategy

Companies maximize their interests when they achieve advantages of cost leadership and differentiation at the same time. Cost leadership means cost reduction, whereas differentiation

本领先和差异领先地位的目标难以实现。部分企业将经营活动集中于某一个或几个特定的购买群、某种产品系列的一个细分区段或某一个细分市场，这就是聚焦战略。这种战略的核心就是专注于某一个或几个特定的消费群体、某种具体的产品线或某个细分市场。聚焦战略可以结合成本领先或差异领先战略实现：成本领先目标聚焦战略寻求在目标市场上的成本优势，差异领先目标聚焦战略则追求目标市场上的产品差异优势（徐惠群，2009）。精品民宿是中国酒店市场近年来的热点，花间堂是其中的成功例子。花间堂旗下客栈定位为高级私人客栈，目标顾客群体是希望体验客栈的个性与文化并同时享受星级酒店的舒适度的高端旅客。在此基础上，花间堂通过修缮丽江的老宅，提供不同的休闲度假活动，成功实现产品的差异化（私人管家，2016）。

2.4.2　拓展性战略

拓展性战略是指某一业务单元被企业评估为具有集中增长的潜力，企业为达成长期目标，针对该业务单元在不同的发展阶段所采取一系列中心明确、相互一致的，以适应拓展市场份额和获取竞争优势并能有效实施的战略。其具体的战略形式包括市场渗透战略、产品创新战略、新市场开发战略和多样化经营战略（图 2-5）。

	现有产品/服务	新产品/服务
现有市场	市场渗透	产品创新
新市场	市场开发	多样化经营

图 2-5　业务单元增长型战略方法选择

来源：Ansoff，H. I.（1957）. Strategies for diversification. *Harvard Business Review*，35(5)，113-124.

1. 市场渗透

市场渗透是指以现有的产品面对现有的顾客，以目前的产品市场组合为发展焦点，通过更大的市场营销力度，提高现有产品质量或服务水准，进一步提高市场份额，力求增大产品的市场占有率的战略方式。采取市场渗透战略，可以促销或提升服务质量等方式说服消费者增加重复购买次数或购买企业提供的多种不同产品。酒店工作人员向住店客人建议购买酒店的其他产品或服务，如纪念品、烟酒、点心或升级至更好的房间就是市场渗透方案之一。

results in price premium, leading to the accumulation of earnings. However, limited by various conditions, achieving both cost leadership and differentiation comprehensively and in long term is difficult. Several companies focus their business on one or several specific buying groups, such as a segment of a certain product line or a market segment, in implementing focus strategy. The core of this strategy is focusing on one or a few specific consumer groups, a specific product line, or a market segment. Focus strategy can be achieved together with cost leadership or differentiation strategy. Cost focus strategy seeks cost advantage in the target market, whereas focused differentiation strategy pursues product differentiation advantage in the target market (Hsu, 2009). Boutique homestay is very popular in the hotel market of China in recent years. Blossom Hill Hotels & Resorts is one of the successful examples. Blossom Hill positions its properties as high-class private inns, which target high-end travelers who want to experience the unique character and culture of the inns while enjoying the comfort of the star hotel. On this basis, Blossom Hill realizes product differentiation by amending the old houses in Lijiang and providing different leisure activities (Butler Service, 2016).

2.4.2 Expansion of the strategic model

Growth strategy refers to a series of clearly focused, consistent, and feasible strategies implemented by a company. These strategies are applied according to the development stage of the business unit when the business unit is assessed as having the focus growth potential. The purpose is to adapt to the expanding market share, gain competitive advantage, and achieve long-term goals of the company. The specific strategies include market penetration, product development, new market development, and diversification (Figure 2 - 5).

	present product/service	new product/service
present market	market penetration	product development
new market	market development	diversification

Figure 2 - 5   Alternatives of business unit growth strategies

Source: Ansoff, H. I. (1957).Strategies for diversification. *Harvard Business Review*, 35(5), 113 - 124.

1. Market penetration

Market penetration refers to selling existing products to current customers. Given the development focused on current product-market portfolio, greater marketing efforts can improve existing product quality or service standards. Thus, market and product shares are increased. Companies that apply the market penetration strategy convince consumers to increase the number of repeat purchase or purchase different products provided through promotion or enhancement of service quality. Market penetration is reflected when hotel staff suggest hotel guests to buy other hotel products or services, such as

吸引现有客人的多次重复消费或针对潜在客人试买消费的促销活动也属此列。市场渗透战略的风险性最小。当企业特定的产品或服务在当前市场中还未达到饱和,用户对产品的使用率还可以显著提高时,企业往往采用市场渗透战略。例如,城市可以吸引商务旅行者带他们家人再来度假。但如果市场已经达到饱和,这种策略可能是回报率最低的。

2. 产品创新

产品创新的核心是企业推出新产品给现有顾客。企业通常以推出全新产品或扩大现有产品的深度和广度给现有的顾客的方式,利用现有的顾客关系来开展营销,增加产品销售量和市场占有份额。新推介的产品既可以是现有产品的升级和改进(如喜达屋旗下的雅乐轩酒店是 W 酒店的延伸),也可以是全新的产品(如希尔顿酒店集团最新品牌 Tru)。旅游经营者不断推出新的旅游目的地,旅游目的地也不断开发新的旅游景点、景区。但产品创新策略风险系数大,因为进行产品开发通常需要大量的研究和开发费用,一旦某项新产品的开发遭受失败的厄运,损失成本非常之高。

3. 市场开发

市场开发是指企业开拓尚未开发或尚未饱和的市场,在不同的地区找到具有相同产品需求的顾客,并为其提供现有产品的战略。其主旨就是将现有产品或服务打入新的市场。采用该战略的企业一般存在过剩的生产能力和营销能力,并且可以得到可靠的、经济的高质量销售网络。该战略要比市场渗透战略风险大,因为如果开拓新市场失败就会给企业带来大量市场开发支出的损失。最常用的市场开发活动是识别新的地区市场,如从欧洲市场向亚洲市场延伸。在酒店业内,连锁经营被认为是有利于市场开发的最主要手段。连锁经营集团向各下属企业提供必要的投资和信心十足的管理人员,这正好解决了市场扩张的两大主要问题——财务和人力资源。近年来各大世界知名酒店集团(万豪、洲际、希尔顿等)纷纷加快在中国酒店业市场的扩张速度就是企业进行市场开发的实例。

4. 多样化经营

多样化经营是指一个企业将新产品投入新市场。提供新产品给新市场具

souvenirs, tobacco, liquor, and snacks, or upgrade to a better room. Marketing penetration strategy is also reflected in promotions that attract repeat purchase of existing customers or initial purchase of potential customers. Market penetration possesses minimum risk. When the specific product or service has not yet reached the saturation stage in the current market, and product usage by customers can be significantly improved, companies often use market penetration strategy. For example, cities can attract business travelers to return for vacation with their families. However, if the market has been saturated, then this strategy may lead to the lowest rate of return.

2. Product development

The core of product development is the introduction of new products to existing customers. Enterprises usually launch new products or expand the depth and breadth of existing products for existing customers and use existing customer relationships to carry out marketing programs. The goal of these strategies is to increase product sales and market share. The new products can be upgrades or enhancements of existing products (e.g., Starwood's Aloft, which is an extension of W hotel) or new products (e.g., Hilton's newest brand, Tru). Tourism operators continue to introduce new tourist destinations, and tourist destinations are constantly developing new tourist attractions. However, product development strategy is risky because it usually requires a large amount of research and development expenses. Once the development of a new product fails, the loss is steep.

3. Market development

Market development refers to the strategy of enterprises to explore the market that has not yet been developed or saturated, find customers with the same demand for products in different regions, and offer existing products to them. The main purpose is to sell existing products or services to new markets. Enterprises that adopt this strategy generally possess excess production capacity and marketing capabilities, and they can access reliable, economical, and quality sales network. This strategy is riskier than market penetration, because failure to exploit new markets can result in a significant loss of market development expenditure. The most commonly used market development activity is to identify new regional markets, such as the extension from European market to Asian one. In the hotel industry, chain operation is the most important means for market development. Chain groups provide necessary investment and confident managers to affiliate companies, thus solving the two main problems of market expansion, namely, finance and human resources. In recent years, the world leading hotel groups (Marriott, InterContinental, and Hilton) have accelerated their market expansion in China's hotel industry, exemplifying market development.

4. Diversification

Diversification refers to the introduction of an enterprise of new products into new markets. Providing new products to new markets has a two-way risk of new product and new

有新产品创新和新市场开发的双重风险,是一种最高风险的战略。企业实行多元化战略,关键是实现所有不同部门的优劣势互补,取得公司整体力量强于各部门力量之和的协同效果。中国的华侨城集团是实行多元化经营取得成功的佼佼者。华侨城集团是国务院国资委直属的大型中央企业,旗下有高科技电子、旅游业、房地产业、酒店业、传媒业等主要产业。华侨城旅游业从兴建中国第一个主题公园——锦绣中华微缩景区起步,相继成功建设了中国民俗文化村、世界之窗、欢乐谷等四大主题公园,并以此形成了一个集旅游、文化、购物、娱乐、体育、休闲于一体的文化旅游度假区。此外,其又先后投资建设了北京华侨城、上海华侨城、成都华侨城、深圳东部华侨城等大型旅游综合项目。华侨城酒店业异军突起,旗下的威尼斯酒店、海景酒店、华侨城大酒店等主题酒店品牌享誉全国,经济型酒店城市客栈成功实现了跨区连锁经营。经过资产整合后的华侨城酒店正呈现出强劲的势头。华侨城国际传媒以其雄厚的实力及专业化运作,逐渐成为业内佼佼者。

此外,战略联盟也是企业常用的战略之一。企业通过与本地或跨国公司组成战略联盟来提高或完善自身的能力和资源。战略联盟通常有四种形式:产品或服务联盟、推广联盟、物流联盟、价格合作。在跨国发展层面,企业在本土以外的国家开展业务可能需要取得许可。此时,与该国本土企业成立合资公司或收购本土供应商能帮助企业符合相应的要求。华住集团与法国雅高酒店集团于 2014 年达成协议组成战略联盟。2016 年年初,华住集团与雅高集团完成交叉持股交割,正式落实长期战略联盟协议。根据协议,华住成为雅高集团部分品牌在中国大陆和台湾地区、蒙古国的总加盟商,并与雅高联合开发部分雅高旗下品牌的酒店(一财网,2016)。

market development. Therefore, this strategy bears the highest risk. The key for companies to implement diversification strategy is to make all different departments complementary to each other's advantages and disadvantages. This relationship can achieve the synergy that the overall strength of the company is stronger than the sum of all departments. China's OCT Group is the leader in business success through implementing diversification operation. The OCT Group is a large enterprise directly affiliated with the State Council State-owned Assets Supervision and Administration Commission. The main business of the group includes high-tech electronics, tourism, real estate, hotels, and media. OCT tourism started with the construction of China's first theme park, the Splendid China Miniature Park, and later successfully built the China Folk Culture Villages, Window of the World, and Happy Valley. These four major theme parks form a cultural tourism resort that combines tourism, culture, shopping, entertainment, sports, and leisure. In addition, the OCT group has invested in the construction of large-scale integrated tourism projects such as Beijing OCT, Shanghai OCT, Chengdu OCT, and Shenzhen East OCT. OCT hotels rise as a new force in hotel industry with its Venice Hotel, Seaview Hotel, OCT Grand Hotel, and other themed hotel brands being famous in the country. Its economy hotel brand City Inn successfully achieved inter-regional chain operations. After asset integration, the OCT hotel is showing a strong momentum. OCT international media is gradually becoming the industry leader with its strength and professional operation.

Strategic alliance is another strategy commonly used by enterprises. A company improves or perfects its capabilities and resources through the formation of strategic alliances with local or international companies. Generally, the four forms of strategic alliances are product or service, promotional, logistics, and pricing collaborations. For international development, companies may need permission to operate in another country. In this case, setting up joint ventures with the country's domestic enterprises or acquiring local suppliers can help companies meet corresponding requirements. Huazhu Hotels Group and AccorHotels Group reached an agreement to form a strategic alliance in 2014. In early 2016, Huazhu and Accor completed the cross-shareholding delivery and formally implemented the long-term strategic alliance agreement. Under the terms of the agreement, Huazhu is the general franchisee of some of the Accor brands in the Chinese Mainland and Chinese Taiwan, and Mongolia, and jointly develops hotel brands of the AccorHotels Group (China Business Network, 2016).

第3章　市场营销信息与调研

 本章要点

- 营销信息系统的组成及信息来源
- 主要市场营销调研的研究方向
- 旅游企业市场营销调研数据收集途径
- 营销效果评估研究的主要方法
- 市场需求预测

随着经济发展和科技进步,旅游市场的竞争愈发激烈,市场营销人员需要通过不断更新的信息来了解和追踪顾客需求、偏好、购买行为等方面的变化,为企业决策提供及时可靠的信息。营销信息系统正是市场营销人员的信息来源。搭建和维护一个高效的营销信息系统需要相应的人员、设备以及对信息的收集、整理、分析和评估。本章将详细介绍营销信息系统的组成、营销研究的步骤、主要信息来源、营销效果评估的方法以及市场需求预测。

3.1　营销信息系统

营销信息系统包括人员和设备,通过对营销信息的收集、整理、分析和评估,向营销决策者提供必要、及时而准确的信息。企业的内部记录、营销情报活动和营销研究是建立企业营销信息系统的基础。

3.1.1　内部记录

内部记录系统的核心是记录企业从收到订单到获得付款的过程,其中包括订单数量、销售总额、价格、成本、库存水平、应收款项、应付款项等一系列数据。系统能够为市场营销人员提供及时和准确的报告,以方便他们了解当

Chapter 3   Marketing Information and Research

 Key points of the chapter

- Components and information sources of marketing information system
- Main research direction of marketing research
- Data collection methods of tourism marketing research
- Evaluation methods of marketing effectiveness
- Forecasting market demand

With the development of economy and the progress of science and technology, competition in the tourism market intensifies. Marketers must understand and track changes in customer demands, preferences, and purchase behaviors through updated information to provide timely and reliable information needed in the decision making of a company. Marketing information system is the information source for marketers. Building and maintaining an efficient marketing information system require relevant personnel and equipment as well as collection, collation, analysis, and evaluation of the information. This chapter explains in detail the components of marketing information systems, steps of marketing research, main sources of information, assessment methods of marketing effectiveness, and market demand forecasting.

3.1   Marketing Information System

Marketing information systems, including personnel and equipment, provide decision makers with necessary, timely, and accurate information through collection, collation, analysis, and evaluation of marketing information. The internal records, marketing intelligence activities, and marketing research are the basis of establishing the marketing information system of an enterprise.

3.1.1   Internal records

The core of the internal record system is to record the process from placing orders to receiving payment, including a series of data, such as order quantity, total sales, prices, costs, inventory level, receivables, and payables. The system provides marketers with timely and accurate reports that can help them to understand how a product was sold at a

时的产品销售情况。市场营销人员通过分析内部记录系统所提供的数据,寻找重要的市场机会或潜在问题。企业一般都会对数据进行储存分类,并建立不同的数据库,如顾客数据库、产品数据库和销售人员信息数据库。这些数据库能够方便营销决策者获取所需的数据,设定相应的目标和计划,并追踪营销活动的进展和成果。此外,掌握统计学方法的分析员能够对这些数据进行挖掘,在不受重视的细分市场、顾客需求或行为趋势等方面获得新的市场前景和其他有益的信息。

酒店及旅游企业的内部数据库信息有诸多来源,如顾客登记和预订记录、销售组合和顾客组合信息、问询记录和拒客记录、投诉处理记录等。这些记录都可以被用作市场营销有用的信息源。零售管理系统(POS)是目前旅游企业使用较多的储存企业内部信息的系统。它由许多以特定软件控制的收银机组成,用来记录出售货品的数量、成本、销售时间、顾客资料等交易资料和销售信息。零售管理系统记录的经营信息涵盖了货品销售数量、销售地点、销售时间、销售地区以及顾客资料等诸多方面,引起了旅游企业经营的革命性变化。例如,美国的菲尔兹饼干(Mrs. Fields' Cookies)拥有一套允许不同分店与总部之间双向交流的综合电脑网络。每个分店每天都会事先收到总部基于历史数据做出的每种产品的预测销售数量,总部也会监控每间分店的实际销售水平并按小时更新其预测。当实际销售量低于期望值时,电脑就会推荐推销技巧来提高销售额,比如在店前提供样品供过往路人品尝等。企业总部市场营销研究部门的审计员、分店经理或市场分析人员能定期从不同的报告中收集信息,识别消费趋势,解决经营中存在的某些问题(徐惠群,2009)。

由于酒店与旅游业提供的产品的特殊性,除了 POS 中记录的销售数据外,关于顾客行为的内部信息也可以帮助营销人员更好地了解顾客的需求和偏好。以丽思卡尔顿的被称为"秘诀系统"的顾客关系管理系统为例。这个全球丽思卡尔顿信息共享的管理系统记录酒店所有客人的投诉和偏好,质量团队负责维护和整合信息。许多时候当酒店员工遇到客人的投诉时,都可以通过查看系统中其他酒店记录下来的信息找到解决方法。

3.1.2 营销情报系统

内部记录系统提供的是营销活动结果的数据,而营销情报系统则是提供营销活动依据的数据。营销情报系统是营销人员收集市场环境变化的过程和

particular time. Marketers can discover important market opportunities or potential problems by analyzing the data provided by the internal record system. Companies typically store and classify data and create different databases, such as customer, product, and salesperson information databases. These databases enable marketing decision makers to access the data they need, set goals and plans, and track the progress and results of marketing campaigns. Analysts who master statistical methods can also exploit these data and gain new market insights and other useful information in less focused segments, customer needs, or behavioral trends.

A number of information sources can be accessed for internal databases of hotel and tourism companies, such as customer registration and booking records, sales mix and customer portfolio information, inquiry records and rejection records, and complaint-handling records. These records can be used as useful information source for marketing. Point-of-sale (POS) system, which is used by many tourism enterprises to store internal information, is composed of many cash registers controlled by specific software. This system is used to record the quantity, cost, transaction time, and customer information of sold goods. POS system records business information, including the quantity, sales venue, sales time, sales region, and customer information of sold goods, causing a revolutionary change in the tourism industry. For example, Mrs. Fields' Cookies in the United States adopts an integrated computer network that allows two-way communication among different stores and headquarters. Each store receives daily forecasted sales figures for each product based on historical data from the headquarters, and the headquarters monitors the actual sales for each store and updates its forecasts every hour. When the actual sales falls below expectations, the computer recommends promotion techniques to increase sales, such as providing samples in front of the store for passersby to taste. Auditors in corporate marketing research departments, store managers, or market analysts regularly collect information from different reports, identify consumption trends, and address operational problems (Hsu, 2009).

In addition to the sales data recorded in POS system, the internal information about customer behavior can enhance the understanding of marketers of customer needs and preferences, given the specific nature of the products offered by the hospitality and tourism industry. For example, the Ritz-Carlton customer relationship management system, which is known as the "Mystique system", is an information-sharing management system that records complaints and preferences from all hotel guests. A quality control team is responsible for maintaining and integrating the information. When a hotel employee encounters a guest complaint, he or she can find a solution by looking through useful information recorded by other hotels in the system.

3.1.2　Marketing intelligence system

The internal record system provides data on the results of the marketing campaign, whereas the marketing intelligence system provides the data that are used as the basis for

信息源。市场情报来自书籍、报纸杂志、贸易出版物、互联网、与顾客交流、与供应商和分销商交流、与其他企业营销人员交流等渠道。根据 Kotler 和 Keller(2006)的研究,企业可以通过六个步骤(见图 3-1)提高营销情报的质量。一些企业有专门的分析员对市场情报进行收集和分析,提取关键的市场环境变化并传递给营销决策者,以确保营销决策者能够接收到最新的市场信息,制定有效的营销策略。

图 3-1　营销情报获取流程

来源：Kotler，Keller（2006）. *A Framework of Marketing Management*（3rd ed）. Upper Saddle Rier，NJ：Pearson Prentice Hall.

　　熟知企业所处的竞争环境也是管理部门在市场竞争中战胜对手的关键。获取竞争对手信息的方法很多,包括分析业内的新闻媒体,登记成为竞争对手的邮件客户从而第一时间获取最新的信息以了解对手的营销活动,以顾客身份前往竞争对手的企业观察、购买及分析竞争对手的产品等。此外,企业还可以通过非正式的交流渠道如与工作人员聊天来获取相关信息。

3.2　营销研究

　　营销研究是企业面对特定市场环境,进行系统化研究设计,收集市场信息并进行分析,获取相应数据和研究结果的过程（Kotler 和 Keller,2009）。营销人员可以使用二手数据(已存在的为其他目的而收集的信息)、一手数据

marketing campaigns. Marketing intelligence system is the process and information sources of marketing personnel collecting market environment changes. Market intelligence comes from channels such as books, newspapers, magazines, trade publications, the Internet, and communication with customers, suppliers, and distributors. Kotler and Keller (2006) claim that companies can improve the quality of market intelligence in six steps (Figure 3 – 1). To ensure that marketing decision makers can receive the latest market information and develop effective marketing campaigns, some companies hire specialized analysts to collect and analyze market intelligence and extract key market environment changes, which are then presented to the marketing decision makers.

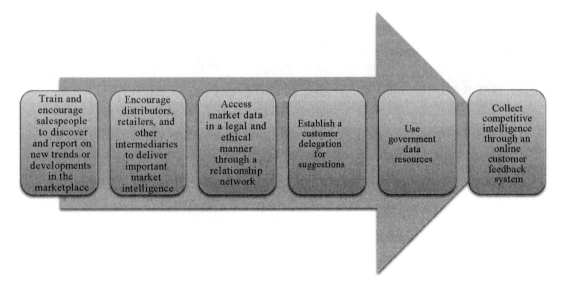

Figure 3 – 1　Marketing intelligence acquisition

Source: Kotler & Keller (2006). *A Framework of Marketing Management*. (3rd ed.) Upper Saddle River, NJ: Prentic Hall.

To win over the opponent in the market competition for management, companies should be familiar with the competitive environment. The following ways can be used to obtain competitor information: analysis of the industry news media, registration as an email subscriber of competitors to obtain updated information and learn their marketing activities, observations as customers at the business of competitors, and purchase and analysis of competitors' products. Enterprises can also obtain relevant information through informal communication channels, such as informal conversations with the staff.

3.2 *Marketing Research*

Marketing research is the systematic research design, market information collection and analysis, and it involves obtaining appropriate data and research results (Kotler & Keller, 2009) when a company is faced with a particular market environment. Marketers can use secondary data (i.e., information already collected for other purposes), primary

（为当前研究目标而专门收集的原始信息），或这两类资料的结合。

3.2.1　二手数据

二手数据的来源非常广泛。在通常情况下，企业会花费销售额的 1%～2% 用于购买外部的市场营销研究公司的服务。市场营销研究公司有三种类型。

（1）信息服务研究公司：此类研究公司收集和分析顾客和贸易的信息，并以此获利。例如 TNS Gallup（盖洛普）、Business Monitor International（BMI，国际商业观察）、Smith Travel Research（STR）。

（2）专项营销研究公司：此类研究公司负责企业指定的研究项目，进行项目设计并汇报结果。例如 Capgemini（凯捷咨询）、Horwath HTL（浩华）。

（3）专业服务研究公司：此类研究公司提供特定类型的研究服务，如田野调查或访谈。例如 Continental Research Corporation。

小型企业同样可以从营销研究公司购买服务或通过其他更为经济的方式进行市场研究，例如：

（1）聘用学生或教授进行营销研究。一些企业通过赞助部分学术或实战商业比赛，以合理的成本获取解决营销问题的新视角。

（2）利用互联网信息。企业可以通过调查竞争对手的网页、监测网上论坛或者取得公开出版物的数据，以低成本获得大量的市场信息。

（3）观察竞争对手。许多小型企业会定期到竞争对手的专营店或餐厅进行观察，体验竞争对手的产品和服务，以获得最新的信息和想法。

除此之外，企业还可通过各种渠道获取一些成本较低的二手数据。这些渠道包括以下几种。

（1）政府部门：政府机构的出版刊物或统计报告是二手资料的重要来源。一般国家或地方政府会对各行业定期进行统计，并公布相关结果。如《加拿大旅游业月度报告》《新加坡旅游业季度报告》《中国社科院旅游绿皮书》《中国旅游研究院旅游服务行业年度报告》等。

（2）行业组织和协会：旅游业的不断发展使得越来越多的非营利性组织和协会也积极参与分析、规划以及推广旅游业的活动，如联合国世界旅游组织（United Nations World Tourism Organization，UNWTO）、国际会议和观

data (i.e., raw information that is specifically collected for current research goals), or a combination of both.

3.2.1 Secondary data

Secondary data comes from a wide range of sources. Typically, companies spend 1% to 2% of their sales on services of external marketing research firms. Marketing research companies can be classified into the three following types.

(1) Information service research companies: This type of research companies collects and analyzes information about customers and trade and profits from it. Examples are TNS Gallup, Business Monitor International, and Smith Travel Research (STR).

(2) Specialized marketing research companies: This type of research companies is responsible for research projects designated by enterprises, carrying out project design and reporting the results. Examples are Capgemini and Horwath HTL.

(3) Professional service research companies: These research firms provide specific types of research services, such as field surveys or interviews. An example is Continental Research Corporation.

Small businesses can also buy services from marketing research firms or conduct market research in other cost-effective ways, such as the following:

(1) Employing students or professors to conduct marketing research: Some companies gain new perspectives to solve marketing problems at a reasonable cost by sponsoring academic or practical business competitions.

(2) Using online information. Companies can access large amounts of market information at low cost by investigating competitors' web pages, monitoring online forums, or obtaining publicly available data.

(3) Observe competitors. Many small businesses regularly inspect competitors' stores or restaurants and experience competitors' products and services to acquire the latest information and ideas.

In addition, companies can obtain different low-cost secondary data through various channels, including the following:

(1) Government departments: Publications or statistical reports of government agencies are important sources of secondary data. National or regional governments gather statistics regularly on various industries and publish the relevant results. Examples are *Canadian Tourism Monthly Report*, *Singapore Tourism Quarterly Report*, *Green Book of China's Tourism by Chinese Academy of Social Sciences*, and *China Travel Agency Industry Development Report published annually by China Tourism Academy*.

(2) Industry organizations and associations: The continuous development of tourism has led to an increasing number of non-profit organizations and associations participating in the analysis, planning, and promotion of tourism, such as the United Nations World

光联合局（International Association of Convention and Visitor Bureau，IACVB）、亚太旅游协会（Pacific Asia Travel Association，PATA）、中国旅游饭店业协会（China Tourist Hotel Association，CTHA）等。世界旅游组织每年会对全球旅游业的发展进行统计并预测趋势。中国旅游饭店业协会对行业数据进行科学统计和分析，对行业发展现状和趋势做出判断和预测，利用中国旅游饭店网和协会会刊《中国旅游饭店》向会员提供快捷资讯，为饭店提供专业咨询服务。同时还公布酒店业各阶段的经营结果和一系列的地方性调研报告。

（3）行业门户网站：酒店业和旅游业的门户网站也是提供有用的旅游与酒店业信息的重要渠道。这种门户网站往往目标明确，提供与其定义相关的具体信息，从其名称就能很明确地辨别出在网站内能获取哪一方面的信息，如环球旅讯、迈点网、品橙旅游、HotelNewsNow、Hotels Editorial 等。

（4）行业刊物：各种各样的旅游业刊物是获取旅游和酒店等信息的有效渠道。这类刊物包括了为读者提供旅游信息的旅游杂志，如 *Travel and Leisure*；针对某一特定旅游产品的旅游休闲杂志，如 *Cruise Travel*；还有学术类期刊，如《中国旅游研究》（*China Tourism Research*）等。

一般来讲，二手资料比一手资料更容易获得，成本较低，甚至有时是零成本，它在企业进行市场营销研究的开始阶段搜寻背景资料时非常有用，可确定问题并对市场营销研究的开展起到指导作用。但由于其本身是为解决其他问题而收集的，资料的种类和来源或许不能完全满足信息搜寻者当前解决问题的需要，在其使用过程中有时需要克服一些与新数据相关的诸如样本错误和偏差问题。例如，非营利组织和以营利为目的的机构即使对同一问题进行调查，其着眼点也可能会不同，从而得出不同的统计结果和解释。在使用二手数据时，弄清楚下列问题有助于增强研究者的信心：

▸ 数据是否和当前研究有关？

▸ 数据中变量的原始定义是否和当前研究中的变量一致？

▸ 数据是否是最新的？

▸ 数据可否通过其他来源加以证实？

▸ 数据是否准确，且无偏见？

3.2.2　一手数据

一手数据是最有效、最明确地收集解决营销问题的信息的方式。一手数据研究（primary research）需经历明确问题与研究目标、确定解决问题的研

Tourism Organization（UNWTO），the International Association of Convention and Visitor Bureau（IACVB），the Pacific Asia Travel Association（PATA），and the China Tourist Hotel Association（CTHA）. Each year，the UNWTO carries out statistics and forecasts the development of the global tourism industry. The CTHA gathers the industry statistics and analyzes the data，makes judgments and forecasts on the status quo and trends in the industry，and provides newest information to members as well as professional consultation service to hotels through its website and the journal of the association. The CTHA also releases the performances of the various stages of the hotel industry and a series of local research reports publicly.

(3) Industry portals：The portals for the hotel and tourism industry also serve as an important channel providing useful information on tourism and hospitality. These portals often serve clear purposes and provide specific information related to their definition. What information can be obtained within the site can be identified from its name（e.g.，Travel Daily，Meadin.com，Pinchain Travel，HotelNewsNow，and Hotels Editorial）.

(4) Industry publications：A wide range of tourism publications offer an effective means to obtain information about tourism and hotels. Such journals include travel magazines that provide tourist information，such as *Travel and Leisure*；travel and leisure magazines for a specific travel product，such as *Cruise Travel*；and academic journals，such as *China Tourism Research*.

Secondary data is more readily available and less costly than primary data，and sometimes it even has zero cost. Secondary data can be useful when a company is searching for background information in the initial stage of marketing research to identify problems and provide guidance for marketing research. However，because secondary data are collected to solve other problems，the types and sources of the data may not fully satisfy the problem that the information searcher needs to solve at present. In the course of using secondary data，overcoming problems such as sample error and deviation problem is inevitable. For example，non-profit and for-profit organizations may differ in focus areas even when investigating the same problem，leading to varying statistical results and explanations. When using secondary data，clarifying the following questions can boost the researcher's confidence：

▶ Are the data relevant to current research?

▶ Is the original definition of the variable in the data consistent with the current study?

▶ Are the data up-to-date?

▶ Can the data be verified by other sources?

▶ Are the data accurate and unbiased?

3.2.2　Primary data

Primary research is the most effective and clear means of collecting information to solve marketing problems. Primary research involves defining problems and objectives，setting research plans to solve problems，collecting and analyzing raw data，and writing a

究方案、收集和分析原始数据以及撰写研究报告的过程。本章下一节的内容将对一手数据研究的具体过程、其在旅游服务业的应用以及怎样检测研究过程等进行详细讨论。本节主要介绍最常见的营销调研问题,包括顾客识别、产品调研、广告设计测试和追踪研究。

1. 顾客识别

企业所拥有的资源及其特点各不相同。企业应当根据自身的优势和劣势找到适合的定位,识别目标市场,与现有顾客建立良性互动的牢固关系。企业应建立客户数据库,通过价值分析,找出最有效的市场营销及产品销售手段,保持顾客的长久品牌忠诚度。对于那些具有消费潜力但尚待发掘的潜在顾客,可以通过企业的营销活动刺激消费,扩大市场占有率。

2. 产品调研

通过一般性的产品调研,企业可以辨别顾客的购买行为,即他们购买的产品和服务、他们是否喜欢企业提供的产品以及他们对企业推出的产品的看法和评价。顾客购买行为或消费者研究可作为市场细分的基础,它可以通过调查顾客中的样本人群来识别重度消费者、中等消费者和轻度消费者以及他们的人口统计特点来完成。另外通过对某个企业和它的顾客的观察来估测产品销售情况也是一种有效研究顾客行为的方式,但得出的结果没有前者精确。实际上我们也经常可以听到经理人用"我们大多数的顾客⋯⋯"来揣测。

3. 广告设计测试

广告概念一般在正式制作推出之前的设计阶段的早期就会被测试以确定它们是否为消费者所接受。这一被称为广告设计测试的做法在制作电视广告时尤其普遍,因为电视广告的制作费用和媒体时间都很昂贵,特别是黄金时段的播放时间。广告设计测试的方式很多,有问卷调查、电子邮件或电话调查。

4. 追踪研究

从广义上看,追踪研究是对同一组消费者在不同的时间点上进行调查和收集资料,然后通过对前后几次调查所得资料的统计分析来探索其消费行为随时间发展而发生的变化,及不同行为之间因果关系的一种研究方式。它可

research report. The next section of this chapter discusses in detail the research process using primarydata, its application in the hospitality and tourism industry, and the ways to detect the research process. This section focuses on the most common marketing research issues, including customer identification, product research, advertising testing, and follow-up study.

1. Customer identification

Enterprises possess different resources and characteristics. Companies should find a proper position based on their own strengths and weaknesses, identify the target market, and establish a solid relationship with existing customers through benign interaction. Companies should establish a customer database and hence identify the most effective marketing and product sale approaches through value analysis to maintain long-term customer loyalty to the brand. For potential customers with untapped consumption potential, companies may stimulate their consumption through marketing campaigns and expand market share.

2. Product research

Through general product research, companies can identify the customer purchase behavior, that is, the products and services they buy, whether they like the product provided by enterprises, and their views and evaluation on the product launched. Customer purchase behavior or consumer research can be used as a basis for market segmentation and can be performed by investigating the sample population of the customer group to identify heavy, medium, and light users and their demographic characteristics. Product research is also an effective means to study customer behavior by assessing the sales of an enterprise and its customers, but the results are not as accurate compared to customer identification. Managers often speculate customer behavior as generalizing "most of our customers...".

3. Advertising testing

Advertising ideas are typically tested early in the design phase prior to formal production and launch to determine whether they are acceptable to consumers. Advertising testing is particularly prevalent for TV commercials, which are expensive to produce and spread in media, especially those broadcasted during prime time. Many methods can be used to design ads, including surveys, emails, or telephone interviews.

4. Follow-up study

Broadly speaking, follow-up study is a research approach that investigates the same group of consumers at different time, collects information, and then analyzes the statistics from several surveys to explore consumers' consumption behavior over time and

以分为首次调查(或称前期调查)和追踪调查(或称后续调查)两个部分。狭义上看,追踪研究仅指的是对前期调查过的消费群体在经过一段时间后进行的第二次(或第 n 次)调查,即仅指后续调查。开展追踪调查的常用方法是基于市场区域的随机抽样样本的一系列调查。首次调查得出的结论为后面的调查研究奠定了比较的基础。接下来的研究是对消费者行为和态度变化的追踪。追踪调查一般被用于识别消费者变化,评估新产品推广、新营销策略实施或者服务质量标准的有效性。不同企业调查的主题可能不同。一般来讲,旅游及酒店企业跟踪研究的主要方向和主体包括顾客类型、品牌知晓度、购买频率和时机、广告认知度和回忆、顾客态度和企业形象、顾客满意度、对服务质量的感知、首选产品/服务的特性,以及不同场合的顾客偏好。

3.3　营销调研过程

　　一般而言,大型企业有内部的营销研究部门。营销研究部门在企业中有着重要的地位,其首要任务是通过内部和外部调查研究,进行顾客群体分析,预测市场发展趋势和变化,进而对企业现有的产品或服务提出改进建议并指引企业如何对顾客进行反馈。Kotler 和 Keller(2009)认为,有效的市场营销研究通过六个步骤获得准确的研究结果。这六个步骤分别是:(1) 确定研究问题、可选决策方案和研究目标;(2) 制订研究计划;(3) 收集数据和信息;(4) 分析数据和信息;(5) 展示研究结果;(6) 做出营销决策。(如图 3-2 所示)

图 3-2　市场营销研究步骤

来源:Kotler,Keller(2009). *Marketing Management*. (13th ed.). Upper Saddle
River,NJ:Pearson Prentice Hall.

3.3.1　确定研究问题、可选决策方案和研究目标

　　确定研究问题及可选决策方案和研究目标是营销研究的第一步,也是最

the causal relationship between their different behaviors. Follow-up study can be divided into two categories: first survey (i.e., pre-survey) and follow-up survey (i.e., post-survey). In a narrow sense, follow-up study refers only to the post-survey, which is the second (or n th) survey taken by the consumer groups after they have taken the first survey. Conducting a series of surveys based on a random sample of market areas is a common method for follow-up surveys. The conclusion of the first survey lays the foundation for the following research. The next study is a follow-up study to monitor changes in consumer behavior and attitudes. Follow-up surveys are typically used to identify consumer changes and evaluate the effectiveness of new product promotions, new marketing strategy implementations, or service quality standards. However, different enterprises may investigate varied subjects. The main research directions and subjects of hotel and tourism companies include customer type, brand awareness, purchase frequency and timing, advertising awareness and recall, customer attitude and corporate image, customer satisfaction, service quality perception, preferred product/service characteristics, and customer preferences on different occasions.

3.3 Marketing Research Process

Large enterprises have internal marketing research departments, which play an important role. The primary tasks of these departments are to conduct internal and external research, analyze customer groups, forecast market trends and changes, provide recommendations to the management for the improvement of existing products or services, and guide concerned personnel to give feedback to customers. Kotler and Keller (2009) argue that effective marketing research achieves accurate results in six steps (Figure 3 - 2). These steps are (1) identifying research questions, decision alternatives, and research objectives; (2) developing the research plan; (3) collecting the data and information; (4) analyzing the data and information; (5) presenting research findings; and (6) making marketing decisions.

Figure 3 - 2　Marketing research steps
Source: Kotler, Keller (2009).*Marketing Management* (13th ed.). Upper Saddle River, NJ: Pearson Prentic Hall.

3.3.1　Identify research questions, decision alternatives, and research objectives

Identifying research questions, decision alternatives, and research objectives is the

重要的一步。过于宽泛或狭隘的研究问题最终都会带来大量不必要或不准确的信息。因此,在制订研究计划前,市场营销人员和研究人员需要一同确定合理的、现实的研究问题。在一些情况下,为了帮助市场营销人员和研究人员确定研究问题,管理层可以向双方说明现有的可选决策方案,然后再以备选方案为基础,确定研究问题。研究目标应当是具体的、以结果为导向的。研究目标有三种:第一种是探索性研究目标,它阐明问题的本质并提供可能的解决方案或新的解决思路。如 Choi 和 Kim(2012)做了关于酒店员工如何看待工作生活平衡的研究,发现"家庭与工作之间的冲突"影响酒店员工的工作满意度,间接影响员工的工作表现。第二种是描述性研究目标,它确定市场需求量及需求特征。如 Han(2002)以上海酒店业为例,研究影响酒店外包的因素,发现酒店会基于提高自身竞争力而实施外包战略。第三种是因果研究目标,它确定关键因素之间的因果关系。如 Mattila(2004)做了关于服务失误与顾客忠诚度之间关系的研究,发现顾客对餐厅的情感会影响到顾客对餐厅服务失误的态度,同时也影响顾客对餐厅的补救措施的感知。

3.3.2　制订研究计划

在确定研究问题后需要制订详细的研究计划,包括所需要的信息类型、数据来源、数据收集方法、采样计划和样本接触方式,并计算所需成本。一手数据和二手数据是研究中的数据来源。通常而言,研究人员会在研究中首先检验大量与项目相关并易于获取的二手数据。如果二手数据的分析结果能够完全或部分解决研究问题,可以相应降低研究对一手数据的需求,从而降低研究项目的成本。如果没有相应的二手数据或者数据本身已经过时、不准确或者不可信,研究人员需要收集一手数据。

市场营销人员常用的一手数据收集方法包括观察、焦点小组访谈、问卷调查和实验研究。

1. 观察

Tischler(2004)提出,在研究观察中,研究人员通过直接观察顾客的购买行为和购物环境,获取一手数据。在一些观察研究中,研究人员会为参与研究的顾客配备记录本,并要求顾客在遇到促使他们购买的因素时,写下他们当时的行为。此外,研究人员可以在餐厅或酒吧中进行非正式的访谈,以获取

first and most important step in marketing research. Too broad or narrow research questions eventually lead to a large amount of unnecessary or inaccurate information. Therefore, marketers and researchers must work together to identify reasonable and realistic research questions before developing a research plan. In some cases, to help marketers and researchers identify research issues, the management can present existing decision alternatives to both parties and then identify research questions based on the alternatives. The research objectives should be concrete and outcome oriented. Research objectives can be classified into three types. The first type is exploratory research objectives, that is, clarifying the nature of the problem and providing possible or new solutions. In their study on how hotel employees perceive work-life balance, Choi and Kim (2012) find that "conflict between family and work" affects the hotel staff's job satisfaction and indirectly influences staff performance. The second type is descriptive research objectives that determine market demand and demand characteristics. Han (2002) takes the hotel industry in Shanghai as an example to study the factors influencing hotel outsourcing. Hotels implement the outsourcing strategy based on the need to improve their competitive power (Han, 2002). The third type is causal research objectives, which determine the causal relationship between key factors. In a study on the relationship between service failure and customer loyalty, Mattila (2004) finds that customers' emotion affect their attitude toward restaurant service mistakes and their perception of the restaurant's service recovery.

3.3.2　Develop the research plan

After a research question is identified, a detailed research plan is developed, including the type of information required, source of the data, method of data collection, sampling plan, and contact methods. The cost is calculated accordingly. Primary and secondary data are the sources of data for the research. Researchers first examine a large amount of secondary data that are easy to access and relevant to the study. If the results of the secondary data analysis can fully or partially solve the research question, then researchers can reduce the demand for primary data, thereby cutting the cost of the research project. If no relevant secondary data are found or the data are outdated, inaccurate, or untrustworthy, then the researchers must collect primary data.

Methods for collecting primary data commonly used by marketers include observation, focus group interviews, surveys, and experimental research.

1. Observation

Tischler (2004) suggests that, in observational studies, researchers obtain primary data by directly observing customer purchase behavior and shopping environment. In some observational studies, researchers provide customers with notebooks and ask them to write down what they do when they encounter the factors that prompted them to buy. Researchers can also conduct informal interviews in restaurants or bars to obtain

相应的信息。在研究时,照片可以提供丰富的信息。

2. 焦点小组访谈

焦点小组访谈的参与者由研究者根据目标顾客群体的人口统计特征和心理学统计特征以及其他相关因素进行挑选。一般情况下,六至八位参与者会在研究人员的引导下,就多种与研究相关的话题进行深度讨论,并获得一定的报酬。焦点小组访谈有助于了解参与讨论的顾客的购买动机和购买行为,但由于参与讨论的人数很少,而且并非随机挑选而来,研究人员要避免将研究结果推广至整个目标市场。

3. 问卷调查

企业通过问卷调查了解顾客群体对于某项产品或服务的知识、信任度、偏好及满意度,并在更广泛的群体中测量这些项目。企业可以采用四种方式进行调查:(1)根据企业需要进行针对性调查;(2)联合其他企业进行综合调查;(3)邀请企业自身或其他企业现有的固定消费者样本回答问题;(4)在大型商场中接触顾客并邀请他们回答问题。企业太频繁地进行调查可能导致顾客反馈率下降,因此,在进行调查研究时,企业应该尽量使调查简短,避免过于频繁地邀请同样的顾客群体参与调查。此外,向参与顾客提供奖励也有助于提高顾客的反馈率。问卷调查是在收集一手数据时最常用的方法。在正式发放问卷前,研究人员需要仔细地设计问卷并对其进行测试和修正。问卷的形式、问题的用词和顺序都会对消费者的反馈产生影响。问卷上的问题分为两种类型——封闭式和开放式。对于封闭式问题,研究人员需要在正式发放问卷前列出所有答案供消费者勾选,而对于开放式问题则需要参与者以文字形式回答问题,其更能体现参与者的想法。

4. 实验研究

实验研究能够验证因果关系,对观察研究结果的不同解释提供证据。一般而言,实验研究中的样本会分为实验组和对照组。研究人员通过控制随机变量,对实验组和对照组进行不同的处理,并测量不同的观察结果在统计学上是否有明显的差异。如果随机变量能够被消除或控制,研究人员可以认为观察结果和处理方法之间有相关关系。有些实验室进行实验需要使用一些技术设备进行辅助,例如使用视速仪测量参与者在看见一个特定的广告或图

information. Photos can provide a wealth of information.

2. Focus group interviews

Participants in focus group interviews are selected by researchers based on demographic and psychographic characteristics of the target customer group and other relevant factors. Six to eight participants participate in an in-depth discussion on various research-related topics under the direction of researchers and receive reward in return. Focus group interviews help to understand the buying motivations and purchase behavior of the participating customers. However, because of the small number of participants and the random selection, researchers should avoid extending the results to the entire target market.

3. Surveys

Companies use a questionnaire to understand customers' knowledge, trust, preference, and satisfaction with a product or service and measure these in a wide community. Enterprise can adopt four following investigation methods. (1) Carry out targeted investigation according to the needs of the enterprise. (2) Conduct a comprehensive survey in conjunction with other enterprises. (3) Invite sample of existing consumers of the enterprise or other companies to answer questions. (4) Approach customers in large shopping malls and invite them to answer questions. Too frequent investigations by enterprises may decrease customer feedback rate. Therefore, during investigation, enterprises should try to make the survey as short as possible and avoid frequently inviting the same customer groups to participate in the survey. Providing incentives to participating customers can also improve customer feedback. Surveys are the most commonly used method for collecting primary data. Before the formal distribution of questionnaire, researchers should carefully design the questionnaire and then test and revise it. The form of questionnaire, as well as the use of words and order of the questions, can affect consumer feedback. Questions are divided into two types, namely, closed and open questions. For closed questions, the researcher needs to list all the answers before formally distributing the questionnaire, whereas for open questions, the participants are asked to answer questions in their own words to better reflect their opinions.

4. Experimental research

Experimental research tests the causality and provides evidence for different interpretations of observational findings. The sample in experimental research are divided into experimental and control groups. By manipulating random variables, researchers treat the experimental and control groups differently and measure whether the differences are statistically significant. If the random variable can be eliminated or controlled, then researchers can imply a correlation between observation and treatment. Some laboratory experiments require the use of technical equipment, such as using visual instruments to measure the interest or emotional changes of participants after seeing a

片后的兴趣或情感变化,并使用皮肤传感器、脑电波扫描仪和全身扫描仪等仪器获取参与者的反应。

选择合适的研究方法和研究工具后,研究人员需要从三个方面制订采样计划。

(1)样本对象:不同的顾客群体有不同的特征和行为模式。因此,在选择样本对象时,研究人员需要根据研究问题选择合适的顾客群体作为样本对象。

(2)样本规模:大规模样本能够提供更为可靠的研究结果。但小规模样本通过合适的抽样方法,同样能够获得可靠的结果。

(3)抽样过程:通常而言,抽样分为概率抽样和非概率抽样。概率抽样包括简单随机抽样、分层抽样和整群抽样。研究人员可以计算样本误差的置信区间,使样本更具有代表性。非概率抽样包括任意抽样(便利抽样)、判断抽样和配额抽样。

3.3.3　调查方法

在营销研究中,样本的接触方式主要包括面对面访谈、电话访谈、邮寄调查以及在线调查。

1. 面对面访谈

面对面访谈是适用性最广的样本接触方式。访谈人员可以提问较多的问题,并记录与参与者相关的观察结果,如穿着和肢体语言。但是,面对面访谈也是成本最高的方法,研究结果还可能受到访谈人员的偏见的影响,并需要更多的计划和管理。面对面访谈有两种形式——约见访谈和拦截式访谈。约见访谈由研究人员约见参与者进行访谈,并提供奖励。拦截式访谈是研究人员在大型商场里或主要街道上拦截路人进行现场访谈。拦截式访谈需要快速进行,而且可能会包括非概率抽样样本。

2. 电话访谈

电话访谈是一种快速获取研究信息的方式。其反馈率一般高于邮寄问卷。在电话访谈中,访谈人员对问题的描述要简洁明了,在参与者不明白问题时进行阐述和解释。然而,由于顾客反感电话营销,电话访谈越来越难以进行。

particular advertisement or picture and obtaining their responses with a skin sensor, brainwave scanner, or a full-body scanner.

After selecting the appropriate research methods and tools, researchers must develop a sampling plan considering the three following aspects.

（1）Sampling units: Different customer groups vary in their characteristics and behavior patterns. Therefore, when selecting sampling units, researchers should select the appropriate customer group according to the research question.

（2）Sample size: Large-scale samples can provide more reliable results, but small-scale samples may also generate reliable results through appropriate sampling.

（3）Sampling procedure: Sampling is divided into probability and non-probability sampling. Probability sampling includes simple random sampling, stratified sampling, and cluster sampling. Researchers can calculate the confidence interval of the sample error to make the sample representative. Non-probability sampling includes accidental sampling （convenience sampling）, judgmental sampling, and quota sampling.

3.3.3 Survey methods

In marketing research, sample contact methods include face-to-face interviews, telephone interviews, mail surveys, and online surveys.

1. Face-to-face interviews

Face-to-face interviews are the most widely used sample contact method. Interviewers can ask many questions and record observations of participants, such as clothes and body language. The drawbacks are that face-to-face interviews are also the most expensive approach, and the results are influenced by the bias of the interviewer. Hence, this method requires additional planning and management. Face-to-face interviews come in two forms, namely, arranged and intercept interviews. For arranged interviews, researchers make appointments with participants for interview and offer them rewards. Intercept interviews are conducted by researchers in large shopping malls or at major streets, intercepting passersby for on-site interviews. Intercept interviews need to be conducted quickly and may involve non-probabilistic sampling.

2. Telephone interviews

Telephone interviews provide a quick means to access research information. The feedback rate is higher than mail questionnaire. In a telephone interview, the interviewer describes the problem concisely and clearly and may explain and elaborate the problem when the participant does not understand it. However, telephone interviews are becoming increasingly difficult due to customer antipathy toward telemarketing.

3. 邮寄调查

邮寄问卷是对非访谈人群进行调查的方式之一。邮寄问卷上的问题需要简单、清晰。但是,邮寄问卷的反馈率较低,且反馈速度较慢。

4. 在线调查

企业有多种方法可以利用互联网进行营销研究,例如在官方网站嵌入问卷并对回答问卷的参与者提供奖励。或者,企业可以在顾客群体经常访问的网页设置链接,邀请访问人群通过回答问题赢取奖品。另外,企业可以通过赞助聊天室或网站主页导入问题,邀请参与者回答。最后,企业可以在网上举行实时顾客讨论或进行在线虚拟焦点小组访谈。除此以外,企业可以利用不同的网站,在不同的时间,提供不同的产品或不同的价格,以此了解产品或价格的效度。在发布新产品之前,企业一般会进行产品测试。与传统的新产品营销研究相比,网上产品测试能够更快速地提供相应的信息。

表 3-1 总结了各种调查方法的优缺点。

表 3-1　各种调查方法的优缺点

方法	优点	缺点
面对面访谈	● 问卷填答完整 ● 应答率相对高 ● 与被访者关系良好 ● 数据收集地点灵活	● 劳力强度大 ● 相对昂贵 ● 访谈者偏差
电话访谈	● 可以随机抽样 ● 计算机辅助电话调查系统减少数据录入的错误	● 过度使用会受到被访者的抵制 ● 时间长于 15 分钟会使被访者疲劳
邮寄调查	● 可以大规模邮寄 ● 对被调查者的干扰最小	● 缺少人际接触 ● 回收率低 ● 更长的数据收集期
在线调查	● 快速完成调查 ● 相对便宜 ● 问卷设计引人注目	● 被调查者样本的代表性 ● 技术限制 ● 难以计算应答率

3. Mail surveys

Mailing questionnaire is one way of investigating people who cannot be personally interviewed. Questions on mail questionnaires should be simple and clear. However, the response rate is low, and the response return is slow.

4. Online surveys

Companies can use the Internet for marketing research in several ways, such as embedding questionnaires on the official website and providing incentives to participants who answer the questionnaire. Alternatively, the company can place links on the pages that the customer groups frequently visit to invite people to answer questions and win prizes. Companies can also invite participants to answer questions by sponsoring a chat room or homepage and importing questions. In addition, companies can conduct real-time customer discussions or focus group interviews online. Moreover, companies can use different sites to provide various products or prices at specific times to understand the product or price validity. Before releasing new products, companies usually carry out product testing. Online product testing can provide the corresponding information more quickly than traditional marketing research for new products.

Table 3 - 1 summarizes the advantages and disadvantages of various survey methods.

Table 3 - 1 Advantages and disadvantages of survey methods

Methods	Advantages	Disadvantages
Face-to-face interviews	● Complete responses to all questions ● Relatively high response rate ● Good relationship with interviewees ● Flexible data collection venues	● Labor intensive ● Relatively expensive ● Interviewer bias
Telephone interviews	● Random sampling ● Uses computer-assisted telephone interview system, which can reduce data entry errors	● Overuse may be resisted by respondents ● Possibility of respondents getting tired if time is longer than 15 minutes
Mail surveys	● Can be mass mailed ● Minimum interferences to respondents	● Lack of interpersonal contact ● Low return rate ● Longer data collection period
Online surveys	● Fast ● Relatively cheap ● Attractive questionnaire design	● Sample representation of respondents ● Technical limitations ● Difficulty in calculating the response rate

3.3.4　收集数据和信息

收集信息阶段一般是营销研究过程中费用最高和最容易出现误差的阶段。在这个阶段有四个主要的问题：（1）一些既定的参与者需要多次联系，或无法参与，需要寻找替代者；（2）部分参与者可能拒绝参与研究；（3）部分参与者可能提供有偏见的或不诚实的回答；（4）访谈人员可能存在偏见或不诚实。

由于计算机和电子通信技术的出现，数据收集方法得到迅速改进。一些电话研究公司在一个集中的地点（例如电话呼叫中心）进行访谈，专业的访谈人员通过屏幕读出问题并将回答录入电脑。这个过程不需要进行编辑或编码，可以减少误差、节省时间并提供所需数据。另外一些研究公司则在购物中心设立互动站点，参与者可以坐在站点内通过屏幕阅读问题，并录入他们的回答。除此以外，企业也可以利用一些网络调查工具来收集需要的数据和信息，例如问卷星、Survey Monkey 等。

3.3.5　分析数据和信息

收集数据和信息后，研究人员首先对数据进行频数分布分析，计算数据的平均数和主要变量的离散程度。然后利用统计学的方法进行分析并建立决策模型，以挖掘更多的研究结果。研究人员会检验不同的假设和理论，利用灵敏度分析测定假设和结论。

3.3.6　展示研究结果

分析数据后，研究人员向管理层展示与主要营销决策相关的研究结果。Fielding（2006）认为，研究人员在将数据和信息转化为对市场的洞察，并向管理层提出建议方面起着越来越重要的作用。同时，研究人员应尽可能以便于理解和有吸引力的方式来展示结果。如果是复杂的、包含丰富信息的、难以用语言或图形表达的研究结果，可以通过可视化的艺术图像进行展示。

3.3.7　做出营销决策

越来越多的企业利用营销决策支持系统帮助营销管理者做出更好的决策。营销决策系统是一个包括数据、体系、工具、技术、软件和硬件的集合。企业通过营销决策系统，从业务和环境中收集并分析相关的信息，然后将结

3.3.4　Collect the data and information

The data collection phase is usually the most expensive and error-prone phase in the marketing research process. This stage contains four main issues. (1) Some participants may be contacted several times, become unable to participate, or need to be replaced by alternatives. (2) Some participants may refuse to participate in the study. (3) Some participants may give biased or dishonest answers. (4) Interviewers may be biased or dishonest.

Data collection methods have improved rapidly because of the advent of computers and electronic communications. Some telephone research companies conduct interviews at a centralized location, such as a call center, where the professional interviewer reads the questions from and writes the answers into the computer. This process eliminates the need for editing or coding, reduces errors, saves time, and provides the required data. Other research firms set up interactive sites in shopping malls where participants can sit and read the screen and enter their answers. Enterprises can also use some online survey tools to collect the required data and information (e.g., Sojump and Survey Monkey).

3.3.5　Analyze the data and information

After collecting the data and information, researchers analyze the frequency distribution of the data and calculate the averages of data and the degree of dispersion of the main variables. Researchers subsequently use statistical methods to analyze and establish decision-making model to explore other research results. Researchers examine different hypotheses and theories and use sensitivity analysis to test hypotheses and conclusions.

3.3.6　Present research findings

After analyzing the data, researchers present to the management the research results related to major marketing decisions. Fielding (2006) argues that researchers play an increasingly important role in translating data and information into market insights and offering suggestions to the management. At the same time, researchers should try their best to present results comprehensively and engagingly. If research results are complex and difficult to express in language or graphs as well as contain rich information, then they can be displayed through visualized artistic images.

3.3.7　Make marketing decisions

A growing number of enterprises use marketing decision support systems to help marketing managers make informed decisions. A marketing decision system is a collection of data, systems, tools, techniques, software, and hardware. Companies collect and analyze relevant information from the business and environment through the marketing

果作为营销行动的基础(Little,1979)。卡夫食品是全球范围内最早利用营销决策支持系统的企业之一。在 20 世纪 70 年代,卡夫食品的营销经理会根据市场竞争的情况,将数据输入决策支持系统,并根据系统给出的结果采取相应的行动。例如,当时奶酪市场的竞争主要集中在 40 盎司(1 盎司=18.35克)包装的奶酪上,营销经理希望了解这种情况在多大程度上会影响企业的16 盎司包装奶酪的销售。随后,营销经理将 40 盎司包装奶酪在过去一年的销售数据以及竞争对手的销售数据输入系统,同时将 16 盎司包装奶酪的数据也输入到系统中,系统根据内置的模型进行估算,通过销售额、市场份额等数据表达估算结果。结果显示,尽管 40 盎司包装奶酪的市场竞争非常激烈,但当卡夫食品销售 1 份 40 盎司包装奶酪时,会同时带来 1.2 份 16 盎司包装奶酪的销售量。另一方面,估算结果显示,16 盎司包装奶酪的市场份额在过去 1 年内提高了 7%。因此,营销经理决定在继续推广 40 盎司包装奶酪的同时,增加对 16 盎司包装奶酪的营销推广(Little,1979)。

3.4　营销生产力评估

营销研究的一个非常重要的目的是衡量营销活动有效性。市场营销人员要对营销投资负责,并且能够向高层管理人员解释营销费用(McManus,2004),即能够对营销生产力进行衡量。营销生产力有三种衡量方法:(1)营销绩效——评估营销效果;(2)营销组合模型——评估市场活动对产品业绩的影响;(3)营销仪表板——及时获得营销效果的工具。

3.4.1　营销绩效

营销绩效是一套帮助市场营销人员衡量、比较和解释营销活动表现的指标。营销绩效包括三个方面。第一,活动绩效,即顾客投诉量、销售额、员工总数、顾客人数、订单数量、新增职位等可被计算的内部或外部项目。第二,会计(运营)绩效。会计绩效有两种较为普遍的计算方式:一是投资回报率和资产回报率;二是项目净现值。投资回报率通常用于计算特定活动或项目在特定时间点所带来的收益。资产回报率则是考虑整个企业利用资产获得收益的效率。净现值对项目的现金流进行评估,以确定项目未来所带来的现金流对企业的价值。第三,成果绩效。营销组合分析是评估营销成果绩效的一种工具。通过分析不同来源的数据,营销组合分析能够更清晰地指出不同

decision system and then use the results as the basis for marketing actions (Little, 1979). Kraft Foods is one of the world's first companies to use marketing decision support systems. In the 1970s, Kraft Foods' marketing managers input data into the decision support system based on the market competition and took corresponding actions according to the results from the system. For example, when competition in the cheese market was concentrated on 40 ounce cheese, the marketing manager wanted to know how much this can affect the sales of 16 ounce cheese. The marketing manager then entered the sales data for 40 ounce cheese in the past year and the competitor's sales data into the system, along with the 16 ounce cheese data. The system estimated the results based on built-in models and calculation of data, such as sales and market share. The results showed that, despite the fierce competition in 40 ounce cheese market, when Kraft Foods sold 40 ounce cheese, 1.2 sales of 16 ounce cheese were also bought. The estimates showed that the market share of 16 ounce cheese increased by 7% in the past year. As a result, the marketing manager decided to increase marketing activities for 16 ounce cheese while continuing to promote 40 ounce cheese (Little, 1979).

3.4 Measuring Marketing Productivity

An important purpose of marketing research is to measure the effectiveness of marketing activities. Marketers should be accountable for marketing investment and able to explain marketing expenses to senior management (McManus, 2004); they must measure marketing productivity. Marketing productivity can be measured in three ways: (1) marketing metrics (assessing marketing effectiveness), (2) marketing mix modeling (assessing the effect of marketing activities on product performance), and (3) marketing dashboards (tools for obtaining timely marketing effectiveness).

3.4.1 Marketing metrics

Marketing metrics are a set of indicators that help marketers measure, compare, and interpret marketing campaigns. Marketing metrics include three aspects. The first aspect is activity metrics, which refer to the internal or external items that can be calculated, such as the amount of customer complaints, sales, total number of employees, number of customers, order quantity, and added positions. The second aspect is accounting (operation) metrics. Calculating accounting metrics involve two common methods, namely, return on investment and return on assets and the net present value of the project. Return on investment is often used to calculate the benefits of a particular activity or project at a given point in time, whereas return on assets is the efficiency of taking advantage of enterprise assets. Net present value assesses the project's cash flow to determine the value brought to the enterprise by the project's future cash flow. The third aspect is result metrics. Marketing mix analysis is a tool to assess the performance of marketing results. By analyzing the data from different sources, marketing mix analysis

营销活动的效度。除此以外,市场营销者可以利用多元分析明确不同的营销元素对营销成果的影响。成果绩效可以从四个方面进行评估:股权价值、顾客终身价值、品牌资产和平衡计分卡。品牌经理可以利用营销绩效制定或调整营销项目,而高层管理人员则利用营销绩效确定财务资源的分配。

3.4.2　营销组合模型

对营销有效性的评估还包括评价不同营销活动的效果。营销组合模型通过分析不同来源的数据,如零售商销售数据、企业货物运输数据、价格、媒体、推广费用等,更清楚地了解特定营销活动的效果(Tellis,2006)。市场营销人员可以通过多变量分析、回归分析等统计学方法,更深入地理解不同变量之间的关系。通过应用营销组合模型,营销者可以更加有效地决定如何在不同的营销方式中分配资源。

3.4.3　营销仪表板

营销仪表板是根据营销业绩和营销组合模型,在企业内部展示实时营销数据的一套系统,用以帮助企业确保正常运营,它同时也是展示企业营销绩效的工具。企业需要在营销仪表板中包含两个重要的营销计分表——顾客表现计分表和利益相关者表现计分表,以反映企业的整体情况,提供早期的警告信号。顾客表现计分表反映企业在顾客满意、顾客流失、新顾客获取等方面的表现。管理层应该时刻注意各项指标,并对表现不合理的项目采取行动。利益相关者计分表是反映与企业有关并影响企业业绩的利益相关者(如员工、供应商、银行、分销商、零售商、股东等)的满意度的工具。与顾客表现计分表一样,对于满意度下降或处于平均水平以下的利益群体,企业应该加倍留意并采取行动。

3.5　市场需求预测

市场需求预测是销售预测的基础。企业在六个产品水平(整体、行业、企业、产品线、产品形式、产品项目)、五个空间水平(世界、洲际、区域、地区、顾客)和三个时间范围(短期、中期、长期)的基础上,共有 90 种不同的方法对需求进行预测。

can point out the validity of different marketing activities. Marketers can also use multivariate analysis to determine the effect of different marketing elements on marketing outcomes. Result metrics can be assessed in four dimensions, namely, equity value, customer lifetime value, brand equity, and balanced scorecard. Brand managers can use marketing metrics to develop or adjust marketing programs, whereas senior managers use marketing metrics to determine the allocation of financial resources.

3.4.2　Marketing mix modeling

Measuring marketing productivity also includes evaluating the effectiveness of different marketing activities. Marketing mix modeling provides a clear picture of the effectiveness of specific marketing activities by analyzing data from different sources, such as retailer sales data, corporate shipment data, prices, media, and promotional costs (Tellis, 2006). Marketers can enhance their understanding of the relationships between variables by using statistical methods, such as multivariate and regression analyses. By applying marketing mix modeling, marketers can effectively decide how to allocate resources to different marketing approaches.

3.4.3　Marketing dashboards

Marketing dashboard is a set of systems that display real-time marketing data within the enterprise based on marketing metrics and marketing mix modeling. The dashboard help enterprises to ensure the normal operation and display the marketing performance of the company as a tool. Companies need to include two important marketing scorecards in the marketing dashboard to reflect the overall condition of enterprises and provide warning signals in the early stage. These scorecards are for customer and stakeholder performance. Customer performance scorecard reflects the performance of the organization in terms of customer satisfaction, customer retention, and new customer acquisition. Management should always pay attention to these indicators and take action on unreasonable items. Stakeholder performance scorecard reflects the satisfaction of stakeholders (e. g. , employees, suppliers, banks, distributors, retailers, and shareholders) who are related to the business and affect the performance of the business. As with the customer performance scorecard, companies should pay attention to and take action on interest groups whose satisfaction falls or is below average.

3.5　Forecasting Market Demand

Market demand forecast is the basis of sales forecast. Market demand can be forecasted through 90 different methods, which are based on six product levels (all sales, industry sales, company sales, product line sales, product form sales, and product item sales), five spatial levels (world, continent, region, territory, and customer), and three time levels (short run, medium run, and long run).

市场的规模取决于特定产品在特定市场上存在的买家数量,通常情况下根据对产品的兴趣及实际购买能力,营销人员将市场划分为四个层级。第一,潜在市场,即对产品有足够兴趣的顾客。然而,顾客兴趣并不足以确定一个细分市场。市场营销人员需要通过顾客群体收入和购买渠道评估这部分顾客是否能够成为一个细分市场群体。第二,有效市场,即对产品有足够兴趣、拥有一定收入并且能够通过一定渠道购买特定产品的顾客。对于特殊产品(如烟草、酒类),企业或政府只销售给特定群体。此时,该特定群体为合格有效市场。第三,目标市场,即企业确定争取的合格有效市场上的一部分顾客。企业将集中其营销和分销资源到目标市场。第四,渗透市场,即企业产品的实际购买顾客群体。图 3-3 说明了这些市场规模之间的关系。

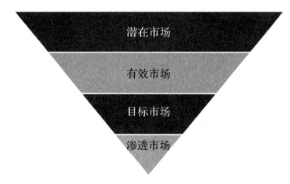

图 3-3　市场规模之间的关系

对市场规模进行计算和预测首先要明确一些关键概念,包括市场需求、市场潜力、企业需求、企业销售预测、企业销售潜力。

1. 市场需求

Kotler 和 Keller(2009)将市场需求定义为在特定的营销项目和市场环境下,在特定的地理区域内,特定的顾客群体在特定的时间范围内购买的产品总量。市场需求并非一个固定的数字,而是在一定条件下的函数,称为市场需求函数。市场份额是现有市场对产品的需求量,而市场渗透率则是现有市场需求和潜在市场需求之间的比例。低市场渗透率表明在市场上的所有企业都有发展的机会,高市场渗透率则说明获取剩余潜在市场的份额将会非

Market size depends on the number of buyers of a given product in a particular market. Typically, marketers divide the market into four sections based on the customers' interest in the product and the actual purchasing power. Potential market is the group of customers who are interested in the product. However, customer interest is insufficient to determine a market segment. Marketers must assess the customers' income and purchase channels to determine whether these customers can become a market segment. Available market refers to customers who are interested in the product, enjoy a certain income, and can purchase the specific product through a certain channel. Some special products (e.g., tobacco and alcohol) are only sold to specific groups by companies or governments. In this case, the specific group are qualified as available market. Target market refers to customers who enterprises are determined to win among the qualified available market. Enterprises focus their marketing and distribution of resources on the target market. Penetrated market refers to customers who are actually buying the products from the company. Figure 3 – 3 illustrates the relationships among these markets.

Figure 3 – 3   Relationships among different markets

Key concepts must be defined before the calculation and prediction of market size, including market demand, market potential, company demand, company sales forecast, and company sales potential.

1. Market demand

Kotler and Keller (2009) define market demand as the total number of products purchased by a particular customer group within a given time period in a given geographical area within a given marketing program and market environment. Market demand is not a fixed number but a function with certain conditions, that is, market demand function. Market share is the demand for a product in the existing market, whereas market penetration index is the ratio between the current and potential market demand. Low market penetration index indicates that all firms in the market have opportunities for growth, and high market penetration index indicates that acquiring

常昂贵。一般而言,当市场渗透率达到高水平时,价格竞争更为激烈,而边际收益逐渐下降。份额渗透率是帮助企业了解现有市场份额和潜在市场份额差距的一个指标。低份额渗透率表明企业有扩大份额的机会。造成低份额渗透率可能有多种原因,如品牌知名度低、产品可达性低、缺乏利益或价格过高。

2. 市场潜力

市场潜力指在特定的市场环境下,当营销支出达到无穷大时,市场需求所达到的极限。产品渗透率是体现市场潜力的一个指标,代表在一定人口中拥有或使用企业产品的人数。一般假设低产品渗透率的市场有更高的市场潜力。

3. 企业需求

企业需求指在一定的时间范围内,企业营销活动所带来的预期市场需求份额。它取决于市场对本企业的产品、服务、价格和营销信息,以及企业主与竞争对手相比较后的感知。如果其他变量都是相等水平,企业的市场份额取决于市场规模和企业营销支出的有效程度。

4. 企业销售预测

企业销售预测指在假定的市场环境和选定的营销计划下,企业预期达到的销售量。通常而言,企业习惯根据销售预测来制订营销计划。然而,这种制订计划的方式是基于企业需求不会扩张或销售预测总量即为国家或区域经济活动总量,而这并不现实。因此,企业应该根据制订的营销支出计划来确定销售预测。在企业销售预测中还有两个重要的概念:销售指标和销售预算。销售指标是产品线、企业部门或销售代表的销售目标。一般而言,销售指标是一种管理手段,管理层设定的销售指标稍高于预测销售额,用以衡量和促进销售代表的工作。销售预算是对销售总量的保守估计,用于采购、生产和现金流方面的决策。一般而言,管理层设定的销售预算稍低于销售预测,以避免过高的风险。

5. 企业销售潜力

企业销售潜力指与竞争对手营销活动相关的企业需求所能达到的极限。

remaining potential market share is very expensive. In general, when market penetration index reaches a high level, price competition intensifies, while marginal returns decline. Share penetration index is an indicator that helps companies understand the gap between their current and potential market share. Low penetration index indicates that firms have an opportunity to increase their share. Low penetration index can be attributed to various reasons, such as low brand awareness, low product accessibility, lack of interest, or high prices.

2. Market potential

Market potential refers to the market demand limit when the marketing expenditure increases to infinity in a specific market environment. The product penetration percentage is an indicator of market potential and represents the number of people who own or use a firm's products in a given population. Markets with low product penetration percentage are assumed to possess high market potential.

3. Company demand

Company demand refers to the expected market share resulting from the marketing activities in a certain period of time. It depends on the market's perception of a company's products, services, prices, and marketing information, as compared to the company's main competitors. If other variables are equal, then the firm's market share depends on the size of the market and the effectiveness of the marketing expenditures.

4. Company sales forecast

Company sales forecast is the sales volume that a firm expects to achieve under the assumed market environment and the selected marketing plan. In general, companies are accustomed to develop marketing plans based on sales forecasts. However, this approach is based on the unrealistic assumptions that the company demand will not expand or that the sales forecast is the total amount of national or regional economic activity. Therefore, enterprises should determine sales forecasts based on a marketing spending plan. Sales forecasting features two important concepts, namely, sales quotas and budgets. Sales quota is the sales target for the product line, company department, or sales representative. Sales quota is a management tool. The management sets sales quota slightly higher than the sales forecast to measure and promote the performance of sales representatives. Sales budget is a conservative estimate of total sales, and it is used for purchasing, production, and cash flow decisions. The management sets the sales budget slightly lower than the sales forecast to avoid excessive risk.

5. Company sales potential

Company sales potential is the limit of company demand associated with the

在大部分情况下,企业销售潜力低于市场潜力,因为每个竞争对手都有忠诚的客户群体。

3.5.1　估算现有需求

市场总体潜力指在一定的环境条件和行业营销活动水平下,一个行业内所有企业在一定时间范围内可实现的最大销售量。其公式如下:

$$市场总体潜力 = 潜在买家数量 \times 平均采购量 \times 产品单价$$

平均采购量可以通过企业现有的销售数据或者营销研究收集的一手数据估算得出。

地区市场潜力是一定地区范围内的市场总体潜力,影响企业对营销预算的分配。有两种主要方法可以测算地区市场潜力,即市场组合和多重因子指数。市场组合法用于了解不同市场的潜在买家总量,并预测买家的潜在采购量。当企业能够列出所有的潜在买家并准确地估算每个买家的购买量时,此方法能够提供准确的结果。然而,相关的数据并不容易获取。多重因子指数主要用于顾客营销方面,最常用的方法是线性指数法。企业列出与地区市场潜力相关的因素,并通过一手数据或二手数据确定每个因素对市场潜力影响的比例,计算每个因素(如人口总数、人均收入、地区酒店客房供应量、季节变化、竞争对手数量等)的市场潜力总量,最后求和得出地区市场潜力。例如在对中国出境旅游市场的大小进行估计时,Li、Harrill 和 Uysal 等(2010)通过对现有文献的梳理,选择了人口数量、经济发展水平、与主要交通枢纽的距离作为主要因素对市场大小进行估计。

除了估算市场和地区的总体潜力外,企业同样需要了解目标市场上的行业销售总量,即估算竞争对手的销售量,涉及行业销售总额和市场份额两个指标。企业可以通过行业贸易总会获得行业销售总额,并将企业自身的业绩与行业总体进行比较。此外,企业可以向营销研究公司购买行业销售总量和品牌销售总量的相关报告,与特定的竞争对手进行比较。

3.5.2　需求预测

在进行需求预测前,企业通常首先准备宏观经济预测,其次是行业销售预测和企业销售预测。宏观经济预测包括通胀、失业率、利率、消费者物价、

competitor's marketing activities. In most cases, company sales potential is lower than market potential, because each competitor possesses a loyal customer base.

3.5.1 Estimating current demand

Total market potential refers to the maximum sales that all enterprises in the industry can achieve within a certain period with specific environmental conditions and level of industry marketing activities. Total market potential can be calculated as follows:

Total market potential

= Potential number of buyers × Average purchases of each customer × Price

The average purchases of each customer can be estimated from existing sales data or primary data collected from marketing research.

Area market potential is the total market potential within a certain area, affecting the distribution of a company's marketing budget. Area market potential can be measured with two main methods, namely, market-buildup method and multiple-factor index method. Market-buildup method is used to understand the total number of potential buyers in different markets and forecast potential buyer purchases. This method can provide accurate results when an enterprise can list all potential buyers and accurately estimate the purchase volume of each buyer. The problem is that relevant data is not readily available. Multiple-factor index method is mainly used for consumer marketing, and the most commonly used method is the linear index method. Companies list the factors associated with area market potential, determine the effect of each factor on market potential with primary or secondary data, calculate the total market potential of each factor (e.g., total population, per capita income, regional hotel room supply, season changes, and the number of competitors), and finally obtain the sum of area market potential. Li, Harrill, Uysal, Burnett, and Zhan (2010) select the population size, economic development level, and distance from the main transportation hubs as the main factors to estimate the outbound tourism market size in China.

In addition, to estimate total market potential and area market potential, companies must understand the target market on the total industry sales; they should estimate sales of competitors in terms of total industry sales and market share. Enterprises can obtain the total industry sales through trade associations in the industry and compare their own performance with that of the industry. Companies can also buy marketing reports related to the total industry sales and total brand sales from industry research firms to compare their performance with those of specific competitors.

3.5.2 Forecasting demand

Before forecasting demand, companies initially prepare macroeconomic forecasts, followed by industry sales forecasts and corporate sales forecasts. Macroeconomic forecasts include inflation, unemployment, interest rates, consumer prices, business

商业投资、政府开销、净出口量以及其他变量。基于宏观经济预测结果，企业再对行业销售总额进行预测，并以此估算企业的销售总额和市场份额。

企业可以在其内部进行需求预测，或向外部资源（如营销研究公司）购买预测数据。所有的预测都基于三种信息，即顾客群体意见、顾客群体行为和过往数据。获得顾客群体意见需要调查买家或相关群体的意见，并结合销售代表意见和专家意见进行分析。调查顾客群体行为需要企业将产品投放至测试市场并记录买家的反馈。此外，企业可以通过分析过往购买行为，进行时间序列分析或需求统计分析，对未来需求进行估算。具体来讲，在进行需求预测时有如下几种方法。

1. 顾客购买意向调查

一些营销研究公司会通过问卷获取消费者的购买意向，并将答案绘制成购买概率量表。此外，调查中还会包括消费者个人现在和将来的财务状况，以及他们对经济的预期。随后，营销研究公司将不同的信息组合，形成消费者信心指数。行业的买家（采购者）信心指数可以以同样的方式进行测算。

2. 销售代表意见

当对买家进行访谈行不通时，企业可以请销售代表估算他们的未来销售额。由于销售代表对企业未来的资源分配和营销计划并不知情，他们的估算可能会过于乐观或过于悲观。此外，销售人员可能会故意提供低估的需求，目的是为了降低自身的销售指标。因此，企业在询问销售代表意见时，应该提供一定的协助或奖励，并进行适当的调整。

3. 专家意见

企业也可以通过行业专家（包括经销商、分销商、供应商、营销顾问和贸易协会）获取对未来需求的估算。一些企业会从知名的经济预测公司购买经济和行业的未来需求预测数据。如果企业邀请专家进行预测，德尔菲法能够帮助企业得到更为准确的预测结果。

4. 过往销售数据分析

时序分析是过往销售数据分析的一种方法，主要是将过去的数据按时间

investment, government spending, net exports, and other variables. Based on the results of macroeconomic forecasts, companies forecast the total industry sales and then estimate the total sales and market share of enterprises.

Companies can forecast demand internally or buy forecasts data from external sources, such as marketing research firms. All forecasts are based on three types of information: customer group opinions, customer group behaviors, and historical data. Obtaining customer group opinions involves investigating the views of buyers or related groups and combining them with the advice of sales representatives and experts for analysis. Investigating customer behaviors requires the company to place the product in the market and record buyers' feedback. Companies can also estimate future demand by analyzing past purchase behavior and conducting time series analysis or demand statistics analysis. Specifically, demand is forecasted through the following means:

1. Customer purchase intention survey

Some marketing research companies obtain consumer purchase intention through questionnaires and set the answers as the purchase probability scale. The survey also includes the present and future personal financial situation of consumers and their expectations of the economy. Subsequently, these marketing research companies combine different information and form the consumer confidence index. The buyer confidence index of the industry can be measured similarly.

2. Sales representative opinion

When interviews with buyers are infeasible, companies can ask sales representatives to estimate their future sales. The estimates of sales representatives may be overly optimistic or pessimistic because they are unaware of the company's future resource allocation and marketing plan. In addition, sales representatives may intentionally report underestimated demand to reduce their own sales targets. Therefore, enterprises should provide assistance or incentives and make the appropriate adjustments when asking sales representatives for their opinions.

3. Expert opinions

Companies can obtain estimates of future demand through industry experts (including resellers, distributors, suppliers, marketing consultants, and trade associations). Some companies buy economic and industry forecasts of future demand from well-known economic forecasting firms. If a company invites experts to predict, then the Delphi method can help the company obtain accurate forecast results.

4. Analysis of past sales data

Time series analysis is a method used to analyze past sales data by dividing past data

分为四个项目(趋势、循环、季节和不规则),并将这些项目用于对未来的预测。指数平滑法是将过去的平均销售量和最新的销售量结合,赋予最新销售量更高的权重,得出对下一阶段销售量的预测。需求统计分析主要对影响销售水平的因素进行测定,然后使用这些因素进行预测。

5. 市场测试

当上述方法都不可行时,企业可以将产品投入市场进行测试,根据测试结果对新产品的销售量做出预测,或估算产品在新销售渠道、新地区的销售情况。

into four items (i.e., trends, cycles, seasons, and irregularities) by time and using these items for future prediction. The exponential smoothing method combines past average sales volume with the latest sales volume, giving the latest sales volume a higher weight, to obtain the sales volume forecast for the next stage. Statistical analysis of demand measures factors affecting the sales level and then use these factors for prediction.

5. Market testing

When the above methods are infeasible, companies can place the product into the market for testing and forecast the sales of the new product according to test results or estimate the sales in new channels or areas.

第4章 消费者市场

 本章要点

- 影响旅游者购买行为的文化因素
- 影响旅游者购买行为的社会因素
- 影响旅游者购买行为的个人因素
- 旅游者主要心理过程与行为相关理论

随着市场竞争的日益激烈,营销人员逐渐意识到获取竞争优势的重要性和必要性。创造和传递顾客价值需要营销人员深入了解现有市场及潜在市场的需要和需求,以及影响需求的环境因素、行为因素以及消费决策过程。企业面临的市场有消费者市场和企业市场,本章侧重于介绍影响消费者市场的因素、主要行为变量以及相关理论。

4.1 消费者行为及其影响因素

消费者行为是关于个人或群体为了满足自身的需要和需求进行的购买、使用、处置产品、服务、意见或体验的行为(Simonson 等,2001)。对消费者行为的研究可以分为三个互相依赖的维度:(1)文化因素;(2)社会因素;(3)个人因素。个体在出生时并不会带有价值观或行为模式,更不会理解何为文化。所有个体都是在成长过程中学习并形成自身的价值观和行为模式的。在此过程中,个体需要与其他个体建立联系。这种联系可以是直接联系(与其他人进行交流)或间接联系(观察他人行为)。因此,社会是个人和文化之间的联结。但是,个体有独立的思考和感受,并不会自主地改变或适应其他文化或价值。在同一个社会中,拥有相同或不同思考和感受的个人间的不断交流和互动,可能会对彼此的价值观和行为模式产生影响。

Chapter 4 Consumer Markets

 Key points of the chapter

- Cultural factors influencing the buying behavior of tourists
- Social factors influencing the buying behavior of tourists
- Personal factors influencing the buying behavior of tourists
- Major psychological processes of tourists and behavior-related theories

As market competition intensifies, marketers are becoming increasingly aware of the importance and necessity of gaining competitive advantage. Creating and delivering customer value require marketers to understand the needs and demands of existing and potential markets, environmental and behavioral factors affecting demands, and buying decision processes. This chapter focuses on the factors influencing the consumer market, main behavioral variables, and relevant theories.

4.1 Consumer Behavior and Its Influencing Factors

Consumer behavior is the act of buying, using, and disposing a product, service, opinion, or experience by an individual or a group to satisfy own needs and demands (Simonson et al., 2001). Research on consumer behavior can be divided into three interdependent dimensions, namely, (1) cultural, (2) social, and (3) personal factors. Individuals are not born with values or behavior patterns, and they do not naturally understand culture. All individuals learn and form their own values and behavior patterns as they grow. In this process, individuals must establish connections with others. The connection can be a direct (to communicate with others) or indirect contact (to observe the behavior of others). Society is the link between an individual and culture. However, an individual possesses independent thoughts and feelings and does not volunteer to change or adapt to other cultures or values. In the same society, individuals with similar or different thoughts and feelings may influence the values and behavior patterns of one other through constant communication and interaction.

4.1.1　文化因素

文化是消费者需求和行为的根本决定因素。Peter 和 Olson(1996)认为,文化是"在一个社会群体中大部分人共同拥有的价值观",同时也是人类行为的蓝图。每种文化都包括了更小范围的亚文化。亚文化体现的是某个社会群体的社会身份和群体特征,如国籍、信仰、种族等。企业通过严谨的研究,发现不同种族或人口特征的细分市场并不一定喜欢或接受面向大众市场的营销广告。因此,进行基于亚文化的多文化营销非常重要。例如香港旅游发展局在 2014—2015 年度的营销活动中,针对内地市场和海外市场的不同文化特征,拍摄了 9 段不同的短片,宣传香港丰富多彩的旅游体验。

社会阶层也是亚文化中的一个重要特征。在社会中具有相同价值观、兴趣和行为特征的人聚集在一起,形成一个社会群体。不同的社会群体持续分化,最终形成不同的社会阶层。社会阶层主要有四个特征:

(1) 不同的社会阶层在衣着、语言模式和休闲偏好方面有明显差异;

(2) 不同的社会阶层中的个体有不同的感知身份——来自上层社会或下层社会;

(3) 社会阶层受到多因素的影响,包括职业、收入、财富、教育和价值导向;

(4) 受社会阶层的流动性和社会平等程度影响,个体可以往上层或下层社会流动。

文化并非一成不变。经济和技术发展、国际交流的增多等因素都会对文化产生影响,文化会因此而发生变化,进而影响消费者的价值观及其行为或偏好。Hsu 和 Huang (2016)研究并总结了现今中国社会的 40 种价值观(见表 4-1),表格中所列的前 20 种价值观与之前的研究(Chinese Culture Connection,1987;Fan,2000)一致。在研究中被提及的现代价值观并不是中国特有的,Hsu 和 Huang(2016)认为这是全球化、大众媒体和社交媒体对中国文化的影响。这些价值观的变化影响了中国消费者的旅游动机、旅游模式和旅游目的地选择。

4.1.1 Cultural factors

Culture is the fundamental determinant of consumer demand and behavior. Peter and Olson (1996) argue that culture is "the meanings that are shared by (most) people in a social group" and a blueprint for human behavior. Each culture includes a small range of subcultures that reflect the social and group identities of a social group, such as nationality, religion, and race. Through rigorous research, enterprises find that market segments with different racial or demographic characteristics may not necessarily like or accept mass market advertising. Therefore, multicultural marketing based on subcultures is crucial. For example, in the marketing campaign for 2014—2015, the Hong Kong Tourism Board (HKTB) produced nine short films according to the different cultural characteristics of the mainland and overseas markets to promote the rich and colorful tourism experience of Hong Kong.

Social class is also an important feature of subculture. People with same values, interests, and behavior characteristics in a community gather to form a social group. Different social groups continue to divide and ultimately form different social classes, which exhibits the four following main features.

(1) Different social classes are significantly different in clothing, language style, and leisure preferences.

(2) Individuals in different social classes possess different perceived identities—from the upper or the lower class.

(3) Social classes are affected by many factors, including occupation, income, wealth, education, and value orientation.

(4) Individuals can move to upper or lower social communities as a result of the mobility of social classes and the level of social equality.

Culture is mutable. Economic and technological development, increased international exchanges, and other factors affect culture. Culture changes, thus affecting the values and behavior or preferences of consumers. Hsu and Huang (2016) study and summarize 40 values in Chinese society today (Table 4 – 1). The first 20 values listed in the table are consistent with previous studies (Chinese Culture Connection, 1987; Fan, 2000). The modern values mentioned in their study are not unique to China, and Hsu and Huang (2016) demonstrate that these values result from the effects of globalization, mass media, and social media on Chinese culture. These changes in values influence the tourism motivation, travel patterns, and destination selection of Chinese consumers.

Table 4 – 1   40 values in Chinese society today

No.	Cultural value	Meaning	Effect on travel behaviors
1	Being considerate of others	Put one's self in others' shoes	
2	Complacency	Be satisfied with one's position in life	
3	Courtesy and morality	Exhibit good manners, comply with regulations, and conform to local customs	

表 4-1 现今中国社会的 40 种价值观

排序	文化价值观	含义	对旅游行为的影响
1	为他人着想	设身处地考虑他人	
2	安于现状	满足于当前的生活状态	
3	道德修养	遵守法规、入乡随俗、行为有礼	不文明的旅游行为
4	务实	脚踏实地不虚荣	
5	诚信	诚实守信	旅游信息来源:信任口碑而非旅行社
6	勤奋/拼搏	为达到目标而努力工作	
7	友善	待人友善,在必要时伸出援手	
8	适可而止	没有过分的欲望	
9	规划	为自身发展设定计划	
10	尊重历史	尊重历史的发展,牢记历史教训	旅游活动:偏好历史遗迹或博物馆
11	自律	规范自身行为,成为别人的行为模范	
12	责任感	对工作和家庭负责任	
13	节俭	避免过度消费	目的地选择:选择物美价廉;旅游模式:寻找价格更低廉的选择;旅游活动:购买便宜的产品
14	健康	拥有健康的体魄	
15	开阔视野/新奇	增长见闻	旅游动机:开阔视野;目的地选择:文化景点;旅游模式:包价旅游;旅游活动:购买特别的产品;重游可能性:低
16	文化/教育	增长见闻,锻炼思考	旅游动机:获取知识
17	安稳	注重个人安全和生活的稳定性	目的地选择:注重安全;旅游模式:包价旅游
18	抱团	建立团体,重视团体努力	
19	妥协	牺牲部分个人利益达成一致	
20	从众	跟随他人的选择	旅游活动:偏好著名景点
21	望子成龙	希望孩子做到最好	

Continued

No.	Cultural value	Meaning	Effect on travel behaviors
4	Down-to-earth	Not caught up in superficial things	
5	Honesty	Conduct business with integrity and keep one's words	Travel info source: trust word-of-mouth（WOM）but not travel agencies
6	Industry · (hardworking)	Work hard to achieve one's goals	
7	Kindness	Be kind to others and lend a helping hand to people in need	
8	Moderation	Not possess excessive desires	
9	Planning	Make plans for one's personal development	
10	Respect for history	Value continuity and never forget history	Travel activity: historic sites and museums
11	Self-discipline	Be able to regulate oneself and set an example for others	
12	Sense of obligation	Be accountable at work and to the family	
13	Thrift	Refrain from excessive consumption	Destination choice: assess value for money; Travel mode: look for cheaper options; Travel activity: shop for good deals
14	Health	Healthy body	
15	Horizon broadening/Novelty	Broaden one's views and have a wide range of experiences	Travel motivation: broaden horizon; Destination choice: cultural attractions; Travel mode: package tour; Travel activity: shop for specialties; Revisit intention: low
16	Knowledge and education	Improve one's knowledge and thinking skills	Travel motivation: gain knowledge
17	Stability and security	Personal safety and stability of life	Destination choice: security as an important criterion; Travel mode: package tours
18	Collectivism	Build in-group cohesiveness and value group effort	
19	Compromise	Accept less than one desire（because of conflicts with others or reality）	
20	Conformity	Do as others have done	Travel activity: famous attractions
21	Devotion to children	Want the best for one's children	

续　表

排序	文化价值观	含义	对旅游行为的影响
22	亲情	与家庭成员保持紧密联系,决定以家庭为重	旅游决策:以家庭为主; 旅游活动:为家庭成员购物
23	孝道/尊老	尊重并照顾长者	
24	友情	交朋友,与朋友互动	
25	和谐	随和,避免冲突	
26	乐观自信	积极、自信	
27	具竞争力	在工作中具有竞争力	
28	遵纪守法	认同遵守法律规定的必要性	
29	便利	无须花费过多的精力就可以达到目标	旅游模式:偏好包价旅游
30	安逸	在舒适的环境中享受生活	
31	名利	富有,具有名望	
32	时尚	了解时尚前沿	
33	享乐	满足物质上的追求	游客更愿意在旅游上花费
34	休闲	放松身心,平衡工作与生活	旅游动机:放松 目的地选择:自然风光 旅游模式:自由行
35	个性/独立/自由	追求自由、独立	目的地选择:氛围自由的目的地 旅游模式:自由行
36	活在当下	享受当前的快乐	
37	攀比/炫富	在物质方面与别人比较,不愿意落后	热衷于在社交媒体上与朋友分享旅游经历
38	生活品质	提高生活的幸福感	
39	私利	满足自身需求	与陌生的同行游客有友好的互动
40	崇洋	希望接触外国文化	

来源:基于 Hsu, C. H. C., & Huang, S. S.（2016）. Reconfiguring Chinese cultural values and their tourism implications. *Tourism Management*,54,230-242.

Continued

No.	Cultural value	Meaning	Effect on travel behaviors
22	Family orientation/kinship	Stay close with family and be family-oriented in one's decisions	Travel decision: family oriented; Travel activity: shopping (for family members)
23	Filial piety	Respect and take care of one's parents and elderly people	
24	Friendship	Make new friends and develop interpersonal relationships	
25	Harmony	Harmonious atmosphere without fighting	
26	Confidence	Be positive and confident	
27	Competitiveness and competence	Have a competitive edge in one's work	
28	Respect for legal practices	Believe in the necessity of abiding by laws and regulations	
29	Convenience	Achieve one's objectives without exerting much effort (related to consumption)	Travel mode: package tour
30	Easy and comfortable	An easy life in a comfortable environment	
31	Fame and fortune	Be rich and famous	
32	Fashion	Grasp the latest trend	
33	Indulgence	Gratify one's (material) desires	Prerequisite to travel: willing to spend
34	Leisure	Relax and enjoy a balance of life and work	Travel motivation: relaxation; Destination choice: natural sceneries; Travel mode: independent
35	Liberation	Have freedom of being independent and true to oneself	Destination choice: democratic societies; Travel mode: independent
36	Live in the moment	Seek pleasure in the present to avoid having regrets in the future	
37	Ostentation	Keep up with the Joneses	Share travel experience with friends on social networks
38	Quality of life	Improve the general well-being of one's life	
39	Self-interest	Satisfy the needs and wants of oneself (money and power)	Friendly casual interactions with stranger/fellow travelers
40	Worship foreign cultures	Exposure to foreign cultures (out of admiration for their advanced developments)	

Source: Based on Hsu, C. H. C. & Huang, S. S. (2016). Reconfiguring Chinese cultural values and their tourism implications. *Tourism Management*, 54, 230 - 242.

4.1.2 社会因素

不同的社会因素会影响消费者的购买行为,如参照群体、家庭、社会角色和社会地位。

1. 参照群体

参照群体是指对消费者的消费态度或行为有直接或间接影响的群体。图 4-1 所示为参照群体的主要类型。对消费者有直接影响的群体称为成员资格型群体,而这个群体又分为首要群体和次要群体。首要群体包括家庭、朋友、邻居和同事等与消费者有持续性、非正式互动的群体。次要群体则更为正式,与消费者有较少的持续性互动,如宗教团体、职业协会或贸易联盟等。

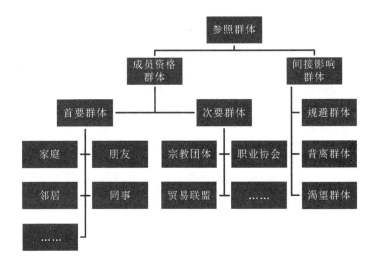

图 4-1 参照群体

来源:Kotler,Keller. (2009). *Marketing Management* (13th ed.).
Upper Saddle River,NJ:Pearson Prentice Hall.

间接影响的群体可能是非消费者所属的群体,或是个体消费者并不愿意成为其中一员的群体。间接影响的群体包括渴望群体,即个体消费者希望加入的群体;规避群体,即个体消费者非其成员,且个体消费者并不认同其价值观、形式或行为的群体;背离群体,即个体消费者所属,但并不认同其价值观、形式或行为的群体。

4.1.2 Social factors

Different social factors, such as reference groups, family, social roles, and social statuses, can influence consumer behavior.

1. Reference groups

A reference group refers to a group directly or indirectly influencing consumer attitudes or behaviors. Figure 4 – 1 illustrates the main types of reference groups. Groups directly influencing consumers, that is, membership groups, are divided into primary and secondary groups. Primary groups include family, friends, neighbors, and colleagues who have continuous and informal interactions with consumers. Secondary groups are more formal and have fewer ongoing interactions with consumers (e.g., religious groups, professional associations, or trade unions).

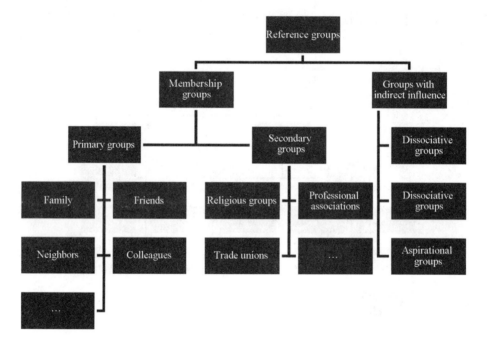

Figure 4 – 1　Reference groups
Source: Kotler, Keller. (2009). *Marketing Management* (13th ed.). Upper Saddle River, NJ: Pearson Prentice Hall.

Groups with indirect influence may be those that consumers do not belong to or that an individual consumer is unwilling to become a member of. These groups include aspirational groups, which individual consumers want to join; dissociative groups, of which individual consumers are not members and do not subscribe to the values, forms, or behaviors of the groups; and disclaimant groups, of which individual consumers belong to but do not agree with the values, forms, or behaviors of the groups.

参照群体对消费者的影响主要有三种方式：(1)消费者对参照群体的消费行为和生活方式的体验；(2)参照群体对消费者的态度和自我概念的影响；(3)消费者希望与参照群体保持一致，对产品或品牌的选择产生偏好。Hsu、Kang 和 Lam(2006)通过对 464 名中国居民进行问卷调查，发现大部分游客在选择旅游目的地时主要听从首要群体的意见。同时，在旅游行业内，不同参照群体对游客的影响取决于游客个人的价值观、性格、动机等心理因素。

除了参照群体，意见领袖同样会影响个体消费者的态度或行为。Schiffman 和 Kanuk(2004)认为，意见领袖是指能够对特定产品或产品类型提供非正式信息或意见的人。通常而言，意见领袖对产品类型有着较高水平的了解和自信，并在社交方面较为积极主动。消费者认为，意见领袖是一个可信的信息源。与意见领袖相比，营销专家同样也是可信的信息来源。但营销专家并不如意见领袖有影响力，因为后者通过亲自使用产品获得了更多的一手信息。对于消费者来讲，意见领袖的信息可以帮助他们缓解在决策前期的紧张和不确定性，尤其对于购买新产品的决策来讲更是如此，所以意见领袖是重要的口碑传播者。新西兰旅游局邀请意见领袖洪晃多次赴新西兰旅游并在其博客上撰文宣传，起到了一定的营销效果。洪晃是中国报纸杂志专栏作家，同时她的博客是国内著名文化女性博客，粉丝数量超过 30 万，博客访问次数超过 1 亿次。2010 年，洪晃发文介绍，2008 年全球第一大乳制品供应商恒天然旗下品牌"安满"邀请她及其他 30 位母亲体验新西兰牧场，并参观安然配方奶粉的制造过程。此后，洪晃连续发布有关新西兰旅游的博客文章，推介新西兰旅游。2012 年，新西兰旅游局与洪晃合作，推出一系列新西兰旅游宣传片。

2. 家庭

在消费者的生命过程中，有两个家庭类型——原生家庭和新生家庭。在原生家庭中，父母对个体消费者的影响最为明显。个体消费者从父母那里获得关于宗教、政治、经济等方面的倾向，建立个人志向、自我认知(Palan 和 Wikes，1997)。新生家庭则对个体消费者日常的购买行为有更为直接的影响。一般而言，妻子是家庭中的主要购买者，在购买决策中扮演越来越重要的地位(Mottiar 和 Quinn，2004)。另一方面，儿童和青少年对家庭消费也有直接或间接的影响。不少学者认为，在过去的几十年中，儿童在家庭旅游

Reference groups can influence consumers through three main approaches. (1) Consumers experience the consumption behaviors and lifestyles of reference groups. (2) Reference groups influence the attitudes and self-concept of consumers. (3) Consumers desire to be consistent with the reference group, and thus establish preferences in products or brands. In their questionnaire survey of 464 Chinese residents, Hsu, Kang, and Lam (2006) find that most visitors follow the opinion of the primary group in selecting a tourist destination. In the tourism industry, the effect of different reference groups on tourists depends on the personal values, personality, motivation, and other psychological factors of tourists.

Apart from reference groups, opinion leaders influence the attitudes or behaviors of individual consumers. Schiffman and Kanuk (2004) indicate that opinion leaders can provide informal information or advice on a particular product or product type. In general, opinion leaders possess a high level of confidence in product types and are socially active. Consumers believe opinion leaders are a trusted information source. Marketing experts are also a trusted information source However, they are not as influential as opinion leaders, who learn hands-on information by using the product personally. For consumers, opinion leaders can help them mitigate tensions and uncertainties in the early stages of decision making, especially in buying decisions of new products. Therefore, opinion leaders are important WOM communicators. Tourism New Zealand invited opinion leader Hong Huang multiple times to visit New Zealand to promote travel experience in her blog, creating a marketing effect. Hong Huang is a Chinese newspaper and magazine columnist, and her blog is a domestically well-known cultural women blog with more than 300,000 fans and over 100 million blog visits. In 2010, Hong Huang released that the largest dairy supplier in the world, Fonterra's brand, Anmum, invited her and 30 other mothers to visit the New Zealand ranch and observe the manufacturing process of Anmum milk powder in 2008. Since then, Hong issued a series of blog articles about traveling to New Zealand to promote the tourism of New Zealand. In 2012, Tourism New Zealand and Hong Huang collaborated and launched a series of New Zealand tourism videos.

2. Family

In the life of a consumer, two types of families are established—the family of orientation and procreation. In the family of orientation, the influence of parents on individual consumers is obvious. Individual consumers obtain religious, political, and economic tendencies from their parents, building personal ambitions and self-awareness (Palan & Wikes, 1997). In comparison, the family of procreation exerts a more direct influence on the daily buying behavior of individual consumers. On one hand, the wife is the primary purchaser of the household and plays an increasingly important role in

决策中的地位已从被忽视的被动体转为活跃的参与者（Howard 和 Madrigal，1990），甚至对于很多家庭来讲，为孩子提供教室外的学习机会，使其增长见识，已成为重要的出游动机（Li、Zhang 和 Cai，2016）。根据同程网的数据，2015 年中国在线亲子旅游市场交易规模达到 114.7 亿元人民币，与 2014 年相比增长了 76.2%。为了吸引亲子市场，广州长隆酒店对客房设有不同主题，如狩猎房、野趣房、白虎房等，以便能够吸引儿童入住。除此以外，长隆酒店还针对儿童提供额外的服务，如提供儿童浴袍、洗漱用品、拖鞋、玩偶等。

3. 社会角色与地位

Kotler 和 Keller（2009）认为，个体消费者在不同的社会群体中有不同的社会角色，而不同社会角色要求个体有相应的行为。另一方面，不同的社会角色也有不同的社会地位。而不同的社会地位对不同的产品和品牌有不同的潜在需求。对于旅游者来讲，旅游不仅仅是休息、放松、猎奇，也是个人社会地位的表现，这会影响目的地的选择（Correia 和 Kozak，2012）。Pappas（2014）的研究结果表明，距离、旅游花费以及目的地与居住地的文化差异对旅游者在出游过程中感知到的社会地位表现程度有正相关关系。

4.1.3　个人因素

消费者决策同样会受到消费者个人特征的影响。个人特征包括年龄、生命周期、职业、经济状况、性格、自我认知以及生活方式与价值观。

1. 年龄与生命周期

消费者对食品、衣饰、家具和休闲活动的偏好与其年龄有关。生命周期同样影响消费者的购买决策。生命周期分为家庭生命周期和心理生命周期。家庭生命周期是指任何时间点上，一个家庭的人数、年龄和性别。心理生命周期则受个人在生命中的经历和转变影响。不同的经历和转变会带来新的需求或偏好的变化。表 4－2 对几个主要的生命周期阶段进行了归纳并分析了各个阶段可能具有的一些建议性消费特点。

purchasing decisions（Mottiar & Quinn，2004）. On the other hand，children and adolescents directly or indirectly influence household consumption. Many scholars believe that the status of the children in family tourism decisions has shifted from neglected passive parties to active participants in the last few decades（Howard & Madrigal，1990）. For many families，providing opportunities for children to learn outside the classroom has become an important motivating factor for traveling（Li，Zhang & Cai，2016）. The data from LY.com show that the business scale of the online parent-child tourism market in China is expected to reach 114.7 billion Chinese yuan in 2015，growing 76.2% than in 2014. To attract families，the Chimelong hotel in Guangzhou features rooms with different themes，such as hunting，wild，and white tiger rooms，to attract children to stay. In addition，this hotel provides additional services for children，such as bathrobes，toiletries，slippers，and dolls.

3. Social roles and statuses

Kotler and Keller（2009）demonstrate that individual consumers engage in different social roles in various social groups，and different social roles require individuals to behave accordingly. Different social roles also have different social statuses，and these social statuses have distinct potential needs of various products and brands. For tourists，tourism is not only a relaxation but also a manifestation of individual social status，which affects destination selection（Correia & Kozak，2012）. Pappas（2014）show that distances，travel costs，and cultural differences between destination and place of residence are positively related to the degree of manifesting social status perceived by tourists during travel.

4.1.3 Personal factors

The decision making of the consumers is also affected by their personal characteristics. These personal characteristics include age，stage in the life cycle，occupation，economic circumstances，personality，self-concept，lifestyle，and values.

1. Age and stage in the life cycle

The preferences of consumers for food，clothing，furniture，and leisure activities are related to their age. The stage in the life cycle also affects their purchasing decisions. The life cycle is divided into family and psychological life cycle. The family life cycle refers to the number，age，and gender of the members in a family at any time. The psychological life cycle is affected by personal life experiences and changes. Different experiences and changes can lead to new demands or altered preferences. Table 4 − 2 summarizes the major life cycle stages and analyzes the possible consumption characteristics of each stage.

表 4 – 2 生命周期和旅游业

生命周期阶段	年 龄	旅游业消费特征
童年		
幼童	4 岁及以下	他们对父母而言是"问题消费者",飞机上需要婴儿位置;酒店里可能需要托婴服务。
孩童	5～12 岁	他们对外出就餐地点的选择有重要影响;度假胜地的酒店为小孩提供娱乐项目。
青少年		
少年	13～15 岁	他们变成了独立的消费者,但是通常没有明显的独立收入;他们对外出旅游有主要影响;饭店有供其独立使用的娱乐设施。
青年	16～18 岁	他们作为独立的消费者,经常做兼职工作;他们对社交活动有很高的需求。
年轻的成年期		
单身年轻人	19～24 岁	他们全职工作或念大学,或半工半读;其收入足以负担例如为了约会等小规模地使用酒店和景区服务;他们和家人一起旅行,旅游开支较少。
年轻夫妇	25～34 岁	他们大多是双收入家庭,但是家庭开支和投资通常减少了可用于旅游的资金;他们对旅游兴趣很大。
中年		
中年早期	35～49 岁	他们的收入大幅增长,但是家里的或在上大学的孩子需要不断的支持;他们对旅游有最大的嗜好。
中年中晚期	50～59 岁	他们的收入达到最高,但有时会提前退休,收入会减少;对旅游有很强的偏好;和年轻一些的中年群体相比,外出就餐相对少了
老年		
老年早期	60～74 岁	他们收入稳定且充足,退休后有充裕的闲暇时间;通常身体健康,充满活力;想要享受生活;出于健康考虑,对饮食有一些特别的讲究。
老年中期	75～84 岁	他们构成了中国日益增长的人口群体,他们有更多的健康问题,通常丧偶独居;身体状况变差;可能需要老人院的护理;在饮食上更加注意。
老年晚期	85 岁及以上	他们在生活上更需要照顾;女性比例高于男性;年老体弱,但有些老人反应灵敏,身体健康;通常需要特殊的饮食和帮助。

来源:徐惠群.(2009).旅游营销.北京:中国人民大学出版社.

Table 4 - 2   Life cycle and tourism

Stages in life cycle	Age	Consumption characteristics in tourism
Childhood		
Toddler	4 and below	They are "problematic consumers" to parents, requiring baby seats on planes and perhaps babysitting service in hotels.
Child	5~12	They exert an important influence on selecting a dine-out place; resort hotels provide entertainment for children.
Youth		
Adolescent	13~15	They become independent consumers but do not have a significant independent income; they have a major impact on travel; hotels features recreational facilities for their independent use.
Teenager	16~18	Independent consumers who often do part-time work; they possess a high demand for social activities.
Young adulthood		
Young single	19~24	They are full-time or part-time working or studying in a university; they have sufficient income to afford use of some hotels and tourism services for occasions, such as dating; they travel with families and spend relatively less on tourism.
Young couple	25~34	Most are double-income families, but household expenses and investments reduce the amount of funds available for tourism; they possess great interest in tourism.
Middle age		
Early middle age	35~49	They experience a large growth in income, but children at home or in college require constant support; they possess the greatest favor for tourism.
Late middle age	50~59	Their income is the highest, but they sometimes retire early and income can be reduced; they possess a strong preference for tourism; they dine out less than the younger middle-aged group.
Elderly		
Early elderly	60~74	Their income is stable and adequate, and they have plenty of leisure time after retirement; they usually healthy and energetic; they want to enjoy life; for health considerations, they have certain diet preferences.
Middle elderly	75~84	They form a growing group in China, and they have health problems and poor physical condition, are often widowed, and live alone; they may require elderly homes for nursing; they pay attention to diet.
Late elderly	85 and above	They need to be taken care of; this group has more women than men; they are old and frail, but some elderly people are responsive and in good health; they usually require special diet and help.

Source: Hsu, C. H. C. (2009). *Tourism marketing*. Beijing: China Renmin University Press.

不同的年龄意味着不同的生理状况、心理状况和收入水平,会产生不同的需求和欲望。青年阶段的人们有足够的时间和精力,有一定的探险或远距离出游的兴趣,但又受经济实力较弱的限制,倾向于购买价格便宜的旅游产品;小型包价度假旅游产品专为现代越来越多的"双职工"家庭设计,把短程旅行与某个成员的商务出行结合起来,解决双方因为工作时间差异而导致的难以一起出行的难题;步入老年阶段后的人们,既有弹性大的时间也有较强的经济实力,对旅游产品需求的品位高,他们需要慢节奏的旅游产品和服务。

随着医疗水平的进步,人们的平均寿命也相应延长,老年人群逐渐庞大。老年人具有充裕的出游时间,并且不受季节限制。他们已经有稳定的储蓄收入,可用于支付旅游费用,加之由于生活环境过于单调,大多数老年人都有利用晚年外出旅游,以实现以往由于工作忙没能实现的外出接触新环境的种种愿望。因此,老年旅游市场,或者说"银发市场",已经开始作为一个新型的游客群体吸引越来越多的营销人员的关注,成为他们开发的主要目标市场之一。淡季的特别促销优惠一般是针对考虑价格成本但在时间上比较自由的群体设计的,这个群体中很多都是老年人。各种针对老年人市场的旅游产品也不断浮出水面,如去哪儿网推出的"夕阳红老年万里行"跟团游,以走访人文景点为主;携程网打造的"爸妈放心游"旅游产品,力图"让旅行带爸妈重温青春的味道";还有驴妈妈网的"乐享爸妈游"以及同程网的"全景敬老游",皆为针对中老年人开发的旅游产品(郑炜,2015)。

2. 职业与经济状况

不同的职业会影响消费者的购买行为和模式,例如,作家偏好文化底蕴深厚的旅游目的地,如国内的北京、上海、凤凰古城,国外的伦敦、维也纳等。市场营销人员可发掘对其产品和服务有较高兴趣的职业群体,制定满足特定职业群体的产品。经济状况包括可支配收入(收入水平、稳定性和时间)、储蓄和财产(包括流动性财产)、债务、贷款能力、消费及储蓄态度。市场营销人员可根据经济指标对产品或服务进行重新设计、重新定位或重新定价,或者推广折扣以继续为目标顾客提供价值。

3. 性格与自我认知

性格是一套区分不同个体的心理特征,这些特征会使个体在面对环境变

Different ages mean varied physiological conditions, psychological conditions, and income levels, resulting in distinct needs and wants. People at the youth stage have enough time and energy and an interest in adventure or long-haul travel, but they are restricted by the relatively weak economic capability and buy cheap tourism products. Small-scale holiday tour package are specifically designed for the increasing double-income family nowadays, combining the short-haul travel with the business trip of a family member to solve the difficulty of couples traveling together because of differences in working hours. People at the elderly stage have both flexible time and strong economic capability. They demand high-grade and slow-paced tourism products and services.

The life expectancy of people is correspondingly extended with medical progress, and the elderly group gradually becomes large. The elderly possess sufficient travel time, and they are not subject to seasonal restrictions. The elderly also own stable income from savings to pay for travel expenses. Moreover, the living environment for elderly people is monotonous and simple.Consequently, the majority of the elderly wish to spend their time in traveling, to realize the desire to explore the new environment that they could not achieve in the past because of their busy work. Therefore, the elderly tourism market, or "silver-hair market" as a new type of tourist groups, attracts an increasing attention of the marketers and becomes one of their main target markets to develop. Off-season promotions are designed for groups that consider the monetary cost while being relatively flexible in time, and many of these groups are from the elderly. All kinds of tourism products for the elderly market have been developed, such as the "sunset elderly journey" tour launched by Qunar to visit the main cultural attractions, the "parent reassurance tour" developed by Ctrip in an attempt to "let travel bring parents to revisit the taste of youth," the "happy parent tour" of Lvmama, and the "full-view elderly tour" of LY.com (Zheng, 2015).

2. Occupation and economic circumstances

Different occupations affect consumer behaviors and purchase patterns. For example, writers prefer travel destinations with a profound cultural background, such as Beijing, Shanghai, Phoenix ancient city, London, and Vienna. Marketers can explore professional groups with high interests in their products and services and develop products that meet the demands of specific occupational groups. Economic circumstances include disposable income (income level, stability, and time), savings and property (including liquidity), debt, lending capacity, and consumption and saving attitudes. Marketers can redesign, reposition or reprice products or services based on economic indicators, or promote discounts to continue providing value to the target customers.

3. Personality and self-concept

Personality is a set of psychological characteristics that distinguish different

化时有一致的、持续的反应。Gover 和 Schoormans（2005）认为，自信、支配性、自主性、尊重、交际、自我保护和适应性都是心理特征的一部分。性格可以作为一个因素，用于分析顾客品牌选择，因为顾客更倾向于选择与自身性格更为相近的品牌。Kotler 和 Keller（2009）将品牌性格定义为一个特定品牌所拥有的一套与人类相似的心理特征。

Sirgy（1982）认为，顾客经常选择和使用与他们实际自我认知（个体实际如何看待自己）一致的品牌。同时，品牌的选择可能是基于顾客的理想自我认知（个体希望如何看待自己）或他人自我认知（个体认为他人如何看待自己）。在不同的情景下或在不同的群体中，消费者有多种自我认知，从而会对产品或服务进行不同的选择。

4. 生活方式与价值观

生活方式是个体在生活中的活动、兴趣和意见模式，其描述的是个体如何与身边的环境进行互动。市场营销人员经常寻找企业产品与特定生活方式群体之间的联系。生活方式可以按照限制来源分为收入限制导向和时间限制导向。一般而言，企业会向收入限制导向的顾客提供低成本的产品和服务。例如，经济型酒店通过减少非必要服务、简化装修等方式降低总成本从而降低房价，为收入限制导向的消费者提供价格低廉的住宿产品。时间限制导向的顾客不希望因为时间上的限制而无法体验产品或服务，因而对价格相对不敏感。旅游在很多时候会成为实现理想生活方式的途径，所以在越来越多的地方出现了介于旅游和移民之间的季节性生活方式旅游，又被称为居住旅游（McWatters，2009；O'Reilly，2007；Tomas，2006）、生活方式移民（Benson，2011；Benson 和 O'Reilly 2009；Sato，2001），或第二家园旅游（Hall 和 Müller，2004；Hiltunen，2007）。季节性生活方式旅游通常会受到气候条件的影响。

价值是一种内心深处的持久的信仰，用于指导人们在面对一系列情境时的行为和判断，这种信仰是超越直接目标而指向生存的终极状态的（Rokeach，1968）。Rokeach（1971）认为，价值可以分为工具性价值和终极价值。工具性价值是道德或能力，是为达到理想化终极状态所采取的行为方式或手段；终极性价值是存在的理想化终极状态和结果，是一个人一生希望实现的目标。价值是影响消费者决策的一个重要因素，也是不同文化背景的

individuals. These characteristics enable individuals to respond to changes in the environment consistently and continuously. Gover and Schoormans (2005) believe that self-confidence, dominance, autonomy, respect, communication, self-protection, and adaptability are part of the psychological characteristics. Personality can be used as a factor in the analysis of customer brand choice, because customers are likely to select the brands that are close to their personality. Kotler and Keller (2009) define a brand personality as a set of psychological characteristics similar to a human being possessed by a particular brand.

Sirgy (1982) contends that customers often select and use brands that are consistent with their actual self-concept (how individuals actually view themselves). Simultaneously, brand choice may be based on the ideal self-concept of the customer (how individuals would like to view themselves) or the self-concept of others (how individuals think others see themselves). In different situations or in different groups, consumers possess varying self-concept to select distinct products or services.

4. Lifestyle and values

Lifestyle is the activity, interest, and opinion patterns in the life of an individual, describing how the individual interacts with the surrounding environment. Marketers often seek for connections between the products of a company and a particular lifestyle group. Lifestyle can be money or time constrained depending on the source of limits. Companies provide low-cost products and services to money-constrained customers. For example, hotels lower their rates by reducing non-essential services and simplifying the interior design to reduce the total cost, providing money-constrained consumers with low-cost accommodation products. Time-constrained customers do not want to miss the experience of the product or service because of time constraints and thus are relatively insensitive to price. Tourism is often the means of achieving the ideal lifestyle. Therefore, the seasonal lifestyle tourism emerges in a growing number of places between tourism and immigration, also known as residential tourism (McWatters, 2009; O'Reilly, 2007; Tomas, 2006), lifestyle migration (Benson, 2011; Benson & O'Reilly 2009; Sato, 2001), or second home tourism (Hall & Müller, 2004; Hiltunen, 2007). Seasonal lifestyle tourism is often affected by climatic conditions.

The value is a deep and enduring faith that guides the behaviors and judgments of a person in the face of a range of situations and that transcends the immediate goal and points to the ultimate state of existence (Rokeach, 1968). Rokeach (1973) believes that values can be divided into instrumental and terminal values. The instrumental value is the morality or ability and is the way or means of behavior in achieving the ultimate state of idealism. The terminal value is the available idealized ultimate state and result and is the life goal for a person to achieve. Values are an important factor influencing consumer decision making and are also the most fundamental determinant of the difference in

消费者行为差异的最根本的决定因素。以内在价值为导向的旅游者由于希望对自己的生活有更多的控制,所以旅游时更希望接触到新鲜事物以获得个人发展,而以外在价值为导向的旅游者相对较被动,并且对外部事件敏感,更倾向于将旅游作为一种体现个人社会地位的途径(Li 和 Cai,2012)。

4.2　消费者主要心理过程

在消费者的心理过程中,主要有四个关键的心理项目——动机、感知、学习和记忆。

4.2.1　动机

在关于人类动机的研究中,有三个最为著名的理论——弗洛伊德(Sigmund Freud,1900)理论、马斯洛(Abraham Maslow,1943)理论和赫茨伯格(Frederick Herzberg,1966)理论。弗洛伊德认为,影响人类行为的心理力量大部分是无意识的,人类不能完全理解,甚至没有意识到自身动机的存在。阶梯技术能够让研究人员更好地追踪人的动机——从工具性价值到终极性价值。动机研究者通常会通过与几十个消费者进行深度访谈,揭示消费者心理上由产品引起的更深层次的动机。另外,研究人员会使用多种不同的投射测验技术,如词语联想、完成语句、图像判读和角色扮演。马斯洛试图解释为什么人类在特定的时间内会被特定的需求所驱动(Maslow,1954)。他认为人类的需求层次是根据迫切程度进行排列的:(1)生理需求;(2)安全需求;(3)社交需求;(4)尊重需求;(5)自我实现需求。人类会首先满足最重要的需求。当最重要的需求得到满足以后,才会满足次重要的需求。赫茨伯格(1966)提出了双因素理论,区分不满因素(引起不满的因素)和满意因素(引起满意的因素)。在市场营销中,缺少不满因素并不足以鼓励顾客购买;而当顾客购买产品时,必须存在满意因素。

在旅游动机研究中,主要的理论包括旅游生涯结构模型、寻求逃离模型和推拉模型。Pearce 和 Caltabiano(1983)在马斯洛理论的基础上,提出了旅游生涯阶梯模型。旅游生涯阶梯模型应用马斯洛五个层次需求,提出旅游动机的五个层次,从低到高分别是放松需求、安全需求、关系需求、自我尊重和发展需求以及自我实现需求。旅游生涯阶梯模型被提出后,很快在实践中被运用,特别是在管理咨询方面(Ryan 和 Glendon,1998)。然而该模型中"阶梯"一词的使用暗含了阶段性,也即旅游者只有在满足了较"低"层次的动机后才会产生较"高"层次的动机,这使得该模型在实践应用过程中的效度往往不尽如人意。此后,Pearce 和 Kim(2005)在旅游生涯阶梯模型的基础上提出

consumer behaviors in the different cultural backgrounds. The intrinsic value-oriented tourists are willing to have access to new things to gain personal development, because these tourists desire to have control over their life. The external value-oriented tourists are relatively passive and sensitive to events, hence they are inclined to use tourism as a means of manifesting personal social status (Li & Cai, 2012).

4.2　Major Psychological Processes of Consumers

Four key psychological items are addressed in the psychological processes of consumers, namely, motivation, perception, learning, and memory.

4.2.1　Motivation

Three of the most famous theories in human motivation research are those of Sigmund Freud (1990), Abraham Maslow (1943), and Frederick Herzberg (1966). Freud believes that most of the psychological forces affecting human behavior are unconscious, and humans cannot fully understand or even realize the existence of their own motives. The laddering technique allows researchers to better track the motivations of people—from the instrumental to the terminal value. Motivation researchers often conduct comprehensive interviews with dozens of consumers, revealing deep psychological motivations of consumers for the product. In addition, researchers use various projective techniques, such as word association, sentence completion, image interpretation, and role play.Maslow (1954) attempts to explain why humans are driven by specific needs at a particular time. He believes that the human needs are arranged in levels according to the urgency, the order is as follows: (1) physiological, (2) security, (3) social, (4) esteem, and (5) self-actualization needs. First, people satisfy the most important needs. Then, when the most important needs are satisfied, people attempt to satisfy the next most important needs. Herzberg (1966) proposed a two-factor theory to distinguish the dissatisfiers (factors that cause dissatisfaction) from the satisfiers (factors that cause satisfaction). In marketing, the lack of dissatisfiers is not enough to encourage customers to buy. Satisfiers must exist when customers buy products.

In tourism motivation research, the main theories include travel career structure, seek-escape, and push-pull models. Pearce and Caltabiano (1983) propose a travel career ladder model based on Maslow's theory. The travel career ladder model adopts Maslow's five levels of demands and proposes five levels of tourism motivations—from low to high being physiological, safety, love and belongingness, self-esteem, and self-actualization needs. The travel career ladder model was soon implemented in practice, especially in management consulting (Ryan & Glendon, 1998). However, the use of the term "ladder" in the model implies the stage, indicating that the tourist has a "high" level of motivation only after satisfying the motivation of the "low" level, which makes the validity of the model often unsatisfactory in the practical process. Pearce and Kim (2005) propose a

了旅游生涯结构模型,该模型更加侧重于动机的结构及模式,而非步骤。根据旅游生涯结构模型,旅游动机是多种受过往出游经验及年龄影响的内在动力的组合,其中逃逸/放松、新奇感、关系以及自我发展是适用于所有旅游者的核心动机。旅游经历丰富的旅游者更加看重通过与当地居民互动及融入大自然来获得自我发展,而旅游经历欠丰富的旅游者则更看重能够带来诸如刺激、个人发展、自我实现、安全、浪漫等体验的出游。

基于内在动机理论,Iso-Ahola(1982)认为,动机是对未来状态的认知,即个体行为的内在动机是对未来的状态可能带来的满意的意识。当潜在满意的意识建立起来后,两种动机力量——寻求和逃离,就会对游客的旅游行为产生影响。换言之,个体参加旅游活动是因为他们认为旅游有可能满足其两种潜在需求:对特定内在奖励的渴求,如自我掌控、具有竞争力的需求(寻求),和想要离开固有环境的外在需求(逃离)。

虽然许多旅游学者都将心理学的理论用作研究基础或研究工具,但他们都无法解释为什么人们想要逃离日常环境或寻求刺激,也无法解释旅游者在生涯阶梯上的前进或后退(Jamal 和 Lee,2003;Ryan 和 Glendon,1998)。为了解决这个问题,一些学者使用社会学的方法来阐释旅游动机(如Britton,1991;Rojek,1995;Wang,2000)。与心理学角度相反,社会学途径强调现代资本主义社会的结构对个人旅游者行为的影响(Jamal 和 Lee,2003)。从社会学角度研究旅游动机最著名的是 Graham Dann 于 1977 年提出的推拉理论。

Dann(1977)认为,推力因素和拉力因素出现在旅游决策的两个阶段中。推力因素是个人内在的因素,它不断向个人灌输想要旅游的渴望。其目标是满足不同的心理需求。拉力因素则是个人外在的因素,强调特定目的地对于个人的好处,并确定个人假期的时间、地点和享受方式。因此,在拉力因素生效前,必须存在推力因素。

Dann 在他对推力动机因素的研究中提出,促使个人旅游的潜在需求包括逃离混乱的日常生活、爱与情感、社交互动、他人认可和自我提升(Dann,1981)。这些需求或渴求与马斯洛的需求层次理论是一致的。在推拉模型中,"推力"概念并非是一个单纯的心理学因素,而是文化和社会环境的组合,

travel career structure model based on the travel career ladder model, further focusing on the structure and patterns of motivations rather than stages. The travel career structure model suggests that the travel motive is a combination of the various motivation factors influenced by past travel experience and age. The core motivations for all tourists are escape/relax, novelty, relationship, and self-development. Tourists with more experience in tourism are more interested in self-development through interaction with the local residents and the integration with nature, while less experienced travelers are more interested in travel experiences that bring stimulation, personal development, self-actualization, security, and romance.

Based on the theory of intrinsic motivation, Iso-Ahola (1982) asserts that motivation is the recognition of the future state, that is, the intrinsic motivation of individual behavior is the sense of satisfaction that may be caused by the state of the future. When the potential consciousness of satisfaction is established, two motivational forces—seeking and escaping—can influence the behavior of tourists. Specifically, an individual participates in tourism because he/she believes that tourism can possibly meet two potential needs, namely, the desire for a specific intrinsic reward, such as self-control, for competitive demand (seeking) and the external demand to leave the current environment (escaping).

Although many tourism scholars use psychological theories as research foundation or tools, these scholars cannot explain why people want to escape from their daily environment or seek excitement, nor can they explain the advance or retreat of travelers on their career ladder (Jamal & Lee, 2003; Ryan & Glendon, 1998). To solve this problem, some scholars use sociological methods to explain the motivations of tourism (e.g., Britton, 1991; Rojek, 1995; Wang, 2000). In contrast to psychology, the sociological approach emphasizes the influence of the structure of modern capitalist societies on the behavior of individual travelers (Jamal & Lee, 2003). The most famous theory of tourism motivation from the sociological viewpoint is the push-pull theory proposed by Graham Dann in 1977.

Dann (1977) believes that the push and pull factors appear in the two stages of tourism decision making. The push factor is a personal intrinsic factor that instills the desire to travel to the individual, aiming to meet the different psychological needs. The pull factor is a personal external factor, emphasizing the benefits of a particular destination to individuals and determining the timing, location, and enjoyment of a personal holiday. Therefore, a push factor must be available before the pull factor becomes effective.

Dann's study of the push factors of motivation (1981) suggests that the potential needs motivating the individuals to travel include escaping chaotic daily life, love and emotion, social interaction, recognition of others, and self-promotion. These needs or aspirations are consistent with Maslow's hierarchy of needs. In the push-pull model, the concept of "push" is not simply a psychological factor but rather a combination of

它促使人们产生旅游的想法(Jamal 和 Lee，2003)。人们通过旅游来满足这些需求并不只是因为人的本性，更因为人们生活于一个由于标准化人际互动而失去一体化力量的社会。因此，人们尝试逃离孤独的感觉和混乱的日常生活。推拉理论的提出，使得人们在对个体出游决策进行研究时可以更多地引入个人的基本需求，而非仅仅依据与营销或目的地属性相关的因素。

4.2.2　感知

感知是人们选择、组织、解读信息以构建关于世界的有意义的想象的过程(Berelson 和 Steiner，1964)。在营销过程中，顾客感知比现实更为重要，因为感知影响顾客的实际行为。人们可以通过三种感知过程——选择性注意、选择性扭曲和选择性记忆对相同的客观对象产生不同的感知。

1. 选择性注意

注意力是人们面对一些刺激因素时对大脑处理能力进行分配的结果。自发性注意是带有目的地关注某种刺激，非自发性注意是被某些人或某些事物所吸引。由于大脑的处理能力有限，每个人都不能完全注意到每天所接受到的全部信息，因此，大脑会筛选出最重要的刺激因素——这个过程称为选择性注意。关于选择性注意，研究人员有以下发现(Kotler 和 Keller，2009)：

(1) 人们更容易注意与现时需求最为相关的刺激。

(2) 人们更容易注意自身所预期的刺激。

(3) 人们更容易注意到有明显偏差的刺激因素。例如，人们会更容易注意到啤酒减价 5 元的广告，而非电脑减价 5 元的广告。

2. 选择性扭曲

即使顾客注意到刺激因素，但他们的理解可能并非与市场营销人员预期的一样。选择性扭曲是对信息进行带有个人偏见的解读的倾向。消费者经常扭曲所接受到的信息，使其与之前所感知的品牌或产品期望相一致(Russo、Meloy 和 Medvec，1998)。

3. 选择性记忆

大部分顾客都不能记住每天所接受到的所有信息，但会记住与其态度或认知相一致的信息，这种现象称为选择性记忆。因此，顾客更容易记住自己所

cultural and social contexts that motivate people to generate travel ideas (Jamal & Lee, 2003). People travel to meet these needs not only because of human nature but also because people live in a society that loses the power of integration given the standardized interaction. Consequently, people aim to escape the feeling of loneliness and chaotic everyday life. Push-pull theory enables the possibility of introducing basic personal needs when studying individual travel decisions rather than only the factors associated with marketing or destination attributes.

4.2.2　Perception

Perception is the process in which people select, organize, and interpret information to construct a meaningful imagination about the world (Berelson & Steiner, 1964). In marketing, customer perception is more important than reality, because perception affects the actual behavior of customers. People can perceive the same object differently through the three perceptual processes, namely, selective attention, selective distortion, and selective retention.

1. Selective attention

Attention is the result of distributing the processing power of the brain when people face some stimuli. Voluntary attention is the attention to a stimulus with purpose, whereas involuntary attention is being attracted by people or objects. No person can fully focus on all the information received daily, because the processing power of the brain is limited. Therefore, the brain screens out the stimulus other than the most important ones; this process is called selective attention. In selective attention, the researchers obtained the following findings (Kotler & Keller, 2009):

(1) The focus on the stimulus that is most relevant to the current demand is easier.

(2) People are likely to focus on the stimulus that meets their own expectations.

(3) People are likely to notice the stimulus with a significant bias. For example, a $5 discount ad for beer is easier to notice than a $5 discount ad for a computer.

2. Selective distortion

The understanding of the customer may not be similar to the expectation of the marketers, even if these customers notice the stimulus. Selective distortions interpret the information with a personal bias. Consumers often distort the information they receive to match the perceived brand or the product expectation (Russo, Meloy & Medvec, 1998).

3. Selective retention

Most customers cannot recall all of the information they receive daily, but these customers remember the information that is consistent with their attitudes or perceptions; this phenomenon is called selective retention. Therefore, the customer can

偏好的产品的优点,而忘记竞争对手产品的优点。

4.2.3 学习

学习理论学者认为,学习是由驱动力、刺激、暗示、反馈和强化等因素相互作用而产生的。驱动力是促进行动的强有力的内在刺激因素;暗示是指决定个人行为的时间、地点和方式的较小的刺激因素。一般而言,顾客会对相似的刺激产生大致相同的行为,这种现象称为一般化。与一般化相反的是差异化。差异化是指人们能够通过学习,认识到同一组刺激中存在的差异,并相应地调整个人行为。市场营销人员可以利用学习理论,在强大的驱动力、鼓励暗示和积极强化下,培养市场对产品的需求。例如携程的广告词"携程在手,说走就走",实际上是在暗示和鼓励消费者在购买旅游产品时选择携程。

4.3.4 记忆

认知心理学者将记忆区分为短期记忆和长期记忆。短期记忆是短暂、有限的信息储存;长期记忆则是持久、无限的信息储存。长期记忆有多种不同的联想模型,其中一种为网络联想记忆模型(Wyer Jr. 和 Srull,1989),如图4-2所示。在此模型中,长期记忆被认为是一套带有节点和链接的网络。节点储存信息,然后通过不同强度的链接进行联系。节点直接的伸展活动流程决定了人们在一定情境下能够回想起的信息量和信息类型。

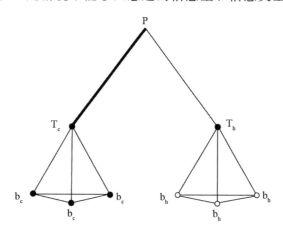

图4-2 网络联想记忆模型

来源:Wyer & Srull.(1989). Person memory and judgment. *Psycholgical Review*,96,58-83.

easily remember the advantages of the product he/she prefers and forget the advantages of the competitor product.

4.2.3 Learning

Learning theory scholars believe that learning is produced by the interaction of factors, such as driving forces, stimuli, cues, feedback, and reinforcement. Driving force is a powerful internal stimulus for action. Cues refer to the small stimuli that determine the timing, location, and manner of individual behavior. In general, the customer produces similar behavior to similar stimuli; this phenomenon is called generalization. In contrast to generalization, differentiation denotes that people can learn to recognize the differences in the same group of stimuli and adjust the individual behavior. Marketers can use the learning theory to nurture the market demand for products by encouraging cues and positive reinforcement with the strong driving forces. For example, the advertisement, "Ctrip in hand, travel right away" is recommending to and encouraging the consumers to select Ctrip when purchasing tourism products.

4.3.4 Memory

Cognitive psychologists divide memory into short- and long-term memory. The short-term memory is brief with limited information storage, whereas the long-term memory is lasting with unlimited information storage. One of the many different association models of long-term memory is the associative network memory model (Wyer Jr. & Srull, 1989) illustrated in Figure 4 – 2. In this model, the long-term memory is considered to be a set of the networks with nodes and links. The nodes store information and then connect through the links with different strengths. The direct spreading activation process of nodes determines the amount and type of information that people can recall in certain contexts.

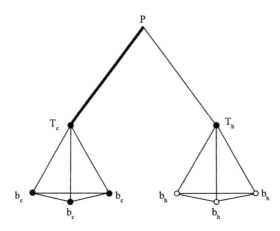

Figure 4 – 2　Associative network memory model
Source: Wyer & Srull. (1989). Person memory and judgment. *Psycholgical Review*, 96, 58 – 83.

在营销管理的框架下，P 代表消费者，而 T_c 和 T_h 是消费者所面对的两种不同的消费情境，B_c 和 B_h 是消费者在两种不同情境下所回想起的关于品牌的内容或产品。

随着目的地间竞争的加剧，营销人员开始关注难忘体验在营销中的作用。难忘体验是指能够被旅游者记住并回忆起的好的旅游体验，也即留存在记忆中的旅游体验（Kim、Ritchie 和 McCormick，2012）。Kim、Ritchie 和 McCormick（2012）认为，难忘体验包含七个维度：享乐的（hedonism）、参与（involvement）、新鲜（novelty）、地方文化（local culture）、休憩（refreshment）、知识（knowledge）以及有意义（meaningfulness）。外部环境、人际接触、消费者的个人特征以及其他与出游相关的要素都会影响消费者难忘体验的获得，Jauhari（2013）提出了服务商（hospitality intelligence）的概念，以描述前线员工需要具备的使消费者获得难忘体验的能力。服务商由三个方面组成，即情商（emotional intelligence）、文化商（cultural intelligence）以及服务体验商（hospitality experiential intelligence）。

In the framework of marketing management, P represents the consumer, T_c and T_h are the two consumption scenarios faced by consumers, and B_c and B_h are the brand contents or products that consumers recall in two situations.

Marketers begin to focus on the role of unforgettable experiences in marketing as the competition among the destinations intensifies. An unforgettable experience is a good travel experience that can be remembered and recalled by tourists and is a travel experience that is retained in memory (Kim, Ritchie & McCormick, 2012). Kim, Ritchie, and McCormick (2012) contend that an unforgettable experience consists of seven dimensions, which are hedonism, involvement, novelty, local culture, refreshment, knowledge, and meaningfulness. The external environment, interpersonal contact, personal characteristics of the consumer, and other travel-related factors can influence in collecting unforgettable experiences for consumers. Jauhari (2013) proposes the concept of hospitality intelligence, which describes the requirements for the frontline employees to provide consumers with unforgettable experiences. Hospitality intelligence is composed of three aspects, namely, emotional, cultural, and hospitality experiential intelligence.

第5章 企业市场

本章要点

- 企业市场的定义及其与消费者市场的区别
- 企业购买决策过程
- 旅游企业主要的企业市场类型
- 企业客户关系维护中重要理论

企业不仅是产品的提供者,也是重要的消费者。企业市场购买数量大,购买能力强,因而也具有更强的议价能力。了解企业市场的特征及其决策过程有助于旅游企业制定相关的营销战略。本章将详细介绍企业市场的特征、与消费者市场的区别、企业购买决策过程、主要企业市场类型及其特点以及企业客户关系维护。

5.1 企业市场特征

Webster 和 Wind(1972)将企业购买定义为企业根据自身需求发掘、评估、选择品牌和供应商,最终购买产品和服务的决策过程,企业市场由此产生。Kotler 和 Keller(2009)认为,企业市场包括为生产、销售、租赁或供应自身产品和服务而购买其他企业的产品和服务的所有需求。与面向消费者市场类似,企业同样需要了解它们的企业顾客,确定双方之间最为重要的价值(Donath,2005)。然而,企业市场在购买者数量、企业顾客关系等方面与消费者市场存在明显差异(表5-1)。

Chapter 5　Business markets

 Key points of the chapter

- Definition of business market and its difference from consumer market
- Business purchase decision-making process
- Major business market types for tourism enterprises
- Essential theories in customer relationship maintenance for business markets

An enterprise is not only a product provider but also an important consumer. The business market buys in large amounts; it possesses strong purchasing power, and thus enjoy strong bargaining power. Understanding the characteristics of the business market and its decision-making process can help tourism enterprises to develop relevant marketing strategy. This chapter explains in detail the characteristics of the business market, its differences with consumer market, business purchase decision-making process, the main types of business markets and their features, and business-to-business customer relationship maintenance.

5.1　Characteristics of Business Markets

Webster and Wind（1972）define organizational buying as the decision-making process in which an organization explores, evaluates, and selects brands and suppliers according to its own needs and ultimately purchases products and services. Kotler and Keller（2009）argue that business market includes all the needs for purchasing other firms' products and services for the production, sale, lease, or supply of the company's own products and services. Similar to consumer-oriented market, companies need to understand their business customers and identify the most important value between them （Donath, 2005）. Despite this similarity, significant differences are observed between business and consumer markets in aspects such as the number of purchasers and customer relationships（Table 5 – 1）.

表 5 – 1　企业市场与消费者市场差异

项　目	企业市场	消费者市场
购买者数量	少	多
单次购买量	多	少
企业顾客关系	密切	疏离
专业采购	有专业的采购代理	一般没有
参与采购决策的人数	多（购买决策中心）	少（家庭或个人）
销售拜访次数	多	少或无
衍生需求	有（需求来自消费者商品）	无
刚性需求	是（大部分对价格不敏感）	不是
需求波动	大（存在加速效应）	小
直接采购	是	不是

来源：Kotler，Keller.（2009）.*Marketing Management*（13th ed.）.Upper Saddle River，NJ：Pearson Prentice Hall.

衍生需求是指企业市场的产品是由消费者产品衍生而来的，例如消费者对酒店的需求带来了酒店对客用品的需求。刚性需求是指产品的价格变动并不显著影响企业市场对产品的需求，如对于展销会参展企业来讲，展销会期间周边酒店价格的波动并不会影响其对产品的需求。需求波动是指企业产品的需求非常容易受到影响，而且影响幅度非常大，存在加速效应。消费品市场需求量的少量增加或减少，都会导致企业市场需求量大幅度地变化。

企业买家的购买决策取决于购买情境，如企业面临问题的复杂程度、购买要求的时效性、决策参与人数、时间限制等。Robinson、Faris 和 Wind（1967）提出企业面临的购买情境主要有三个：直接重购、修改重购和新购买。直接重购是指采购部门根据日常安排，重新订购货品如办公用品，并在经批准的列表上选择供应商的过程（Kotler 和 Keller，2009）。在此过程中，供应商专注于保证货物和服务的质量，并经常提出建立自动订货系统以便节省双方时间。而外部供应商（并不在批准列表上的供应商）则尝试提供新的产品或利用顾客对现有供应商的不满，争取进入批准列表并获取小量的订购，再逐步扩大自身的市场份额。

Table 5 - 1   Differences between business and consumer markets

Items	Business markets	Consumer markets
Number of purchasers	less	more
Buying quantity per purchase	more	less
Business-customer relationship	close	distant
Professional purchasing	professional purchasing agents	usually none
Number of people influencing buying decisions	more (buying decision center)	less (family or individual)
Sales calls	more	less or none
Derived demand	yes (from consumer goods)	none
Inelastic demand	yes (mostly insensitive to prices)	no
Fluctuating demand	large (there is acceleration effect)	small
Direct purchasing	yes	no

Source: Kotler, Keller. (2009). *Marketing Management* (13th ed.). Upper Saddle River, NJ: Pearson Prentice Hall.

Derivative demand means that the product for the business market is derived from the consumer goods. For example, consumer demands for the hotel introduce the hotel's demands for guest supplies. Inelastic demand implies that the product price changes do not significantly affect the business market demand for products. For example, price fluctuations of surrounding hotels during a fair do not affect exhibitors' demand for the product. Fluctuating demand indicates that the demand for business goods is easily affected, and the effect is substantial because of an acceleration effect. A small increase or decrease in the market demand of consumer goods leads to significant changes in business market demand.

The purchasing decisions of business buyers depend on the buying situation, such as the complexity of the problem faced by the enterprise, the newness of the purchase requirements, the number of participants in decision-making processes, and the time constraints. Robinson, Faris, and Wind (1967) argue that the three main buying situations for firms are straight rebuy, modified rebuy, and new task. The straight rebuy is the process by which the purchasing department reorders products (e.g., office supplies) and selects suppliers from an approved list based on routine arrangements (Kotler & Keller, 2009). In this process, suppliers focus on maintaining the quality of goods and services and often propose the establishment of automatic order systems so that both sides can save time. External suppliers (i.e., those not on the approved list) try to provide new products or exploit customer dissatisfaction with existing suppliers, gain entry into the approved list and get a small order, and then gradually expand their market share.

修改重购是指买家对产品的规格、价格、运输要求或其他项目提出修改要求,再进行订购的过程(Kotler 和 Keller,2009)。整个流程通常需要买卖双方的人员参与。当买家提出修改要求时,内部供应商(在批准列表上的供应商)会变得非常紧张,想要维持双方的合作关系。而外部供应商则可以根据要求推出更好的产品以赢得业务。修改重购在酒店行业非常普遍。例如,酒店根据企业每年的用房量,与企业商定协议价格。第二年,如果企业实际用房量超出协议用房量,企业可能会要求酒店提供更优惠的协议价格。在传统制造业中,修改重购可能只是由买家向卖家提出,但在酒店行业中,修改重购可以是双向的。如果企业的实际用房量并没有达到协议用房量,酒店可能会提高该企业的协议价格。

新购买是指采购商第一次购买产品或服务(Kotler 和 Keller,2009)。Bunn(1993)认为,在新购买决策过程中,参与决策的人数、决策所需的信息量以及成本或风险的大小,都会影响决策所需要的时间。在新购买情境下,采购者需要确定产品的规格、价格限制、运输条款和时间、服务条款、付款方式、订购数量、合格供应商和优先供应商等要素。最终,新购买会逐渐变为直接重购,变成日常采购行为。新购买对市场营销人员来说既是机会也是挑战。企业的新购买决策过程一般有五个阶段,即意识、兴趣、评估、试用和采用(Ozanne 和 Churchill,1971)。在这五个阶段中,不同要素在不同阶段有着不同的地位:大众媒体在意识阶段有重要影响;销售人员在兴趣阶段扮演重要角色;而评估阶段需要可靠的技术资源作为支持。

一些专业采购商希望卖家能够提供一体化购买方案,这种一体化购买方案称为系统化购买(Kotler 和 Keller,2009)。在系统化购买中,买家向主要承包商提出一个项目的投标。主要承包商赢得投标后与买家签订合同,并承担完成项目的责任。同时,赢得投标的主要承包商可以将项目中的部分次要任务转包给次级承包商,但需要提供完善的质量控制方案,以保证项目的完成质量。部分卖家认识到系统化购买成了一种市场趋势,故将系统化购买方案变为一种营销工具,称为一体化销售(Kotler 和 Keller,2009)。系统化销售的一种类型为系统化合同,即在合同期内个体卖家向顾客提供维护、修理、运营等服务,并为顾客管理部分工具或库存。通过系统化购买与销售,买家

The modified rebuy is the process by which buyers request changes in the specifications, prices, transportation requirements, or other elements of the product before ordering them (Kotler & Keller, 2009). The entire process typically involves both buyers and sellers. When a buyer makes an amendment request, the internal supplier (i.e., the supplier on the approved list) becomes nervous and wants to maintain the relationship, whereas external suppliers propose better products according to the request to win business. The modified rebuy is common in the hotel industry. For example, a hotel negotiates contract price with a company according to its annual booking of hotel rooms. The next year, the company may require the hotel to provide a more favorable contract price when the actual amount of room booking exceeds the agreed amount. In the traditional manufacturing sector, a modified rebuy may only be proposed by the buyer to the seller. By contrast, in the hotel industry, a modified rebuy can be two-way. If the actual amount of room booking does not meet the agreement, then the hotel may increase the company's contract price.

A new task is a purchase of a product or service for the first time (Kotler & Keller, 2009). Bunn (1993) argues that the number of people involved in decision making, the amount of information required for decision making, and the scale of costs or risks in the new-task decision-making process can affect the time required for decision making. In a new task scenario, a buyer must determine the product specifications, price limits, transport terms and conditions, service terms, payment methods, order quantity, qualified suppliers, and preferred suppliers. Ultimately, the new task gradually becomes a straight rebuy as a daily purchasing behavior. The new task is both an opportunity and a challenge for marketers. The new-task decision-making process of an enterprise features several stages: awareness, interest, evaluation, trial, and adoption (Ozanne & Churchill, 1971). Different elements acquire various positions in these five distinct stages. Mass media exerts a significant effect in the awareness stage. Sales staff plays an important role in the interest stage. The evaluation stage requires reliable technical resources as support.

Some professional buyers want sellers to provide an integrated purchase plan, which is called systems buying (Kotler & Keller, 2009). In a systems buying, the buyer proposes a bid to the prime contractors. The prime contractor wins the bid and signs a contract with the buyer and assumes responsibility for completing the project. At the same time, the prime contractor winning the bid can subcontract some of the secondary tasks of the project to the subcontractors, but the quality control program is required to ensure the quality of the project. Some sellers recognize systems buying as a market trend, thus turning a systems buying program into a marketing tool called systems selling (Kotler, Keller & Brady, 2009). One type of systems selling is systems contracting, in which individual sellers provide maintenance, repair, and operation services to customers and manage part of the tools or inventory for the customer. In systems buying and selling,

能在减少采购和管理成本、降低采购价格等方面获益，而卖家则能够降低运营成本和减少文书工作。

5.2　企业购买过程

通常而言，企业的采购决策会由一个专门的群体制定，Webster 和 Wind（1972）将这个决策群体称为购买决策中心。购买决策中心的成员一般有七种不同的角色，他们有共同的目标，共同承担决策所带来的风险。

（1）发起人：要求购买某种产品或服务的企业内部使用者。

（2）使用者：使用产品或服务的人。

（3）影响者：通过确定产品规格、为评估产品或服务选项提供相应信息，对购买决策产生影响的人。一般而言，技术人员是非常重要的影响者。

（4）决策者：决定产品要求或供应商的人。

（5）批准者：批准决策者或采购者行动的人。

（6）采购者：取得批准，对供应商进行选择，并制订购买条款的人。采购者在选择供应商和谈判方面起主导作用，部分时候能够帮助决策者制订产品要求或规格。

（7）看守者：防止卖家接触购买决策中心成员的人，例如采购代理、前台接待员或接线员。

购买决策中心通常由不同的利益、权力、背景和追求的人员组成，这些成员在决策时会根据不同的条件做出决定。在购买决策中心，不同动机、感知和偏好的采购者会有不同的采购风格。

（1）"简约"型。

（2）"自我专家"型。

（3）"追求最好"型。

（4）"一站式采购"型。

（5）"分析"型：部分年轻高学历的采购者在选择供应商前，会利用电脑对每个供应商的方案进行严密的分析。

（6）"粗鲁"型：一些老派的采购商会利用一些卖家提出的优惠条件，向其他卖家提出更优惠的要求。

个人的需求会影响个人的行为，包括争取从企业中为个人获得最大化的回报。因此，为了保证企业能够达成目标，企业利益不会因为个人行为而受到损害，企业需要对购买决策流程和结果进行规范，因为决策实现的是企业和

buyers can benefit from reduced procurement and management costs and lower procurement prices, while sellers can reduce operating costs and paperwork.

5.2 *Business Buying Process*

In general, business buying decisions are made by a specialized group referred to as the buying center (Webster & Wind, 1972). Members of the buying center play seven different roles. They share a common goal as well as the risk of decision making.

(1) Initiator: An internal user of a business that requires the purchase of a product or service.

(2) User: A person who uses the product or service.

(3) Influencer: A person who influences the purchase decision by determining the product specification and providing information to evaluate the product or service option. A technician is an important influencer.

(4) Decider: A person who determines the product requirements or the supplier.

(5) Approver: A person who approves the actions of decision makers or purchasers.

(6) Buyer: A person who gets the approval, selects the suppliers, and develops the terms of the purchase. Buyers play a leading role in selecting suppliers and negotiating and, in some cases, help decision makers to formulate product requirements or specifications.

(7) Gatekeeper: A person who prevents sellers from reaching people who are members of the buying center, such as a purchasing agent, receptionist, or operator.

A buying center is usually made up of people with different interests, powers, backgrounds, and aspirations, who make decisions based on different conditions. At the buying center, buyers with different motivations, perceptions, and preferences possess different buying styles.

(1) "Keep-it-simple" buyers.

(2) "Own-expert" buyers.

(3) "Want-the-best" buyers.

(4) "Want-everything-done" buyers.

(5) "Analyst" buyers: Some young and highly educated buyers use the computer for a rigorous analysis of each vendor's proposal when choosing suppliers.

(6) "Toughies" buyers: Some old-fashioned buyers will use some of the terms the seller offers to ask other sellers to offer more favorable terms.

Individual needs can affect individual behaviors, including striving to maximize returns for the individual from the firm. Therefore, to ensure that enterprises can achieve their goals and their interests will not be damaged by personal behaviors, companies need to standardize buying decision-making process and results, because the decision is to meet both business and personal needs. In a buying decision-making process, a buyer is not purchasing the final product but solutions to the company's

个人两方面的需求。在企业的购买决策中,采购者最终所购买的并不是产品,而是购买企业经济和战略问题的解决方案,同时它也是实现决策中心成员的个人成就以获取奖励的过程。在这种情境下,企业的购买决策是"理性的",也是"感性的"(Ward 和 Webster,1991)。因此,市场营销人员在进行营销前,需要明确以下问题:谁是主要决策参与者?这些人影响哪种决策?影响的程度有多大?他们使用的评估因素有哪些?

不同规模的卖家对于如何接触购买决策中心群体有不同的方法,小规模的卖家专注于接触关键购买决策影响者,而大型卖家则利用多层次深度销售接触更多的决策参与者。企业需要通过更多的自身宣传项目,接触更多潜在的购买决策影响者,以保持现有顾客对企业的认知(Webster 和 Wind,1972)。

在选择最终供应商时,购买决策中心需要关注供应商的交货能力、价格和供应商的名气。同时,购买决策中心需要应对以下问题。

(1)价格压力与提高生产力。采购中心经常会被企业要求降低采购品的价格,他们可以通过不同的方式来解释现有价格是否已经处于足够低的水平,例如所有权总成本、产品生命周期成本等,并将这些成本与竞争对手进行对比。

在提高生产力方面,采购中心需要注重以下因素:采购品能有助于提高日常运营效率;有足够的数据对企业的运营与管理进行分析;有合适的分析工具;实时的库存管理。

(2)供应商数量。通常而言,企业在发展过程中会逐渐减少供应商的数量。因此,供应商数量同样符合 20/80 法则,即 20% 的供应商提供 80% 的采购品。这样的供应商需要有稳定的质量、低廉的价格、不断提高的表现和庞大的供货系统。企业也会在生产过程中不断和供应商进行沟通。

(3)当企业选择最终供应商后,需要定期审视供应商的表现。评估供应商表现的方法有三种:采购中心联系最终使用者并要求使用者对供应商进行评估;采购中心通过权重计分的方法对供应商在不同方面的表现进行评价;采购中心将现有供应商的失误转化为采购成本,进行汇总,并提出新的采购方案。对供应商的表现进行评估会导致三种结果:采购商与供应商继续合作、修改合作方式或终止合作。

economic and strategic problems as well as the process to achieve individual accomplishment and obtain rewards for members of the decision-making center. In this context, the firm's buying decisions are "rational" and "emotional" (Ward & Webster, 1991). As a result, marketers must answer the following questions before marketing: Who is the primary decision maker? What kind of decisions do these people influence? What is the extent of the effect? What are the evaluation factors they adopt?

Small sellers focus on reaching key decision-making influencers, whereas large sellers use multiple levels of in-depth selling to reach many decision makers, depending on how sellers of different scales have access to the decision-making center members. Companies should rely on their own promotion programs to reach out to many potential decision-making influencers and retain the company perception of their existing customers (Webster & Wind, 1972).

In choosing the final supplier, the purchasing decision center needs to focus on the supplier's delivery capacity, price, and reputation. At the same time, buying decision-making centers need to address the following issues:

(1) Price pressures and improving productivity: Buying centers are often asked to lower the price of goods they purchase, and they can explain in various ways whether the price is already sufficiently low, such as the total cost of ownership and the life-cycle cost of the product, and compare these costs to competitors.

In terms of improving productivity, the buying center should focus on the following factors: purchased goods, which can help improve the efficiency of day-to-day operations, sufficient data to analyze the operation and management of the enterprise, appropriate analysis tools, and real-time inventory management.

(2) Number of suppliers: Normally, companies gradually reduce the number of suppliers during business development. Therefore, the number of suppliers also complies with the 20/80 rule, which means that 20% of the suppliers provide 80% of the purchased goods. These suppliers must offer stable quality, low price, continuously improving performance, and large supply system. Enterprises also continue to communicate with suppliers during production.

(3) When an enterprise chooses the ultimate supplier, it needs to regularly review the supplier's performance. The performance of a supplier can be evaluated in three ways. The buying center contacts the end user and requires the user to evaluate the supplier. The buying center evaluates the supplier's performance in various aspects through the weighted-score method. The buying center translates existing supplier failures into purchasing costs, aggregates them, and proposes new purchase plans. Evaluating the supplier's performance can lead to three outcomes. That is, the buyer and the supplier continue to work together, modify the mode of cooperation, or terminate the cooperation.

5.3　旅游企业的主要企业市场

5.3.1　团队商务市场

对于旅游企业来讲一个重要的企业市场是团队商务市场。团队商务或会议市场比消费者市场需要更完备的设施、技术支持以及服务。由于场地的预订和使用通常间隔较长时间，目的地和酒店需要与顾客保持紧密的交流，了解顾客不断变化的需求，密切关注市场变化，从而保证服务质量。根据参与人数可以将会议分为两种：普通会议（出席人数一般为 1 万人以下）和全市性会议（出席人数为 1 万人或以上）。普通会议只需要一家或几家酒店的会议设施即可满足需求，而全市性会议则需要全市的酒店共同接待。从会议主题类型来看，团队商务市场通常包括四种：大会，协会会议，公司会议，以及社会、军事、教育、宗教等团体的会议或是联谊会（SMERF）。

大会通常需要完善的会议设施，酒店一般需要提供进行委员会会议、全体会议、分组讨论、小型展览等项目的场地和相关设施。协会会议通常需要较长的策划和准备时间，许多大型协会的大会需要两年至五年的时间进行组织和策划，有的甚至需要 10～15 年的准备时间。对于协会来讲，大会的注册费、展览场地的租金是主要的收入来源。由于协会的大会参与者是自发参会的，酒店应该协助会议策划者吸引会员参与会议，例如向会议策划者介绍本地的景点、提供活动建议、协助策划会后活动等。除了组织所有会员参加的大会外，协会的管理委员会还会定期举办会议，商讨协会相关事宜。例如旅行及旅游研究协会（Travel and Tourism Research Association，TTRA）在世界各洲有不同的分会，每年各分会都会派代表到总部参加协会会议。

公司会议的类型包括培训、管理和计划。由于公司会议对于员工来讲是不可选择而必须参加的，不需要进行营销，因此公司会议的预订和准备时间一般只有几周，很多公司都会聘请大型代理来策划和执行公司会议，如美国运通、Carlson Wagonlit、Consortia、中青旅会展、深圳新境界会展等。这些代理提供差旅管理和会议策划服务。一般而言，公司希望会议能够有效率，

5.3 *Major Business Markets for Tourism Enterprises*

5.3.1 Group business markets

For tourism enterprises, group business market is an important business market. The group business or conference market needs more sophisticated facilities, technical support, and services than the consumer market. As the booking and use of venues are usually separated by longer periods, the destination and the hotel should keep in close contact with the customers, understand the changing needs of customers, and pay close attention to market changes to ensure the quality of service. Conferences can be divided into two categories according to the number of participants: ordinary (usually less than 10,000 attendees) and city-wide conferences (10,000 attendees or more). An ordinary conference only needs one or several hotels' conference facilities to meet the demand, whereas a city-wide conference will need all the hotels in the city to accommodate. In terms of conference theme, the group business market includes four kinds of conferences: conventions, association meetings, corporate meetings, and social, military, educational, religious, or fraternal (SMERF) meetings.

Conventions usually require comprehensive conference facilities. Hotels need to provide venues and related facilities for committee meetings, plenary meetings, group discussions, and small exhibitions. Association meetings usually require a longer planning and preparation time. Many meetings of large associations need two to five years to organize and plan, and some even need $10 \sim 15$ years as preparation time. For the association, the registration fee for the conference and the rent for the exhibition venue are the main sources of income. As participants attend the meeting on a voluntary basis, the hotel should assist the meeting planners to attract members to participate, such as meeting the planners to introduce the local attractions, provide activity suggestions, and help plan post-event activities. In addition to organizing the conference for all members to participate, the association's management committee holds regular meetings to discuss matters related to the association. For example, the Travel and Tourism Research Association (TTRA) has various chapters in different continents. Each year, representatives of the chapters attend the conference organized by the TTRA headquarters.

Types of corporate meetings include training, management, and planning. Since corporate meetings are not optional for employees and do not require marketing, corporate meetings are typically booked and prepared for weeks. Many companies hire large agents to plan and execute corporate meetings, such as American Express, Carlson Wagonlit, Consortia, China Youth Travel Service Convention and Exhibition, and Shenzhen Xinjingjie Convention and Exhibition. These agents provide travel management and meeting planning services. Companies want the conference to be efficient and meet

并完成既定目标。

SMERFs 是社会企业(social)、军队(military)、教育机构(educational)、宗教团体(religious)和联谊会(fraternal)的简称。这些小型团体对房价和餐饮价格都非常敏感。酒店在接待这些团体时,通常会考虑提供一些折扣,如基于预订的房间数量提供免费房晚、免费或折扣餐饮等。由于 SMERFs 是价格敏感群体,他们在入住或会议时间方面都非常灵活,以确保自己能够获得最优惠的价格。因此,SMERFs 是酒店周末或淡季时很好的生意补充。

不同的组织和会议对场地有不同的要求,会议策划公司的偏好也会影响目的地和酒店的选择。表 5-2 所列为不同类型会议对酒店设施的关注。

表 5-2　不同类型会议的目的地和酒店偏好

会议类型	目的地	酒店
大会	1. 交通方便程度 2. 会展设施数量 3. 酒店数量 4. 本地景点与活动 5. 支持服务	1. 会议设施空间和数量 2. 价格 3. 客房质量 4. 餐饮质量 5. 对账流程
协会会议	1. 会展设施数量 2. 酒店设施数量 3. 位置 4. 交通方便程度 5. 本地景点	1. 会议设施空间和数量 2. 客房质量与数量 3. 餐饮质量 4. 价格 5. 对账流程
公司会议	1. 环境 2. 位置 3. 交通方便程度 4. 本地景点 5. 会展设施数量	1. 客房质量 2. 餐饮质量 3. 价格 4. 无线上网服务 5. 会议设施空间和数量
SMERFs 会议	1. 位置 2. 交通方便程度 3. 本地景点 4. 环境	1. 价格 2. 会议设施空间和数量 3. 客房清洁度 4. 餐饮质量 5. 过往体验

来源:整理自 Elston, K. & Draper, J.(2012). A review of meeting planner site selection criteria research. *Journal of Convention & Event Tourism*, 13, 203-220.

商务旅游目的地通常会有专门的为城市和酒店制订的面向团队商务市场的营销计划,并为团队商务市场提供配套服务。例如,在美国,许多城市都有会议与游客局(Convention and Visitor Bureau,CVB),其主要负责营销研

its stated goals.

SMERFs (i.e., social, military, educational, religious, and fraternal organizations) are small groups that are sensitive to room prices and food and beverage prices. The hotel typically consider discounts for these groups, such as free nights and free or discounted meals based on a certain amount of room nights booked. SMERFs are price-sensitive groups and are flexible in terms of check-in or meeting time to ensure that they get the best possible price. As a result, SMERFs are a great business complement to the hotel during weekends or off-season.

Various organizations and meetings have different venue requirements. The event organizing company's preferences also affect the choice of the destination and the hotel. Table 5 - 2 lists the focuses on hotel facilities for different types of meetings.

Table 5 - 2 Destination and hotel preferences of different types of meetings

Meeting format	Destination	Hotel
Convention	1. Convenience of local transportation 2. Number of meeting facilities 3. Number of hotels 4. Local scenery and activities 5. Support services	1. Space and number of meeting facilities 2. Price 3. Quality of room 4. Quality of food and beverage 5. Reconciliation process
Association meeting	1. Number of meeting facilities 2. Number of hotel facilities 3. Location 4. Convenience of local transportation 5. Local scenery	1. Space and number of meeting facilities 2. Quality and quantity of room 3. Quality of food and beverage 4. Price 5. Reconciliation process
Corporate meeting	1. Environment 2. Location 3. Convenience of local transportation 4. Local scenery 5. Number of meeting facilities	1. Quality of room 2. Quality of food and beverage 3. Price 4. Free WIFI 5. Space and number of meeting facilities
SMERF meeting	1. Location 2. Convenience of local transportation 3. Local scenery 4. Environment	1. Price 2. Space and number of meeting facilities 3. Room cleanliness 4. Quality of food and beverage 5. Past experience

Source: Based on Elston, K. & Draper, J. (2012). A review of meeting planner site selection criteria research. *Journal of Convention & Event Tourism*, 13, 203 - 220.

Business tourism destinations usually have a special marketing plan designed for the city and hotels targeting the business market and provide support services for the group business market. For example, in the United States, many cities have the Convention and Visitors Bureau (CVB), which is responsible for marketing research and marketing.

究和市场推广。这类机构有的通过酒店或城市收入税项支持,有的由政府资助,由商会、旅游局或者政府运营。会议或展览策划者通过此类机构获得目标举办城市的交通、酒店等信息,而酒店也能通过此类机构获取相关会议或展览的最新消息。因此,会议占业务比重较大的酒店应该与此类机构保持良好的关系。

香港旅游发展局在会展旅游业务方面积极联系全球各大专业团体和活动主办机构,吸引他们到香港来举办会展活动。旗下的"香港会议及展览拓展部"采取了三方面的策略,即强化伙伴关系、积极向外推介及展示优势。

1. 强化伙伴关系

香港会议及展览拓展部与"全球会议业领袖国际会议筹组人协会"签订了三年的合约。同时,也继续与"American Society of Association Executives""Global Conference Network""Helms Briscoe"及"International Congress and Convention Association"紧密合作。通过这些战略伙伴的庞大网络,香港会议及展览拓展部可以向其成员宣传香港。

2. 积极向外推介

香港会议及展览拓展部积极参加不同地区市场的主要展销会和活动,从而联系国际买家、企业和会展奖励旅游代理。

3. 展示优势

香港会议及展览拓展部举办工作坊,展示香港会展奖励旅游产品、地点和发展。此外,它还为中国内地的会展奖励旅游代理举办访港交流活动,以及为奖励中国内地、印度和印度尼西亚的代理而举办"香港会议及奖励旅游挑战赛"。

新加坡成立了"新加坡会展业务局"向全世界推广新加坡的会展业务。新加坡会展业务局与当地的旅游企业合作,推出了两个专门针对会展的项目——新加坡奖励旅游项目和新加坡会展优先项目。奖励旅游项目主要是为奖励旅游游客提供独特的包价旅游项目,以提升他们在新加坡的旅游体验;会展优先项目则是为会议或展览的组织者节省成本,并提供更为顺畅的会展策划与执行体验。

对于协会会议策划者而言,最重要的目的地因素是酒店和设施的数量、

Some of these institutions are supported by hotels or city income tax, and some are supported by government funding and run by chambers of commerce, tourism authorities, or governments. Meetings or exhibition planners get information of the city's transportation and hotels through such institutions, and hotels can get an up-to-date information about meetings or exhibitions the same way. Therefore, hotels with meetings accounted for a large proportion of the business should maintain a good relationship with such institutions.

The Hong Kong Tourism Board (HKTB) is actively engaged with MICE and event organizers in the MICE sector, attracting them to Hong Kong for convention and exhibition events. The subordinate Meetings and Exhibitions Hong Kong (MEHK) office has adopted three strategies, namely, fostering the partnerships, outreaching, and showcasing.

1. Fostering partnerships

MEHK has signed a three-year contract with the International Association of Professional Congress Organizers. Meanwhile, they also continue to work closely with the American Society of Association Executives, the Global Conference Network, the Helms Briscoe, and the International Congress and Convention Association. Through the vast network of these strategic partners, MEHK can promote Hong Kong to their members.

2. Outreaching

MEHK actively participates in the major trade fairs and events in various regions to contact international buyers, companies, and MICE agencies.

3. Showcasing

MEHK organizes workshops to showcase the products, locations, and development of MICE tourism in Hong Kong. It also organizes Hong Kong visiting tours for MICE agents from the Mainland of China as well as Top Agent Awards Program to reward MICE agents from Hong Kong, the Mainland of China, India, and Indonesia.

Singapore has set up the Singapore Exhibition & Convention Bureau (SECB) to promote Singapore's convention and exhibition business worldwide. In conjunction with the local tourism industry, the SECB launched two exclusive programs for exhibitions and conventions, namely, the Singapore Incentives & Rewards Program and the Singapore MICE Advantage Program. The incentive and reward program is designed to provide unique travel packages to enhance the travel experience of tourists in Singapore. The advantage program aims to save the cost of meeting or exhibition organizers and provide a smooth planning and execution experience.

For association meeting organizers, the most important destination criteria are the

交通便捷性、与大部分参与者所在城市的距离和交通费用。在选择酒店方面，与普通会议相似，食品质量、价格、会议室、对账流程等因素是协会会议策划者最为看重的。公司文化对于选择酒店也有重要影响，酒店销售人员需要了解客户的公司文化，发掘酒店能够提供的潜在价值，提高客户对酒店的满意程度。

5.3.2　奖励旅游

奖励旅游是企业以独特的旅游体验作为激励员工或是认可员工表现的一种管理手段。（国际奖励旅游管理者协会，2014）随着经济收入的增加、工作强度的增大，对于很多企业和员工来讲，奖励旅游已逐渐成为双方都认可的最好的奖励方式（Rogers，2013）。2011 年美国有 66000 场奖励活动（Sanders，2011）。2008 年在澳大利亚接待的入境奖励旅游游客花费高达 10 亿元人民币。

由于这种旅游的特殊性质，企业会关注目的地及酒店为员工带来的激励作用，而获奖员工会关注目的地及酒店是否能够满足其内在和外在的出游需求。Mair（2015）认为，奖励旅游的场地选择及组织应当能够满足员工的成就感、自我尊重、了解目的地、与同事交流互动以及自我意识增强的需求，通常情况下，国外的奢华目的地会受到获奖员工的青睐，能起到更好的激励效果。

奖励旅游可以由公司内部人员进行策划，也可以通过奖励旅游策划公司或旅行社进行策划和执行。现今的趋势多是交由奖励旅游策划公司或旅行社安排（Trottman，2003），其中一个原因是很多奖励旅游策划公司或旅行社会提前买断航班座位或酒店的房间，再以包价的形式向公司销售。这种方式比公司内部人员进行策划、询价更有效率。另一方面，奖励旅游策划公司能够提供多个目的地选择，企业能够选择其中最有特色的。因此，酒店应该与奖励旅游策划公司以及公司内部的决策者保持紧密合作。通常而言，奖励旅游策划者是按照人均消费额来计算奖励旅游的预算的，酒店销售人员需要以相同的方式计算成本并提出报价。

对于奖励旅游策划者来讲，在选择目的地时需要考虑企业的属性、奖励旅游的规模、该企业过往奖励旅游经验以及访问过的目的地、预算以及企业要达到的目的。例如销售型企业会选择经典或热门的目的地，而金融类及信息技术类企业则会选择小众但是单价更高的目的地作为员工的奖励。对于

number of hotels and facilities, convenience of transportation, distance from most of the participants' cities, and costs of transportation. In selecting hotels, similar to the ordinary meeting, food quality, price, conference room, reconciliation process, and other factors are the most important to meeting planners. Corporate culture also has a significant impact on the choice of hotel. Hotel sales staffs must understand the customer's corporate culture, explore the potential value the hotel can provide, and improve customer satisfaction with the hotel.

5.3.2   Incentive travel

Incentive travel is a management tool of companies to encourage employees or recognize employees with a unique travel experience (Society of Incentive Travel Executives, 2014). With increased income and enhanced work intensity, incentive travel has become the best reward for many businesses and employees (Rogers, 2013). In 2011, the United States held 66,000 incentive events (Sanders, 2011). In 2008, Australia received inbound spending up to 1 billion Chinese yuan from incentive travelers.

The special nature of this type of tourism causes companies to be concerned about the incentives of destinations and hotels for employees, and award-winning staff will be concerned about whether the destination and the hotel are able to meet their internal and external travel needs. Mair (2015) argues that site selection and organization of incentive travel should be able to satisfy employees' needs for sense of achievement, self-esteem, opportunity to learn about the travel destination, interacting with the travel group, and prestige and ego enhancement. Luxury destinations in foreign countries will be usually favored by award-winning staff, having a better incentive effect.

Incentive travel can be planned by the company's internal staff or be planned and executed by incentive travel planning companies or travel agencies, with the latter being the trends nowadays (Trottman, 2003). One of the reasons is that many incentive travel planners or travel agencies buy out airline seats or hotel rooms in advance and then offer them to the company in the form of packages. This approach is more efficient than the company's internal staff planning and inquiry. On the contrary, incentive travel planning companies can provide multiple destination options; hence, companies can choose one of the most distinctive destinations. Therefore, the hotel should work closely with incentive travel planning companies and decision makers within the company. In general, incentive travel planners calculate the incentive travel budget based on per capita spending. The hotel sales staff must calculate the cost in the same way and provide the quote.

Incentive travel planners should consider the attributes of the company, the size of the incentive travel, the past experience of the incentive travel of the company, the destination the company has visited, the budget, and what the company wants to achieve. For example, sales-oriented firms choose the classic or popular destinations, whereas financial and information technology companies choose a niche but more

规模较大的奖励旅游,航班频繁的目的地更受欢迎,因为把客人输送到目的地是奖励旅游策划者首先要考虑的因素。亚洲某生产销售美容保健器械的公司为奖励销售业绩良好的员工,展现企业实力,推广企业文化,委托一家旅行社策划 500 人的奖励旅游,出游时间在四月份。考虑到企业属性(销售型企业)以及团队规模,最后选中巴厘岛为目的地。首先因为巴厘岛在东南亚度假海岛中属于高端热门产品;其次,巴厘岛的酒店选择众多,且 4 月属于巴厘岛的雨季,房价合理;再次,飞往巴厘岛的航班较多,且有免费落地签证;最后,在公布的三个目的地中(巴厘岛、岘港、沙巴),巴厘岛最受获奖员工的欢迎,得票最高。

5.4　企业顾客关系维护

企业在选择供应商时最看重其企业信用。企业信用具体体现在三个方面,即企业专业度、企业可信度以及企业吸引力。为了提高合作的效率,供应商和顾客都在探索如何更好地维持双方的关系,从而减少或避免风险及不确定性(Rinehart、Eckert 和 Handfield 等,2004)。目前学术界关于企业顾客关系方面主要有两个理论。一是交易成本经济学。交易成本是指产品或服务从一个企业转移到另外一个企业,其中包括搜索成本、合约成本、监督成本和执行成本(Dyer,1997)。主流经济学认为,市场上所有的单位都能够在没有成本的情况下获取所有关于产品和价格的信息。业务单元能够完全了解产品和业务条款,供应商和顾客之间不存在信息不对称,因而,市场上所有的单位都被假设为是完全理性的。而交易成本经济学认为,市场上所有的单位做出完全理性决策的能力都受到限制,因为所有的单位的精神资源(注意力)都是有限的,无法处理市场上所有的信息。在此情境下,有限理性可以被视为市场上所有单位在有限的条件下争取最优结果,或者是在认知系统的限制下争取次优结果(Todd 和 Gigerenzer,2003)。根据交易成本经济学,买卖双方之间的差异(语言、文化、技术)、交易和协定的流程都可能出现不确定性,这导致企业可能采取机会主义行为,只让其中一方得益。有限理性的提出说明,买家和卖家之间可能存在信息不对称,掌握更多信息的群体可能存在机会主义行为,从而导致市场失效的风险升高。

expensive destination as a reward for employees. Destinations with frequent flights are more popular for larger-scale incentive travels, because delivering guests to destinations is a primary consideration for incentive travel planners. An Asian company producing and selling beauty and healthcare equipment commissioned a travel agency to plan the incentive travel for 500 people in April to reward employees with good sales performance, show the strength of the company, and promote corporate culture. Considering the company's attributes (sales-oriented) and the team's size, they ultimately selected Bali. First, Bali has high-end popular resort products among the islands of Southeast Asia. Second, Bali has many hotels to choose from, and they are at reasonable prices in April, which is the rainy season in Bali. Moreover, there are many flights to Bali, with free visa upon arrival. Finally, among the three destinations announced (Bali, Da Nang, Sabah), Bali is the most popular to the award-winning staff, winning the highest votes.

5.4 *Business-to-Business Customer Relationship Maintenance*

The most important factor to companies in choosing suppliers is the corporate credibility. Corporate credibility is embodied in three aspects, namely, corporate expertise, corporate trustworthiness, and corporate likability. To improve the efficiency of cooperation, both suppliers and customers are exploring how to better maintain the relationship and reduce or avoid risks and uncertainties (Rinehart, Eckert & Handfield, et al. 2004). At present, two theories are used in the academics about business-customer relationship. The first is transaction cost economics. Transaction costs refer to the costs of transfer of a product or service from one enterprise to another, including search costs, contracting costs, monitoring costs, and enforcement costs (Dyer, 1997). Mainstream economics holds that all units in the market can obtain all the information about the product and the price without costs. The business unit is fully aware of the product and business terms, and no information asymmetry is observed between the supplier and the customer. Therefore, all units on the market are assumed to be completely rational. Transaction cost economics argues that all units in the market are limited in their ability to make rational decisions, because all units have limited mental resources (attention) that cannot handle all of the information on the market. In this context, bounded rationality can be considered as all units in the market that strive for optimal results under limited conditions or seek suboptimal results under the constraints of the cognitive system (Todd & Gigerenzer, 2003). According to transaction cost economics, the differences between buyers and sellers (language, culture, and technology), transactions, and agreement processes are likely to be uncertain, leading to opportunistic behaviors that only benefit one of the companies. The reason of bounded rationality is that information asymmetry may exist between buyers and sellers, and the risk of market failure may increase due to the possibility of opportunistic behaviors in groups with more

交易成本除了存在于企业之间，同样也存在于企业与员工之间。员工的出差费用是企业成本的一部分，然而企业中负责差旅管理的员工无法获得或整理市场上所有机票或酒店客房的价格信息，但经常出差的员工在这方面可以获得比企业更多的信息。这就造成了企业和员工之间的信息不对称，员工能够以此通过差旅报销让自身获益。因此，差旅管理显得非常必要。

中国商旅市场总量 2015 年超过 15000 亿元人民币（品橙旅游，2016），但大、中、小型各类企业存在着系统繁复、成本高、差旅管理服务跟不上等一系列问题。同时，商旅市场上存在众多服务商，但集中度远低于以德、法、英为代表的欧洲市场。针对以上情况，阿里巴巴集团旗下的阿里商旅推出企业移动差旅整体解决方案，基于手机 App 提供一站式移动差旅服务，降低了差旅管理的综合成本，例如：

- 采购成本——阿里商旅提供多种航司协议机票、协议酒店、促销活动
- 时间成本——移动差旅整体解决方案可让员工随时随地完成差旅操作
- 人力成本——员工自助操作，无须专人专职代订
- 系统成本——免费的企业级差旅管理系统
- 财务成本——企业差旅报表、统一报销凭证、实时对账系统

第二种企业顾客关系理论是互助理论。Kotler 和 Keller（2009）认为，交易成本理论关注"反信任"领域（即企业内的员工都是机会主义者），而互助理论则关注"信任"领域。互助可以分为战略互助（主要）和行业互助（次要）。战略互助是指互助网络内的成员都被认为是核心企业，在这个网络中有清晰的规则指引所有成员应如何进行信息分享活动。战略互助由网络中的核心成员发出信号，指明何种行为、活动或体系是合适的。相反，行业互助则是由一群拥有互相独立的资源、相互之间有活动联系的成员建立的（Lundgren，1993）。在行业互助中，企业与顾客的关系是相互合作而不是控制（Ritter，1999）。为了更好地维持这种关系，一定程度的信任和信息分享是必需的。因此，战略互助强调的是协调和控制，而行业互助强调的是信任和"敏感/机密"

information.

Transaction costs exist not only between enterprises but also between the enterprise and its employees. The travel expenses of employees are part of the costs of an enterprise. Employees who are in charge of the travel management do not have access to information on all air tickets or hotel rooms in the market, but those employees who travel for business regularly can obtain more relevant information than the firm. This situation creates an information asymmetry between the firm and its employees, and employees can reap benefits through travel expense reimbursement. Therefore, travel management is crucial.

The total size of China's business travel market in 2015 is over 1.5 trillion Chinese yuan (Pinchain Travel, 2016). However, a series of problems are observed, such as complicated systems, high costs, and poor travel management services for large, medium, and small enterprises. At the same time, despite the many service providers in the business travel market, the concentration is far lower than the European market with Germany, France, and the United Kingdom as the representatives. In view of this situation, Alibaba Group's Ali business travel launched the overall solution for mobile travel, based on the mobile app, to provide one-stop business travel services, reducing the overall cost of travel management. These services are as follows:

● Buying cost: Ali business travel provides a variety of agreements in airline tickets, hotel agreements, and promotions.

● Time cost: The mobile travel total solution allows employees to complete business travel transactions anywhere and anytime.

● Labor cost: Staff self-service means no need for special full-time agents to manage the bookings.

● System cost: Business travel management system is free at the enterprise level.

● Financial cost: Business travel statements, unified reimbursement voucher, real-time reconciliation system are available.

The second theory of business-to-business customer relationship is network theory. Kotler and Keller, (2009) argue that the transaction cost economics focuses on "anti-trust" (i.e., employees are opportunists in the firm), whereas network theory focuses on the "trust." Networks can be divided into strategic (primary) and industrial (secondary). In strategic network, members of the cooperative network are considered core enterprises, and the rules are clear in this network to guide all members on how to share information. In this network, the core members release signals to indicate what behavior, activity, or system is appropriate. On the contrary, the industrial network is established by a group of members with independent resources and active contacts with each other (Lundgren, 1993). In this network, the relationship between the business and the customer is mutual cooperation rather than control (Ritter, 1999). To maintain this relationship effectively, a certain degree of trust and information sharing is necessary.

信息的交换。整体而言,两种互助都可以理解为是企业之间长期的协议,使得这些企业能够获得长期的可持续竞争优势(Jarillo,1988)。

商业关系中存在的由于信息不对称带来的风险或者不确定性对于商业合作伙伴或者行业之间的信任有着重要的影响(Giddens,1990)。它可能严重损害商业关系,使得交易或协定的谈判的正面或负面影响不能被正确估计(Le Flanchec,2004)。不确定性可能导致非理性的决策,以及商业伙伴之间非理性的交易结果。为此,供应链管理、供应商早期参与和采购联盟都是促进更紧密关系的部分办法(Buvik 和 John,2000)。许多企业采用了纵向协调的方式来对企业客户关系进行维护。建立信任是建立长期、健康和良好合作关系的先决条件。Cannon 和 Perreault(1999)的研究发现,企业之间的关系基于供给的重要性、需求方在采购过程中所面临的障碍以及买卖双方的互动程度可以分为以下八种类型:

(1)基本购买与销售——企业之间有日常的合作和信息交换。

(2)骨架关系——企业之间需要互相适应,减少合作和信息交换。

(3)契约交易——企业之间的关系是基于正式的合同,相互之间的信任程度、合作和互动会逐渐减少。

(4)顾客供给——在传统市场中,两家企业在相同的目标市场,提供相似的产品。双方之间竞争大于合作。

(5)合作系统——在合作系统内的双方在运营方面形成统一,但是在法律渠道或适应方面却无法达成系统共识。

(6)相互协作——双方之间有更多的信任和承诺,逐步形成真正的合作关系。

(7)互相适应——买卖双方进行很多基于双方关系的协调,但没有形成强制的信任或合作。

(8)顾客为王——卖家主动适应顾客需求。

通过纵向协调,买卖双方都可以为双方创造更多的价值(Narayandas 和 Rangan,2004)。纵向协调能够使企业之间建立良好的企业顾客关系,但同时也可能会导致买方或卖方对应成本,也即针对特定企业或价值链合作方所

Therefore, the strategic network emphasizes coordination and control, whereas the industrial network emphasizes trust and the exchange of "sensitive/confidential" information. As a whole, both types of networks can be understood as long-term agreements between enterprises, enabling them to achieve long-term sustainable competitive advantages (Jarillo, 1988).

Risks or uncertainties in business relationships that arise from information asymmetries exert important influence on trust between business partners or between industries (Giddens, 1990). It can seriously undermine business relationships, so that the positive or negative effects of negotiations on deals or agreements cannot be properly estimated (Le Flanchec, 2004). Uncertainty can lead to irrational decisions, as well as irrational trading results, among business partners. Thus, supply chain management, early supplier engagement, and purchasing alliances are some of the ways to promote closer relationships (Buvik & John, 2000). Many companies adopt vertical coordination to maintain business customer relationships. Building trust is a prerequisite in establishing long-term, healthy, and cooperative relationships. Cannon and Perreault (1999) find that the relationships between firms can be divided into the following eight types based on the importance of supply, the obstacles of the demand side during procurement process, and the interaction between buyers and sellers:

(1) Basic buying and selling: Daily cooperation and information exchanges are observed between the enterprises.

(2) Bare bones: Enterprises need to adapt to each other and reduce cooperation and information exchange.

(3) Contracting transaction: The relationship between enterprises is based on a formal contract. The degree of mutual trust, cooperation, and interaction will be gradually reduced.

(4) Customer supply: In the traditional market, the two companies provide similar products to the same target market. Competition between them is greater than cooperation.

(5) Cooperative systems: The two partners in the cooperative system are united in the operational aspects, but they are unable to reach a systemic consensus on legal channels or adaptation.

(6) Collaborative: The two partners have more trust and commitment and gradually form a real relationship.

(7) Mutually adaptive: Buyers and sellers conduct a lot of coordination based on the relationship between the two sides, but did not form a mandatory trust or cooperation.

(8) Customer is king: Sellers take the initiative to adapt to customer needs.

In vertical coordination, buyers and sellers can create more value for both parties (Narayandas & Rangan, 2004). Vertical coordination can lead to good business customer relationships and may lead to relevant costs for buyers or sellers, that is, additional costs

产生的额外费用的增高（Rokkan、Heide 和 Wathne，2003）。

在酒店行业，协议客户（公司住房协议或会议业务协议）是酒店最重要的企业客户之一。酒店与协议客户之间的合作是通过签订合同建立的，日常的关系维护主要通过酒店销售经理进行客户拜访，以及接待协议客户入住酒店来完成。根据 Cannon 和 Perreault 的企业关系理论，酒店和协议客户之间只是契约交易的关系，双方之间没有建立更为紧密的关系。然而，酒店有能力通过努力和团队协作，在日常的关系维护中与企业客户建立更多的信任。广州银行是广州丽思卡尔顿酒店的协议客户，酒店销售经理得知广州银行行长即将入住酒店，首先通过行长秘书了解到行长喜欢以新鲜茶叶泡茶。随后，销售经理联系客房部，将广州银行行长所写的书提前放到房间，并将房间内的茶包更换为新鲜茶叶。接着，销售经理联系前厅部，为客人办理客房内入住手续。广州银行行长入住后非常满意酒店的安排，决定将银行以后的差旅住宿和会议都安排在丽思卡尔顿酒店。

for a particular company or value chain partner (Rokkan，Heide & Wathne，2003).

In the hotel industry，the contract guest (corporate booking contract or conference business contract) is one of the hotel's most important business customers. The cooperation between the hotel and the contract guest is built by establishing the contract. The daily relationship maintenance mainly relies on the hotel sales manager visiting customers as well as accommodating contract guests to stay at the hotel. According to Cannon and Perreault's theory of business relationships，the relationship between the hotel and the contract guest is only a contractual transaction，and the two parties do not establish a closer relationship. However，the hotel has the ability to work with the team through collaboration and gain more trust in the daily maintenance of business-to-business customer relationships. Bank of Guangzhou is a contract guest of the Ritz-Carlton，Guangzhou. The hotel sales manager knew that the president of Bank of Guangzhou would soon stay in the hotel. He first learned through the secretary that the president liked to make tea with fresh tea leaves. The sales manager then contacted the housekeeping department to place the book written by the president of Bank of Guangzhou into the room and replace the tea bags in the room with fresh tea leaves. Consequently，the sales manager contacted the front office to arrange in-room check-in for the guest. After the arrival，the president of Bank of Guangzhou was very satisfied with the arrangements of the hotel and decided to commission all the business travel accommodations and conferences of Bank of Guangzhou to the Ritz-Carlton Hotel.

第6章　市场差异化及定位

本章要点

- 市场细分的定义及其重要性
- 市场细分遵循的具体标准
- 微观市场营销的四个层级
- 目标市场的选择

　　随着旅游市场竞争越来越激烈，企业逐渐意识到竞争优势的重要性和必要性。"以消费者为中心"成了旅游服务业内公认的经营理念。为了成为具有竞争优势的企业，企业首先要明确"到底谁才是企业的消费者"。毕竟企业的经营不能立足于社会中的所有人群，而应该找准企业能最好服务的某个或某几个群体。这也就是营销学中的市场细分——市场上具有若干相同或相似特点并且对营销方式的反应相同或相似的人群。具有不同需要、特征或行为，因而需要不同产品或营销组合的不同的人群则分属于不同的市场细分。

　　市场细分的重要性主要体现在下面几个方面。第一，确定企业所面对的消费群体，从而提升企业竞争力。通过市场细分可以找到具体的消费市场，使得经营者和营销人员能够更加有针对性、更加有效地制定决策，在特定市场提升品牌的认知度和品牌资产，从而提升企业竞争力。第二，进行市场细分有助于企业的市场扩张。例如，企业可以在现有的基于地理分布的市场细分基础上，向周边市场扩张，或在现有的基于人口统计特征的市场细分的基础上进行市场扩张。例如喜达屋集团旗下的 W Hotel 和 Aloft 分别面向高端年轻市场和中端年轻市场。第三，市场细分有助于更好地与目标市场沟通以及维护顾客关系，了解顾客希望从产品中获取的价值、愿意支付的价格以及希望获得服务的地点等。

Chapter 6   Market Differentiation and Positioning

 Key points of the chapter

- ■ Definitions and importance of market segments
- ■ Bases for market segmentation
- ■ Four levels of market segmentation
- ■ Selection of target markets

With increasing competition in the tourism market, companies gradually realize the importance and necessity of competitive advantages. "Customer-centric" has become a recognized business philosophy in the tourism service industry. To gain competitive advantages, a company must first identify the "actual consumers" of the company. After all, business operations cannot be based on all the people in society; but it should identify the one or several groups that the company can serve the best. These groups are called market segments in marketing—groups of people in the market with the same or similar characteristics and the same or similar responses to marketing. Diverse groups of people vary in their needs, characteristics, or behaviors. Thus, they demand different products or marketing mixes and are divided into different market segments.

The importance of market segmentation is reflected in the following aspects. First, determining the consumer groups for a company enhances the competitiveness of the company. Through market segmentation, a company can identify specific consumer markets, making the operators and marketers more targeted and more effective in decision-making to enhance brand awareness and brand equity in specific markets, thereby enhancing the competitiveness of the company. Second, market segmentation supports the company's market expansion. For example, companies can expand into markets based on geographically distributed market segments, or expand into market segments based on demographic characteristics, such as Starwood's W Hotel and Aloft, which target the high-end and mid-tier young markets, respectively. Third, segmentation improves communication with the target market and maintains customer relationships, by understanding the value customers want from the product, the price they are willing to pay, and the location where the service is desired.

6.1 市场细分的原则和类型

在进行市场细分时,首先基于特定的细分基础将市场划分为具有共同特征的人群,然后挑选出企业能够向其提供最优价值的细分市场。企业的市场可以分为消费者市场和组织型消费市场。

6.1.1 消费者市场

消费者市场的细分有两组不同的标准:(1)描述性特征——地理细分、人口统计特征和心理统计特征细分;(2)行为特征——消费者反馈。

1. 地理细分

地理细分将市场分为不同的地理单元来进行分析,例如国籍、地区或城市。企业可以选择在其中一个或几个区域进行运营,也可以进入所有区域市场,但企业需要注意不同地区之间的差异。地区营销是地理细分市场中最为常用的营销方式,企业在特定的邮政编码区域内进行营销。在地区营销中,很多企业会利用地图软件来识别客人的地理位置来源。一些地区营销研究会把地理分布数据和人口统计数据结合起来,对消费者及其区域进行更为详细的分析。这种分析被称为地理人口细分——通过人们的生活地区对消费者进行分析(Sleight,2004)。

从地理的角度,旅游包含三个主体:目的地、客源地、两地之间的路线(Leiper,1979)。旅游消费的异地性使得目的地和客源地之间的距离、路线、交通等成为消费者在选择目的地时的重要考虑因素。Cai 和 Li(2009)的研究发现,距离是一种简单而有效的市场细分方法,旅行距离不同的旅游者在人口统计变量、旅游动机以及旅游行为方面均存在显著差异。鉴于此,在旅游规划中通常使用地理要素作为依据,将市场细分为入境市场和国内市场,国内市场又分为周边市场、区域市场、远程市场。

2. 人口统计特征细分

人口统计特征细分将市场分为不同的人口特征来进行分析,例如年龄、家庭规模、生命周期、性别、收入、职业、教育等。由于人口特征与消费者的需求密切相关,且易于统计,因此在市场营销研究中最为常用。人口统计特征中的年龄与生命周期、性别、收入、年代以及社会阶层是常用的细分依据。

6.1 Bases and Types for Market Segmentation

When conducting market segmentation, the market is first divided into groups with common characteristics based on a specific segmentation basis. Then, the market segments for which the company can provide the best value are selected. Companies' markets can be classified into consumer markets and organizational markets.

6.1.1 Consumer markets

Market segmentation for consumer markets has two distinct sets of criteria: (1) descriptive characteristics—geographical, demographic, and psychographic characteristics-and (2) behavioral characteristics—consumer responses.

1. Geographic segmentation

Geographic segmentation divides the market into different geographical units, such as nationality, region, or city. Businesses can choose to operate in one or several areas, or can access all regional markets, but companies must be aware of the differences between regions. Regional marketing is the most common way of marketing in geographically segmented markets where the business is marketed in specific zip code areas. In regional marketing, map software is used by various companies to identify the customers' locations. Several regional marketing studies combine geographical distribution data with demographic data for a more detailed analysis of consumers and their regions. Such analysis is called geodemographics segmentation—analysis of consumers through their living areas (Sleight, 2004).

From a geographical point of view, tourism consists of three subjects, namely, the destination, the source market, and the route between the two places (Leiper, 1979). The allopatric nature of tourism consumption makes the distance, route, and transportation between the destination and the source market important considerations when consumers choose destinations.Cai and Li (2009) find that distance is a simple and effective method of market segmentation. They also discovered that significant differences exist in the demographic variables, travel motivation, and travel behaviors for tourists with different travel distances. Accordingly, tourism planning is usually based on geographical factors to divide the market into the inbound and the domestic markets, with the domestic market divided into peripheral, regional, and remote markets.

2. Demographic segmentation

Demographic segmentation analyzes and divides the market into different demographic characteristics, such as age, household size, life cycle, gender, income, occupation, and education. Demographic characteristics are closely related to consumer demand, and given that their statistics are readily available, they are the most commonly used features in

（1）年龄与生命周期阶段

消费者的消费能力和需求会随着年龄而变化。生命周期阶段决定了这一时期消费者主要关心的问题。然而，心理特征上的差异可能导致基于年龄和生命周期的市场营销分析失效。

（2）性别

根据基因和社交的影响，男女之间有着不同的态度和行为（Cunningham 和 Roberts，2006）。基于性别的产品或服务差异化在服装、理发、化妆品和杂志等行业中已经有很长的应用历史。性别差异在住宿方面的表现也很明显。女性商务客人一般把房间的温馨氛围、人性化、细节性的服务以及价格因素作为衡量酒店的标准。客房内是否有熨斗、熨衣板、送餐服务以及浴袍等也是重要的考虑因素。但男性住店客人则一般考虑更多的是服务质量以及配套商务设施（McCleary、Weaver 和 Li，1994）。然而，单纯地将产品定位为男性使用或女性使用已经不足以满足市场的需求。男性和女性个人用品市场都出现了市场分裂的趋势，即女性使用较多的产品也可能存在男性使用者。媒体能够帮助市场营销人员更容易地接触目标性别市场。

（3）收入

基于收入进行市场细分在汽车、服装、化妆品、理财服务和旅游行业有着相当长时间的历史。在部分情况下，一些企业专注于低收入细分市场，因为低收入市场的竞争压力较小或者消费者忠诚度更高（Van Hoffman，2006）。而另外一些企业则在溢价商品和服务市场中获得成功。除此以外，企业发现所在市场逐渐变成"沙漏型"，即中产阶级的消费者同时对溢价和低价商品都存在需求（White 和 Leung，2002）。

（4）年代

不同年代的消费者受到其成长时代的深刻影响，他们有着相同的大众文化、政治和经济体验，以及相似的观点和价值观。市场营销人员经常会在广告中利用目标年代群体中突出的偶像或形象进行营销。不同年代群体之间有明显的差异，但同时也会相互影响。

（5）社会阶层

市场营销人员通过部分宏观标准来对社会阶层进行分类，如职业、教育、家庭收入和财产价值。每个社会阶层在阶层内部都有一套明显影响购买决策的价值观。

marketing research. The demographic characteristics of age and life cycle, gender, income, generation, and social class are commonly used as segmentation basis.

(1) Age and life cycle stage

A consumer's spending power and demands change with age. The life cycle stage determines the major concerns of consumers during this period. However, differences in psychological characteristics may lead to failure of marketing analysis based on age and life cycle.

(2) Gender

Different attitudes and behaviors exist between men and women, depending on their genetic and social influences (Cunningham & Roberts, 2006). Differentiation of products or services based on gender has a long history of application in clothing, hairdressing, cosmetics, and magazines. Obvious gender differences also occur in terms of accommodation. Female business guests regard the warm atmosphere of the room, humanity, detailed services and price factors as standards for assessing hotels. Whether the rooms have an iron, ironing board, room service, and bathrobes are also important considerations. By contrast, male guests are generally more concerned about the quality of service and affiliated business facilities (McCleary, Weaver & Li, 1994). However, simply positioning the product for male or female use is no longer sufficient to meet the needs of the market. Both male and female personal product markets have a trend of market fragmentation, that is, products used more by females may also have male users. Moreover, media can assist marketers to more easily reach the target gender market.

(3) Income

Market segmentation based on income has long been applied in the automotive, clothing, cosmetics, financial services, and travel industries. In some cases, firms focus on low-income segments where competition is less intense or consumer loyalty is higher (Van Hoffman, 2006). Other companies are successful in the premium goods and services market. In addition, companies are discovering that the market is becoming "hourglass," that is, middle-class consumers are demanding both premium and low-price goods (White & Leung, 2002).

(4) Generation

Consumers at different generations are profoundly influenced by their era of growth. They share the same popular culture, political and economic experiences as well as similar perspectives and values. Marketers often utilize prominent idols or images of the target generation in advertising. Significant differences occur between generations, but they also mutually influence each other.

(5) Social class

Marketers classify social classes by certain macro criteria, including occupation, education, household income, and property values. Within each class, a set of values influence purchasing decisions.

3. 心理统计特征细分

心理统计特征细分是指根据不同的心理/性格特点、生活方式或价值观，将消费者分为不同的组别。对心理特征群体的研究主要集中在两方面——消费者整体生活方式研究和特定产品研究。前者着重于通过一些普遍的特征对人口进行分类，如"对创新的接受程度""以家庭为中心"等。后者则专注于研究上述特征对消费者购买决策的影响（Kotler 和 Keller，2009）。一般而言，营销研究人员通过三个主要因素来描述个人的生活方式和所属心理特征群体：（1）活动（activities，A），指消费者从事与旅游相关的活动；（2）兴趣（interests，I），指消费者对主题旅游产品感到兴奋，并产生特殊且持续性的注意；（3）观点（opinions，O），指消费者对于与主题旅游相关的事件所表达的看法，包括解释、期望及评价。换句话说，营销人员可以从某人从事活动的范围（包括工作和社交方面的诸多活动，如娱乐、体育以及度假偏好）、所感兴趣的事项，以及各项意见的表达，来衡量他的生活形态（曹胜雄、赖璟锋和邱博贤，2006）。

通过 AIO（Activities-Interests-Qpinions）研究定位市场能更好地洞察诸多要素，如消费群体的时间或价格敏感度、冒险精神或自信心，他们是否喜欢冒险，是否是冲动型购物者，生活态度是乐观还是悲观等问题，都能通过心理研究得到答案。米歇尔于 1978 年基于对约 1600 户美国家庭的调查研究，设计出基于人口统计、价格观念、倾向和生活方式变量的 VALS（values and lifestyles）综合型消费者分类系统，开始应用于商业并被国外 200 多家公司和广告代理商运用于营销实践中（吴垠，2005）。2015 年改良后的 VALS 系统（SBI International，2015），仅基于与消费有关的自我导向意识和可用资源两个维度将美国具有不同生活态度和消费行为及决策形式的成年消费者分为 8 个消费群体，并在欧美得到了广泛应用。这八个群体包括创新者、思考者、实现者、体验者、相信者、奋斗者、创造者、和生存者。

自我导向指的是消费者的态度和购买的行为。原则导向型个体的购买决策依据其本身的信念，不理会他人的观点和看法。地位导向型消费者的购买决策参照周围有过类似购买经历的同级的消费观点，往往趋向于购买同辈先前购买过且感觉满意的产品和服务。行动导向型购买者所购买的产品会对他们周围的人产生影响，他们渴望社会或生理方面的活动，追求多样性且承担风险的意愿强。

3. Psychographic segmentation

Psychographic segmentation divides consumers into different groups based on various psychological/personality traits, lifestyles, or values. Studies on psychographic groups focus on two aspects, namely, the consumer's overall lifestyle and specific product research. The former focuses on the classification of the population using general characteristics, such as "the acceptance of innovation" and "family-centered". The latter focuses on the effect of such characteristics on consumer purchasing decisions (Kotler & Keller, 2009). Marketing researchers usually describe individual lifestyles and psychographic characteristics of groups through the following three main factors. (1) Activities (A) refer to the consumer's activities related to tourism. (2) Interests (I) indicate aspects which consumers are excited about in themed tourism products and which produce special and lasting attention. (3) Opinions (O) pertain to the consumers' expressed views toward events related to themed tourism, including interpretations, expectations, and evaluations. Marketers can measure an individual's lifestyle from the scope of a person's activities (including work and social activities, such as entertainment, sports, and vacation preferences), matters of interest, and expressions of opinions (Cao, Lai & Qiu, 2006).

Targeting the market through Activities-Interests-Opinions (AIO) research provides better insight into many factors such as consumer groups' time or price sensitivity, risk-taking, or self-confidence. Do they like adventures? Are they impulsive shoppers? Is their attitude toward life optimistic or pessimistic? Such questions can be answered through psychological research. Based on a survey of about 1,600 American families in 1978, Michelle devised the VALS (values and lifestyles) framework, a comprehensive consumer classification system based on demographics, price perceptions, tendencies, and lifestyle variables. The framework began to be applied to business and has also been used by over 200 foreign companies and advertising agencies in marketing practices (Wu, 2005). The 2015 modified VALS framework (SBI International, 2015) divided US adult consumers with different lifestyles, consumer behaviors, and decision-making styles into eight consumer groups based on two dimensions: consumption-related self-orientation and resources. The VALS framework has been widely used in Europe and the United States. These eight groups include innovators, thinkers, achievers, experiencers, believers, strivers, makers, and survivors.

Self-orientation refers to consumers' attitude and purchasing behaviors. Principle-oriented individuals make purchasing decisions based on their own beliefs and ignore others' views and opinions. Status-oriented consumers make purchasing decisions with reference to the consumption views of their counterparts with similar purchasing experiences, and they tend to buy products and services that peers have previously purchased and perceived as satisfactory. Products purchased by action-oriented consumers have an effect on people around them. Such consumers are eager for social or

可用资源是心理上、生理上以及物质形态方面的资源的全面综合，包括教育、收入、自信、健康、购买愿望、智力和能力水平（SBI International，2015）。

4. 行为特征细分

行为特征细分根据消费者的知识、态度、使用方式或反馈进行分类。除此以外，购买决策角色也是行为特征中的一个重要因素。通常而言，消费者在购买决策中有五种不同的角色——发起人、影响者、决策者、购买者和使用者。所有角色的决策过程和最终的消费者满意度有重要影响。在构建细分市场的过程中，一些行为变量会被作为主要的参考因素，如场合、动机、使用者状态、使用频率、购买者准备阶段、忠诚度和态度。

（1）场合

场合的分类可以根据消费者生命周期中的不同阶段或其他方面进行，例如消费者在青少年、建立家庭等不同时期会面对不同的场合。又或是依据消费者产生需求、购买或使用产品时的情境来确定场合，并对消费者进行分类。旅游和酒店行业一般是通过节事对消费者进行细分并进行相应的营销活动的。例如中国游客倾向在农历新年期间外出旅游，香港唯港荟酒店（Hotel ICON）在 2016 年春节前 1 个月，特别针对国内游客提供 15% 的早鸟优惠。

（2）动机

并非所有购买了产品的消费者都需要同样的购买动机。基于消费者动机对其进行细分有助于更加有效地为目标市场提供并宣传满足其偏好和所追寻的利益的产品。

（3）使用者状态

所有的产品都会有非使用者、曾经使用者、潜在使用者、第一次使用者和规律使用者。对于企业而言，吸引潜在使用者是营销的一个最重要的目的。而在吸引曾经使用者，甚至是非使用者方面，最重要的一点是了解这些消费者不使用产品的原因。

（4）使用频率

不同的产品使用者可以根据使用频率分为轻度使用者、多次使用者和惯常使用者。惯常使用者的数量通常在市场中只占很小的一部分，但相当大比例的购买量是由这些消费者所贡献的。市场营销人员更偏好于吸引一个惯常使用者而非多个轻度使用者。

physiological activities, pursue diversity, and express extreme willingness to take risks. Resources (in the framework) represent a comprehensive synthesis of the psychological, physiological, and physical aspects of resources, including education, income, confidence, health, purchasing aspirations, intelligence, and competency levels (SBI International, 2015).

4. Behavioral segmentation

Behavioral segmentation classifies consumers according to their knowledge, attitude, use patterns, or responses. Decision role is also an important factor in behavioral characteristics. Consumers usually have five different roles in purchasing decisions—initiator, influencer, decider, buyer, and user. Both the decision-making process of all the roles and the final consumer satisfaction have important effects. In building market segments, several behavioral variables are used as primary reference factors, namely, occasions, motivations, user status, usage rate, buyer-readiness stage, loyalty status, and attitude.

（1）Occasions

Occasions can be categorized according to different stages or other aspects of the consumer's life cycle. For example, consumers may encounter different situations in different periods, such as adolescence and establishing families. Occasions can also be determined by situations where consumers generate demand for, purchase, or use the products, thereby allowing for the classification of consumers. The tourism and hospitality industry normally segment consumers based on festivals and events and conduct marketing campaigns accordingly. For example, Chinese tourists tend to travel during the Lunar New Year period. Thus, Hotel ICON provided a 15% early-bird discount for domestic tourists in the first month of 2016 before the Lunar New Year.

（2）Motivations

Not all consumers who purchase a product need the same motivation to buy. Segmenting based on consumer motivations facilitates more effective delivery and advertisement of products that meet the preferences and interests of the target market.

（3）User status

All products have non-users, former users, potential users, first-time users, and regular users. For businesses, attracting potential users is one of the most important marketing purposes. As to attract former users and even non-users, the most crucial aspect is to understand why such consumers do not use the product.

（4）Usage rate

According to frequency of use, different consumers can be classified into light, medium, and heavy users. The number of heavy users usually represents a small fraction of the market, but a significant percentage of purchases are contributed by these consumers. Marketers prefer to attract one heavy user rather than multiple light users.

（5）购买者准备阶段

市场中的消费者对于产品的认知程度是不一样的。有些消费者不知道企业的产品，有些意识到有这个产品，有些听说过这个产品，有些对产品有兴趣，有些希望获得产品，有些准备购买产品。不同阶段的消费者数量对市场营销人员制定不同的营销项目有影响。

（6）忠诚度

根据不同的品牌忠诚度，消费者可以被分为以下四种类型（Brown，1953）。

1）核心忠诚者：一直只购买一个品牌的产品的消费者；

2）多元忠诚者：忠诚于两到三个品牌的消费者；

3）转移忠诚者：忠诚度从一个品牌转移到另一个品牌的消费者；

4）多变者：不忠诚于任何品牌的消费者。

（7）态度

消费者对于购买产品的态度有五种：热情、积极、中立、消极和厌恶。企业在不同态度的消费者身上所花费的时间也不一样。以投票为例，候选人会感谢热情的支持者并提醒他们投票，鼓动积极支持者投票，尝试争取中立选民但并不会花费时间改变反对和厌恶选民的态度。

6.1.2　组织型消费市场

与消费者市场类似，组织型消费市场同样可以通过地理分布、利益和使用频率等变量进行分类。表 6-1 是对这类市场细分的归纳。

表 6-1　组织型消费市场细分主要变量

地理分布	
1	行业：企业服务哪个行业？
2	企业规模：企业服务哪种规模的公司？
3	地点：企业服务哪个地理区域的公司？
运营因素	
4	技术：企业应该专注于何种技术？
5	使用者或非使用者：企业应该服务重度、中度还是轻度使用者，或是非使用者？
6	消费者能力：企业应该为消费者的需求提供少数还是多种服务？

（5）Buyer-readiness stage

Consumers in the market have different levels of awareness for products. Consumers can thus be classified as: unaware of the product, aware of the product, heard of the product, interested in the product, want to get the product, and ready to buy the product. The number of consumers at different stages influence marketers to develop different marketing projects.

（6）Loyalty status

According to different loyalty statuses, consumers can be divided into the following four types （Brown, 1953）.

1）Hard-core loyals: Consumers who always only buy products of one brand.

2）Split loyals: Consumers who are loyal to two to three brands.

3）Shifting loyals: Consumers whose loyalties shift from one brand to another.

4）Switchers: Consumers who are not loyal to any brand.

（7）Attitude

Consumers possess five attitudes toward buying products: enthusiastic, positive, neutral, negative, and hostile. The time that companies spend on consumers with dissimilar attitudes also differ. Taking votes as an example, candidates thank enthusiastic supporters and remind them to vote, encourage positive supporters to vote, and try to convince neutral voters. However, they do not spend time changing the attitude of negative and hostile voters.

6.1.2 Organizational markets

Similar to consumer markets, organizational markets can be classified by geographical distribution, interests, and usage frequency of use. The following table summarizes these market segments.

Table 6 - 1　Major segmentation variables for organizational markets

Demographic	
1	Industry: Which industries should we serve?
2	Company size: What size companies should we serve?
3	Location: What geographical areas should we serve?
Operating variables	
4	Technology: What customer technologies should we focus on?
5	User or non-user status: Should we serve heavy users, medium users, light users, or non-users?
6	Customer capabilities: Should we serve customers needing many or few services?

续　表

	购买途径
7	采购职能组织：企业应该服务采购职能高度集中的还是分散的公司？
8	权利结构：企业应该以服务工程为主还是财务为主的公司？
9	现有关系：企业应该服务关系密切的公司还是对企业最有利的公司？
10	采购政策：企业应该服务偏好租赁、服务合同、购买系统或是密封投标的公司？
11	采购标准：企业应该服务追求质量、服务或是价格的公司？
	情境因素
12	紧急情况：企业应该服务需要快速、紧急运输或服务的公司？
13	特殊应用：企业应该专注于产品的某种应用或者能让产品应用于所有情况？
14	订购规模：企业应该专注于少量订购还是大宗订购？
	个人性格
15	买卖双方相似性：企业应该服务与自身人员和价值有相似性的企业？
16	对待风险的态度：企业应该服务承担风险或逃避风险的顾客？
17	忠诚度：企业应该服务对供应商有高忠诚度的企业？

来源：Bonoma，T. V. & Shapiro，B. P.（1983）. *Segmenting the Industrial Market*. Lexington，MA：Lexington Books.

表6-1列出了营销人员在确定企业目标细分市场和客户前需要注意的问题。四大因素之间存在循序渐进的关系——企业需要先确定目标市场的范围，然后明确企业以何种服务或产品满足何种规模、何种使用频率、何种采购途径的顾客。

6.2　市场细分的层级

市场营销的开端是大众市场营销，企业提供大众化的产品，利用大众化的销售渠道将产品推广给所有的顾客。大众化市场营销实际上是一种成本最优化战略。然而，随着供给的增多，市场竞争变得越来越激烈，顾客希望花同样的价钱获得更多的价值，标准化产品和服务逐渐难以满足顾客的需求。

Continued

	Purchasing approaches	
7	Purchasing-function organization: Should we serve companies with highly centralized or decentralized purchasing organization?	
8	Power structure: Should we serve companies that are engineering dominated, financially dominated, and so on?	
	Purchasing approaches	
9	Nature of existing relationship: Should we serve companies with which we have strong relationships or simply go after the most desirable companies?	
10	General purchasing policies: Should we serve companies that prefer leasing? Service contract? Systems purchases? Sealed bidding?	
11	Purchasing criteria: Should we serve companies that are seeking quality? Service? Price?	
	Situational factors	
12	Urgency: Should we serve companies that need quick and sudden delivery or service?	
13	Specific application: Should we focus on a certain application of our product rather than all applications?	
14	Size of order: Should we focus on large or small orders?	
	Personal characteristics	
15	Buyer-seller similarity: Should we serve companies whose people and values are similar to ours?	
16	Attitude toward risk: Should we serve risk-taking or risk-avoiding customers?	
17	Loyalty: Should we serve companies that show high loyalty to their suppliers?	

Source: Bonoma, T. V. & Shapiro, B. P. (1983). *Segmenting the Industrial Market*. Lexington, MA: Lexington Books.

Table 6 - 1 lists the questions marketers must address before determining the company's targeted segments and customers. A sequential relationship exists among the four factors; companies must first determine the scope of the target market, and then what services or products the company should provide to satisfy customers with what size, what usage rate, and what procurement channels.

6.2 Levels of Market Segmentation

The beginning of marketing is mass marketing. Companies provide mass products and use mass channels to promote their products to all customers. Mass marketing is actually a cost-optimization strategy. However, with the increase in supply, market competition intensifies. Customers want to pay the same price for more value. Satisfying customers' needs becomes gradually difficult for standardized products and services.

因此,更多的企业转向微观市场营销。微观市场营销一共有四个层级:细分市场、利基市场、本地市场和个人市场。

6.2.1　细分市场

细分市场是指一组拥有相似需求的消费者。细分市场营销有利于企业进行差异化,并向消费者提供符合其关键价值的产品,进而从竞争中脱颖而出。然而,即使是在同一个细分市场内,并非所有的消费者都需要一样的产品。因此,Anderson 与 Narus(1995)提出灵活性市场感知价值产品的概念来迎合细分市场中的所有消费者。灵活性市场感知价值产品包括两个部分:(1)基础解决方案——细分市场中所有成员都认可其价值的产品和服务;(2)消费者价值选择——细分市场中部分顾客所需求的价值。消费者所选择的价值可能会带来额外的收入。

细分市场可以通过不同的方式进行,其中一种方式为偏好细分。同质偏好指细分市场中所有消费者有大致相同的偏好;分散偏好则是所有成员之间存在巨大的偏好差异;群体性偏好指细分市场中有一部分消费者有相同的偏好。

6.2.2　利基市场

利基市场相对于细分市场更为微观,包括的是一群专门寻求特定利益或价值的消费者。通常而言,利基市场的整体购买量较少,但具有一定的市场规模、利润和增长潜力。市场营销人员通过对细分市场进行进一步的区分来识别利基市场。诞生于 1998 年的安缦酒店通过低调奢华的设计风格、充分彰显目的地自然及人文环境的选址、宁静与平和的环境以及注重隐私的服务倡导一种独特的,远离喧嚣的生活方式,使其迅速成为高端旅游细分市场青睐的宠儿,在短短十几年间迅速拥有了数量巨大的拥趸——安缦痴(Aman Junkie)。正如安缦的创始人 Adrian Zecha 所说,"这不意味着我们比大的酒店好,因为我们很小。我们是与众不同的,就是这样。安缦酒店响应当代生活方式,所以我们提供一种无尽的生活享受。"随着营销效率的提高,以往被认为规模太小的利基市场可能会变得更有价值(Blattberg 和 Deighton,1991)。互联网的出现和不断发展使得在互联网上建立商店成为可能,很多小型的企业在开始时通过建立网上商店,对某一个利基市场进行营销。在传统市场中,大部分的销售额是由少部分的热门产品所产生的,其他非热门产品所产生的销售额很少,从而形成"长尾现象"。亚马逊网站的出现降低了小

Therefore, more companies turn to micromarketing, which involves four levels: market segments, niches, local areas, and individuals.

6.2.1　Market segments

Segment refers to a group of consumers with similar needs. Segment marketing can allow companies to differentiate themselves and provide consumers with products that satisfy their key value. Consequently, they can stand out from the competition. However, even with the same market segment, not all consumers need the same product. Therefore, Anderson and Narus (1995) propose the concept of flexible market-perceived value offering to cater to all consumers in the market segment. The flexible market-perceived value product consists of two parts: (1) a naked solution—products and services in which all members of the segment recognize the value and (2) discretionary value options—the value needed by part of the market segment. The value chosen by the consumers may generate additional revenues.

Segmentation can be conducted in different ways, one of which is a preference segment. Homogeneous preference indicates that all consumers in the segment have roughly the same preference, whereas diffused preference means a notable difference in preference among all members. Finally, clustered preference suggests that some consumers in the segment share the same preference.

6.2.2　Niche markets

Niche market is more micro than segment, and it includes a group of consumers who are looking for a specific benefit or value. The overall purchase of a niche market is small, but it has a certain market size, profit, and growth potential. Marketers identify the niche market by further distinguishing the market segments. Aman Hotel, established in 1998, promotes a unique lifestyle away from the hustle and bustle of city life through a low-key luxury design style, site selection that fully demonstrates the natural and cultural environment, a quiet and peaceful environment, and services which uphold privacy. Thus, it quickly gained favor in the high-end tourism segment and attracted a considerable number of supporters, the Aman Junkies, in a short period of over 10 years. "It does not mean we are better than large hotels because we are small. We are different, that's it. The Aman Hotel responds to contemporary lifestyles so we provide endless enjoyment of life", stated Adrian Zecha, founder of Aman. As marketing efficiency increases, niche markets previously considered too small can become more valuable (Blattberg & Deighton, 1991). The emergence and growth of the Internet made it possible to build stores online, and many small businesses have begun to market a niche market through online stores. In the traditional market, most of the sales are generated by a small number of popular products, while other non-popular products generate very few sales, resulting in the "long-tail theory". The arrival of Amazon reduced the

型企业产品推广成本,使得小型企业的好产品能够通过互联网被消费者了解甚至是购买。同时,消费者通过亚马逊网站能够以较低的信息搜索成本获得更多的选择,因此,利基市场的价值得到提升。

6.2.3　本地市场

本地市场营销体现了"草根营销"的趋势(Kotler 和 Keller,2009)。企业的营销活动专注于尽可能贴近本地市场的个体消费者,并建立个人的情感联系。相对于全球范围或国家范围内的广告或营销,本地市场营销更能满足本地市场的独特需求,从而提升消费者对企业产品的感知价值。例如,四川省双流县的农家乐以有机葡萄园、枇杷园、蔬菜园等观光农业为主,每年双流政府都会投入 1000 多万元举办节庆,几乎每个月都有一个与乡村旅游或农家乐有关的节庆,节庆主要面对的是四川的本省游客(国家旅游局,2016)。但在另一方面,本地市场营销也带来一些风险,如因企业的生产工厂与目的地市场不一定在同一区域,产品在物流方面的成本与风险会相应提高。侧重本地市场会导致制造成本的提高,从而降低企业的规模经济,而过于强调本地市场营销也可能会限制营销企业的整体品牌形象。

6.2.4　个人市场

市场细分的最终层级称为"个人市场""个性化营销"或"一对一营销"(Peppers 和 Rogers,2001)。个性化的趋势使得企业寻求通过范围经济将市场进行细分(Anderson 和 Narus,1995)。个性化将大规模定制与个性化营销相结合,让消费者能够根据自己的选择设计具有感知价值的产品。当一家企业能够在一对一的层面上回应消费者对产品和信息个性化的需求时,个性化企业随之形成。除了消费者市场外,个性化对于公司市场同样重要。

6.3　目标市场选择

为了确保目标市场的有效性,在进行市场细分时要遵循五个基本标准:第一,可测量性,即细分市场的规模、购买力和特征都能被测量;第二,充实性,细分市场规模要足够大,而且有足够的盈利能力;第三,可进入性,细分市场易于接触并提供服务;第四,差异性,细分市场易于被识别,并且市场内的

promotion costs for small enterprises, making good products from small businesses appreciated or even purchased by consumers through the Internet. Simultaneously, consumers are able to access more choices from lower information search cost through Amazon. As a result, the value of niche markets has increased.

6.2.3 Local markets

Local marketing reflects the trend of "grassroots marketing" (Kotler & Keller, 2009). Corporate marketing campaigns focus on individual consumers who are as close as possible to the local market, and they build personal emotional connections. In contrast to global or national advertising or marketing, local marketing can better meet the unique needs of the local market, thereby enhancing consumers' perceived value of the companies' products. For example, the agritainment properties in Shuangliu County, Sichuan Province, focuses on organic grapes, loquat farms, vegetable farms, and other sightseeing agriculture. The Shuangliu Government annually invests over 10 million yuan to hold festivals and events. A festival or event related to rural tourism or agritainment occurs almost every month. Such festivals and events primarily target local visitors from Sichuan Province (National Tourism Administration, 2016). However, local marketing also generates certain risks. For example, given that the production plant and the destination market are not necessarily in the same region, the product's cost and the risk on logistics increase accordingly. Focusing on the local market increases the manufacturing costs, and thus reduces the company's economies of scale, whereas too much emphasis on local marketing may also limit the overall brand image of the business.

6.2.4 Individual markets

The final level of market segmentation is called "segments of one" "customized marketing" or "one-to-one marketing" (Peppers & Rogers, 2001). The customization trend has led firms to seek market segmentation through economies of scope (Anderson & Narus, 1995). Customization combines mass customization with customized marketing so that consumers can design products with perceived value according to their own choices. When a company can respond to consumers' needs for customized products and information at a one-on-one level, it becomes a customized company. Aside from the consumer market, customization is equally important for the organizational market.

6.3 Target Market Selection

To ensure the effectiveness of target markets, market segmentation should follow these five basic criteria by being measurable, substantial, accessible, differentiable, and actionable. First, market size, purchasing power, and characteristics must be measurable. Second, market segments should be substantial or large enough and have sufficient profitability. Third, market segments must facilitate easy access and provision of services. Fourth, market segments must be

成员能够对不同的营销组合元素或项目产生不同的反馈;第五,可操作性:
企业能够制定有效的营销项目来吸引和服务细分市场。除此之外,在评估不
同的细分市场时,企业需要关注两大因素,即细分市场的整体吸引力和企业
目标与资源。有吸引力的细分市场不一定符合企业的长期目标,或者企业可
能缺乏在此细分市场中提供优质价值的一种或多种能力。

万豪酒店集团在开发万怡(Courtyard by Marriott)品牌时,聘请外部市
场营销研究人员进行市场调查。研究发现,商务旅客和旅游者都对当时的酒
店设施不满意,因为他们都在为自己不使用的设施而付费(例如泳池、商务中
心等)。研究结果显示出一个新的细分市场,从而促成有限服务市场的诞生。
当时酒店行业并没有相应的品牌服务这一细分市场,因此,万豪集团通过建
立万怡品牌进入这一细分市场。

企业在选定目标市场后,需要决定如何在目标市场中进行定位。有多种
方法帮助企业进行市场定位,其中一种方法为需求细分法。需求细分法一共
可采用七个步骤(见表6-2)。

表6-2　需求细分法的实施步骤

步骤	名称	实施内容
1	需求细分	根据相似的需求以及消费者在解决特定购买问题时所寻求的利益,将消费者分为不同的细分市场。
2	识别细分市场	通过人口统计特征、生活方式和使用行为等因素,识别每个需求细分市场的特点和可行性。
3	细分市场吸引力	利用细分市场吸引力指标(如市场增长、竞争激烈程度和市场可进入性),确定每个细分市场的整体吸引力。
4	细分市场营利能力	确定细分市场的营利能力。
5	细分市场定位	根据细分市场内消费者的需求和特征,制定"价值定位"和产品—价格定位。
6	细分市场测试	制定细分市场的"串联图板",测试每个细分市场定位战略的吸引力。
7	营销组合战略	将细分市场定位战略扩展至整个营销组合:产品、价格、推广和渠道。

来源:Best,R. J.(2005). *Market-based Management*(4th ed.). Upper Saddle River,
NJ:Prentice Hall.

differentiable, that is, easily identified. Members of the market can then have different responses to different marketing mix elements or programs. Finally, market segmentation should be actionable, meaning companies can develop effective marketing programs to attract and serve market segments. When evaluating different market segments, companies must also focus on two factors: the overall attractiveness of the market segments and corporate objectives and resources. Attractive segments do not necessarily meet the long-term goals of the business, or companies may lack one or more capabilities to deliver high-quality value in this market segment.

When developing the Courtyard by Marriott brand, the Marriott Hotel Group employed external marketing researchers. Their study discovered that business travelers and tourists were both unsatisfied with the hotel facilities at that time because they were paying for facilities that they did not use (such as swimming pools, and the business centers). Results showed a new market segment, thus leading to the birth of the limited service segment. Back then, the hotel industry had no corresponding brand serving this market segment. Consequently, the Marriott Group entered the market segment by building the Courtyard brand.

After selecting the target market, companies must decide how to position themselves in the target market. Numerous ways can support companies for market positioning, one of which is the needs-based market segmentation approach. This needs-based market segmentation approach involves seven steps(Table 6 - 2).

Table 6 - 2 Steps of needs-based market segmentation approach

Step	Them	Contents
1	Needs-based segmentation	Group customers into segments based on similar needs and benefits sought by customers in solving their particular consumption problems.
2	Segment identification	For each needs-based segment, determine which demographics, lifestyles, and usage behaviors make the segment distinct and identifiable (actionable).
3	Segment attractiveness	Using predetermined segment attractiveness criteria (such as market growth, competitive intensity, and market access), determine the overall attractiveness of each segment.
4	Segment profitability	Determine segment profitability.
5	Segment positioning	For each segment, create a "value proposition" and product-price positioning strategy based on that segment's unique customer needs and characteristics.
6	Segment "acid test"	Create "segment storyboard" to test the attractiveness of each segment's positioning strategy.
7	Marketing-mix strategy	Expand segment positioning strategy to include all aspects of the marketing mix: product, price, promotion, and place.

Source: Best, R. J. (2005). *Market-based Management* (4th ed.). Upper Saddle River, NJ: Pearson Prentice Hall.

雅高酒店集团于 2012 年根据集团对中国旅游者行为特征的分析,推出针对中国市场的全新品牌——美爵(Grand Mercure)。雅高酒店集团认为,中国顾客有以下特征:

- 相对其他国家的消费者而言,中国顾客对舒适、灵活和娱乐休闲方面的要求更高。

- 他们认为人们普遍认为国际品牌应当在各个方面树立标杆,尤其是服务。

- 通常认为法国和欧洲的品牌优雅、简约而且时尚。

- 历史悠久的品牌通常被认为拥有卓越的品质和高标准。

- 入住的酒店级别代表了社会地位。

- 中国顾客最重视的问题是保护隐私。

- 倾向中式餐馆、更大的卧房和 KTV 等设施。

2014 年在中国酒店市场上,75% 的酒店为非连锁酒店。而在市场结构方面,国际品牌酒店只占市场整体的 5%。由此可以看出,中国消费者对酒店的需求和市场供给之间存在明显的差距。因此,雅高集团对美爵品牌的定位是:根据中国消费者需求量身打造的国际酒店品牌,专注于为富有经验的中国旅行者寻找他们熟悉的文化体验。美爵品牌完美契合中国宾客的期望,同时营造充满魅力的体验与纯正本地化的品牌形象。美爵酒店在不同的运营地(亚太、沙特阿拉伯和巴西)引入原汁原味的当地文化,构建独特的品牌形象。

例如,新加坡美爵酒店主打广东传统美食和点心,而其酒吧的特色饮品为新加坡司令鸡尾酒;智利圣地亚哥美爵酒店专门为中国客人提供中式茶包,酒店礼宾部提供圣地亚哥游览路线图。这些酒店体现了美爵品牌在照顾中国消费者需求的同时,提供当地文化的体验。

企业在进行市场细分时,可以选择不同的市场细分战略达到扩大市场份额、提高收入等目的。这些市场细分战略包括单一细分市场、选择性专业化、产品专业化、市场专业化和全市场覆盖。

6.3.1　单一细分市场

企业能够通过在单一市场上进行集中性营销获得大量关于此细分市场需求的知识,同时也能够实现品牌的市场拓展。此外,企业可以利用产品、分销渠道和推广的专业化在细分市场中获得经济效益。企业在细分市场中成为领导者时可以获得高额投资回报。然而,单一细分市场存在明显的风险,

In 2012, the Accor Hotels Group launched a new brand, Grand Mercure, for the Chinese market, based on the Group's analysis of Chinese tourists' behavior characteristics. The Accor Hotel Group believes that Chinese customers have the following characteristics:

- Consumers in China have a higher demand for comfort, flexibility, and recreation than consumers in other countries.

- They think that there is a general perception that international brands should set the benchmark in every aspect, especially in terms of services.

- They consider French and European brands as elegant, simple, and stylish.

- They deem brands with a long history as having superior quality and high standards.

- The hotels they stayed are believed to represent social status.

- Privacy is of primary importance for Chinese customers.

- They display preference for Chinese restaurants, larger bedrooms, KTVs, and other facilities.

In 2014 in the Chinese hotel market, 75% of the hotels are non-chained hotels. In terms of market structure, the international brand hotels make up only 5% of the overall market. Hence, a clear gap exists between Chinese consumers' demand for hotels and the market supply. Therefore, the Accor Group's positioning for the Grand Mercure brand is a specifically tailored international hotel brand according to the needs of Chinese consumers, emphasizing familiar cultural experiences for experienced Chinese travelers. The Grand Mercure brand perfectly fits the expectations of Chinese guests and simultaneously creates a charming experience and a brand image of authentic localization. Grand Mercure builds its unique brand image through the introduction of authentic local culture at different locations (Asia Pacific, Saudi Arabia, and Brazil).

For example, the Grand Mercure Hotel in Singapore is dedicated to traditional Cantonese food and dim sum, while its specialty drink at the bar is the Singapore Sling. The Grand Mercure Santiago de Chile offers Chinese tea bags for Chinese guests and the concierge provides a travelling route map of Santiago. These hotels reflect the Grand Mercure brand in catering to Chinese consumers' demands while providing local cultural experiences.

Companies can choose diverse market segmentation strategies to expand market share, increase revenues, and fulfill other objectives. Such strategies include: single-segment concentration, selective specialization, product specialization, market specialization, and full market coverage.

6.3.1　Single-segmentation concentration

Companies can acquire extensive knowledge on the demand of one market segment through concentrated marketing in a single market; they can also realize market expansion of their brands. In addition, companies can use specialization of products, distribution channels, and promotion in the market segment to obtain economic benefits. When a company becomes a leader in the market segment, it can earn a high return on

如细分市场衰退或竞争对手进入细分市场。因此,很多企业偏好将风险分散,将业务拓展至多个细分市场。如果企业选择在多个细分市场发展业务,管理层需要留意细分市场对成本、业绩表现和技术的影响。另外,企业可以选择在特级细分市场开展业务,而非专注于孤立的细分市场。特级细分市场是一组拥有可开发的相似性的细分市场。例如,很多交响乐音乐会的目标顾客是有广泛文化兴趣的消费者,而非经常出席音乐会的人。

6.3.2　选择性专业化

企业选择进入数个具有吸引力且合适的细分市场。这些细分市场相对于其他细分市场没有或很少有协调性,但每个细分市场都有足够的盈利空间。这种多元化细分市场战略能够有利于企业分散风险。

6.3.3　产品专业化

产品专业化指企业制造一种特定的产品并向不同的细分市场销售产品。根据不同市场的需求,企业可以提供不同型号或不同功能的同款产品,并在此产品市场中建立品牌声望。产品专业化的风险是企业所提供的产品容易被全新的技术所取代。

6.3.4　市场专业化

市场专业化指企业专注于满足一个特定消费者群体的多种需求,并在此消费者群体中建立品牌声望。另外,凭借着在消费者群体中的声誉,企业可以成为其他产品进入此消费者市场的渠道。市场专业化的风险在于消费者群体规模的缩小或预算的缩减。

6.3.5　全市场覆盖

只有非常大型的企业拥有实施全市场覆盖的能力,如微软、通用汽车和可口可乐。在全市场覆盖战略中,企业面向所有消费者群体提供所有他们需要的产品。这些大型企业有两种方式来覆盖所有市场:标准化营销和差异化营销。标准化营销是指企业忽略所有细分市场的差异,并向所有细分市场提供同一种产品。企业设计产品,制订营销计划,赋予产品一个优质的形象,以吸引尽可能多的消费者。标准化营销依赖于大众分销和大众广告。由于产品种类单一,企业能够在研发、生产、库存、运输、营销研究、广告、管理等方

investment. However, obvious risks are present in a single segment, such as a recession in the market segment or competitors entering the market segment. Thus, many companies prefer to diversify risks and expand into multiple segments. If a company opts to develop its business in multiple segments, management must tackle the effect between market segments on cost, performance, and technology. In addition, companies can choose to conduct business in super-segments, rather than focusing on isolated segments. A super-segment is a group of segments with similarities that can be developed. For example, many symphony concerts are aimed at consumers with a wide range of cultural interests instead of focusing on those who regularly attend concerts.

6.3.2　Selective specialization

Companies can choose to enter a number of attractive and appropriate market segments. Such segments have little or no synergy with other segments, but each market segment has sufficient profitability. This diversified market segmentation strategy can be conducive for companies to diversify their risks.

6.3.3　Product specialization

A company manufactures a specific product and sells it to different market segments. Based on different market needs, the company can provide the same type of products with different models or diverse functions, and establish brand reputation in that product market. The risk of product specialization is that the product provided by the company may be easily replaced by brand-new technologies.

6.3.4　Market specialization

Companies which focus on meeting the multiple needs of a specific consumer group can build brand reputation within that consumer group. Moreover, with their reputation in the consumer group, such companies can become the market channel for other products to enter that particular consumer group. The risk of market specialization is the reduction in the size of the consumer group or the reduction in budget.

6.3.5　Full market coverage

Only very large enterprises, such as Microsoft, General Motors, and Coca-Cola, have the ability to implement full market coverage. With the full market coverage strategy, companies provide all consumer groups with all the products they need. Such major companies have two ways to cover all the markets: undifferentiated marketing and differentiated marketing. Undifferentiated marketing means that companies ignore the differences in all market segments, and provide the same product to all of them. Companies design the product and generate marketing plans to create a high-quality image for the product in order to entice as many consumers as possible. Undifferentiated marketing relies on mass distribution and mass advertising. With a single product or product type, companies can reduce costs in research and development, production, inventory, transportation, marketing research, advertising, management, and other

面降低成本。因此,企业能够将低成本转化为低价格,赢得价格敏感市场。

　　差异化营销则是企业为不同的细分市场提供不同的产品。一般而言,差异化营销相对于标准化营销能够获得更高的销售收入。但同时,差异化营销的成本也高于标准化营销。企业需要注意市场是否被过于细分,如果出现这种情况,企业需要考虑进行反向细分以扩大消费者规模。例如,强生公司将婴儿洗发露的目标市场扩展至成年人(Kotler 和 Keller,2009)。

areas. Consequently, companies are able to convert low cost to low price to win price-sensitive markets.

By contrast, differentiated marketing indicates that companies provide different products for different market segments. Differentiated marketing usually generates higher sale revenues, compared to undifferentiated marketing. The cost of differentiated marketing is also higher than that of undifferentiated marketing. Companies must note whether the market is too fragmented, and if so, they must consider counter-segmentation to expand the size of consumers. For example, Johnson & Johnson extended the target market for baby shampoos to adults (Kotler & Keller, 2009).

第 7 章　品牌战略管理

本章要点

- 品牌及品牌化
- 目的地品牌化
- 品牌资产管理
- 品牌塑造策略

随着市场竞争的加剧,品牌在旅游企业和目的地营销中的作用日益凸显。通过品牌化及品牌战略管理,企业或者目的地能够更有效地进行市场细分与营销沟通,与消费者建立情感连接,从而在竞争中脱颖而出。本章将介绍品牌及品牌化的概念,品牌资产管理,目的地品牌化,以及品牌塑造策略。

7.1　品牌及品牌化

品牌是一个或一组特定产品、服务的名字、符号、标志、设计、形象或这些要素的组合,用以辨认产品,并使之与竞争对手的产品及服务区别开来。品牌体现的是消费者在其生命周期内对于产品或服务的累积的信任。品牌是基础的、理性的和真实的,而且与产品或服务的表现有关。品牌通常包含四个组成部分(Kotler 和 Keller,2009):第一是品牌个性,即企业对自身产品或服务进行定位的方式;第二是品牌形象,即消费者对品牌个性的感知,它是关于品牌的视觉或语言表达,用以与消费者建立心理或情感联系,从而留在消费者的记忆中(Coop,2005);第三是品牌承诺,即市场营销人员对于品牌应当向消费者所提供的价值的愿景;最后是品牌知识,指的是消费者记忆中与品牌相关的内容,如消费者想到丽思卡尔顿,就想到卓越的酒店服务。而品牌化是运用某一标签或(名称)短语去反映品牌定位,以快速而简明地传达

Chapter 7　Strategic Brand Management

 Key points of the chapter

- Brand and branding
- Destination branding
- Managing and measuring brand equity
- Branding strategies

With intensified market competition, the role of brand in tourism companies and destination marketing has become increasingly prominent. Through branding and brand strategy management, companies or destinations can effectively conduct market segmentation and marketing communication as well as establish emotional connections with consumers to stand out from the competition. This chapter introduces the concept of brand and branding, brand equity management, destination branding, and branding strategy.

7.1　Brand and Branding

A brand is the name, symbol, logo, design, image, or combination of these elements of one or a group of particular products or services; it identifies the product and distinguishes it from its competitors' products and services. Brand reflects the cumulative trust of the product or service from consumers in its life cycle. Apart from being foundational, rational, and real, brand is related to the performance of the product or service. Branding consists of four components (Kotler & Keller, 2009). The first component is brand identity, that is, the way companies position their products or services. The second component is brand image or the consumer's perception of brand image. Brand image concerns the brand's visual or language expression to establish a psychological or emotional contact with consumers, thereby enabling the product to remain in the consumers' memory (Coop, 2005). The third component is brand promise, which is the marketers' vision of the value the brand should deliver to the consumers. The

所定位内容的基本要义,从而使所提供的利益能够易于(为旅游消费者所)了解和记忆(李天元,2007)。简言之,品牌化就是一种把自己的一项或一系列产品/服务与竞争对手的产品/服务区分开来的方法(张颖,2003)。

定位和品牌化概念起源于消费品的市场营销战略(Chernatony、Drury和 Segal-Horn,2003),强调的是消费品的差异化,也即区别于其他同类产品的特性。随着服务产业重要性的不断扩大及市场的成熟,服务业企业也愈来愈要求认识到本产品不同于其他产品的独一无二的特质。Chernatony 和 Segal-Horn(2001)指出,品牌化中对这些差异性的应用的主要意义在于,虽然所有的品牌都是无形的,但服务品牌代表了服务中的某些无形因素,而产品品牌代表了产品的部分有形成分,它尤其适用于旅游环境中的产品差异化。所谓定位,就是识别和确定某一产品或服务的重要品质,以便能够以有意义的方式向消费者展现其有别于竞争产品或服务的特色或内含利益(李天元,2007)。所以,"差异化"成为旅游产品定位的关键点,它使企业的产品从众多的同类产品中凸显出来,体现出自身的竞争优势。品牌化则使之在旅游消费者心目中建立起一个与众不同的形象,并留下良好的回忆。一旦与此形象相关的旅游产品的名字、标识或口号被呈现,消费者就能回忆其产品。

品牌化的最终目的是在一定程度上通过感情吸引消费者,使消费者与品牌之间建立一种超越物质满意的,深厚、长久、亲密的关系(Morrison 和 Crane,2007)。Kunde 和 Cunningham(2002)提出了品牌宗教模型,用以描述品牌在消费者生活中五个不同阶段的角色。较弱的品牌只是"产品或服务",没有超越其功能的内涵。"品牌概念"在情感上能够引起消费者的共鸣,并鼓励其更多地参与。"企业概念"指品牌能够反映企业的战略,表达企业的哲学。达到"品牌文化"的品牌成为消费者日常生活中的一部分。而模型的最终阶段是"品牌宗教",消费者将品牌视为一种生活方式。如图 7-1 所示。

酒店业的品牌化始于 20 世纪初。当时,一些酒店如斯塔特勒(Statler)酒店和丽兹(Ritz)酒店把分属于不同城市的酒店联系起来,一致采用同一个品牌,品牌在酒店业中的重要效用便引起了关注。纵观中国酒店业的发展,从"中国酒店的历史博物馆"(1863 年兴建于天津的利顺德大饭店)开始,到 1982 年香港半岛集团管理北京建国饭店,再到如今全球十大酒店集团均已落户中国,与本土诸多酒店集团展开激烈竞争,国外品牌的进入带动了中国

last one is brand knowledge, which refers to part of consumer's memory related to the brand. For example, when consumers think of Ritz-Carlton, they think of excellent hotel services. Branding employs a label or a (name) phrase to reflect brand positioning and to quickly and concisely convey the basic meaning of the positioning so that the benefits can be easily understood and memorized (by tourism consumers) (Li, 2007). Branding is distinguishing one or a series of products/services from competitors' products/services (Zhang, 2003).

The positioning and branding concept originated in the marketing strategy of consumer goods (De Chernatony, Drury & Segal-Horn, 2003), with emphasis on differentiating consumer goods or distinguishing their characteristics from other similar products. As the importance of the service industry continues to expand and the market matures, service companies increasingly recognize the unique characteristics of services different from other products. De Chernatony and Segal-Horn (2001) suggest that the main significance for applying these differences in branding is that despite the intangibility of all brands, service brands represent some intangible components in the service, and product brands represent some tangible components in the product. Such significance is particularly suitable for product differentiation in a tourism environment. Positioning means identifying and determining the important quality of a product or service to enable meaningful unravelling of its distinctive characteristics or implied benefits compared with competitive products or services to consumers (Li, 2007). "Differentiation" becomes the key point of tourism product positioning enabling the company's product to stand out from many similar products, thereby reflecting its own competitive advantages. Branding aims to establish a different image for the product and leave a good memory in the consumers' mind. After presenting the name, logo, or slogan of the tourism product associated with the image, consumers can recall the product.

Branding ultimately aims to attract consumers' emotion to a certain extent and establish a deep, long-term, and intimate relationship beyond the material satisfaction between consumers and the brand (Morrison & Crane, 2007). Kunde and Cunningham (2002) propose a brand religion model to describe the role of brands in five different stages of a consumer's life. Weaker brands are simply "products or services" that do not go beyond their functional connotations. The "concept brand" can appeal to consumer's emotions and encourage increased participation. "Corporate concept" means that a brand can reflect a company's strategy and express its philosophy. Brands achieving the "brand culture" become part of the consumers' daily life. The final stage of the model is "brand religion," where consumers view a brand as a way of life (Figure 7 - 1).

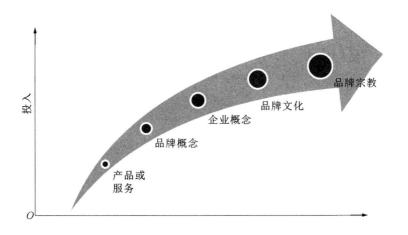

图 7 - 1 品牌宗教模型

来源：根据 Kunde & Cunningham. (2002). *Corporate Religion*. Harlow，
England：Financial Times Prentice Hall.

本土酒店品牌化的建设，也加快了中国酒店业与国际接轨的步伐。在餐饮业，百年老店北京的全聚德、杭州的楼外楼、西安的同盛祥都是享誉全国的知名品牌，品牌连锁企业在旅游业中发挥了日益重要的作用。

品牌的作用可以从消费者角度和企业角度进行解读。从消费者角度来看，品牌代表特定水平的质量和满意度，因而能够简化购买决策，降低风险（Suri 和 Monroe，2003），使得消费者能够轻松地选择某种产品或服务（Erdem，1998；Erdem 和 Swait，1998）。从企业角度，通过注册品牌商标，企业能够对产品或服务的特征进行法律保护（Bagley，2005），并通过品牌扩展和授权获得更多发展机会。成功的品牌所传递的价值和信息是竞争对手无法复制的，它可以为企业带来强大的竞争优势（Klein，2000）。其不仅可以帮助企业将产品和服务与竞争对手进行区分，还能够使企业在分销渠道和供应商方面获得强大的支持。一个成功的品牌帮助企业更好地对市场进行细分，向不同的目标市场提供不同的产品或服务，从而提高营销传播的效率，最终提高顾客的忠诚度。喜达屋酒店及度假村集团就是偏向于使用多品牌策略来满足不同细分市场需求的典型例子。集团旗下共有 10 个品牌，其中 5

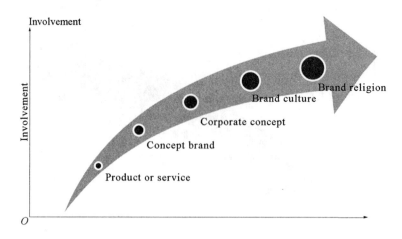

Figure 7 – 1   Brand religion model

Source: Kunde & Cunningham. (2002). *Corporate Religion*. Harlow, England: Financial Times Prentice Hall.

Hotel branding began in the early 20th century when some hotels, such as Statler and Ritz connected hotels in different cities together under the same brands, thereby instigating popular concern on the brand's importance in the hotel industry. Throughout the development of China's hotel industry, from the Astor Hotel (利顺德大饭店) built in Tianjin in 1982, the "China Hotel History Museum," to the management of the Beijing Jianguo Hotel by the Hong Kong Peninsula Group in 1982, and, now, the entry of the world's top 10 hotel groups to China and their fierce competition with many local hotel groups, the entry of foreign brands lead to the development of China's domestic hotel brands as well as the speeding up of the pace of China's hotel industry to match international standards. In the food and beverage industry, the century-old Beijing Quanjude, Hangzhou Louwailou, and Xi'an Tongshengxiang, are all well-known brands in the nation. Brand chain businesses have been playing an increasingly important role in the tourism industry.

The role of a brand can be interpreted from the perspectives of consumers and companies. From a consumer perspective, brands represent a certain level of quality and satisfaction, which simplifies the purchasing decisions and reduces risks (Suri & Monroe, 2003) to facilitate easy options for consumers when choosing a product or service (Erdem, 1998; Erdem & Swait, 1998). From a company perspective, companies can protect the characteristics of products or services by registering brand names (Bagley, 2005) and gain further development opportunities through brand extension and licensing. Successful brands deliver values and information preventing competitors from replicating them, which is a competitive advantage (Klein, 2000) assisting companies not only in differentiating their products and services from their competitors but also in obtaining strong support from distribution channels and suppliers. A successful brand assists companies to effectively segment the market, offer different products or services to different target markets to improve the efficiency of marketing communication, and ultimately improve customer loyalty. Starwood Hotels and Resorts is a typical example of adopting a multi-brand strategy to meet the needs of different market segments. The group has 10 brands, with five core brands. With its high-end positioning and prestigious

个核心品牌。瑞吉（St. Regis）以其高端的定位和尊贵的服务品质展示着豪华的品牌地位，喜来登（Sheraton）为商务客户带来周全、便利与高效的舒适环境，威斯汀（Westin）、W 酒店及雅乐轩（Aloft）等品牌在某些地域组成了一个不同档次的酒店群落，成为这些区域酒店业务的垄断者。品牌也有助于新业务的开展和新产品的引进。当假日酒店集团决定进入有限服务酒店市场时，它引进的新品牌假日快捷（Holiday Inn Express）的迅速发展很大程度上归功于假日集团长时间积累起来的声誉和形象。

7.2　目的地的品牌化

目的地的品牌化是目的地营销中非常重要的一部分。香港作为亚洲主要旅游目的地之一，一直很重视自身的品牌管理。从 2011 年起，香港旅游发展局以"香港：亚洲国际都会"作为香港旅游的品牌，搭建全新的推广平台，凸显香港多元化的旅游特色。香港的目的地品牌营销策略由产品导向转变为旅客体验导向。香港的品牌主要凸显四个特点。（1）精彩不息：在香港这个活力十足的不夜城，时刻都能带来新鲜不同的体验，让旅客尽享日与夜的精彩。（2）迷人对比：古今中西、城市郊野，种种对比强烈的元素在香港相互碰撞、影响，既有火花，也能包容，给旅客无限的惊叹。（3）多元紧凑：旅客在香港，能以有限时间享受多种不同的体验。因为没有一个城市像香港一样，拥有如此丰富多元的旅游体验，而且都近在咫尺。旅客可以轻松、快捷又安全地畅游，随时发现新的惊喜。（4）潮流尖端：走在时代尖端的香港，汇聚世界潮流与各地精华，同时也能创造出与众不同的自我风格，为各地旅客带来炫酷的产品和体验（Hong Kong Tourism Board，2016）。

香港旅游发展局每年都会推出不同的营销活动以推广"香港：亚洲国际都会"这一品牌，如表 7 - 1 所示。

表 7 - 1　香港旅游发展局品牌推广活动

年份	活动主题	内容
2010—2011	2010 年香港节庆年	在全球推出以"中西融和·无尽精彩"为主题的广告，向旅客介绍香港全年不绝的中西节日和盛事。 六个推广时段，包括传统文化汇、夏日盛会、万圣狂欢月、美酒佳肴月、缤纷冬日节及新春节庆。 推出多款与传统节气有关的手机游戏，提升旅客对香港节气的兴趣。 联合业界伙伴，为旅游业争取商机，并全力开拓"一程多站"及会展和邮轮旅游的潜力。

service, St. Regis demonstrates its status as a luxury brand. Sheraton provides a comprehensive, convenient, efficient, and comfortable environment for business travelers. The Westin, W, and Aloft brands form a distinctively different group of hotels in some regions and become the monopolies of the hotel business in these regions. The brand further contributes to the development of new businesses and the introduction of new products. When the Holiday Inn Group decided to enter the limited service hotel market, the rapid development of the newly introduced brand Holiday Inn Express largely owes to the reputation and image built over a long time by the Holiday Inn Group.

7.2 *Destination Branding*

Destination branding is crucial to destination marketing. As one of the major tourist destinations in Asia, Hong Kong has consistently placed utmost importance to its own brand management. From 2011 onwards, the HKTB adopts "Hong Kong: Asia's World City" as the brand of Hong Kong tourism, building a new platform for promotion to highlight Hong Kong's diversified tourism features. Hong Kong's destination brand marketing strategy changes from product-oriented into visitor-experience-oriented. Hong Kong's brand highlights four major DNAs, namely, (1) non-stop intensity: a city that never sleeps; Hong Kong is bursting with an energy unfailingly exhilarating visitors. Dull moments do not exist here; (2) fascinating contrasts: East, West, urban, natural, modern, or ancient; in Hong Kong, strikingly different worlds coexist, thereby offering visitors an amazing array of contrasting experiences; (3) compact variety: Hong Kong makes life easier for travelers! No other place packs such a variety of rich and diverse experiences into an area extremely easy and fast to explore; (4) distinctly trendy: by adopting and adapting global trends, Hong Kong nurtures its own unique style to offer products and experiences sought after the world over (Hong Kong Tourism Board, 2016).

The HKTB launches various marketing campaigns to promote the brand "Hong Kong: Asia's World City" every year, as provided in Table 7 – 1.

Table 7 – 1   Branding campaigns of the Hong Kong Tourism Board

Year	Theme	Contents
2010—2011	Festive Hong Kong 2010	Global launching of advertisement themed as "Hong Kong. A World of Celebrations" to introduce the year-long sequence of eastern and western festivals and events in Hong Kong. Six promotional periods, including Cultural Celebrations, Summer Spectacular, Halloween Treats, Wine & Dine Month, Winter Fest, and Chinese New Year. Launching of different mobile games related to traditional festivals to increase visitors' interest in Hong Kong's festivals. Together with industry partners, to seek business opportunities for the tourism industry and to explore the potential of "Multi-Destination" and exhibition and cruise tourism.

续　表

年份	活动主题	内容
2011—2012	香港：亚洲国际都会	应不同客群包括年轻、家庭及年长客群的兴趣及喜好，旅游发展局制作了不同版本的宣传资料，展现香港在全年不同时段均有无尽精彩的事物。 　　借助本土人气卡通人物"麦兜"，宣传香港的旅游景点和亲子游活动，希望吸引更多内地及台湾的家庭旅客访港。
2012—2013	Every Moment Is a Different World	推出了全新面貌的 DiscoverHongKong.com 网站。 　　推出分别以中年和家庭客群为对象的宣传短片，鼓励他们来港旅游。
2013—2014	香港·味道	针对中国内地市场，《香港·味道》美食艺术展在北京、上海、成都与厦门举行。 　　展览采用互动形式，共设四个展区："美食之最大赏互动投影区"利用虚拟科技把得奖菜式送到观众面前；"经典茶餐厅展区"通过情景模拟带出香港情怀；台湾陶艺家朱芳毅作品展让粤式点心与艺术结合；还有"粥粉面饭影音录像区"专题介绍四大香港美食。
	笑出·快乐香港	通过一系列电视广告，传达友善待客的信息，鼓励本港市民与旅客增进交流。 　　成效：《笑出·快乐香港》宣传短片通过 YouTube 及其他网上平台观看次数如下： 　　中国内地：540 万； 　　台湾地区：250 万； 　　东南亚：880 万。
2014—2015	我在香港之时	制作了九个以地道香港玩家为主角的品牌短片，与香港 18 个区的旅游达人合作，带领游客深入香港社区，并推出有三合一功能的 App"香港·我的智能行程"，使得游客可以定制个性化行程。

Continued

Year	Theme	Contents
2011—2012	Hong Kong: Asia's World City	The HKTB has produced different editions of promotional materials for different groups, including youngsters, families, and elderly visitors, to show an endless array of exciting events throughout the year in Hong Kong. Promotion of Hong Kong's tourist attractions and family activities, with the assistance of a local popular cartoon character named, "McDull," hoping to attract more the Mainland of China and Taiwan's family visitors to Hong Kong.
2012—2013	Every Moment Is a Different World	Launching of a brand new website, DiscoverHongKong.com. Launching of promotional videos targeting middle-aged and family customers to encourage them to travel to Hong Kong.
2013—2014	Taste of Hong Kong	To target the Chinese mainland market, the "Taste of Hong Kong" exhibitions were staged in Beijing, Shanghai, Chengdu, and Xiamen. The exhibition adopted interactive approaches with the following four exhibition areas: "a simulated dining experience" was used to bring the award-winning dishes to the audience through virtual technology; "a mock-up of a cha chan teng corner" brought out Hong Kong sentiment by simulating the situation; an exhibit from Taiwanese ceramic artist Zhu Fangyi showcased the combination of Cantonese dim sum and art; and a "documentary area for congee, rice noodles, noodles, and rice" introduced the four most famous Hong Kong cuisines.
	happy@hongkong	A series of TV commercials to convey the message of friendly hospitality to encourage greater interaction between Hong Kong people and visitors. Results: The number of times viewed for the "happy @ hongkong" promotional videos on YouTube and other online platforms are as follows: the Mainland of China: 5.4 million Taiwan: 2.5 million Southeast Asia: 8.8 million
2014—2015	My time for Hong Kong	HKTB produced nine brand short films featuring authentic Hong Kong players, worked with the tourism experts from Hong Kong's 18 districts to bring tourists deeply into Hong Kong communities, and launched a three-in-one App "My Hong Kong Guide," enabling visitors to plan personalized trips.

续　表

年份	活动主题	内容
2015—2016	香港 Fun 享夏日礼——大买·爱吃·玩不停	夏季一向是香港旅游的旺季,香港旅游发展局于 2015—2016 年度推出了"香港 Fun 享夏日礼——大买·爱吃·玩不停"大型活动,包括丰富的旅游体验及大量的购物优惠。配合此项活动进行的整合营销,包括全新宣传短片《大买·爱吃·玩不停》、社交媒体营销、线下推广、公关活动等。

　　2014—2015 年,香港旅游发展局推出新的品牌推广活动"我在香港之时",让旅客能充分感受到在香港每一刻都可以拥有惊喜而多变的体验。该活动通过数码媒体推广、公关宣传、业界合作及其他途径,大力宣传香港现有的旅游体验。

　　在市场推广方面,香港旅游发展局将重点放在制作以香港旅游体验为主,具有互动性质的内容的短片,并有效传达给消费者。根据重点,香港旅游发展局主要推出了三项活动,包括短片《我在香港之时》(*My time for Hong Kong*)、当地人带路活动,以及《香港·我的智能行程》应用程序。

　　在宣传媒介方面,香港旅游发展局利用了 YouTube、区域电视网路、DiscoverHongKong. com、Facebook、官方微博、Twitter、Instagram 和 Pinterest 等社交媒体。在推广期间,所有活动一共获得了 1504 篇媒体报道,宣传效益达 1200 万港元,并获得 7.44 亿曝光次数,以及 1700 万次的短片浏览量。《香港·我的智能行程》应用程序下载量达到 85000 次,其中 84% 用户表示容易使用,82% 表示会推荐给朋友。DiscoverHongKong.com 网站浏览次数达到 6550 万次。同时所有社交媒体平台的"粉丝"达 370 万人(香港旅游发展局,2015)。

　　此外,香港旅游发展局也在公关宣传方面采取了一系列的行动,包括邀请名人分享对香港的看法、邀请摄影师 Murad Osmann 及其女友拍摄影片等。影片制作完成后为新闻机构如路透社、法新社和 Getty Images 等提供材料。同时,具有广泛覆盖网络的全球和区域电视网络也是香港旅游发展局的合作对象。Discovery Networks 旗下的 TLC 亚洲频道合作制作名为 *My Taste of Hong Kong* 的系列节目。推广期间 Murad Osmann 拍摄的相片共赢得 160 万个"赞"并吸引了超过 2 万个评论,宣传效益超过 400 万港元。另外,香港旅游发展局通过通讯社,将"香港除夕倒数"和"新春国际汇演之夜"

Continued

Year	Theme	Contents
2015—2016	Hong Kong Summer Fun"Shop. Eat.Play"	Summer is constantly a peak season for Hong Kong tourism. HKTB launched the Hong Kong Summer Fun"Shop. Eat. Play" in 2015—2016，including a wealth of travel experiences and several shopping offers. Integrated marketing was conducted with the campaign，including the new "Shop. Eat. Play" TV commercial，social media marketing，offline promotions，and public relations activities.

In 2014—2015，the HKTB launched a new branding campaign called "My time for Hong Kong" to allow visitors a full experience of Hong Kong's possible moment-to-moment surprises and varied experiences. It vigorously promoted the existing travel experiences in Hong Kong through digital media，public relations，industry cooperation，and other means.

With regard to marketing，the HKTB focused on the production of interactive contents featuring travel experiences in Hong Kong and effectively communicating them to consumers. With such focus，the HKTB launched three major activities，including the short film titled，*My time for Hong Kong*，the "Hong Kong Insiders' Guide" campaign，and the "My Hong Kong Guide" App.

On the media side，the HKTB utilized social media，such as YouTube，regional television networks，DiscoverHongKong. com，Facebook，official Weibo，Twitter，Instagram，and Pinterest. During the promotional period，all activities received 1,504 media coverage，HK $ 12 million in publicity value，744 million impressions，and 17 million video views. The "My Hong Kong Guide" App was downloaded 85,000 times，with 84% of downloaders saying it was easy to use and 82% saying it would be recommended to friends. DiscoverHongKong.com website received 65.5 million page views. Simultaneously，the number of "fans" on all the social media platforms were up to 3.7 million (HKTB，2015).

The HKTB also took a series of actions in publicity，including inviting celebrities to share their views on Hong Kong and inviting photographer Murad Osmann and his girlfriend to make films. This completed film production provided materials to news organizations，such as news agencies，including Reuters，Agence France-Presse，and Getty Images. At the same time，global and regional television networks with extensive coverage were partners of the HKTB. A series of programs entitled，*My Taste of Hong Kong* were produced with Discovery Networks' TLC Asia channel. During the promotional period，Murad Osmann's photos won 1.6 million "likes" and attracted over 20,000 comments，generating over 4 million Hong Kong dollars in publicity value. In addition，the HKTB cooperated with news agencies to bring "Hong Kong New Year's Eve Countdown" and "Chinese New Year Parade" to a worldwide audience，generating a

的盛况带给全世界观众,并分别带来 2.31 亿港元及 3.6 亿港元的宣传效益。

在会展旅游业务方面,香港旅游发展局强化与业界伙伴的关系,与全球会议业领袖国际会议筹组人协会签订了三年的合约。同时,也继续与 American Society of Association Executives、Global Conference Network、HelmsBriscoe 及 International Congress and Convention Association 紧密合作。通过这些策略伙伴的庞大网络,向它们的会员宣传香港。同时,香港旅游发展局积极参加不同地区市场的主要展销会和活动,从而联系国际买家、企业和会展奖励旅游代理,并通过举办工作坊展示香港会展奖励旅游产品、地点和发展。此外,香港旅游发展局也为中国内地的会展奖励旅游代理举办访港交流活动,以及为奖励中国内地、印度和印度尼西亚的代理而举办"香港会议及奖励旅游挑战赛"。

针对不同的市场,香港旅游发展局也采取了不同的策略。例如,针对中国内地市场,香港旅游发展局拍摄并发布微电影《我在香港之时》及《忆城·香港篇》。两部微电影观看次数超过 1600 万(数字来自土豆网 2014 年 8 月至 10 月和爱奇艺 2015 年 1 月至 2 月),总宣传效益达 5000 万港元。此外,香港旅游发展局也拍摄了四集名人豪华游轮之旅的节目,宣传香港为首选游轮度假目的地。仅一个月节目的观看次数即达 240 万。考虑到支付宝在内地的影响力,香港旅游发展局开发了《香港·优惠》App,并与支付宝进行合作。

除了香港以外,世界其他知名旅游目的地同样通过发起针对不同客源市场的营销活动推广目的地品牌。日本是澳大利亚的一个主要客源国。2014 年一共有超过 32.6 万名日本游客到澳大利亚旅游,旅游花费超过 14 亿澳元。2015 年,澳大利亚旅游局针对日本年轻一代以及善用社交网络的游客推出"GIGA Selfie"黄金海岸自拍活动。游客只要站在黄金海岸指定的地点,利用"GIGA Selfie"智能手机应用程序就可以进行自拍。自拍完成后,游客就会收到一条链接进行分享(Ryan,2015)。

7.3　品牌资产管理

品牌资产及其价值是消费者对品牌的反应,体现在消费者对品牌的思考、感受和行动上,也反映品牌在价格、市场份额和盈利能力等方面对企业的贡献。如今,品牌对提高企业的财务价值有非常重要的作用。对企业而言,品牌代表的是能影响消费者行为的、有着巨大价值的法定财产。品牌能够被收购和销售,并且能够为企业带来可持续的收入。以顾客为基础的品牌资产

publicity value of 231 million and 360 million Hong Kong dollars, respectively.

In the MICE sector, the HKTB strengthened its relationship with industry partners and signed a three-year contract with the International Association of Professional Congress Organizers (IAPCO). HKTB further continued to work closely with the American Society of Association Executives, Global Conference Network, HelmsBriscoe, and the International Congress and Convention Association to promote Hong Kong to their members through the vast networks of these strategic partners. Simultaneously, the HKTB actively participated in major trade fairs and events in different regions to reach international buyers, businesses, and exhibition incentive travel agents. The board also organized workshops to showcase the products, locations, and development of MICE tourism in Hong Kong. The HKTB also organized inbound exchange activities for MICE agents in the Mainland of China, as well as the Top Agent Awards Program to reward agents in the Mainland of China, India, and Indonesia.

For different markets, the HKTB adopted different strategies. For example, the HKTB filmed and published micro films titled *My time for Hong Kong* and *Yicheng Hong Kong* for the Mainland of China's market. The total number of views for the two micro films was over 16 million from Tudou (August to October 2014) and iQiyi (January to February 2015), with a total publicity value of 50 million Hong Kong dollars. Furthermore, the HKTB also launched a four-episode program of celebrities' cruise trips to promote Hong Kong as a premier cruise destination. The number of views reached a total of 2.4 million in a month. In light of Alipay's influence in the Mainland of China, the HKTB developed the "Hong Kong Value Offer" App and cooperated with Alipay.

Apart from Hong Kong, other well-known tourist destinations in the world also launched many marketing campaigns targeting different source markets to promote destination brands. Japan is one of Australia's major source countries. Over 326,000 Japanese tourists visited Australia in 2014, with tourism spending over 1.4 billion Australian dollars. In 2015, Tourism Australia launched the "GIGA Selfie" campaign in Golden Coast, targeting a younger and social media-savvy generation from Japan. Visitors can use the "GIGA Selfie" smartphone App to take a selfie as long as they are standing on designated locations in Golden Coast. Once the selfie is completed, visitors receives a link to share it (Ryan, 2015).

7.3 *Managing and Measuring Brand Equity*

Brand equity and its value are the consumers' responses to the brand reflected in consumer's thoughts, feelings and actions toward the brand, including the brand's contribution to the company in terms of price, market share, and profitability. Today, the brand plays an important role in improving the financial value of a company. For the company, the brand represents the influence on consumer behavior and is a statutory asset with great value. Brands can be acquired and sold and can bring sustainable business

是衡量品牌成功度的真正指标,这种品牌资产包括四个维度:品牌忠诚度、品牌知名度、感知质量以及品牌联系(Aaker,1991)。

品牌忠诚度是指消费者在购买决策中,多次表现出来的对某个品牌有偏向性的(而非随意的)行为反应。它是一种决策和评估的行为过程,也是一种心理态度过程。品牌忠诚度的最终衡量指标是顾客的重复购买以及口碑推介。品牌忠诚度的形成不完全依赖于产品的品质、知名度、品牌联系及传播,它与消费者本身的特性密切相关,形成于消费者的实际使用经历。品牌忠诚度的建立需要一个过程,一般经过购买前的认知、购买时的体验和购买后的偏好三个主要步骤。首先,产品的广告或其他沟通方式使得消费者从未知到知之,即识别;其次,成功的经营和持续的营销刺激购买行为的完成,用自身的体验检测识别阶段形成的价值期望;最后,体验过后的高满意度和价值衡量才可能建立起消费者对该品牌的偏好,即使支付更高的价格也愿意(Heskett、Sasser 和 Hart,1990)。

品牌知名度是所有销售活动的基础,比如在广告的 AIDA(Attention,Interest,Desire,Action)层级原理中,广告的目标首先是要引起注意即产生知觉,然后激发兴趣,再创造欲望,最后带来顾客行为。品牌知名度是品牌体现在目标对象的头脑中的强度,其目标并非一般的知觉,而是指品牌因为其指定的目的而被记忆。企业应通过重复的品牌展现以及品牌与相关产品类别的强烈的联系来增强顾客对品牌的熟悉程度。

感知质量是指顾客所感知的某一品牌在同类别产品中的优越程度。由于较高的感知质量意味着更高的要价,感知质量成为企业财务表现的重要的贡献者。但是,因为各种原因市场所感知的品牌质量有可能与实际的质量并不相符,这些原因包括以前经历的低劣质量、质量的感知来源于原先以为并不重要的属性、消费者信息处理的不完善等。顾客所感知的质量是否正确并不重要,重要的是什么是顾客的真实感受。

品牌联系或品牌形象是存在于记忆中的与品牌有关的任何联系,它存在于消费者的头脑中并参与信息的处理过程。品牌联系包括对各种功能性和情感性属性的联系,其中一些代表了关键的购买决策标准。传统的品牌定位观点认为,定位应聚焦于某一个或几个代表核心购买理由的联系,但是更为

incomes. Customer-based brand equity is a genuine measure of a brand's success comprising the following four dimensions: brand loyalty, brand awareness, perceived quality, and brand associations (Aaker, 1991).

Brand loyalty refers to consumers' repetitive biased (rather than random) behavior responses to a certain brand during decision marking. It is a process of decision making and assessment as well as psychological attitude. The ultimate measure of brand loyalty is the repeat purchase of customers and word-of-mouth referral. The formation of brand loyalty is not entirely dependent on product quality, reputation, brand contact, and communication. Brand loyalty isclosely related to the characteristics of consumers themselves and is formed in consumers' actual user experience. The establishment of brand loyalty requires a process including three major steps, namely, pre-purchase perceptions, purchase experiences, and post-purchase preferences. First, the product advertising or other means of communication transform consumers from unknown to known, that is, identification. Second, the successful operation and continuous marketing stimulate the completion of purchase behavior to evaluate the expected value formed during the identification stage with their own experiences. Finally, a high degree of satisfaction and value evaluation after the purchase tend to establish a consumer preference for the brand, even if it requires a higher price (Heskett, Sasser, & Hart, 1990).

Brand awareness is the basis for all sales activities. For example, in the advertising's AIDA principle, advertising primarily aims to attract attention, namely, generate awareness, then stimulate interest, create desire, and finally bring customer action. Brand awareness is the strength of the brand embodied in the mind of the target subject. Its goal is not the general perception but the brand memorized due to its designated purpose. Businesses should reinforce customer familiarity with the brand by repeating brand presence and strong connections between brand and related product categories.

Perceived quality refers to consumers' perceived superiority of a brand within the same product category. Perceived quality becomes an important contributor to the financial performance of a company, given that higher perceived quality means a higher price. However, the perceived brand quality of the market may be inconsistent with the actual quality for various reasons, including poor quality previously experienced, perceived quality originated from attributes that were not previously important, and imperfect consumer information processing. The accuracy of the perceived quality of customers does not matter but the customers' genuine feelings.

Brand associations or brand images are any brand-related links existing in memory, which exist in the consumers' mind and participate in the processing of information. Brand associations include links to various functional and emotional attributes, some of which represent key criteria for purchase decision. The traditional brand positioning view suggests that positioning should focus on one or several representative links to core purchase reasons. Nevertheless,

关键的是品牌联系应当是有力的、积极的和独特的。

Hsu、Oh 和 Assaf（2012）的研究指出，在酒店企业中，品牌资产还应包含管理信任及品牌可靠度。管理信任指的是消费者对品牌管理能力的感觉、信心以及依赖的意愿。在选择酒店品牌时，消费者对于品牌的管理风格的了解会影响其决策。品牌可靠度是指消费者对于品牌是否能够提供一致的、符合预期的服务的感知和信心，反映了品牌在不同时间场合提供一致的产品和服务的能力。一个可靠的品牌能够在任何时候、任何场合提供符合其品牌承诺及消费者预期的产品和服务，从而唤起消费者对品牌的信任及忠诚度。

由于品牌资产是一项有益的战略资源，并影响营销决策，市场营销人员需要了解：（1）品牌资产的来源及其如何影响企业的利益，这一点可以通过品牌审计进行测量；（2）这些资源和结果如何随时间变化，这一点可以使用品牌追踪进行衡量。品牌审计是一个基于消费者角度的评估程序，用以评估品牌的健康程度，发掘品牌资产的来源，并向企业提供如何提升或改变其品牌资产的建议。经常对品牌资产进行品牌审计有利于市场营销人员更负责、更积极主动地管理品牌。另一方面，品牌审计对于营销经理而言，在制定营销方案、选择营销组合变量和进行策略改变时，能提供非常有用的基础信息。品牌追踪则是有规律地不断从消费者的反馈中获取量化数据并进行解读，在一些关键维度为营销人员提供与品牌和营销活动相关的、持续的、基础的信息。品牌追踪是掌握消费者在何地购买、购买量多少、品牌价值在哪些方面被创造等信息的一种方式，帮助营销人员进行决策。

品牌资产和品牌表现的评估主要有四个阶段（Keller，2000）.

1. 企业与营销经理

营销项目及相关的企业运作需要从定量（量化因素，如营销费用）和定性（营销项目流程清晰、具一致性）两方面进行管理。

2. 消费者的思考与感受

个人消费者的性格、市场竞争和其他的环境因素都会影响消费者的感受。个人感受和他人感受都会影响消费者对品牌的思考。

strong, positive, and unique brand associations are essential.

Hsu, Oh, and Assaf (2012) emphasize that brand equity should also include management trust and brand reliability in hotel companies. Management trust refers to consumer's feelings, confidence, and willingness to rely on brand management ability. When choosing the hotel brand, consumers' understanding of the brand management style influences their decision making. Brand reliability refers to the perception and confidence of consumers whether the brand can provide consistent services in line with expectations, reflecting the brand's ability to provide consistent products and services at different times. A reliable brand can provide products and services matching its brand promise and consumer expectations at any time and any location, thus evoking consumers' brand trust and loyalty.

Given that a brand equity is a useful strategic resource and influences marketing decisions, marketers must understand: (1) the sources of brand equity and how they affect the interests of the business, which can be measured by brand audit and (2) the manner in which these resources and results change over time, which can be measured through brand tracking. Brand audit is a consumer-based assessment process assessing the health of a brand, identifying the sources of brand equity, and providing advice on how to enhance or change its brand equity. Frequent brand audits of brand assets assist marketers enhance their accountability and proactive attitude in managing the brand. Alternately, brand audit provides extremely useful basic information for marketing managers when developing marketing programs, selecting marketing mix variables, and making strategic changes. Brand tracking is a regular and constant feedback from consumers to obtain quantitative data, interpret, and provide marketers with continuous basic information related to marketing activities in some key dimensions. Brand tracking is a method of understanding where consumers are, how much they buy, and where brand values are being created, to help marketers make decisions.

The assessment of brand equity and brand performance has four main stages (Keller, 2000).

1. Business and marketing managers

Marketing projects and related business operations must be managed both quantitatively (quantitative factors, such as marketing expenses) and qualitatively (clear and consistent marketing project processes).

2. Consumers' thinking and feelings

Individual consumer's personality, market competition, and other environmental factors affect consumers' feelings. Personal feelings and feelings of others both affect consumers' thoughts of the brand.

3. 消费者的行为

消费者购买产品或服务影响企业的收入、市场份额和其他判断品牌成功的因素。另一方面,消费者其他的行为(如口碑)则对品牌未来的发展有着重要的影响。

4. 资本市场的反应

除了企业内部的财务表现,品牌同样可以通过企业股票价格和市场资本价值来进行评估。

7.4　品牌塑造策略

品牌塑造策略在旅游业中变得日益普遍和重要,各企业塑造品牌的形式也呈现出多样化的趋势。不仅企业可以品牌化,单个产品(如麦当劳的巨无霸)或单项服务(如迪士尼的快速通行证 FASTPASS)也可以品牌化。旅游业最常见的三种品牌塑造模式是品牌联合、多品牌策略和品牌延伸。

Interbrand 机构(2016)将品牌联合定义为两个或者两个以上消费者高度认可的品牌进行商业合作的一种方式,其中所有参与品牌的名字都被保留。它既可以指两个或多个不同主体的品牌间的联合,即品牌联合化,也可以是供应商为其下游产品中必需的原料、成分和部件建立品牌资产的成分品牌化。品牌联合化主要用于异业捆绑联盟,相互联合的品牌通常经营不同的业务,双方之间不存在竞争。例如可口可乐和九城运行的魔兽世界的联合促销模式,广州花园酒店行政楼层提供法国欧舒丹的护肤用品,银行的信用卡中心与航空公司、酒店或餐厅间的联合促销手段。

旅游线路的制定不仅包括游览的景区,还包括住宿、交通和饮食等部分。所以,很多旅行社与知名酒店、航空公司或餐厅联合,利用它们的名气提升线路质量和档次。例如,某些旅行社制定的"入港旅游豪华团"行程中,安排乘坐国泰航空的航班和半岛酒店的住宿。旅行社可以利用酒店、航空公司或餐厅的良好品牌形象来提升自己品牌的评价,提升本身的形象与知名度。总之,品牌联盟的优点在于形成交叉品牌信任度和认可度,促成品质认知的转移与品牌评价的提升。

3. Consumer behavior

Consumers' purchase of products or services affects companies' revenues，market share，and other factors determining the success of a brand. Alternately，other consumer behavior（such as WOM，Word of Mouth）significantly influences the future development of a brand.

4. Capital market reaction

Apart from the internal financial performance，a brand can be evaluated through corporate stock prices and market capital values.

7.4　Branding Strategies

Branding strategy has become increasingly popular and important in the tourism industry. The way in which companies shape their brands further shows a trend of diversification. Not only companies can be branded，individual products（such as McDonald's Big Mac）or individual services（such as Disney's FASTPASS）can also be branded. The three most common branding strategies in the tourism industry are co-branding，multi-branding，and brand extension.

Interbrand（2016）defines co-branding as a method of business collaborations between two or more highly recognized brands，with the names of all participating brands retained. This co-branding can refer to the combination of two or more different brands from different entities，namely，composite co-branding. It can also be ingredient co-branding in which suppliers establish brand equity for the necessary raw materials，components，and parts in their downstream products. Composite co-branding is mainly used for horizontal bundle alliance. Brands associated with each other operate different businesses；and no competition exists between each other. Examples are the joint promotion model of Coca-Cola and the World of Warcraft operated by The 9，the executive floor of Guangzhou Garden Hotel provides French L'Occitane skin care products，and the joint promotions between bank credit card center and airlines，hotels，or restaurants.

Tourism planning routes include the scenic areas as well as the accommodation，transportation，food and beverage，and other components. Therefore，many travel agencies collaborate with well-known hotels，airlines，or restaurants，to enhance the quality and grade of the route by utilizing their reputation. For example，some travel agencies develop the"luxury inbound tour group" itinerary，with Cathay Pacific flights and accommodation at the Peninsula hotel. Travel agencies can utilize the good brand image of hotels，airlines，or restaurants to enhance the evaluation of their own brands，images，and reputation. In short，a brand alliance advantageously forms cross-brand trust and recognition to promote the transfer of quality awareness and upgrade brand

多品牌策略指一个企业使用多个品牌，每一品牌面对的细分市场明确，相互之间一般不存在竞争。温德姆酒店集团拥有多个酒店品牌，不同的品牌代表着不同类型的酒店服务产品，包括豪华酒店温德姆至尊（Wyndham Grand）、全面服务酒店温德姆（Wyndham）、高中价套房酒店灏沣温德姆（Hawthorn Suites by Wyndham）、优质酒店爵怡温德姆（TRYP by Wyndham）、有限服务酒店蔚景温德姆（Wingate by Wyndham）、经济型酒店速 8（Super 8）等。华住酒店集团也是国内酒店集团实施多品牌策略的代表，旗下包括高端品牌禧玥、度假品牌漫心、中端品牌全季和星程、经济型品牌汉庭和海友客栈。多品牌策略主要被运用于经营业务比较多的大型企业。百胜餐饮集团是全球餐厅网络最大的餐饮集团，在全球 100 多个国家拥有超过 34000 家连锁餐厅和 85 万多名员工。其旗下包括肯德基、必胜客、塔可钟、A & W 及 Long John Silver's 五个世界著名餐饮品牌，分别在烹鸡、比萨、墨西哥风味食品及海鲜连锁餐饮领域名列全球第一。

对制成品而言，家族品牌就是同一公司的不同产品所使用的共同品牌。所谓产品线延伸（也即相关延伸）就是指用母品牌作为在原产品大类中针对新细分市场开发的新产品品牌。产品线延伸策略主要有三种模式：向上延伸、向下延伸和双向延伸。不管采取何种延伸模式，企业都是以本身的核心价值为主要依据的。随着单体酒店经济实力的增长和各项资源的积累，在资本逐利动机的驱动下，酒店集团的出现是一种必然现象。酒店集团的家族品牌一般表现为酒店集团的公司名称，如万豪酒店集团的万豪（Marriott）品牌和希尔顿酒店集团的希尔顿（Hilton）品牌。基于家族品牌的品牌线延伸策略越来越广泛地被酒店集团采用。运用家族品牌结构虽然可以用酒店集团悠久的历史、深刻的企业文化背景为酒店产品提供足够的信誉保证，然而随着集团业务向不同档次的细分市场扩展，单一的家族品牌往往难以与集团的多元化酒店产品兼容。尤其是原本在高档和豪华市场竞争的酒店集团在进入中低档酒店市场时使用公司品牌，很容易影响原有的良好形象，造成品牌认知的模糊。岭南酒店集团旗下拥有花园酒店、中国大酒店、东方宾馆等国内知名的五星级酒店，在进入经济型连锁酒店市场时，集团采用"岭南佳园"这一名称作为品牌。这一策略让消费者将"岭南佳园"这一品牌与岭南集团相联系，影响了岭南集团的品牌形象。

evaluation.

Multi-brand strategy refers to a business employing multiple brands; each brand clearly targets the market segments, and no competition typically exists between each other. Wyndham Hotel Group has a number of hotel brands. Different brands represent different types of hotel service products, including luxury hotels Wyndham Grand, full-service hotels Wyndham, mid to upscale suite hotels Hawthorn Suites by Wyndham, quality hotels TRYP by Wyndham, select service hotels Wingate by Wyndham, and economy hotels Super 8. Huazhu Hotels Group is also an example of domestic hotel groups implementing a multi-brand strategy, including high-end brand Joya Hotel, resort brand Manxin, midscale brands JI Hotel and Starway Hotel, as well as economy brands Hanting and Hi Inn. Large enterprises with many businesses adopt a multi-brand strategy. Yum Group is a food and beverage group with the largest global restaurant network, consisting of over 34,000 chain restaurants and over 850,000 employees in over 100 countries. This restaurant network has five world famous food and beverage brands, namely, KFC, Pizza Hut, Taco Bell, A&W, and Long John Silver's, which globally rank number one in their respective areas in chicken, pizza, Mexican cuisine, and seafood chains.

As for manufactures, a family brand is the single brand used for different products by the same company. The so-called product line extension (i.e., related extension) refers to the use of the parent brand as the new brand for the new product developed for new market segments within the original product category. The product line extension strategy has the following three main modes: up-market stretch, down-market stretch, and two-way stretch. Regardless of the adopted extension mode, companies are based on their own core values. The growth of economic strength and the accumulation of various resources for stand-alone hotels driven by the profit motive of capitals enable the inevitable emergence of hotel groups. The hotel group's family brand generally shows the name of the hotel group, such as the Marriott Hotel Group's Marriott brand and the Hilton Hotel Group's Hilton brand. Hotel groups increasingly make extensive use of the brand line extension strategy based on the family brand. Despite the sufficient credit guarantee expected when utilizing family brand structure from the long history of a hotel group and a profound corporate cultural background, gaining compatibility between a single family brand with the group's diversified hotel products is frequently difficult. In particular, when a hotel group originally competing in the high-end and luxury markets enter the middle and low rated hotel markets, utilizing the group's brand easily affects the original good image, consequently creating confusion in brand awareness. The Lingnan Hotel Group owns Garden Hotel, China Hotel, Dong Fang Hotel, and other well-known domestic five-star hotels. However, when entering the economy chain hotel market, the Group adopted "Lingnan Garden" as the name of the brand. This strategy allows consumers to associate the brand "Lingnan Garden" with the Lingnan Group, which affects Lingnan Group's brand image.

自 20 世纪 80 年代大量酒店品牌并购活动开始以来,酒店集团的品牌线延伸策略尤为突出。酒店集团常见的品牌延伸策略有:

(1) 使用完全不相关的独立品牌名称。如精品国际酒店集团(Choice Hotel)采用的就是独立品牌结构,旗下所有品牌毫无关联,包括住宿旅馆(Sleep Inn)、舒适旅馆(Comfort Inn & Comfort Suites)、质量旅馆(Quality Inns,Hotels & Suites)、号角酒店 (Clarion Hotels)、经济客栈 (Econo Lodge)、罗德威旅馆(Rodeway Inn)和长期套房酒店(Mainstay Suites)等。

(2) 在保持家族品牌名称的基础上加入新的名称元素,即"主品牌+亚品牌"结构。凯悦酒店集团的三个品牌柏悦酒店 (Park Hyatt Hotels)、君悦酒店(Grand Hyatt Hotels)和凯悦酒店(Hyatt Regency Hotels)就属此类。

(3) 采用"受托品牌"结构,即"独立品牌+ by + 授权品牌"的形式。例如,喜达屋酒店集团 (Starwood Hotels & Resorts Worldwide)的福朋喜来登品牌(Four Points by Sheraton)和万豪集团的万怡品牌 (Courtyard by Marriott)和万枫品牌(Fairfield Inn by Marriott)即是使用受托品牌的结构。

品牌化建立在对消费者需求及市场规则充分认识的基础上,因此一个在本地市场成功的成熟品牌在新兴市场进行扩张时通常会水土不服。基于对万豪酒店集团在中国的品牌扩张的研究,Wong 和 Wickham (2015)提出了一个包含了六个资源前因变量和五个能力前因变量的酒店品牌资产的拓展模型(见图 7 - 2)。

这六个资源前因变量是:

(1) 财务资本。财务资本能够让酒店集团开展关键的市场营销研究(例如如何确定在中国市场的定位)以及相关的能力建设,使得万豪能够一直达到其市场定位的目标,并不断发展。

(2) 内部关系。内部关系是指万豪集团内关键业务部门(如人力资源、财务、采购、市场销售、市场研究和物业开发等)能积极建立并维持相互之间的良好关系,这使得万豪能够获得主要管理人员的支持和贡献,从而实现其市场定位。

(3) 内部运营系统及项目。万豪能够对其内部的运营系统及项目建立完整的知识体系(如哪个业务部门管理哪个系统或项目),并协助相应的部门建立支持集团取得目标市场定位的知识和目标。

(4) 国际品牌声望。国际品牌声望能够让万豪借助自身已有的国际范围内的声誉,在国内不同等级的城市建立市场定位,并获得本地新兴细分市场的业务。

(5) 人力资本。中国酒店行业缺乏具有技能的人才,而人力资本让万豪

Considering that several hotel brand merger and acquisition（M&A）activities began from the 1980s, the hotel groups' brand line extension strategy has become particularly prominent. Hotel groups follow three common brand extension strategies.

（1）Utilizing a completely independent brand name. For example, the Choice Hotel adopts an independent brand structure with all its brands unrelated, including Sleep Inn, Comfort Inn and Comfort Suites, Quality Inns, Hotels and Suites, Clarion Hotels, Econo Lodge, Rodeway Inn, and Mainstay Suites.

（2）Maintaining the family brand name as the basis and adding a new element, that is, the "main brand + sub-brand" structure. Hyatt Hotels' three brands, namely, Park Hyatt Hotels, Grand Hyatt Hotels, and Hyatt Regency Hotels, are the examples.

（3）Employing "endorser brand" structure, that is, "independent brand + by + endorser brand." For example, Four Points by Sheraton of Starwood Hotels and Resorts Worldwide and Courtyard by Marriott and Fairfield Inn by Marriott of Marriott use an endorser brand structure.

Branding is based on a thorough understanding of consumer needs and market rules; thus, a well-established brand succeeding in the local market frequently fails when expanding in emerging markets. Using a study of Marriott's brand expansion in China as basis, Wong and Wickham（2015）present an extension model of hotel brand equity, including six antecedent resources categories and five antecedent capabilities（Figure 7 - 1）. These six antecedent resources categories are as follows：

（1）Financial capital：This category enables the hotel group to conduct key marketing research（e.g., how to position itself in the Chinese market）and related skills building to enable Marriott's consistent achievement of its market positioning goals and enduring progress.

（2）Internal relationships：This category refers to those key business units within the Marriott Group（e. g., human resources, finance, purchasing, marketing, market research, and property development）are actively involved in establishing and maintaining good relationships with each other, possibly enabling Marriott to gain the support and contribution of key management personnel in achieving its market positioning.

（3）Internal operating systems and programs：Marriott can build a complete knowledge system（e.g., which business unit manages which system or project）for its internal operating systems and projects and assist the corresponding departments in establishing knowledge and objectives on frameworks supporting the group to achieve the target market position.

（4）International brand reputation：This category enables Marriott to establish market positions in the different levels of cities in the country through its existing international prestige and gain access to the local emerging market segments.

（5）Human capital：China's hospitality industry lacks skilled labor, and human

能够在高度竞争的劳动市场具有强大的竞争力。

（6）本地利益相关者关系管理。万豪能够有效地为本地政府官员和关键的利益相关者带来利益，并建立可持续的关系，因为利益相关者对万豪在中国内地及香港地区的成功至关重要。

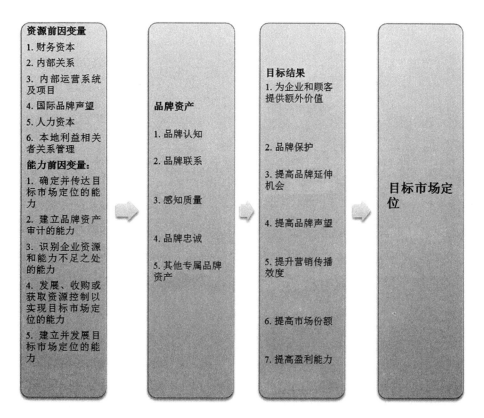

图 7-2　酒店品牌资产拓展模型

来源：Wong，T. & Wickham，M.（2015）. An examination of Marriott's entry into the Chinese hospitality industry：A Brand Equity perspective. *Tourism Management*，48，439-454.

另外五个能力前因变量是：

（1）确定并传达目标市场定位的能力。这种能力让万豪能够最有效地分配其财务资本，并从中国政府所规划的市场发展中识别最新的市场机会。

（2）建立品牌资产审计的能力。这种能力使万豪能够根据其自身资源和能力，有效地分配其财务资本进行内部市场研究。

（3）识别企业资源和能力不足之处的能力。万豪能够通过此能力识别不同的业务部门在争取和维持其目标市场定位时的作用。另外，这种能力让万豪能够识别其现有资源的不足之处，通过投入资金等必要的行动来克服缺点。

capital allows Marriott to be competitive in a highly competitive labor market.

(6) Domestic stakeholder relationship management: Marriott is able to effectively bring benefits and build sustainable relationships with local government officials and key stakeholders, considering the stakeholders' essential role on Marriott's success in the Mainland of China and Hong Kong.

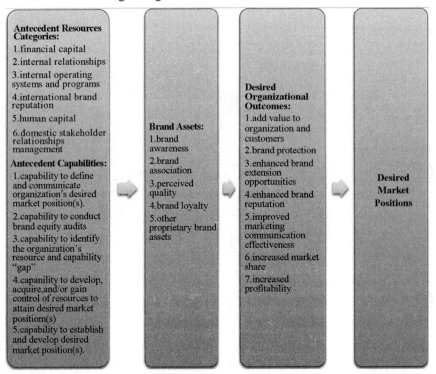

Antecedent Resources Categories:
1. financial capital
2. internal relationships
3. internal operating systems and programs
4. international brand reputation
5. human capital
6. domestic stakeholder relationships management

Antecedent Capabilities:
1. capability to define and communicate organization's desired market position(s).
2. capability to conduct brand equity audits
3. capability to identify the organization's resource and capability "gap"
4. capanility to develop, acquire,and/or gain control of resources to attain desired market positiom(s)
5. capability to establish and develop desired market position(s).

Brand Assets:
1. brand awareness
2. brand association
3. perceived quality
4. brand loyalty
5. other proprietary brand assets

Desired Organizational Outcomes:
1. add value to organization and customers
2. brand protection
3. enhanced brand extension opportunities
4. enhanced brand reputation
5. improved marketing communication effectiveness
6. increased market share
7. increased profitability

Desired Market Positions

Figure 7 – 2 An extended model of hotel brand equity

Source: Based on Wong, T. & Wickham, M. (2015). An examination of Marriott's entry into the Chinese hospitality industry: A Brand Equity perspective. *Tourism Management*, 48, 439 – 454.

The five antecedent capabilities are as follows:

(1) Capability to define and communicate organization's desired market positions: A capability allowing Marriott to allocate its financial capital most effectively and identify the latest market opportunities from the planned market development by the Chinese government.

(2) Capability to conduct brand equity audit. A capability allowing Marriott to allocate its financial capital effectively for internal market research based on its own resources and capabilities.

(3) Capability to identify the organization's resources and capabilities "gap": Marriott can use this capability to identify the role of different business units in achieving and maintaining its target market position. Moreover, this capability allows Marriott to identify the shortcomings of its existing resources and overcome the shortcomings through investment and other necessary actions.

（4）发展、收购或获取资源控制以实现目标市场定位的能力。这种能力使万豪能够高效地对业务部门进行资源的重新分配。

（5）建立并发展目标市场定位的能力。万豪能够通过这种能力为其品牌资产战略分配必要的财务资本，在不断变化及高度竞争的新兴市场中实现并维持其目标市场定位。

旅游业，特别是酒店业，是一个市场分割明显、竞争性大的行业。在这种竞争的环境中，品牌塑造成了一个树立差异化形象的主要手段，也成了建立消费者忠诚度的基础。因此，塑造品牌成了众多旅游企业经营的主要策略之一。品牌带来的经济效益是塑造品牌形象的主要动力，其在旅游服务业中的重要性更是明显。其中一个最可能的原因是旅游产品的无形性特点。不管是锦江、全聚德、国旅，还是国航、故宫，品牌都是识别它们与相似产品的主要标志，是将它们与相应的竞争对手区别的主要因素。任何一个旅游企业要想在市场上脱颖而出，体现出自身与他人的差异，鲜明的品牌形象是关键。

（4）Capability to develop, acquire, and/or gain control of resources to reach desired market positions: A capability enabling Marriott to efficiently re-distribute resources to business units.

（5）Capability to establish and develop desired market positions: Marriott can use this capability to allocate the necessary financial capital to its brand equity strategy to achieve and sustain its target market position in a changing and highly competitive emerging market.

The tourism industry, especially the hotel industry, is a highly segmented and highly competitive industry. In this competitive environment, branding becomes a primary method for differentiation and the basis for the establishment of consumer loyalty. Therefore, branding becomes one of the main strategies of many tourism businesses. The economic benefits brought by brands is the main force to drive branding. Its importance is apparent in the tourism industry. One of the most likely reasons is the intangible nature of tourism products. Whether it is Jinjiang, Quanjude, CTS, Air China, or the Palace Museum, brand is the main sign identifying them from similar products and the main factor distinguishing them from corresponding competitors. For any tourism companies to stand out in the market and to differentiate them from others, a distinctive brand image is the key.

第 8 章　产品开发及管理

本章要点

- 旅游产品的组成与分类
- 旅游包价产品
- 旅游产品的生命周期
- 旅游目的地的生命周期
- 新产品开发

产品和服务是任何一个旅游企业经营的关键。在市场竞争中，企业需要根据市场和竞争对手的变化，调整自身的定位和差异化战略，而这就涉及产品的开发和管理。体验经济时代，消费者消费观念和方式及其需求结构、内容、形式也发生了显著变化，这使得"体验创造价值"的经营理念成为旅游与酒店企业在涉及产品和开展经营活动时最重要的影响因素，而注重顾客的参与性、互动性以及个性化的情感需求成为体验经济下旅游产品的基本特征。本章探讨旅游产品的定义和组成，产品生命周期理论和旅游目的地生命周期理论，以及旅游产品的开发。

8.1　旅游产品的组成

8.1.1　产品的定义及分级结构

Kotler、Armstrong 和 Brown 等（1998）将产品定义为"能被投入某个市场并引起人们的专注、占有、使用或消费，从而可能满足某种欲望或需求的一切事物的总和。它包括有形物品、服务、人员、地点、组织和理念"。它既包括具有物质形态的产品实体，又包括非物质形态的服务。由于产品的最终目的

Chapter 8　Product Development and Management

 Key points of the chapter

- Components and classification of tourism products
- Package tour
- Tourism product life cycle
- Tourilm destination life cycle
- New product development

Products and services are the key to any travel business. To survive market competition, companies must adjust their positioning and differentiation strategies according to the changes in the market and competitors. These strategies involve product development and management. In the era of experience economy, consumers' consumption attitudes and patterns as well as the structure, content, and form of their demand have significantly changed, and, thus, the business philosophy of "experience creates value" becomes the most important influencing factor for tourism and hotel companies with regard to products and operating activities. The focus on customers' participation, interaction, and personalized emotional needs is the basic characteristic of tourism products under experience economy. This chapter discusses the definition and components of tourism products, product life cycle theory, and tourism destination life cycle theory, and tourism product development.

8.1　Components of Tourism Products

8.1.1　Definition of "product" and product hierarchy

Kotler, Armstrong, and Brown, et al. (1998) define a product as "anything that can be offered to a market for attention, acquisition, use or consumption that might satisfy a want or need. It includes objects, services, persons, places, organizations and ideas." It includes both the physical form of product entities and the non-material form of services. Many scholars classify a product according to the market demand that the product can meet, because the ultimate goal of the product is to satisfy the needs and wants of the market segmentation. Day, Shocker, and Srivastava (1979) suggest classifying products into

是为了满足细分市场的欲望和需求,许多学者根据产品所能满足的市场需求来对产品进行分类。Day、Shocker 和 Srivastava(1979)建议基于每项产品所满足的不同需求对产品进行层级分类。在同一个产品级中,每一项产品或可以满足一个具体的需求,或可以被其他产品替代。Kotler 和 Keller(2011)认为,构建产品分级系统要从消费者最基本的需求出发,根据需求的广度、深度和复杂度,以及可以满足需求的产品的丰富度来决定产品家族的分级数量。一个产品家族包含所有的可以满足同一个核心需求的产品类别,一个产品类别包含一组具有特定功能连贯性的产品。产品系列指一组功能接近的产品,而产品种类是指一组具有相同形态的产品。图 8-1 所示为六个层级的产品分级结构。

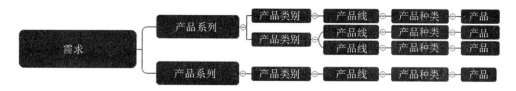

图 8-1　产品层级

来源:Kotler,P.& Keller,K. L.(2011). *Marketing Management*(14th ed.).
Upper Saddle River,NJ:Prentice Hall.

8.1.2　旅游业产品分类

与一般产品不同,旅游业中的"产品"需要采取全面化和综合化的观点,即 Middleton 和 Clarke(2001)所定义的"整体旅游产品"概念:"旅游产品是指一次旅游体验的周期,这个周期开始于旅游者离开长久居住地,直至他/她回到长久居住地为止。"联合国世界旅游组织(2008)把旅游产品定义为旅游者在目的地参与的所有活动,也即任何目的地的所有被旅游者使用的设施和参与的活动都属于旅游产品。因此旅游业中的"产品"是个综合性概念,它涵盖了有形机构、服务、招待、自由选择和顾客参与等多方面的元素。有形产品形成了所有旅游体验的核心,它可以是天然的(如瀑布、岩洞)或人造的(如主题公园);固定的(如酒店)或流动的(如飞机);持久的(如博物馆)或短暂的(如春节)。

在此"整体旅游产品"的综合性归纳之下,个体旅游企业的产品一般有更具体、更详细的产品构成。虽然旅游目的地提供一系列能满足旅游者欲望和需求的产品,但独立的旅游企业提供的产品更加具有针对性,如航空公司专于交通、酒店则专于住宿等。这些单独的企业建立各自的功能执行过程以适应各自对应的特殊市场区域。基于 Kotler 和 Keller 的产品层级框架,McKercher

hierarchies based on the different needs that each product satisfies. Any product within the same product class can meet a specific need or be replaced by other products. Kotler and Keller (2011) argue that building a product hierarchy should start from the most basic needs of consumers to determine the levels of a product family based on the breadth, depth, and complexity of needs as well as the richness of products that satisfy the needs. A product family encompasses all product classes that satisfy a single core need. A product class includes a set of products with specific functional coherence. A product line refers to a group of products with a similar function, and a product type refers to a group of products with one similar form. Figure 8 – 1 shows a six-level product hierarchy.

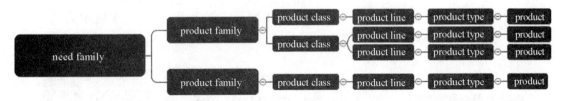

Figure 8 – 1　Product hierarchy

Source: Kotler, P. & Keller, K. L. (2011). *Marketing Management* (14th ed.). Upper Saddle River, NJ: Prentice Hall.

8.1.2　Classification of tourism products

Different from the general product, the definition of "product" in the tourism industry should adopt a comprehensive and integrated view, that is, the "overall tourism product" concept defined by Middleton and Clarke (2001). "As far as the tourist is concerned, the product covers the complete experience from the time he leaves home to the time he returns it." The United Nations World Tourism Organization (2008) defines tourism products as all activities in which a tourist participates at a destination, that is, all facilities used and activities participated by tourists at any destination are tourism products. Therefore, "product" in tourism is a comprehensive concept, consisting of various elements including the tangible institutions, services, hospitality, freedom of choice, and customer participation. Tangible products form the core of all travel experiences, which can be natural (e.g., waterfalls and caves) or man-made (e.g., theme parks); fixed (e.g., hotels) or mobile (e.g., aircraft); or longstanding (e.g., museums) or temporary (e.g., the Spring Festival).

Under the comprehensive concept of "overall tourism products," individual tourism companies have specific and detailed product compositions. Although destinations offer a range of products that meet the needs and wants of tourists, independent tourism companies offer products that are more relevant, for example, airlines are specific for transportation and hotels are for accommodation. These individual firms establish their own functional execution processes to suit their corresponding specific market areas. Using Kotler and

（2016）提出了旅游产品家族框架，包括 5 个需求家族，25 个产品家族，87 个产品类别。5 个需求家族分别是愉悦、意义追寻、个人学习发展、自然以及商务。图 8-2 所示为旅游产品分类图。

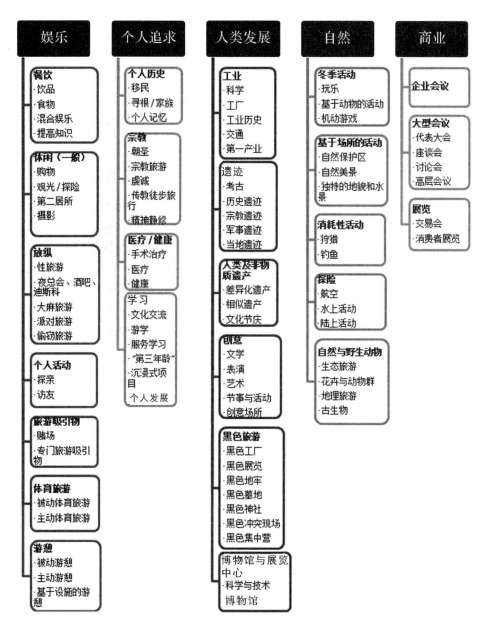

图 8-2 旅游产品分类图
来源：根据 McKercher，B. (2016). Towards a taxonomy of tourism products. *Tourism Management*，54，196-208.

Keller's product hierarchy framework as basis，McKercher（2016）proposes a framework for tourism product family，which includes 5 need families，25 product families，and 87 product categories. The five need families are pleasure，personal quest，human endeavor，nature，and business. Figure 8 – 2 shows a tourism product taxonomy.

Figure 8 – 2   A tourism product taxonomy

Source：McKercher，B.（2016）.Towards a taxonomy of tourism products. *Tourism Management*，54，196 – 208.

旅游产品也可根据其在旅游者消费全过程中起到的作用分成核心服务或利益、必需的便利服务和附加产品或称外延产品三部分。核心服务是旅游产品提供给顾客的最基本的价值和利益。酒店的核心服务是客房，旅游胜地的核心服务是景区景点，餐厅的核心服务则是食品和饮料。

便利服务是核心服务之外必须存在的服务项目，有了这些项目，旅游企业才能顺利运作。例如，酒店必须有前厅才能为客人办理入住，有客房部才能清洁客房，餐厅要有厨房才能准备餐点。这些都是为提供核心服务必须存在的服务项目。旅游企业也可凭借这些便利服务体现出自身特色。如区别于后台厨房的透明厨房、古典风格的大厅装饰或中国特色的宴会厅等。

附加产品或称外延产品是在顾客购买旅游产品时所获得的全部附加服务和利益的总和。它也是旅游企业用以实现产品差异化的重要手段。某些酒店提供的票务代理服务或是当地旅游陪同服务、航空公司提供的酒店预订服务或纪念品订购服务、餐厅的免费停车服务等都可能属于附加产品的内容。预订系统是酒店业内最强有力的辅助服务之一。预订服务的便捷、周到和准确对于区分它和其他的连锁酒店非常重要。但随着越来越多的酒店提供预订服务，这项服务也逐渐失去了特色。所以很多连锁酒店和餐厅提供的常客计划或常客俱乐部即成为附加产品内容之一。它主要通过对顾客的忠诚度管理来提供附加服务。

附加服务需要有形的辅助商品的维持。例如，会员卡是常客俱乐部的有形支撑，而预定或确认方面的信函则是预订系统必需的。总而言之，住宿、交通、食物等是常见的核心旅游产品，而这些核心产品又需要如前厅、客房之类的便利服务才能使之成功传递。附加产品如常客俱乐部积分或奖励是旅游产品营销的重要支撑，也是体现产品特色和个性的关键。

8.1.3　旅游包价产品

旅游者在出游过程中会把旅途中遇到的所有感受和体会都视为整体旅游活动中的组成部分。前往机场的出租车、飞机上的观景、酒店的迎接、床铺的舒适度、餐饮的口味和服务方式等均属于这项整体旅游产品的组成部分，

Tourism products can also be divided into three parts according to their roles in the whole process of tourists' consumption, that is, the core services or benefits, necessary facilitating services, and augmented products. Core services are the most basic value and benefits that tourism products provide to customers. The core service of a hotel is the guest room, the core service of a tourist destination is scenic spot attraction, and the core service of a restaurant is food and drink.

Facilitating services are those that must exist in addition to core services. Tourism companies can operate smoothly only with these services. For example, the hotel must have the front office for guests to check in and the housekeeping department to clean rooms, and restaurants must have a kitchen to prepare meals. These services are necessary to provide the core services. Tourism companies can also rely on these services to reflect their own features, such as a transparent kitchen different from the kitchen at the back of the house, classical-style hall decorations, or Chinese-style banquet hall.

The augmented products or services is the sum of all the additional services and benefits that customers receive when they purchase a travel product. It is also an important means for tourism companies to achieve product differentiation. Ticketing services or local tourist escort services offered by some hotels, hotel reservation services or souvenir bookings offered by airlines, and free parking at the restaurant may be part of the augmented product. The reservation system is one of the most powerful augmented services in the hospitality industry. The convenience, courteousness, and accuracy of booking services are important to distinguish one from other hotel chains. However, as a growing number of hotels offer reservation services, this service has gradually lost its specialty. Therefore, the loyalty program or frequent customer club offered by many hotel chains and restaurants become part of the augmented product. It provides additional services primarily through management of customer loyalty.

The augmented services require the maintenance of tangible facilitating product. For example, membership cards are the tangible support of frequent customer club, whereas booking or confirmation letters are required for the reservation system. Overall, accommodation, transportation, and food are common core tourism products, and the delivery of these core products requires facilitating services such as the front office and rooms. The augmented products (e.g., loyalty club points or incentives) are important support for tourism product marketing and key to reflect the product specialty and personality.

8.1.3 Tour package

Tourists treat all experiences and feelings during a trip as an integrated part of the overall travel activities during travel. The taxi to the airport, the view on the plane, the greeting of the hotel, the comfort of the bed, and the tastes and service style of the hotel all belong to the components of the overall tourism products, and eventually form the

并最终形成旅游者对此次旅行经历的总体印象。因此营销人员通常会把目的地或酒店提供的各种产品组合成一个可销售的"产品包",以便其足以满足对应的市场消费群体的欲望和需求,这种产品被称之为"旅游包价产品"。这种方法与零售市场上盛行的"产品捆绑销售"策略相似。

　　旅游包价产品是指旅游企业将一系列旅游产品和服务整合成一个以统包的价格出售的组合产品,其中,参与组合的各项单独产品和服务的成本不分开计算。项目策划是一种补充性的营销技术,它开发出各种特殊的活动和/或事件以增加旅游包价产品的价值并增加购买者的支出。度假包价产品在旅游销售额中占有很大比例。包价产品功能全面,购买方便,这也是其主要的吸引力之一。产品组合使得各种旅游服务提供商(如交通、住宿、餐饮、娱乐和零售商)通过协同方式获利,并因为能服务于更广泛的旅游消费群而形成规模经济效益。例如,团体旅游包价一般成为旅游目的地在旅游淡季吸引客人时常采用的批发销售形式。不同的旅游业务经营商之间相互合作以填充淡季闲置的容量。他们以较低价格形成包价旅游产品,吸引旅游者批量购买,从而解决淡季获利率低的问题。事实上,控制整个包价产品供应和分销的商业吸引力使得越来越多的旅游企业纵向联合(如 Thomson 旅游集团),以减少交易成本,促成较低价的产品投入、优先考虑首选目的地,并增强了协调性以及市场竞争力。例如,同程旅游网通过"包园"模式(即企业直接向旅游景点购买一定量的门票,再进行分销),与全国超过 300 个旅游景点进行合作,实现较低的产品成本,同时获得这些旅游景点的优先合作权。在获取了大量的上游供应商资源后,同程旅游网推出了"1 元门票"活动,将供应商资源转化为实际的市场竞争力。艾瑞咨询发布的《2015 年中国在线旅游度假行业研究报告》显示,同程旅游网占据中国在线旅游周边游市场份额的15.8%(艾瑞咨询,2015)。

　　商品销售全球化的持续增长导致消费者对消费的产品和服务有越来越多的选择。同样地,"需求跟随供应"的经营观念已经不再是旅游业经营的主导,相反,旅游企业现在需要首先识别旅游者的旅行体验需求,并据此开发供应和传递的高级技巧,并随着需求不断升级。包价旅游的发展性特征正好反映了这种趋势。Host(2004)列举了五种影响包价旅游产品发展的主要要素。

tourist's overall impression for this trip experience. Therefore, marketers usually combine a variety of products offered by destinations or hotels into a salable "product package," so that it is sufficient to satisfy the needs and wants of the corresponding market consumer groups. This kind of product is called a "tour package." This approach is similar to the "bundling" strategy prevalent in the retail market.

A tour package is a product package into which a tourism company combines a series of tourism products and services selling with a package price, where the cost of the individual products and services that are included in the bundle is not calculated separately. Programming is a supplementary marketing technique that develops a variety of special activities and/or events to increase the value of tour package products and increase the expenses of consumers. Holiday package products account for a large proportion of tourism sales. Package products have comprehensive functions and are easy to buy, which is one of its main attractiveness. The product combination enables various tourism service providers (e.g., transport, accommodation, food and beverage, entertainment, and retailers) to make profits with a synergy and to achieve economies of scale because of their ability to serve a wide range of tourism consumers. For example, a group travel package becomes a popular form of wholesale to attract customers during the off-season for tourist destinations. Different tourism operators cooperate with one another to fulfill the idle capacity during the off-season. They form tour packages with lower prices to attract tourists to make bulk purchase to solve the low-profit problem during the off-season. In fact, the commercial attractiveness of controlling the entire supply and distribution of tour package products makes the vertical integration of tourism companies (e.g., Thomson Travel Group) to reduce transaction costs, facilitate the input of lower-cost products, give entrance priority to preferred destinations, and enhance coordination and market competitiveness. For example, LY.com adopts a "block booking" model (that is, companies directly purchase a certain amount of tickets from tourist attractions, and then distribute) and cooperates with more than 300 tourist attractions to achieve lower product costs while obtaining a cooperative priority with these tourist attractions. With access to a large number of upstream supplier resources, LY.com introduces the "1 dollar tickets" activity, transforming the supplier resources into actual market competitiveness. The *2015 China Online Vacation Industry Report* from iResearch shows that LY.com occupies approximately 15.8% market share of the China online travel market (iResearch, 2015).

The continued increase in the globalization of merchandizing has led to increasing choices of products and services for consumers. Similarly, the idea of "demand following supply" is no longer the dominant principle in the operations of tourism companies. Instead, tourism companies now need to first identify tourists' needs for travel experiences and accordingly develop and constantly upgrade advanced skills in supply and delivery. The development characteristics of tour package reflect this trend. Host (2004)

（1）家庭。当今家庭时间明显缺乏。社会竞争激烈，日常生活倍受压力，家庭相聚的时间愈显宝贵。家庭出游为各成员均提供了有价值且优质的时间支配。

（2）体验。体验旅游是快速发展的旅游潮流之一。各种主题明确的、多层次的体验旅游模式鼓励旅游者通过积极参与体验旅游来获得乐趣，而不再是被动的观光者。例如，"到农民家里体验田园生活"的农家乐游，自驾车旅游以及登山、探险游等。

（3）技术和"人力元素"。网络已经成为人们搜索、挑选以及购买旅游包价产品的主要平台，如艾派迪和携程。这就对旅游企业如何在保持高水平服务的同时充分利用网络的优势提出了新的挑战。

（4）灵活性及个性化。识别旅游者的需求之后的下一步工作即是找出能适应这些需求的更广泛的解决方法。基于一个足够宽泛的活动选择菜单，旅游企业定制出能适应目标群体或个人的产品。这个过程涉及旅游企业间新的合作关系的形成以实现产品的灵活性和个性化。例如，游轮公司与其他交通企业合作以实现旅游者全线交通转移的便利，包括离开居住地、登上游轮、离开游轮直至回到原居住地。

（5）控制。安全问题是旅游者关注的主要问题。旅游者对旅游经历中安全控制的感知变得越来越重要。旅行策划者和/或旅游经营商的专业性可以在很大程度上减轻旅游者在旅行途中形成的安全方面的压力。

8.2　产品生命周期

Raymond Vernon 于 1966 年在其《产品周期中的国际投资与国际贸易》中首次提出产品生命周期（PLC）理论。该理论认为产品的生命周期是有限的，在不同的销售阶段，企业有不同的挑战、机遇和问题，因而产品的利润会出现相应的变化，需要有不同的营销、财务、制造、采购和人力资源战略对产品进行支持。在此基础上，产品的生命周期一般可分成四个阶段：引入期、成长期、成熟期和衰退期（如图 8 - 3 所示）。PLC 理论最先应用于时尚型产品，后亦被运用于旅游服务产品。

lists five key factors that influence the development of tour package products:

(1) Family. Family time is obviously lacking nowadays. With fierce social competition and daily life under great pressure, the family time together becomes more valuable. Family trips provide a valuable and high-quality discretionary time to all the family members.

(2) Experience. Experience tourism is one of the rapidly developing trends in tourism. Various experience tourism models with clear themes and multiple layers encourage visitors to experience the fun of travel through active participation instead of being a passive sightseer. For example, rural tourism to "experience the farm life at the farmers' homes," self-driving tourism, hiking, and adventure tours.

(3) Technology and "manmade element". The Internet has become the major platform where people search information for, select, and purchase tour package products, such as Expedia and Ctrip. This idea brings new challenges to tourism companies on how to make full use of the advantages of the Internet at the same time maintaining a high level of service.

(4) Flexibility and personalization. The next step after identifying the tourists' needs is to find broader solutions to accommodate those needs. Based on a sufficiently broad selection of activities, tourism companies can tailor the products to suit the needs of target groups or individuals. This process involves the formation of new partnerships between tourism companies to achieve product flexibility and personalization. For example, cruise lines work with other transportation companies to facilitate full-line transfers of travelers, including departure from their places of residence, boarding, departure from the cruise, and return to their original places of residence.

(5) Control. Safety issues are the main concerns of tourists. Tourists' perceptions of security control in travel experiences are becoming increasingly important. The professionalism of travel planners and/or tour operators can greatly reduce the pressure on travelers regarding security during trips.

8.2 *Product Life Cycle*

Raymond Vernon (1966) first propose the product life cycle (PLC) theory in his *International Investment and International Trade in the Product Cycle*. The theory suggests that the product life cycle is limited. At different stages of sales, companies have different challenges, opportunities, and problems; the product profits therefore experience corresponding changes, requiring different marketing, finance, manufacturing, procurement, and human resource strategies to support the product. Based on this, the product life cycle can normally be divided into four stages, namely, introduction, growth, maturity, and decline (Figure 8 – 3). PLC theory was first applied to fashion products and later in tourism service products.

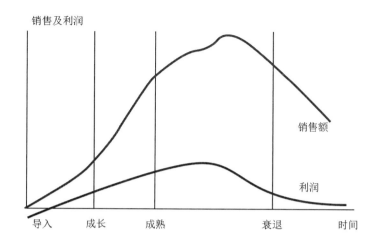

图 8-3　产品生命周期

来源：Kotler，P. & Keller，K. L.(2012). *Marketing Management*（14th ed.）. Upper Saddle River，NJ：Pearsom Prentice Hall.

　　当新产品刚导入时，只有一些爱冒险的创新者可能会尝试。由于产品刚刚被引入市场，销售增长缓慢。同时，大量的费用被用于市场推广。因此，产品在此阶段一般处于亏损或利润较低的状态。随着产品开始进入成长期，更多的人成为早期的接受者而尝试产品。因为销售额增加，产品的盈利状态持续改善。当大众市场开始使用，产品就进入了成熟期。此时，产品已经接触到大部分潜在消费者，因而销售增长缓慢。同时，由于市场竞争加剧，销售额增长率下降，竞争也容易导致营销成本增加，边际利润率逐渐减少。但随着越来越多的竞争者出现，当市场上的供过于求现象越来越明显，直至饱和甚至过度，产品会慢慢变成廉价物品直至消亡，即进入了衰退阶段。

　　产品生命周期可以应用于一个行业、一个概念、一个品牌、一个特定产品，或一个旅游目的地。如在美国，家庭自助餐厅的概念产生于 20 世纪 70 年代，然后流行，但到了 80 年代末期就逐渐消失了。很多没有随消费者偏好的改变而改变的餐厅也在自助餐厅业内消亡了。20 世纪末，高档咖啡馆作为一种新鲜事物出现在中国的一些大城市。现在，即便在小城镇，也有两三家咖啡馆服务于大众市场，由此表明，高档咖啡馆已处于成熟期。

　　对于处于不同产品生命周期不同阶段的企业，其产品选择战略各有不同。在产品导入阶段，企业需要决定何时将产品引入市场。成为市场的先行

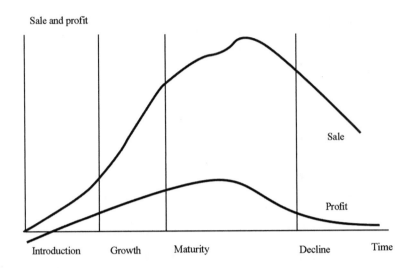

Figure 8 - 3　Product life cycle

Source: Kotler, P. &, Keller, K.L. (2012). *Marketing Management* (14th ed.). Upper Saddle River, NJ: Pearsom Prentice Hall.

When a new product is introduced, only some adventurous innovators may try. As the product is just introduced to the market, sales growth is slow. At the same time, a large amount of expenses is used for marketing. Therefore, at this stage, the product is generally at a status of loss or low profit. As the product turns into the growth stage, more people become early adopters and try out the product. The product profitability continues to improve because of the increase in sales. When the mass market begins to use it, the product enters the maturity stage. At this point, the product is exposed to the most potential consumers, so sales growth is slow. At the same time, with increased market competition, decline of sales growth rate, and increased marketing costs easily brought by competition, marginal profit level gradually reduces. However, with many competitors, when market oversupply becomes very obvious, until saturation or even excessiveness, the product gradually becomes cheap goods until it disappears, that is, enters the declining stage.

The product life cycle can be applied to an industry, a concept, a brand, a specific product, or a tourist destination. In the United States, the concept of family cafeteria originated in the 1970s and then became popular, but by the end of the 1980s it gradually disappeared. Many restaurants that did not change with the change in consumer preferences also died in the cafeteria industry. At the end of the 20th century, premium cafe as a new thing appeared in some of China's major cities. Nowadays, even in small towns, two or three cafes are serving the mass market, which shows that premium cafe is already at the maturity stage.

For different companies at different stages of the product life cycle, their product selection strategies are different. At the product introduction stage, companies need to

者能够获得巨大的优势，这些优势主要来自于消费者对先行者品牌的记忆、先行企业率先从市场需求中获取信息、消费者在选择上的惯性以及先行者的营销信息传播。但这些优势同时伴随着高风险和高花费。如果企业选择成为市场的跟随者，可以带来更好的技术、产品质量或者品牌优势，同样有益于企业的成长。

在市场成长阶段，新的消费者开始购买企业的产品，销售额增长速度很快。同时，新的竞争对手会进入市场，推广自身的产品，并扩大分销渠道。在价格方面，产品的价格与引入阶段大致一样或稍有下降。企业会继续保持较高水平的营销推广花费，以应对市场竞争并继续对市场进行教育。在此阶段，由于销售量增长速度超过市场推广花费的增长，同时单位产品的制造成本快速下降，利润获得增长。但是，企业需要关注市场增长速度的变化，以应对产品生命周期阶段的变化。企业在市场成长阶段会面临是选择市场份额还是选择高额利润的问题。企业可以通过在提高产品质量、推广和分销渠道等方面提高花费而获得市场份额上的主导地位，这种做法放弃了现阶段的利润，而寄希望于下一阶段更高的利润。

在市场成熟阶段，销售增长速度变得缓慢，产品的特性和市场接受程度也进入相对成熟的阶段。这一阶段的持续时间比导入阶段和成长阶段要长，对于市场营销经理来说也有更多的挑战。市场成熟阶段可以进一步细分为三个阶段。第一是细分增长阶段，销售增长率开始下降，缺乏新的销售渠道，并出现新的竞争对手；第二是细分平缓阶段，市场趋于饱和，人均销售增长率变得平缓，大部分的潜在消费者已经尝试使用过产品，转变为实际消费者，未来的销售来源主要是人口增长和替代需求；第三是细分衰退阶段，绝对销售额开始下降，消费者转向市场上的其他产品。细分衰退阶段是产品进入成熟周期后竞争最为激烈的阶段。销售下降导致行业产能过剩，进而引发更为激烈的竞争，例如争夺利基市场、价格战、提高宣传及研发费用等。最终，市场上会出现具有主导地位的企业，通过获取或保持市场份额，以保持企业自身可持续的竞争优势。对于大部分企业而言，他们可以选择成为这些具有主导地位的企业，通过大量的销售和较低的成本来获得利润；又或是实行利基市场战略，以较低的销售量获取高额的利润。

decide when to introduce the product into the market. The market forerunner can get huge advantages. These advantages are mainly from the consumers' memory of the pioneer brand. The market forerunners at the earliest obtain information from the market demand, such as desired product attributes or characteristics, consumer inertia, and pioneer marketing information communications. However, these advantages are accompanied with high risk and high cost at the same time. If companies choose to become market followers, then they can acquire better technology, product quality, or brand advantages, which are beneficial to company growth.

At the market growth stage, new consumers begin to buy the product and sales grow rapidly. At the same time, new competitors enter the market, promoting their products and expanding distribution channels. In terms of price, the price of the product is about the same or slightly lower than at the introduction stage. Companies continue to maintain a high level of marketing expenses in response to market competition and continue to educate the market. At this stage, because the rate of growth for sales is more than the cost of marketing whereas the unit product cost rapidly decreases, profit grows. However, companies need to focus on changes in market growth rate in response to changes in the product life cycle stage. At the market growth stage, companies face the choice of market share or high profits. Companies can gain market dominance by increasing costs to improve product quality, promotion, and distribution channels. These variables discourage profits at the current stage and hopes for higher profits at the next stage.

At the maturity stage, sales growth becomes slow. The product characteristics and market acceptance also enter a relatively mature stage. This stage is longer than the introduction and growth stages and is more challenging for marketing managers. The maturity stage can be further divided into three sub-stages. The first is the growth maturity sub-stage, when the sales growth rate begins to decline, with the lack of new sales channels and the emergence of new competitors. The second is the stable maturity sub-stage, when the market tends to saturation; sales growth rate per capita becomes flat; most potential consumers have tried to use the product, transforming into actual consumers; and the sources of future sales are mainly from population growth and alternative needs. The third is the declining maturity sub-stage, when absolute sales begin to decline and consumers turn to other products in the market. Declining maturity sub-stage is the most competitive stage after the product enters maturity.Decline in sales lead to oversupply in the industry, resulting in more intense competition, such as competition for niche markets, price wars, and increased promotion and R&D expenses. Ultimately, a dominant company emerges in the market through acquiring or retaining the market share to maintain their own sustainable competitive advantage. For most businesses, they can choose to become the dominant player in the business, by making profits through large sales and lower costs or by pursuing a niche marketing strategy to capture high profits at lower sales volumes.

在市场成熟阶段，有三种方式可以帮助企业对品牌的发展方向进行改变，从而提高销售额和利润。第一是市场调整，企业可以尝试扩大成熟产品的市场规模来提高销售量，而销售量的提升来自于品牌使用者的数量和使用频率。企业可以通过将非使用者转化为使用者，开拓新的细分市场，或是吸引竞争对手的市场来提高销售量，以及通过鼓励消费者在不同情境下使用产品，在同一情境下消费更多的产品，或者鼓励消费者创造性地使用产品来提高使用频率。例如，众多国际知名酒店集团不断开拓中国以及东南亚市场就是市场调整策略的体现。朗廷酒店集团 CEO 罗伯特·沃曼（Robert A. Warman）表示，朗廷酒店集团未来将重点发展中国的二、三线城市。

第二种方式是产品调整，可以通过质量提升、特征提升或是风格改进来实现。产品调整可以集中在三个方面：（1）质量提升——提高产品性能；（2）特征提升——在规格、重量、材料、配件等方面加入新的特征，从而提升产品在用途、安全和便捷等方面的表现；（3）风格改进——提高产品的美观程度。当产品生命周期概念应用于单个品牌时，情况完全不同。餐厅经历消费者的接受周期，但是像麦当劳、汉堡王和必胜客等持久品牌带来的经验阻止了品牌的衰落。当销售额开始下降时，公司应该重新审视他们的产品和概念，通过增添新元素或者引入新产品，或者两者同时进行来彻底改造。喜达屋酒店及度假村集团在 2015 年 8 月对原有品牌喜来登（Sheraton）进行升级，推出喜来登大酒店（Sheraton Grand）。喜来登大酒店与原有喜来登品牌相比，有更优质的服务、更精致高雅的客房设计、更高端的酒店配套设施等要素。

第三种方式是营销项目调整，通过调整营销组合中的一个或多个元素，实现提升销售的目的，例如价格、分销渠道、广告宣传、产品推广、人员配备、服务等。收益管理是酒店行业中调整营销项目的体现，酒店通过优化产品价格、分销渠道、细分市场等要素，实现收益和利润的最大化。

大部分企业并没有为处于衰退周期的产品设立合适的战略。对于企业而言，处于衰退周期的产品存在高昂的潜在成本，如时间成本、决策成本、品牌形象成本等。因此，企业应该识别并及时处理处于衰退周期的产品。在识别处于衰退周期的产品方面，企业可以通过设立一套识别系统来发现此类产品，如产品委员会（Kotler，1965）。其次，企业需要了解市场的退出壁垒，较

At the maturity stage, three ways help companies to change the direction of brand development to increase sales and profits. The first is market modification. Companies can try to expand the market size of mature products to increase sales, whereas sales increase from the number of brand users and the frequency of use. Businesses can increase sales by turning non-users into users, opening up new segments, or attracting competitors' markets; by encouraging consumers to use the product in different contexts and to use more products in the same context; or by encouraging consumers to use the product creatively to increase the frequency of use. For example, many renowned international hotel groups continue to explore China and Southeast Asia markets, which is an example of market adjustment strategies. Robert A. Warman, CEO of The Langham Hotels and Resorts, said that the Langham Hospitality Group will focus on the development of China's second- and third-tier cities in the future.

The second way is product modification, which can be achieved through quality improvement, feature enhancement, or style improvement. Product modification can be concentrated in three areas: (1) quality improvement to improve product performance; (2) feature enhancement to add new features in specifications, weight, materials, or accessories to enhance product use, safety, convenience, and other aspects of performance; and (3) style improvement to improve the aesthetic level of the product. When the concept of product life cycle is applied to a single brand, the context is completely different. The restaurant experiences consumers' acceptance cycle, but the experiences brought by McDonald's, Burger King, Pizza Hut, and other enduring brands prevent the brand from declining. When sales begin to decrease, companies should re-evaluate their products and concepts and completely reinvent by adding new elements or introducing new products, or both. In August 2015, Starwood Hotels and Resorts upgraded the original Sheraton brand and introduced the Sheraton Grand. Compared to the original Sheraton brand, Sheraton Grand consists of new elements such as better services, more exquisite and elegant room design, and higher-end supporting facilities.

The third way is marketing mix modification. It achieves the purpose of increased sales by adjusting one or more elements in the marketing mix, such as price, distribution channel, advertising, product promotion, staffing, and services. Revenue management is an example of marketing mix modification in the hotel industry. Hotels achieve maximum revenues and profits by optimizing product prices, distribution channels, market segments, and other elements.

Most companies do not have the right strategy for products at the declining stage. For businesses, products at the declining stage have high-potential costs, such as time, decision, and brand image. Therefore, companies should identify and timely handle products at the declining stage. For identifying products at the declining stage, companies can set up a set of systems to identify such products, for example, the Product Committee (Kotler, 1965). Then, companies need to understand the market barriers to exit. Lower

低的退出壁垒有利于企业退出市场,或吸引其他已退出市场企业的消费者(Harrigan,1980)。在选择合适的战略前,企业需要对行业吸引力及行业内自身竞争力进行评估。收割和剥离是企业和产品退出市场的方法之一。一般而言,企业采取收割和剥离战略时,会在保持销售额的情况下,逐步降低产品或业务的成本。首先减少的是研发成本,其次是设备。随后,企业会开始降低产品的质量,缩减销售人员的规模以及减少广告宣传费用。如果产品依然有强大的分销渠道或良好的品牌声誉,企业可以将之剥离,向其他企业销售此产品或品牌。

8.3　旅游目的地生命周期

基于产品生命周期概念,Butler(1980)提出了与之对等的旅游目的地生命周期理论,即"旅游地生命周期演化模型",并受到广泛的关注和应用。虽然该模型随后被冠之以"旅游区生命周期""度假地生命周期"和"巴特勒时序"等不同名称,但文献里最广泛采用的还是"旅游目的地生命周期"。在此,我们即采用此术语。

旅游目的地生命周期概念为目的地的不同发展阶段的营销和管理提供了一个基本框架。随着旅游目的地的不断演化,其所存在的环境性因素也相应产生不同的变量。目的地管理者应运用营销和管理技巧将目的地所处环境中的这些政治、经济、社会/文化和技术硬件变量有效结合,开展营销。根据 Butler,旅游目的地的演化要经过探索阶段、参与阶段、发展阶段、巩固阶段、停滞阶段、衰落或复苏阶段 6 个阶段(如图 8-4 所示)。

(1)探索阶段:只有数量有限的探险型游客,且分布零散;对当地的自然或文化感兴趣,与当地居民接触频繁。旅游目的地的自然和社会经济环境受旅游的影响甚微。

(2)参与阶段:旅游者的人数逐渐增多,吸引当地居民开始向旅游者提供一些简易设施。旅游者与当地居民的接触依旧频繁。旅游旺季逐渐形成,广告也开始出现。某种程度上改变了当地的社会生活并对当地的基础设施造成部分压力。

(3)发展阶段:旅游者人数迅速上涨,与当地的长住居民人数相比有过之而无不及。吸引众多外来投资和外来企业提供设施设备。交通和基础设

exit barriers can help companies exit the market or attract other consumers from companies that have already left the market (Harrigan, 1980). Before choosing the right strategy, companies need to assess the attractiveness of the industry and their own competitiveness within the industry. Harvest and divestment are one of the ways in which companies and products exit the market. In general, when harvest and divestment strategies are in place, companies gradually reduce the cost of their products or business operations while maintaining the sales. The first is to reduce R&D costs, followed by equipment. Subsequently, companies begin to reduce the product quality, the size of the sales staff, and advertising costs. If the product continues to exhibit a strong distribution channel or a good brand reputation, then companies can divest it and sell the product or brand to other companies.

8.3 *Tourism Destination Life Cycle*

Based on the concept of product life cycle, Butler (1980) suggests the equivalent tourism destination life cycle theory, namely "a tourist area cycle of evolution," which is widely concerned and applied. Although the model was later called "tourist area life cycle" "resort life cycle" "Butler Sequence" and other different names, the one most widely used in the literature is "tourism destination life cycle." This term is used here.

The tourism destination life cycle provides a basic framework for the marketing and management of the destinations at different stages. With the continuous evolution of a tourism destination, the environmental factors where it exists also produce different variables accordingly. Destination managers should use marketing and management techniques to effectively combine these political, economic, social/cultural, and technological hardware variables in the destination's environment for marketing. According to Butler, the evolution of a tourist destination passes through six stages (Figure 8 - 4): exploration, involvement, development, consolidation, stagnation, decline, and rejuvenation.

(1) Exploration: Only a limited number of adventurous tourists, with fragmented distribution, have interest in local nature or culture and frequent contact with local residents. This stage has little impact on the natural and socio-economic environment of the tourist destination.

(2) Involvement: The number of tourists gradually increases, attracting local residents to start providing some simple facilities to tourists. The contact between tourists and local residents is still frequent. Tourism season gradually forms, and advertising begins to appear. It changes the local social life to some extent and brings some pressure to local infrastructure.

(3) Development: The number of tourists rises rapidly and may be equal to or even larger than the number of local residents. It attracts a large number of outside investment and companies to provide facilities and equipment. Transportation and infrastructure

施等有了极大的改善,广告推广力度也大大增强。当地管理部门失去控制能力,开始推广人造景点。

（4）巩固阶段：目的地经济发展与旅游业息息相关。游客增长率已经下降,但总游客量将继续增加并超过长住居民数量。为了扩大市场范围,延长旅游季节,吸引更多的远距离游客,广告营销的范围进一步扩大。当地居民对旅游者的到来已产生反感。以前的设施降为二级设施,已不再是人们向往的地方。

（5）停滞阶段：旅游环境容量已达到或超过最大限度,导致许多经济、社会和环境问题的产生。游客数量达到最大,使得旅游市场在很大程度上依赖于重游游客、会议游客等。自然或文化景点被人造景观所取代,接待设施出现过剩。

（6）衰落（曲线 E）或复苏（曲线 A）阶段：如图 8 - 4 所示,在衰落阶段,旅游者被新的目的地所吸引,只留下一些周末度假游客或不留宿的游客。大批旅游设施被其他设施所取代,房地产转卖程度相当高。这一时期本地居民介入旅游业的程度又恢复增长,他们以相当低的价格去购买旅游设施。此时原来的旅游目的地或成为所谓的"旅游贫瘠地"或完全与旅游脱节。另一种可能是旅游目的地在停滞阶段之后进入复苏期。这有两种途径：一是改造旅游吸引物或开发出新的旅游产品；二是通过营销沟通活动开发出新的旅游者市场。

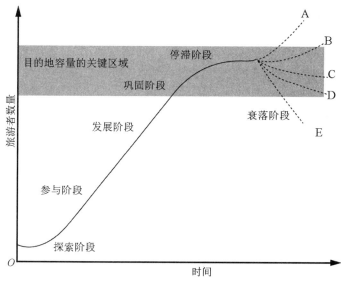

图 8 - 4　Butler 旅游目的地生命周期模型

资料来源：Butler，R. W. (1980). The concept of a tourist area cycle of evolution：implications for management of resources. *Canadian Geographer*，24(1)，5 - 12.

have been greatly improved. Advertising and promotion efforts have greatly enhanced. The local authorities lose control and start promoting man-made attractions.

(4) Consolidation: The economic development of the destination and tourism is closely related. Visitor growth has declined, but the total number of tourists continues to increase and exceeds the number of local residents. Advertising and marketing further increase to expand market coverage, extend the tourism season, and attract more long-distance visitors. The local residents feel discomfort with the arrival of tourists. Previous facilities are downgraded to secondary facilities and no longer a desirable destination.

(5) Stagnation: The tourism environment capacity has reached or exceeded the maximum, resulting in many economic, social, and environmental problems. The number of tourists reaches the highest, making the tourism market to reply on re-visitors and conference visitors to a large extent. Natural or cultural attractions are replaced by man-made landscapes, and the reception facilities are oversupplied.

(6) Decline (curve E) or Rejuvenation (curve A): As shown in finure 8 – 4, during the decline stage, tourists are attracted to a new destination, leaving only weekend visitors or non-stay tourists. A large number of tourist facilities have been replaced by other facilities. Real estate resale is at a very high level. During this period, the involvement of local residents in the tourism industry has resumed growth. They purchase tourist facilities at a very low price. The past tourist destination may become a so-called "tourism slum" or be completely out of touch with tourism. Another possibility may be that the tourist destination enters the rejuvenation stage after the stagnation stage in two ways: one is the renovation of tourism attractions or development of new tourism products and another is the development of a new tourist market through marketing communication activities.

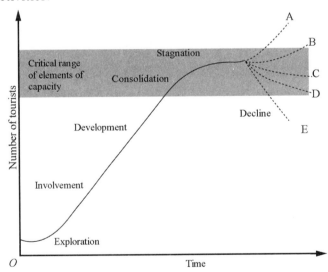

Figure 8 – 4   Butler tourism destination life cycle mode

Source: Butler, R. W. (1980). The concept of a tourist area cycle of evolution: implications for management of resources. *Canadian Geographer*, 24 (1), 5 – 12.

旅游目的地在生命周期后期还可能出现其他现象：图 8 - 4 中曲线 B 代表继续增长，但增长幅度减缓；曲线 C 指经过最初的调节性下降，回复到更稳定的游客量水平；而曲线 D 表示市场以缓慢速度下滑。

与其他理论化模型一样，Butler 的旅游目的地生命周期模型是基于一个理想化的经营环境之上的。这既是该模型的一个优点也是一项缺陷。说是缺陷是因为目的地的环境实际上是不断变化着的，任何一个目的地的经营都不会处于一种完全稳定的经营状况中。但它的优势则体现在，该模型为目的地的实际生活阶段提供了衡量和比较依据。Butler 模型建立于一系列的假定条件之上。首先，所有目的地仅朝一个方向发展。其次，模型中并不考虑政治、经济、社会和技术环境因素的影响。第三，模型是立足于南美和欧洲旅游环境开发出来，然而随后世界其他地区如亚洲和中东的旅游和酒店业以日渐上升的速度迅猛发展。实际上，我们认识到旅游目的地的发展并非一定是个单向直线型过程，有时候两个阶段向前发展，但紧跟着一个阶段倒退。同样地，除了地理环境可能影响模型的实际解释和应用之外，其他环境因素如政治、经济、文化和技术等方面的影响也是必需的考虑因素（Harrison，1995）。已经有很多目的地对该模型进行了实质性验证，其中包括云南的民族文化旅游（Dong、Morais 和 Dowler，2003）。

8.4　新产品开发

在竞争越来越激烈的市场环境下，企业应该围绕核心产品提供额外的有形（设计、包装）或无形（礼貌、高效的服务）的特征或利益，以创造出能满足市场的产品。Kotler 和 Keller（2009）认为，在产品开发中，企业需要明确了解消费者感知价值在不同层面的诉求，发掘消费者感知价值，进而对产品进行分类，以明确产品所需要具备的特征。

Kotler 和 Keller（2009）认为产品存在五个不同的层级，而消费者对于不同层级的产品的感知价值也存在差异。核心价值是指消费者购买产品所获得的价值；基本价值是指由核心价值转化而来的最基本的产品；期望价值是指消费者在购买产品时所期望获得的一系列价值，在添加这些价值后，基本

The tourism destination at the end of the life cycle may also face other possibilities: Curve B shows a continued growth but with a lowering growth rate. Curve C indicates that the market returns to a more stable level of visitors after the initial adjusted decrease. Curve D represents a market downturn with a slow rate.

Similar to other theoretical models, Butler's travel destination life cycle model is based on an ideal operating environment. This is one of the advantages and also one of the disadvantages for the model. It is a disadvantage because the destination environment is actually constantly changing. Any destination cannot be under completely stable operating conditions. However, its advantage is that the model provides a measurable and comparative basis for the real-life stages of destinations. The Butler model is based on a set of assumptions. First, all destinations are moving toward one direction only. Second, the model doesn't consider the influence of other factors, such as political, economic, social, and technological environment. Third, the model was developed based on the tourism environment in South America and Europe. However, tourism and hospitality in the rest of the world, such as Asia and the Middle East, later develop rapidly at an ever-increasing rate. The development of tourist destinations is regarded as not necessarily a one-way linear process and that it sometimes has two stages of development but followed by a stage backward. Similarly, other environmental factors such as political, economic, cultural, and technological influences are necessary considerations in addition to the influence of geographical conditions on the actual interpretation and application of the model (Harrison, 1995). A number of destinations have empirically validated the model, including Yunnan's ethnic cultural tourism (Dong, Morais & Dowler, 2003).

8.4 New Product Development

In an increasingly competitive marketplace, companies should provide additional tangible (design and packaging) or intangible (courteous and efficient service) features or benefits surrounding the core products to create products that meet the market demand. Kotler and Keller (2009) argue that in product development, companies need to clearly understand the appeals of customer perceived value at different levels, to explore customer perceived value, and then classify the products, and to clearly understand the required characteristics for products.

Kotler and Keller (2009) argue that five different levels of products and differences are present in customer perceived value at different levels of products. The core value refers to the benefit that the consumer obtains from buying the product. The basic value is the most basic product converted from the core value. The expected value is a series of value that the consumer expects to obtain when purchasing the product. After adding the value, the basic product is transformed into an expected product. The added value is the value that the consumer receives beyond the expected value after purchasing the product. The potential value is a combination of all additional items beyond the consumer's

产品将会转化为期望产品;附加价值是指消费者在购买产品后,获得的超出期望的价值;潜在价值是组合所有超出消费者期望的附加项目,能够进一步满足消费者需求,并使企业或产品在市场竞争中脱颖而出的价值。当市场上的产品都具有额外满足消费者需求的特征时,市场竞争会更为激烈,同时也要求企业进行产品差异化。在这种情况下,市场营销人员需要了解产品使用者的消费模式,也即终端消费者是如何获取和使用具有感知价值的产品的。除此以外,市场营销人员要测量每种不同的附加项目及其潜在利益是如何影响生产成本的。随着消费者不断提高自身对产品花费的感知价值期望,附加项目及其潜在价值会逐渐成为消费者在购买产品时的参考标杆。

　　旅游新产品的开发是与市场调研、可行性分析相结合进行的。市场调研工作是研究和分析顾客的基础,是准确识别顾客在享受服务或想要服务的过程中所遇"问题"的关键。Urban 和 Hauser(1993)指出,产品开发是从理解个体消费者的具体要求到鉴定与这些要求相关的产品属性的有序过程。这些独特且突出的产品属性代表产品的竞争优势,一旦被识别,它们就可以作为塑造品牌和定位的基础。正如目的地生命周期模型所示,新产品具有转型作用,能够使某个组织或目的地复苏。开发新产品是一个过程,其中涉及人的参与。我们应该特别注意到,这里的"产品"既包括有形产品,也包括服务。开发新产品一般包括以下几个步骤(如图 8-5 所示)。

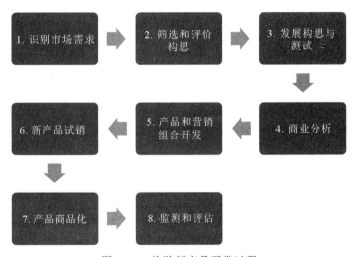

图 8-5　旅游新产品开发过程

1. 识别市场需求

有创意的构思产生于对不断变化的市场需求的反应。对市场上供需状

expectation to further satisfy the consumer's needs and for the company or the product to stand out in market competition. When the products in the market all have additional features to meet consumer demand, the market competition intensifies and requires product differentiation for companies. In this case, the marketers need to understand the consumption patterns of the product users, that is, how the end consumers obtain and use products with perceived value. In addition, marketers should measure how each of the various additional items and their potential benefits affect production costs. As consumers continue to increase their expectation on the perceived value of the product costs, additional items and their potential value gradually become consumers' benchmark reference when purchasing products.

The development of new tourism products is combined with market research and feasibility analysis. Market research is the base for research and analysis of customers, which is key to accurately identify "problems" that customers may encounter in the state of enjoying services or wanting services. Urban and Hauser (1993) point out that product development is a systematic process from understanding individual consumers' specific requirements to identifying product attributes that are relevant to these requirements. These unique and prominent product attributes represent the competitive advantage of the product. Once identified, they can be used as the basis to shape the brand and positioning. As the destination life cycle model shows, new product has a transformational effect that enables the recovery of an organization or destination. The development of new products is a process that involves human participation. In particular, the "product" here includes both tangible products and services. The development of new products generally includes the following steps (Figure 8 - 5).

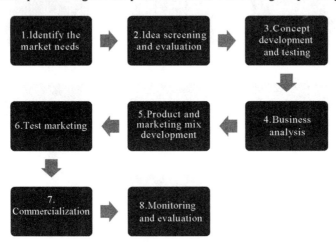

Figure 8 - 5   Development process of new tourism products

1. Identify the market needs

Creative ideas arise from the responses to changing market needs. A comprehensive

况差距的全面理解尤为关键,企业有可能从这些差距中找出新的竞争优势,发现新的机遇。尤其要注意的是,识别需求是以市场为导向的,因为任何有关新产品开发的构思只有得到顾客的认可才能发挥作用。

2. 筛选和评价构思

经过上一阶段收集到的关于新产品的构思并非都是可行的。企业需要对所有的构思进行详细、周密的分析判断。考虑的因素有:企业资源的总体评价、组织的发展规划和目标、财务可行性分析、竞争状况和环境因素分析等。通过评估找出符合企业自身资源和发展战略,能强化企业营销组合的价值和潜力的构思,放弃那些不可行的构思,以免造成时间和成本的浪费。

3. 发展构思与测试

通过筛选,企业确定最具潜力的构思并对其进行检测。此阶段的主导原则是"顾客定义产品"。市场调研信息应被充分利用以识别现有产品和顾客需求之间的差距,因为新产品正是以这些差距为主要依据的。产品的详细情况,如产品特征和传递给顾客的利益在这一阶段得以确定。

4. 商业分析

这是预测一种旅游产品概念在市场中的适应性及发展能力的阶段。旅游产品理念一经确定,企业要对这种产品的潜力的原始猜想进行再回顾,以适应市场需求。商业分析主要围绕选定的产品理念的经济效益展开,包括收益率和可持续发展性,开发和投入旅游新产品的资金风险和机会成本,预测环境及竞争优势的变化对产品发展潜力的影响。风险分析亦是此阶段的关键。通过对已经投入的资金的计算,企业在此做出决策,可能是:(1)增加投资并继续将该新产品理念转变成现实产品的开发过程;(2)停止继续投资,该产品的开发工作就此结束。

5. 产品和营销组合开发

这是把旅游新产品理念转化为新产品实体的过程。当企业决定继续开

understanding of the gap between supply and demand in the market is particularly critical, and companies are likely to find new competitive advantages and discover new opportunities from these gaps. Noting that identifying needs should be market-oriented is important, as any idea of new product development can only be effective if it is recognized by the customer.

2. Idea screening and evaluation

Not all of the ideas for new products collected through the previous step are feasible. Companies need to conduct detailed analysis and evaluation of all the ideas, considering the following factors: the overall evaluation of company resources, organizational development plans and objectives, financial feasibility analysis, competition, and environmental factor analysis. Through the assessment, ideas that are in line with company's own resources and development strategies and strengthening the value and potential of the company's marketing mix are identified while abandoning those non-feasible ideas to avoid waste of time and cost.

3. Concept development and testing

After screening, companies identify the most promising ideas and test them. The dominant principle at this stage is "customer defined product." Market research information should be fully used to identify the gap between the existing products and customer needs because the new product is mainly based on these gaps. The details of the product, such as the characteristics of the product and the benefits delivered to the customers, are determined at this stage.

4. Business analysis

In this stage, companies predict the adaptability and development ability of a tourism product concept in the market. Once a concept of tourism product is confirmed, the company needs to review the original conjecture of the potential of this product to adapt to market demand. Business analysis focuses on the economic benefits of selected product concepts, including yield and sustainability, the financial risks and opportunity costs of developing and investing in new tourism products, and the impact of changes in environment and competitive advantages on the potential of product development. Risk analysis is also key at this stage. Based on the calculation of the funds already invested, the company can make the following possible decisions: (1) increase the investment and continue the development process to transform the new product idea into the real product and (2) stop the investment. The product development process ends here.

5. Product and marketing mix development

In this process, companies transform concept of new tourism product into a real new

发既定的新产品理念时,企业将产品与运营部门和营销部门结合以决定产品的整个生产和营销工作。同时也涉及新产品与现有产品的有效营销捆绑,以实现协调。这样才能保证企业充分调配资源以确保新产品的成功。

6. 新产品试销

在此阶段,企业把开发出来的旅游新产品投放到与之对应的、具有代表性的市场范围内进行实验性销售,观察消费者的反应,从而使新产品失败的风险最小化。此阶段的主要作用在于:(1)检测新产品在正常市场营销环境下可能的销售量和利润额;(2)了解新产品及其组成的营销组合中的不足,加以改进;(3)为预测旅游新产品的开发效果提供证据。

7. 产品商品化

这是新产品从小批量试销到全面营销的阶段。试销成功的新产品在此阶段被全面投入目标市场,即为前面章节我们提及的新产品的导入阶段。此阶段,管理者应制定一个完整的产品上市方案,包括投入新产品的时间、目标市场、促销方法、销售渠道等方面的决策,即何时、何地、由谁用何种方法以何种价格投入什么市场的问题。与大多数耐用品不同的是,旅游产品的上市地点往往取决于目的地所处的位置。旅游与地域的紧密联系性意味着旅游企业不是将新产品引入目标人群,而是将目标人群吸引向新产品。

8. 监测和评估

仅仅将新产品投入市场并期望其营销表现能符合企业所预测的那样是不够的。企业一旦将新产品导入市场,就要对它们的销售表现进行谨慎的监测和评估。典型的评估因素包括销售量、市场份额、投资回报率、收益率、与现有产品相比新产品的销售量和收益率所占的份额和顾客反馈信息。基于这些数据,营销经理制定出当前和未来的产品供应决策。它显示了新产品开发过程的周期性特征,因为既有产品的开发不仅为未来产品开发提供经验教训,还能提供刺激因素推动开发进程。

product. When the company decides to continue developing the established new product concept, the company combines the product with operating departments and marketing departments to determine the product's entire production and marketing. At the same, this process involves the effective marketing bundle between the new product and existing products to achieve coordination. This is the only way that the company fully deploys resources to achieve success of the new product.

6. Test marketing

At this stage, the company put the new tourism product developed into its corresponding and representative market for experimental sales to observe the consumer responses, so that the risk of new product failure can be minimized. The main goal of this stage is (1) to detect the potential sales and profits of the new product under normal marketing environment, (2) to understand and then improve the deficiencies of the new product and its composition of the marketing mix, and (3) to provide evidence for forecasting the results of new tourism product development.

7. Commercialization

This stage is where a new product goes from a small-volume test marketing to a comprehensive marketing. At this stage, a successful new product is fully launched into the target market, or the introduction stage of the new product mentioned in the previous section. At this stage, management should develop a complete product launching plan, including the time to launch the new product, the target market, sales methods, distribution channels, and other decisions, that is, a question of when, where, by whom, and by which method at what price to launch the product to what market. Unlike most durable goods, the place where tourism products are marketed usually depends on the location of the destination. The close relationship between tourism and geographical areas means that tourism companies do not introduce new products into the target group but instead attract the target group to new products.

8. Monitoring and evaluation

Simply launching the new product in the market to expect its marketing performance to match with what the company predicts is not enough. Once the new product is introduced into the market, careful monitoring and evaluation of its sales performance is necessary. Typical assessment factors include sales volume, market share, return on investment, rate of return, share of new product sales and profitability relative to existing products, and customer feedback. Based on these data, the marketing managers set out current and future product supply decisions. This process shows the cyclical nature of the new product development process. Product development provides not only experiences for future product development but also incentives to drive the development process.

在产品导入期,以受欢迎程度和盈利能力两个指标来评价产品的吸引力。评价一个潜在的新产品的最后一个因素是它的独特性。虽然,增加新产品有可能是对竞争者成功经营而做出的防御性回应,但更可取的是拥有一个能在市场上提出新理念而不只是说"我也有"的产品。例如拥有亚洲第一的医疗体系的新加坡近年来采取了多种措施,大力发展医疗旅游。这些措施包括:(1)放宽签证申请程序——以中国为例,中国公民申请新加坡签证非常方便,只需身份证、户口本复印件、在职证明,通过指定旅行社即可申请十年内多次入境的新加坡旅行签证。如果确需在新加坡进行治疗或休养,新加坡医院也会协助外国公民办理医疗签证的申请手续。(2)加快医疗技术创新——新加坡政府允许企业和公共部门科研机构的科学家合作进行创新性研究。另一方面,医疗技术公司也可以与医院合作进行新系统和解决方案的测试。因此,很多全球医疗设备大公司在新加坡投资开展研发活动,例如Becton Dickinson 及西门子医疗系统在新加坡成立了拥有超过 50 名研究人员的合作研发中心。(3)建立医疗研发基地——启奥生物医药园(Biopolis)是新加坡政府专为生物医药研发而建的科研城,旨在促进各科研机构之间的合作。研究人员能够利用医药园内的各种最先进的科学设施与服务,降低企业研发成本,缩短研发时间。除此之外,政府还鼓励修建医疗酒店综合体,为医疗旅游游客提供完善周到的医疗服务。如 2015 年开业的 Farrer Park Connexion 即为亚洲首例医疗酒店综合体,包括一个医疗中心、一家医院和一家酒店。投资 38 亿元人民币(8 亿元新币)的 Farrer Park Connexion 医疗综合体占地 1.36 公顷,可以提供除妇科、儿科外所有的医疗服务,配套的酒店为病人家属提供住宿服务,酒店的餐厅为病人和医院员工提供配餐,并可为病人家属提供健康烹饪课程。目前新加坡每年大约有 40 万国外患者到新加坡接受眼、心脏、大脑疾病和癌症等在内的一系列医学治疗。2014 年新加坡在医疗旅游方面的收入达到 4592 亿元人民币(约 750 亿美元)。

开发新产品存在的一个潜在问题是蚕食,即新产品可能吞食现有产品的销售额,而不是靠吸引新顾客增加销售额。尽管有蚕食的危险,但处于高度竞争的市场上的企业还是要采用增加新产品的方式作为应对竞争的一种防

At the product introduction stage, the attractiveness of the product is evaluated by two indicators, namely, the degree of popularity and profitability. The last factor in evaluating a potential new product is its uniqueness. While adding new products may be a defensive response to the successful operation of a competitor, to have a product that can introduce a new idea in the market rather than just "I also have this product" is more desirable. For example, Singapore, which has Asia's the best health care system, has taken various measures in recent years to develop medical tourism. These measures include (1) the relaxation of visa application procedures. Take China as an example. Chinese citizens can conveniently apply for a Singapore visa. They only need their identity card, a copy of household register, and proof of employment when applying through designated travel agents for a multiple-entry Singapore tourism visa with a 10-year validity. Singapore will also assist foreign citizens to apply for medical visas if they actually need to take treatment or stay for sanitarium. (2) The innovation in medical technology is accelerated. The Government of Singapore allows scientists from companies and public sector research institutes to collaborate on innovative research. Conversely, medical technology companies can also cooperate with the hospitals for the testing of new systems and solutions. As a result, many global medical equipment companies have invested in R&D activities in Singapore. For example, Becton Dickinson and Siemens Healthineers set up a cooperative R&D center with more than 50 researchers in Singapore. (3) A medical R&D base is established. Biopolis is an R&D center that the Singapore government built for biomedical R&D, aiming to promote cooperation among R&D institutions. Researchers can take advantage of the most advanced science facilities and services in the center to reduce R&D costs and development time. In addition, the government also encourages the construction of medical hotel complex to provide comprehensive and thoughtful medical services to medical tourists. Farrer Park Connexion, which opened in 2015, is Asia's first medical hotel complex, comprising of a medical center, a hospital, and a hotel. The Farrer Park Connexion Medical Complex (with a total investment of 3.8 billion RMB, or 800 million Singapore dollars), covers 1.36 hectares, providing all medical services except gynecology and pediatrics. The affiliate hotel provides accommodation for patients' families. The hotel's restaurants cater for patients and hospital staff and provide healthy cooking courses for the patients' families. At present, approximately 400,000 foreign patients visit Singapore each year for a series of medical treatment, including eyes, heart, brain, and cancer. The revenues for Singapore's medical tourism in 2014 amounted to RMB 459.2 billion (approximately 75 billion US dollars).

A potential problem with the development of new products is cannibalization, that is, new products may cannibalize the sales of existing products rather than attract new customers to increase sales. Although there is risk of cannibalization, companies in highly competitive markets should adopt the methods of adding new products as a defense

御措施。并且新产品的提供往往能因为自身的差异性和新颖性保留住现有顾客或吸引新顾客。连锁企业引入新产品相对来说比较复杂,因为新产品不仅要符合企业的品牌形象,保持品牌的核心价值,还必须在广大的消费者人群中受到检测和评价。但在单体企业,新产品的开发过程并不十分正式,因为管理者可以凭借自己的经验作出判断,并且新产品投入市场后被顾客接受的可能性也不会有太大的压力。虽然分析没那么规范,但是应该要考虑前述同样的基本因素。

measure. Besides, the provision of new products often can retain existing customers or attract new customers because of their differentiation and novelty. Introducing new products is relatively more complex for chain companies because the new product not only needs to be in line with the corporate brand image and maintain the brand's core values, but also must be tested and evaluated in a vast number of consumers. However, for standalone enterprises, new product development process is not very formal because management can make judgments based on their own experiences and there is not much pressure for the possibility of consumers' acceptance after the new products are launched to the market. As the analysis is less formal, the same basic considerations mentioned above should be considered.

第9章　价格与定价

本章要点

- 旅游产品定价概论
- 旅游产品定价的影响因素：企业定价目标与需求测算
- 旅游产品定价的影响因素：成本计算与竞争分析
- 旅游产品定价的计算方法
- 旅游企业收益管理

　　价格是营销组合中唯一一项能够产生利润的要素，与产品特征、品牌形象、促销活动相比，价格也是最灵活的要素。价格在很大程度上反映了产品意图传递的价值定位，因此，定价是一个非常复杂的决策过程。在定价决策中，营销人员应当综合考虑公司的营销战略、目标市场特征、品牌定位、市场竞争等要素。本章综合介绍旅游企业在制定价格时需要考虑的因素，包括定价目标对定价策略选择的影响，需求、成本、竞争分析，旅游价格的计算方法，如何对新产品进行定价，以及收益管理的运作，以获取更高的利润。

9.1　旅游产品定价概论

　　价格是用于支付货物或服务的货币数量，是货物或服务价值的体现。价格有多种表现形式，如租金、学费、工资、佣金等。价格的组成包含不同的部分，如货物或服务的成本、销售人员的佣金、税费等。通常而言，价格是买方是否购买的决定因素之一。在市场环境中，顾客和采购商有众多的渠道能够接触价格信息，并获得价格折扣。在消费者和市场竞争的压力下，零售商在必要时会采取降价的方式来应对竞争。与此同时，零售商会向生产商施加压力，以获取更低的成本价。在此情况下，大量折扣和销售推广成了市场的一

Chapter 9 Price and Pricing

 Key points of the chapter

- Introduction to tourism product pricing
- Factors affecting tourism product pricing: Enterprises'pricing objectives and demand
- Factors affecting tourism product pricing: Cost calculation and competitive analysis
- Pricing methods for tourism products
- Tourism enterprise revenue management

Price is the only factor in the marketing mix that can generate profits. Price is the most flexible element compared with product characteristics, brand image, and promotional activities. Price, to a large extent, reflects the value proposition conveyed by the product; therefore, pricing is a complicated decision-making process. For pricing decisions, marketers should consider the company's marketing strategy, target market characteristics, brand positioning, market competition, and other factors. This chapter introduces the factors to consider when setting the price, including the effect of pricing objectives on pricing strategy; demand, cost, and competition analyses; travel price calculation methods; new product pricing; and the use of revenue management to obtain higher profits.

9.1 Introduction to Tourism Product Pricing

Price is the amount of money used to pay for the goods or services. The price reflects the value of commodities and has various forms, such as rent, tuition, wages, and commissions. The composition of price consists of different parts; including the cost of goods or services, commission for sales staff, and taxes. Price determines whether a buyer will purchase the product. In a market environment, consumers and buyers access the price information and price discounts through many different channels. With the pressure from consumers and market competition, the retailers lower the price to cope with the competition and simultaneously put pressure on manufacturers to obtain a lower cost price. In this case, large discounts and sales promotion become characteristics of the market. The consumers tend to aggressively obtain price information through their previous shopping experiences, formal communications (advertising, sales calls, and

部分特征。消费者往往会积极地获取价格信息,通过他们以前的购买经验、正式交流(广告、销售拜访和小册子)、非正式交流(朋友、同事或家人)、销售点、网上资源或其他因素来解读价格(Ofir 和 Winer,2002)。

消费者根据其对价格的感知以及他们所认为的货物或服务应有的实际价格,而不是销售人员所说的价格,来做出购买决定。消费者的意识中有价格门槛,低于价格门槛下限的货物或服务会被认为是质量低劣甚至是不可接受的,而高于价格门槛上限的货物或服务则可能被认为是定价过高。消费者对于价格的感知通常有三个来源:参考价格、价格—质量推断以及价格暗示。参考价格是存在于顾客记忆中某特定商品的价格,抑或是来自于外部的价格参考标准,如"建议零售价"。市场营销人员常常通过设定较高的"建议零售价",或者是暗示产品已经打折,又或是暗示竞争对手价格更高来影响消费者对参考价格的判断,从而操纵参考价格。表 9－1 列出了常见的消费者参考价格。

表 9－1　常见消费者参考价格

● 公平价格
● 常见价格
● 消费者最近一次为产品所付的价格
● 上限价格(消费者愿意支付的最高价格)
● 下限价格(消费者愿意支付的最低价格)
● 竞争对手价格
● 未来期望价格
● 通常折扣价格

来源:根据 Winer,R. S.(1988). Behavioral perspectives on pricing:buyers' subjective perceptions of price revisited. In T. Devinney(Ed.),*Issues in Pricing*:*Theory and Research*(pp. 35－57). Lexington,MA:Lexington Books.整理

价格有时会被认为是质量的象征,尤其是在奢侈品行业中。例如,高价的车被认为是高质量。然而,当消费者能够接触到其他能够体现产品质量的信息时,价格作为质量体现的重要性会明显下降(Kotler 和 Keller,2009)。在旅游行业中,高价的旅游产品同样被认为有高质量,例如高价的旅游团在行程中一般没有购物点,或者会入住高星级酒店。鸿鹄旅游的主打产品"环游世界 80 天"是旅游产品中高价高质量的代表,其费用为每人 138 万元人民币,国际来回航段全程使用商务舱,全程入住五星级地标酒店。营销人员还可通过价格提示影响消费者购买行为。价格提示有多种不同的形式,例如价

brochures), informal communications (friends, colleagues, or family), POS, online resources, or other factors (Ofir & Winer, 2002).

Consumers make purchasing decisions based on their perception of the price and what they think the actual price of goods or services should be, rather than what salespeople offer. Consumers perceive a price threshold. Goods or services with prices lower than the threshold have poor quality and are unacceptable, whereas those with prices higher than the threshold are overpriced. Consumers' perception of price normally originates from three sources: reference price, price-quality inference, and price cues. The reference price is either the price of a particular product that exists in the customer's memory or an external price reference such as "suggested retail price". Marketers often manipulate the reference price to influence the consumer's judgment by setting a higher "suggested retail price," which implies that the product is already discounted or the prices of competitors are higher. Table 9 – 1 shows the common reference price for consumers.

Table 9 – 1　Common reference price for consumers

● fair price
● typical price
● last price paid
● upper-bound price (the highest price that consumers are willing to pay)
● lower-bound price (the lowest price that consumers are willing to pay)
● competitor prices
● expected future price
● usual discounted price

Source: Adapted from Winer, R. S. (1988). Behavioral perspectives on pricing: buyers' subjective perceptions of price revisited. In T. Devinney (Ed.), *Issues in Pricing: Theory and Research* (pp. 35 – 57). Lexington, MA: Lexington Books.

Price is occasionally considered a symbol of quality, especially in the industry of luxury goods. For example, expensive cars are considered of high quality. However, when the consumers gain access to other information that reflects the quality of the product, the importance of the price as a symbol of quality is significantly reduced (Kotler & Keller, 2009). In the tourism industry, high-price tourism products are also considered of high quality; for instance, high-price tour packages do not include shopping in the itinerary or stay in high-star hotels. The flagship product of Honghu Tour "Travel Around the World in 80 Days" is an example of high-price and high-quality tourism product. The cost is RMB 1.38 million per person. The package includes business class return ticket for the international flights and a stay at five-star landmark hotels during the entire trip. Marketers also influence the consumer buying behavior through

格结尾。数字"9"是非常常见的价格结尾,如 9.9 元、299 元等。Anderson 和 Simester(2003)认为,"9"字成为常见的价格结尾是因为它传递了一种打折或讨价还价的信息。除了价格结尾,促销标志和时间(库存)限制也能促进消费者的购买行为(Howard 和 Kerin,2006)。酒店客房促销也经常利用时间限制吸引消费者购买,例如喜达屋酒店集团在每年暑假前都会进行火热促销,许多热门酒店都会提供七折至八折优惠,但促销时间只有 5 天,而且入住时间也只限为每年 7—9 月。

9.2　价格制定的影响因素

企业在多种情况下需要制定价格,如新产品发布、已有产品推向新渠道或新市场,又或是企业参加竞标等。在这些情况下,企业需要决定产品的质量和价格定位。通常而言,企业制定价格首先需要确定定价目标,了解需求,计算成本,并分析竞争对手的产品、成本和定价。这些因素都会对旅游产品价格的制定产生影响。

9.2.1　确定定价目标

企业首先要对产品进行定位。企业拥有越清晰的目标,越容易对产品进行定价。从营销理论来讲,定价是为了实现市场目标的决策,它跟企业的经营战略密切相关。多元化企业一般把明确的定价目标作为公司政策内容之一;而一些小型的单体企业可能对定价目标并没有明确的政策说明。但这并不代表这些单体企业就没有定价目标,它们的定价也会遵循固有的模式和依据,只是这些一般隐含在实际的定价行动中。根据企业经营战略的不同及其定价目标,价格的制定有五种导向,即生存、销售、利润、竞争以及形象。这五种定价方式孰优孰劣,很难一概而论,关键要看企业自身的产品特性及其所处市场的营销环境。

1. 生存导向定价

当企业面临产能过剩、市场竞争激烈或消费者需求变化时,企业生存成为主要的定价目标。只要产品价格能够支付可变成本和部分固定成本,公司即可实现生存的目标。然而,企业生存只是一个短期的目标,长远而言,企业必须学习如何提高产品价值,否则将面临倒闭。

price cues. Price cues have many different forms, such as the end of the price. The number "9" is common at the end of the price, such as 9.9 and 299 yuan. Anderson and Simester (2003) argue that "9" is the common end of price because this number conveys a message of discount or bargain. In addition to the end of price, promotional signs and time (inventory) restrictions promote the consumer buying behavior (Howard & Kerin, 2006). Hotel room promotions often use time constraints to encourage the consumers to purchase. For example, Starwood Hotels annually release hot promotions before the summer holidays. Many popular hotels provide 20% to 30% discount; however, the duration of promotion is only five days and the check-in time is only limited to July to September each year.

9.2　Factors Affecting Pricing

Companies need to set prices in many situations, such as the release of new products, promoting new products to new channels or new markets, or participating in bidding. Under these circumstances, companies need to determine the quality of products and price positioning. Generally speaking, when setting the price, the company first needs to determine the pricing objectives, understand the demand, calculate the cost, and analyze the competitors' products, costs, and prices. These factors affect the formulation of tourism product prices.

9.2.1　Determining the pricing objectives

The company must first position its product. A clear company objective leads to easier product pricing. From the marketing theory, pricing is a strategy to achieve market objectives and is closely related to the business strategy of the company. A diversified business normally sets clear pricing objectives as part of the company policy. Although some small standalone businesses may not have clear pricing objectives, their pricing follows the inherent pattern and basis, which are generally implied in the actual pricing action. According to different business strategy and pricing objectives, price setting has five directions: survival, sales, profits, competition, and image. Determining the best pricing method is difficult. The most suitable pricing method depends on the product characteristics and the marketing environment where the company competes.

1. Survival-oriented

Survival becomes the main pricing objective when the enterprises are faced with overcapacity, fierce competition in the market, or changes in consumer demand. As long as the product price covers the variable costs and some fixed costs, the company achieves the goal of survival. However, the survival of the company is only a short-term goal. In long term, the companies must learn how to improve the product value; otherwise, the company will face closure.

2. 销售导向定价

销售导向定价即市场份额最大化,是指企业的定价以扩大销售量为主要目标,保持或扩大市场占有率是其主要出发点。这些企业相信,销售量越高,单位成本越低,同时长期利润也会越高。一般来说,处于导入期的产品为了迅速扩大市场占有率,常以低价渗透来最大限度地扩大销售量。大部分酒店在新开业之时都会采用此策略以获得一定的市场份额。成熟的市场环境中的产品为了保持市场份额和尽可能地扩大销售量,也常采取低价策略。但销售导向的定价往往以降低旅游产品的利润水平为代价。选择这一定价目标时,旅游企业必须:(1)目标市场价格敏感度高,低价能产生吸引力;(2)备有大量生产的物质条件,总成本的增长速度低于总产量的增长速度;(3)低价能够击败现有和潜在的竞争者。

3. 利润导向定价

利润导向定价就是追求利润最大化,这几乎是所有旅游企业都希望实现的目标。虽然利润导向并不一定意味着高价,但二者常常结合在一起。以利润为导向的经营者,较倾向于选择高价策略,特别是当旅游产品具有独特性和不可替代性,或处于供不应求的状态时,情况就更是如此。产品的差异性和独特性或优质化是利润导向型定价策略里极其重要的因素。迪斯尼乐园就是采用高价策略的成功案例。上海迪斯尼乐园正式开业当日的票价高达499 元,但是门票在开始销售当日就已经被抢购一空。最大利润有长期利润和短期利润之分,还有全部产品的总体利润和单个产品利润之别。有的企业以获取长期的、总的最大利润为目标,考虑长远利益,既考虑到吸引与保持购买者、扩大销售,又能使企业获得最优的经济效益。而有的企业为了在短期内实现利润最大化,更多地采用高价策略以促成短期目标的实现。

4. 竞争导向定价

竞争导向定价即市场价格最大化,是指企业以竞争对手的价格为依据来制定本企业产品价格的定价方法,也称随行就市定价法。产品的最终价格是

2. Sales-oriented pricing

Sales-oriented pricing is also named maximum market share. In this pricing, the main goal of the company is to expand the sales. Maintaining or expanding the market share is the main starting point. These companies believe that a higher sales volume will lower the unit cost and consequently produce higher longer-term profits. In general, products in the introduction stage often use low price penetration to maximize the sales volume and rapidly expand the market share. Most hotels in the opening period use this strategy to obtain a certain market share. Products in a mature market environment also often use the low-price strategy to maintain market share and maximize the sales volume. However, sales-oriented pricing often leads to the reduced profitability level of tourism products. In selecting this pricing objective, the tourism enterprise must satisfy three conditions. (1) Target market has high price sensitivity and a low price can produce attractiveness. (2) With the condition to conduct mass production, the growth rate of total costs is lower than that of the total output. (3) The low price defeats the existing and potential competitors.

3. Profit-oriented pricing

Profit-oriented pricing is also named maximum profit. This pricing is the pursuit of profit maximization, which is the goal of nearly all tourism companies. Although profit orientation does not necessarily indicate high prices, the two factors are often combined. Profit-oriented operators are inclined to choose high-price strategies, especially when the tourism products are unique and irreplaceable or in a state of short supply, which is a more likely situation. Product differentiation and uniqueness/quality are important factors in profit-oriented pricing strategies. Disneyland is a successful case of adopting the high-price strategy. The ticket price for Shanghai Disneyland on the official opening day is as high as 499 yuan; however, the tickets were immediately sold out on the day of the sale. The highest profits are divided into long-term and short-term profits. The overall profit of all products is different from the profit of individual product. Some companies consider the long-term interests and set the goal to obtain long-term and total maximum profit; these companies consider attracting and maintaining the buyers, expanding the sales, and enabling the companies to obtain the best economic benefits. However, some companies often use the high-price strategy to achieve short-term goals and short-term maximizing of profits.

4. Competition-oriented pricing

Competition-oriented pricing is also named maximum market price. In this method, the price of the firm's products is based on the price of competitors, also known as going-rate pricing method. The final price of the product is mainly determined by the

由竞争来决定的,而不是劳动力和原材料的成本,这主要是为了保护市场份额。这种方法不仅在旅游业,在其他服务行业中也广被应用。以竞争为导向的价格决策有两种:对等定价和持续降价。对等定价的"价格标杆"通常是同业内的龙头企业,如某大型景区或某知名酒店集团。在国内旅游业,景区和酒店业较常见的是对等定价,而旅行社的持续降价现象则比较多。在酒店行业中,客房或餐饮产品的定价方法之一为市场竞争定价法,酒店将自身产品与竞争对手进行比较,综合考虑各种因素后,以竞争对手的产品价格为基准进行定价。当某个旅游区域内各大景区所占有的市场份额相对稳定时,景区之间常会出现某种默契,采取对等定价的方式,应对竞争或者回避竞争。对等定价的优点是经营者更趋于将市场竞争注意力转移到非价格要素上,如提升服务质量、开发新产品、加强市场宣传、改进客户服务等,即我们所说的"非价格竞争"。提升店内就餐环境就是餐厅的非价格竞争的行为,酒店连锁加大广告和促销活动的力度亦是如此。

5. 形象导向定价

形象导向定价即产品品质领先,把价格作为向消费者传递信息的载体,以价格塑造产品或品牌的形象。产品的价格形象包括价格水平、价格形式的确定和变动,它综合反映了企业经营理念、定位目标、服务质量以及企业管理能力等,成为企业形象的重要组成部分。因此,产品形象定价紧密围绕企业的定位策略、价格—质量关系以及消费者的感知而展开。价格不仅是反映企业整体形象的组成部分,而且是传递产品和服务质量信息的主要载体。因此,企业在确定价格目标的过程中,对价格传递给消费者的有关旅游产品和服务的"信息"(产品性质、质量等)的管理是关键。例如,星巴克将自身定位为咖啡店中的品质领导者,把品质、豪华的感受、高价格与忠诚的顾客基础结合在一起,为企业带来更好的业绩和利润(Silverstein 和 Fiske,2003a;2003b)。

9.2.2 测算需求

不同的价格会带来不同层次的需求,因而对企业的营销目标有不同的影响。在一般情况下,价格与需求呈负相关关系。也就是说,需求随着价格的

competition, not the cost of labor or raw materials, to protect the market share. This approach is applied in the tourism industry and other service industries. Price-oriented strategies can be classified into two types: price matching and continuous discounting. The "price benchmark" for price matching is usually the industry's leading firms, such as a large scenic spot or a well-known hotel group. In the domestic tourism industry, price matching is more common in scenery sites and the hotel industry, whereas continuous discounting is more common in travel agencies. In the hotel industry, market competition pricing is one of the pricing methods for the rooms and food & beverage products. Hotels compare their own products with competitors', consider various factors, and then set the price based on the competitor's product price used as a benchmark. When the market shares for various scenic spots within a large tourist area are relatively stable, a consensus among the scenic spots is formed; the price matching method is used to cope with or avoid the competition. The advantage of price matching is that the operators tend to shift the focus of market competition to non-price elements, such as improving service quality, developing new products, enhancing promotions, and improving customer service, which is called "non-price competition." Non-price competition behavior includes improving the dining environment for restaurants, as well as increasing the advertising and promotion for hotel chains.

5. Image-oriented pricing

Image-oriented pricing is also named product-quality leadership. In this method, price is the information carrier to consumers. The image of the product or brand is created through the price. The image of the product price includes the price level, as well as the determination and change of the price. The price image reflects the company's business strategy, positioning goal, service quality, and enterprise management skills, and thus becomes an important part of the company image. Therefore, the image-oriented pricing closely depends on the company's positioning strategy, price-quality relationship, and consumer perceptions. Price is not only a reflection of the overall image of a company, but also a major carrier to convey the information of the product and the service quality. Therefore, the key in determining the pricing objectives is to manage the "information" (product nature, quality, etc.) of the relevant tourism products and services, which is delivered to consumers by the price. For example, Starbucks positions itself as a quality leader among cafes; quality, a sense of luxury, high prices, and a loyal customer base were combined to bring better business performance and profitability to the company (Silverstein & Fiske, 2003a; 2003b).

9.2.2 Calculating the demand

Different prices create different levels of demand and thereby have different influences on the marketing objectives of the companies. In general, price is negatively

变化而成反向变化,价格越高,需求越低;价格越低,需求越高。另一方面,价格与需求是正向关系,价格随着需求的变化而成正向变化,需求越大,价格越高;需求越小,价格越低。以酒店客房的需求与房价的关系为例,当商务酒店的周末房价同工作日价格无差异时,其周末住房率就难以得到提高,因为与工作日相比较而言,周末属于入住的淡季,较低的价格才是吸引力的关键。如果周末提供低价房,可能会刺激都市居民来酒店内聚友休闲或家庭聚会,从而使入住率上升,需求增加。

价格与需求之间的关系可以用需求弹性反映。所谓需求弹性是指产品需求量的变化对价格变化的反应程度,它是指导产品定价的重要理论依据(崔志军,2004)。需求的价格弹性等于需求量变化的百分比除以价格变化的百分比。用计算公式表示为

$$E_d = \frac{\Delta Q_d}{\Delta P_d}$$

其中:E_d 为需求弹性;Q_d 为产品数量;P_d 为产品单价。

E_d 表示当价格上升或下降百分之一时,需求量减少或增加的百分比。当 $|E_d| < 1$ 时,称需求是缺乏弹性的。此时,需求量变动的幅度小于价格变动的幅度;当 $|E_d| > 1$ 时,称需求是富有弹性的,此时,需求量变动的幅度大于价格变动的幅度(廖世超,2002)。当 $|E_d| = 1$ 时,称需求为单位弹性,此时,需求量变动的幅度与价格的变动幅度相同,总收入不变(崔志军,2004)。需求弹性不同,价格变动引起的销售量的变动不同,总收益的变动也就不同。我们可根据需求弹性制定出产品价格变动的策略。虽然对某些缺乏弹性的产品采取提价策略可增加总收入,但对于另一些需求为单位弹性的产品,价格的变动实际上对需求的影响不大,因此单位弹性的产品价格应保持不变。对于富有需求弹性的旅游产品可考虑采取降价策略,以增加销售量,通过薄利多销的方式使总收入增加(崔志军,2004)。

企业对产品的定价要特别注重消费者对价格的重视程度,即价格敏感度。不同的细分市场对产品价格差异的反应可能不同。消费者价格敏感度较低的情况有:(1)市场上只有很少甚至没有替代品或竞争者;(2)消费者

correlated with demand, that is, the demand inversely changes with the change of price. A higher price indicates lower demand, whereas a lower price indicates a higher demand. On the contrary, demand has a positive relationship with price. The price changes positively as the demand changes: a greater demand indicates a higher price; whereas a lower demand indicates a lower price. An example is the relationship between the demand for hotel rooms and room rates. When a business hotel has similar room rates for weekends and weekdays, the weekend occupancy is difficult to increase because the weekend is a low season compared with workdays. A lower price is the key for attractiveness. However, providing low prices during the weekend stimulates the city residents to stay at the hotel for friendly or family gatherings, which thereby increases the occupancy and the demand.

The relationship between price and demand is reflected in the elasticity of demand. The elasticity of demand refers to the responsiveness of product demand to a change in price; this concept is an important theoretical base and guide in product pricing (Cui, 2004). Price elasticity of demand = Percent change in demand / Percent change in price. The elasticity is shown in the following formula:

$$E_d = \frac{\Delta Q_d}{\Delta P_d}$$

where E_d = demand elasticity, Q_d = quantity of product, and P_d = unit price of product.

E_d shows that the percentage decreases/increases in demand when the prices increase/decrease by one percent. When $|E_d| < 1$, the demand is inelastic. In this case, the level of demand change is smaller than that of the price change. When $|E_d| > 1$, the demand is elastic. In this case, the level of demand change is larger than that of the price change (Liao, 2002). When $|E_d| = 1$, the demand is unit elastic, indicating that the level of demand change is the same as that of the price change and the total income remains unchanged (Cui, 2004). When the elasticity of demand is different, the demand changes caused by the price changes and the total income changes are also different. We can formulate strategies to change the product prices according to the demand elasticity. Although increasing the price for some inelastic products increases the total revenue, the price change has little effect on the demand for other products with unit elasticity. Therefore, the price for products with unit elasticity should remain unchanged. For tourism products with high elasticity of demand, a price reduction strategy can be used to increase the sales. Total revenue is increased through small profits over a large quantity (Cui, 2004).

The product pricing of a company should especially consider the level of attention of consumers to price, that is, price sensitivity. The reaction of different market segments to price differences may vary. The situation in which the price sensitivity of consumers is low includes the following: (1) only a few or no substitutes or competitors exist in the

没有注意到价格较高;(3)消费者改变其消费习惯的速度很慢;(4)消费者认为较高的价格是合理的;(5)价格仅仅是产品生命周期内(获取、使用、维护)总成本的一部分。比如,周末客房的需求随着价格的变动呈现出弹性特点;相反地,工作日阶段市中心的酒店客房的需求则在短期内无太大的弹性变动,即价格的变动对需求的影响不大。因为工作日入住的主要是商务旅行者,他们更注重的是商务设施的便利和入住的即时性,对价格的敏感度较低。

根据价格敏感度的高低,可将消费者市场划分为四种。

1. 价格型消费者

价格型消费者寻求购买低价的产品,根据以往的经验确定自己的品牌感知和购买价值取向。只要这些产品的质量能够达到大部分品牌或供应商所提供的可以接受的最低质量水平即可,不会为更高的品质和声誉支付更高的价格。

2. 价值型消费者

价值型消费者注重价格和价值的双向利益,愿意花时间和精力进行同类产品衡量,只有在认为某产品具有高于其他替代品的附加价值之后才会做出购买决策。

3. 关系型消费者

关系型消费者对某一品牌已经建立了良好的忠诚度乃至强烈的偏好。如果其偏爱的品牌的价格没有超出所认知的合理范围,就会在没有考察替代品的情况下购买该产品。

4. 便利型消费者

便利型消费者对品牌之间的价格和品质差异不大关注,在购买前不会考察替代品的价格和性能,仅从便利的角度出发购买那些营销渠道简便的品牌。当时间紧迫或支出很小时,便利型消费行为就显得更为普遍(王馨馨,2001)。

价格敏感度并不是一成不变的,不同的社会和经济环境会影响人们对价格的关注度。相对来说,在经济繁荣时期,人们似乎对高档餐饮的价格不太在乎;但在经济衰退期,很多高档餐厅的价格却成为一个障碍,餐厅不得不调

market; (2) consumers are unaware that the price is higher; (3) the speed of consumers to change their consumption habits is low; (4) consumers consider that the higher price is reasonable; (5) the price is only a part of the total cost during the product lifetime (access, use, maintenance). For example, the demand for weekend rooms is elastic as prices change; conversely, the demand for hotel rooms in the city center during the weekday period is less elastic in the short term, implying that price changes exert an insignificant effect on demand. Most of the customers that stay during weekdays are business travelers. They pay considerable attention to the convenience of business facilities and the immediacy of stay, and their price sensitivity is low.

Consumers can be divided into four segments based on their price sensitivity level.

1. Price-oriented consumers

Price-oriented consumers seek to buy low-price products and determine their brand perception and consumption value orientation based on past experiences. It is acceptable as long as the quality of these products could achieve the minimum acceptable quality level that the majority of brands or suppliers can provide. They would not pay higher price for higher quality and reputation.

2. Value-oriented consumers

Value-oriented consumers focus on the two-way benefits of price and value. They are willing to spend time and effort to evaluate similar products and make a purchase decision only when a product is judged to be of higher value added than other alternatives.

3. Relationship-oriented consumers

Relationship-oriented consumers have already established good loyalty to a certain brand and even a strong preference. If the price of their preferred brand does not exceed the perceived reasonable range, they will purchase the product without examining the alternatives.

4. Convenience-oriented consumers

Convenience-oriented consumers are not concerned about the price and quality differences among brands. They do not evaluate the price and performance of alternatives before buying them. They simply purchase brands with easy marketing channels from a point of convenience. Convenience-oriented consumer behaviors become prevalent when time is tight or spending is small (Wang, 2001).

Price sensitivity is not static. Different social and economic environments affect the attention of people to price. During economic boom, people seem to be less concerned about the prices of upscale food and beverage; by contrast, during recession, the price of many upscale restaurants becomes an obstacle. The restaurants have to adjust the menu by introducing some

整菜单，引入一些较低价的菜肴，去掉昂贵的菜品。由于经济条件和社会环境的变化，人们会接受价格变动的价格范围，即价格敏感度的范围也会改变。当价格波动超出了该范围，产品可能会被视为定价过高或者过低。

在古典经济学理论中，在自由市场条件下价格和需求是呈反向变化关系的。当产品或服务价格上涨，需求下降，购买该产品或服务的消费者数量随之减少。策略上来说，从旅游地潜在的环境和社会影响方面考虑，这个显而易见的原理可被旅游地管理部门用来控制游客数量以免超过实际接待能力。同样，该原理也可用以隔离某些与目的地形象和定位明显不相符的细分市场区域。这些现象都是符合逻辑的。但在某些情况下也会出现产品或服务价格上涨，需求也随之增长直至后来才缓慢减少的现象，即产品或服务价格定得越高越能畅销。这种现象被称为凡勃伦效应（Veblen，1899）。

凡勃伦效应的命名源于美国经济学家凡勃伦（1899）出版的《有闲阶级论》中的"炫耀性消费理论"。他指出，社会中的炫耀性消费现象即社会个体沉湎于铺张浪费型的购买活动以达到体现自身社会身份（如权势、地位、荣誉和成功）的目的。具体到现今的旅游业，旅游者力求通过某些旅游活动，如到某个特别的旅游地观光、在某个特殊的酒店住宿等来显示自身的社会地位、权威和价值的消费行为可被认为是"炫耀性消费"。价格—需求间的反向变化理论不适用于这类旅游者。他们追求高消费，愿意花费高价格购买某些特别的旅游产品和服务，实现自身炫耀的目的。所以，旅游企业在制定市场营销策略时也应该考虑到这种"炫耀性消费"的可能性以及炫耀性消费顾客所占市场需求的比例。

有效的定价来自于企业对消费者在购买决策中使用的价格信息和非价格信息的了解。非价格信息包括顾客评价、顾客推荐度、酒店级别、酒店品牌等。Noone和McGuire（2013）的研究发现，消费者在选择酒店时都会利用三种非价格信息，即顾客评论、顾客评分和酒店品牌名称进行决策，其中顾客评论是消费者在选择酒店时最具影响的因素。另外，当消费者根据上述的非价格信息认为能够获得超凡的体验时，会更倾向于为酒店产品支付高价。除此以外，Yang、Mueller和Croes（2016）的研究发现，即使是处于交通不便地区的酒店，如果酒店能获得较高的顾客网络评价，同样能够获得较高的平均房价。

less expensive dishes and removing expensive dishes. The fluctuation range of price changes, that is, the range of price sensitivity, which people could accept will also change due to the changes in economic conditions and social environment. When prices fluctuate beyond that range, the product may be viewed as overpriced or underpriced.

In classical economic theory, the changes in prices and demand are inversely related under free-market conditions. When the price of a product or service rises, demand declines and the number of consumers who purchase the product or service decreases. This obvious principle can be used by tourism authorities to control the number of tourists to be not in excess of the actual receiving capacity in view of the potential environmental and social impact on the tourism destinations. This principle can also be adopted to isolate some of the market segments that clearly do not match with the destination image and positioning. These phenomena are logical. However, under certain circumstances, when the price of a product or service increases, the demand will also increase until a slow decline at a later stage, that is, a product or service is more popular with higher price. This phenomenon is called the Veblen effect (Veblen, 1899).

The name of the Veblen effect is derived from the "conspicuous consumption theory" mentioned in *The Theory of the Leisure Class* published by the American economist Veblen (1899). He emphasized the phenomenon of conspicuous consumption in the society, that is, individuals indulge in extravagant purchasing activities to show their social identity (e.g., power, status, honor, and success). Specific to the current tourism industry, the consumption behavior that tourists seek to show their own social status, authority, and value through certain tourism activities, such as traveling to a particular special tourist destination and staying in a particular special hotel, can be considered "conspicuous consumption." The reverse-change theory of price-demand is not applicable to such type of tourists. They pursue high consumption and are willing to spend high prices to purchase certain special tourism products and services to achieve the purpose of showing off. Therefore, tourism companies should also consider the possibility of such "conspicuous consumption" and the proportion of conspicuous consumption consumer in the market when formulating marketing strategies.

Effective pricing comes from the understanding of the price and non-price information that consumers use in decision making. Non-price information includes customer comments, customer recommendation, hotel ratings, and hotel brands. Noone and McGuire (2013) found that consumers use three types of non-price information—customer reviews, customer ratings, and hotel brand name to make purchase decisions, among which customer review is the most influencing factor when consumers select hotels. When the consumers perceive that they could acquire a superior experience based on the abovementioned non-price information, they will be inclined to pay high prices for hotel products. Yang, Mueller, and Croes (2016) also found that hotels located in areas with poor accessibility can achieve high average room rates if the hotels receive

企业可以利用不同的方法来预估产品的需求。这些方法包括以下几种。

（1）问卷调查：帮助企业测算消费者在不同价格下的购买量。但是，这种方法容易低估消费者在高价格下的购买意愿，企业难以设定更高的价格。

（2）价格测试：企业在同一个商店中对同一商品在不同时间收取不同的价格，以确定价格如何影响销售量。

（3）历史数据分析：对过往价格、销售量及其他因素的分析以理解这些变量之间的关系。用于分析的数据可以是纵向数据（历史数据）或交叉数据（同一时间不同地点的数据）。企业需要安排专门的人才去建立合理的模型，选取合适的数据，再利用合适的数据分析技术，才能获得正确结果。

9.2.3 计算成本

市场需求决定企业产品的价格上限，成本则决定产品价格的下限。产品的价格必须足以包含该产品的全部成本，并酌情加入适当的资金成本报酬率，才能涵盖企业营运时所付出的努力与承担的风险。一般而言，企业设定的价格包含了生产、分销和销售的成本，以及相应的回报。旅游产品的成本是开发、创造及实现旅游产品使用权转移这个过程中所支付的各种费用的总和，包括固定成本和变动成本两部分。

固定成本，也称为管理成本，是指那些不会因为销售量多寡而改变的、企业即使不提供服务也要继续（至少在短期内）承受的成本，比如建筑物租金、设备折旧费、公用事业费、基本员工薪金、资本的成本等。

变动成本则是指同企业所服务的顾客数量或生产的服务数量相关、随着销售量多寡而改变的各种成本，如旅游产品或餐饮产品的原材料费、酒店内的客房用品、导游时间和服务传递场所的清洁维修等成本。

总体来说，旅游产品具有高固定成本和低变动成本的特殊性。总成本中既有旅游设施的物化劳动转移部分，也有旅游企业职工劳动报酬的补偿部分。所以，劳动力成本、固定资本成本和原材料成本就成为产品价格的成本因素中的三个重要方面。劳动力成本是旅游企业产品价格中的重要考虑因素，因为劳动力的薪金直接与企业的固定成本联系。旅游企业，尤其是酒店和餐厅，都属于劳动力密集型企业。据浩华统计，中国内地所有四、五星级酒店客房的人

high online customer ratings.

Companies can use different methods to estimate the demand for products. These methods include the following.

(1) Questionnaire: This method helps companies to measure the quantity of purchase by consumers at different prices. However, this method may easily underestimate the willingness of consumers to pay for high prices. Companies may hardly set a higher price.

(2) Price test: Companies can charge different prices for the same product during different times at the same store to determine how price influences the sales volume.

(3) Historical data analysis: Analyzing historical prices, sales volume, and other factors helps understand the relationship among these variables. The data used for the analysis can be longitudinal data (historical data) or cross-sectional data (data of different places at the sametime). Companies must possess special talents to establish a reasonable model, select the appropriate data, and use the appropriate data analysis techniques to obtain correct results.

9.2.3　Calculating the cost

Market demand determines the price ceiling of a product, and cost determines the price floor of the product. The product price must be sufficient to cover the full cost of the product and, where appropriate, the appropriate rate of return on capital costs to cover the operating effort and commitment of risks for the business. The prices set by a firm generally include the costs of production, distribution, and sales, as well as the corresponding returns. The cost of tourism products is the total sum of expensed paid during the process of developing, creating, and realizing the transfer of right to use tourism products, including the two parts of fixed costs and variable costs.

Fixed costs, also known as administrative costs, are those that do not change with the amount of sales and that the company continues to bear (at least in the short term) even when not providing services, such as building rents, equipment depreciation, utilities, basic staff salaries, and capital costs.

Variable cost refers to the cost associated with the number of customers served or the number of services produced by the company and that changes with the amount of sales, such as the cost of raw materials for tourism products or food and beverage products, the cost of room supplies, the time of tour guide, and the cleaning and maintenance costs of service delivery places.

Tourism products have special characteristics, with high fixed costs and low variable costs. The total cost contains not only the part for the transfer of materialized labor via tourism facilities, but also the part for labor remuneration. Therefore, labor, fixed capital, and raw material costs become three important factors for the cost element of product price. Labor cost is the most important factor to be considered for the price of tourism products because the wages of workers are directly linked with the fixed costs of

工配比达 1.66 人/间,三星级达 1.33 人/间;所有四、五星级酒店里餐位的人工配比为 0.27 人/座,三星级酒店为 0.16 人/座。这一比例明显高于国际平均水平,同时也高于亚洲平均水平。劳动力工资和培训管理费等在企业的固定支出中占很大比例,成为旅游产品价格中关键的一部分(搜狐旅游,2007)。

此外,固定资产是旅游企业资产的主要组成部分,需要企业大量的资金投入,所以,资本成为影响旅游产品价格的另一个因素。资本密集型的旅游企业难以完全靠自身积累作为投资,所以在把自己的资本充分运用起来的同时,还要进行多元化的融资。融入的资本的可获得性和受利率影响的程度影响着旅游产品的总成本,进而影响产品价格。贷款的比例越高,受利率变化的直接影响就越大。当利率较低时,贷款较易获得,资本供给相对丰裕;反之,则会因为资本供给的紧张导致企业扩张更困难、更昂贵。资产使用效率的高低,不仅反映了旅游企业产品的经营水平,而且还将影响全部资本的获利能力。

经验曲线和目标成本是企业衡量成本使用的主要方法(Kotler 和 Keller,2009)。

1. 经验曲线

企业在生产过程中,随着累积产量不断增加,平均固定生产成本会不断下降(如图 9-1 所示)。这样的曲线被称为经验曲线或学习曲线。图中 B 点为企业累积产量达到 10 万个单位时,平均固定生产成本为 10 元,当企业累积产量达到 20 万个单位时,平均固定生产成本降为 9 元(即 A 点)。当企业累积产量达到 40 万个单位时,平均固定生产成本到达 T_1 点,即每单位平均固定生产成本为 8 元。

2. 目标成本

固定成本随着生产规模和经验而改变,企业也可以通过设计师、工程师和采购代表的共同努力来降低固定成本,这种方法称为目标成本法(Sivy,1991)。企业需要测算每个成本要素,如设计、生产、销售等,并考虑以不同的方式来降低成本,使得最终成本能够控制在目标成本的范围内。

the companies. Tourism firms, particularly hotels and restaurants, are labor-intensive enterprises. The statistics from Horwath HTL indicates that the total hotelstaff per available room in China are 1.66 for four- to five-star hotels and 1.33 for three-star hotels; the total food and beverage staff per seat are 0.27 for four- to five-star hotels and 0.16 for three-star hotels. These ratios are significantly higher than the international average and the Asian average. Labor wages and training management fees are accounted for a large proportion of company-fixed expenses and become key parts of the price for tourism products (Sohu Tourism, 2007).

Fixed assets are the main components of the assets of tourism companies. They require large capital investment, so the capital investment becomes another factor affecting the price of tourism products. Capital-intensive tourism companies cannot fully rely on their own accumulation as investment; therefore, apart from fully utilizing their own capitals, they also undergo diversified financing. The availability of capital and the degree to which it is affected by the interest rate influence the total cost of tourism products, which in turn influences product price. When the proportion of the loans is high, the direct influence from changes in interest rates is significant. When the interest rate is low, loans are easy to obtain and the capital supply is relatively abundant. On the contrary, the tight supply of capital will make the expansion of companies difficult and expensive. The efficiency of capital utilization not only reflects the management level of tourism businesses, but also will affect the profitability of all capitals.

Experience curve and target costing are the major methods used by firms to measure costs (Kotler & Keller, 2009).

1. Experience curve

In the production process, as the accumulated production increases, the average fixed cost will continue to decline (Figure 9 - 1). Such a curve is called an experience curve or a learning curve. At the point B in the figure, the average fixed cost is 10 yuan when the accumulated production reaches 100, 000 units. When the accumulated production reaches 200,000 units, the average fixed cost is reduced to 9 yuan (i.e., point A). When the accumulated production reaches 400,000 units, the average fixed cost is at the T1 point, that is, the average fixed cost per unit is 8 yuan.

2. Target costing

Fixed costs can change with the scale of production and experience. Companies can reduce fixed costs through the joint efforts of designers, engineers, and procurement representatives. This approach is called target costing (Sivy, 1991). Companies need to measure each cost element, such as design, production, and sales, and consider different ways to reduce costs, so that the final cost can be controlled within the target cost range.

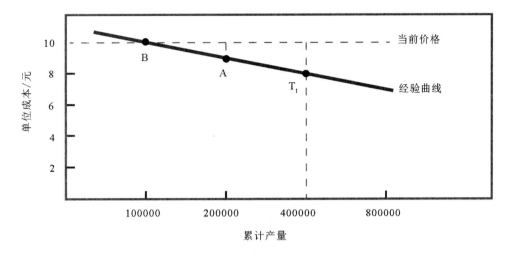

图 9-1　经验曲线
来源：Kotler，P.，Keller，K.(2009). *Marketing Management*（13th ed.）
Upper Saddle River，NJ：Pearson Prentice Hall.

9.2.4　竞争分析

在分析市场需求和企业成本后，企业得出可能的价格范围。然而，企业必须把竞争对手的成本、价格和可能的应对行动也考虑在内。企业应该首先考虑与产品可能价格范围最接近的竞争对手的定价。如果企业的产品包含了竞争对手所没有的特征，企业应该评估这些特征对于消费者的价值，并将这些价值加入到价格中。反之，如果竞争对手的产品包含企业所没有的特征，企业要将相应的价值从价格中减去。然后，企业可以确定自身产品的定价应该是高于还是低于竞争对手，又或是与竞争对手持平。因此，充分了解竞争者的成本和价格，以及竞争者对企业定价策略的反应至关重要。那么企业如何才能预测竞争对手的反应？一种方法是假定竞争对手有一套标准的体系来应对一个价格的设定或改变。另外一种方法是假定竞争对手将每个价格差异或变化都作为一个新的挑战，并根据当时的自身利益做出应对。然后，企业需要研究竞争对手目前的财政状况、最近的销售量、客户忠诚度和企业的目标。如果竞争对手的目标是市场份额最大化，它可能会调整价格差异，以应对这样的变化（Ailawadi、Lehmann 和 Neslin，2001）。如果竞争对手的目标是利润最大化，它可能会提高广告花费或提升产品质量。

经济学家根据参与竞争企业的多少和产品的差异程度，将市场分为四种类型：完全垄断市场、寡头垄断市场、垄断竞争市场和完全竞争市场。不同的

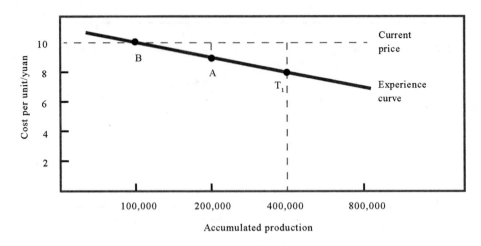

Figure 9 – 1   Experience curve

Source: Kotler, P. & Keller, K. (2009). *Marketing Management* (13th ed.) (p. 585). Upper Saddle River, NJ: Pearson Prentice Hall.

9.2.4　Competitive analysis

After analyzing the market demand and the business cost, the companies can acquire a possible price range. However, companies must consider the costs, prices, and possible responses of competitors. Companies should first consider the pricing of the competitors with closest prices to the possible price range of a product. If the products of a company include features that competitors do not have, they should evaluate the value of these features to consumers and add those values to the price. Conversely, if the product of a competitor contains a feature that the company does not have, then the company should subtract the corresponding value from the price. Companies can determine if their product price should be higher than, lower than, or the same as that of the competitors. Therefore, a good understanding of the cost and price of competitors, as well as the responses of competitors to pricing strategies, is important. How can companies predict the reaction of competitors? One approach is to assume that competitors have a standard set of systems to deal with the set of or change in a price. Another one is to assume that each competitor takes each price difference or change as a new challenge and reacts to it in light of its own interests at that time. Afterward, companies need to study the current financial situation of competitors, namely, recent sales, customer loyalty, and business goals. If the goal of the competitor is to maximize market share, then it may adjust the price difference to cope with such a change (Ailawadi, Lehmann & Neslin, 2001). If the goal is to maximize profits, then it may increase advertising cost or improve product quality.

Economists divide the market into four types based on the number of firms participating in the competition and the degree of product differentiation. They are pure

市场竞争状况决定着企业定价的自由程度,因此企业的定价策略与外部市场上的竞争结构之间有着密切的关系。

1. 完全竞争市场

完全竞争市场是一种竞争不受任何阻碍、干扰和控制的市场,既没有政府的干预,也没有企业或集团的集体联合行动对市场机制作用造成阻碍。完全竞争必备以下四个特点:有众多彼此竞争、市场份额比例相当的旅游者和旅游经营者;经营的旅游产品同质或同一;资源完全自由流动,可自由进入和离开市场;具有充分且畅通的市场信息。在完全竞争环境下,企业的定价一般以市场价格为基准,不会高于市场价格,因为消费者可以在众多的替代品中选择。

2. 完全垄断市场

完全垄断市场是指某旅游产品完全由一家企业所控制,且没有任何替代品,因而完全垄断企业对产品的价格和产量有很大的控制权。完全垄断市场很少见,只见于某些国家特许的独占企业,如公用事业(包括邮政、电话、自来水等企业)、对某种产品拥有专利权或拥有独家原料开采权的企业。在旅游业中,某些独有的旅游资源开发成的旅游产品会形成垄断产品,从而在一定程度上形成完全垄断市场。如中国的长城、埃及的金字塔等都具有世界上独一无二的特色。

3. 垄断竞争市场

垄断竞争市场上既有垄断又有竞争,是一种介于完全竞争和完全垄断之间的市场类型。其特点是:产品之间存在差别;同类产品拥有的经营者较多,进出该市场比较容易。经营者的同类旅游产品所存的差异往往是形成价格差别的关键,这些差异可体现在质量、特征或式样等方面。从总体上看,旅游市场是一个垄断竞争的市场,尤其是旅游目的地市场既有垄断也有竞争。垄断性主要表现在:首先,旅游产品具有差异性,即每个国家或地区的旅游

monopoly, oligopolistic monopoly, monopolistic competition, and pure competition. Different market competition conditions determine the degree of freedom for pricing, so the pricing strategy of enterprises is closely related to the competitive structure of the external market.

1. Pure competitive market

A pure competitive market is a market where in competition is free from any obstruction, interference, and control. Neither government intervention nor collective action of enterprises or groups exists to hinder the market mechanism. Pure competition must satisfy the following four characteristics: many tourists come, and several tourism operators with similar levels of market share compete with one another; their tourism products are homogeneous or the same; resources are completely with free mobility, that is, free to enter and leave the market; sufficient market information exists. In a pure competitive environment, the company pricing is generally based on market prices, not higher than the market price, because consumers can select from a large number of alternatives.

2. Pure monopoly market

A pure monopoly market is where tourism products are entirely controlled by one firm and no other substitutes exist. Therefore, a pure monopoly company has a high degree of control over product prices and the quantity of production. Pure monopoly market is rare, only existing in some exclusive enterprises with special state permissions, such as public utilities (including postal services, telephone, and water) or companies with the patent for a certain product or with exclusive mining rights to raw materials. In the tourism industry, some tourism products developed from unique tourism resources will form monopoly products, thus becoming a pure monopoly market to a certain extent. For example, the Great Wall in China and the pyramids in Egypt are some of the unique features all over the world.

3. Monopolistic competitive market

Monopoly and competition occur in the monopolistic competitive market, which is a type of market between pure competition and pure monopoly. Its characteristics are as follows: differences exist among products; similar products have many operators, and they are relatively easy to enter or leave the market. Differences among the operators of similar tourism products are often the key to the formation of price differences. These differences can be reflected in the quality, characteristics, or styles. The tourism market is generally a monopolistic competitive market, especially for the tourist destination market where both monopoly and competition exist. Monopoly is mainly reflected in the following aspects. First, tourism products are different, that is, the tourism resources of

资源状况不可能是完全相同的,从而导致每一种旅游产品都有其个性和特征。于是,旅游产品之间的差异在一定程度上形成了一种垄断。其次,政府的某些政策限制形成一定的垄断。例如政府对外资参与当地旅游业经营的限制等。再次,由于非经济因素限制,旅游者不能完全自由选择旅游产品,也不能随意进入任何旅游目的地。

4. 寡头垄断市场

寡头垄断市场指为数不多的旅游经营者控制了行业绝大部分旅游供给的市场结构。每个大企业在行业中都占有相当大的份额,以致其中任何一家经营者的产量或价格变动都会影响旅游产品的价格和其他经营者的销售量。这是介于完全垄断市场和垄断竞争市场之间的一种市场形式。旅游产品市场上存在着寡头。如同一旅游线路,有不同的旅行社在经营;同一航线,有不同的航空公司参与竞争,但经营者的数量往往有限,这些旅游产品都是寡头的例子(陈波翀,2003)。此外,航空运输市场属于寡头垄断型。竞争是市场经济的特点,没有竞争,就没有市场经济。但航空运输业属于资金、技术、信息密集型行业,要求一定的规模经济性。如果采取完全竞争模式,或采用竞争垄断模式,过度的竞争将造成对资源的严重浪费和对生产的破坏。目前在我国的航空运输市场上以国航、东方、南方三家航空企业集团为龙头的寡头垄断格局已基本形成。从本质上讲,市场既有竞争,又有垄断,航空寡头垄断市场属于不完全垄断市场。

9.3　旅游产品定价方法

旅游产品定价方法包括成本导向定价法、边际贡献定价法和需求导向定价法。

9.3.1　成本导向定价法

成本导向定价法是以旅游产品的成本为基础来制定产品价格的方法。它以旅游产品单位成本为基本依据,加上预期的利润额作为产品的销售价格,是旅游企业最常用的定价方法。售价与成本之间的差额即利润称为"加成"。基本计算公式如下:

$$单位产品的价格 = 成本 + 成本 × 加成率(成本利润率)$$

$$= 成本 × (1 + 加成率)$$

each country or region cannot be exactly the same, thereby leading to its own personality and characteristics for each tourism product. The differences among tourism products form a monopoly to a certain extent. Second, some of the government restrictions form a certain monopoly, such as the restrictions of the government on the participation of foreign enterprises in local tourism operations. Third, tourists cannot select any tourism products freely and enter any tourist destinations because of noneconomic factors.

4. Oligopolistic monopoly market

Oligopolistic monopoly market refers to the market structure in which a small number of tourism operators control the most tourism supply in the market. Each large enterprise in the industry occupies a considerable portion of share, so that the changes in any one of the operators in production or price will affect the price of tourism products and the sales volume of other operators. This market type is formed between pure monopoly and monopolistic competition. Oligopolies occur in the tourism product market. For example, for the same tour routes, different travel agencies operate; for the same routes, different airlines compete, but the number of competitors is often limited. These tourism products are oligopolistic examples (Chen, 2003). The air transport market is an oligopoly. Competition is the characteristic of the market economy. If competition does not occur, market economy does not exist. However, the air transport industry is a capital-, technology-, and information-intensive industry and requires a certain degree of economies of scale. Excessive competition will result in a serious waste of resources and destruction of production if a pure competition mode or a monopolistic competition model is adopted. The air transport market in China has basically formed an oligopolistic monopoly structure, with Air China, China Eastern, and China Southern as three leading aviation groups. In nature, the market has both competition and monopoly. The aviation oligopoly market is not an entirely monopolized market.

9.3 Pricing Methods for Tourism Products

Pricing methods for tourism products include cost-based pricing, contribution margin (CM) pricing, and demand-based pricing.

9.3.1 Cost-based pricing

Cost-based pricing is based on the cost of tourism products to develop product prices. This method is based on the unit cost of tourism products plus the expected profit amount as the sales price of the product. This pricing method is the most commonly used by tourism companies. The difference between selling price and cost is called "markup." The basic formula is as follows:

$$\text{unit product price} = \text{cost} + \text{cost} \times \text{markup percentage (profit margin)}$$
$$= \text{cost} \times (1 + \text{markup percentage})$$

1. 成本加成定价法

成本加成定价法把所有为生产某种产品而发生的耗费均计入成本，计算单位产品的变动成本，合理分摊相应的固定成本，再按一定的目标利润率来决定价格。其计算公式如下：

$$P = \frac{\left(\dfrac{F_c}{Q} + V_c\right)(1 + R_P)}{1 - T_s}$$

其中：P 为旅游产品价格；Q 为预计销售量；F_c 为固定成本；V_c 为单位变动成本；R_p 为成本加成率（利润率）；T_s＝营业税率。

例　某宾馆有客房 600 间，全部客房年度固定成本总额为 3000 万元，单位变动成本为 80 元/(间·天)，预计全年客房出租率为 70%，成本利润率为 30%，增值税率为 6%，试求客房的价格。

解　根据所给数据和公式，计算如下：

$$P = \frac{\left(\dfrac{30000000}{600 \times 365 \times 70\%} + 80\right)(1 + 30\%)}{1 - 6\%} = \frac{358.4}{0.94} = 381.3(\text{元/间 · 天})$$

2. 目标收益定价法

目标收益定价法又称投资收益率定价法，是根据企业的投资总额和预期总销量，确定一个目标收益，作为定价的标准。其中，因为目标利润 P_f 是企业"必须拥有"的部分，所以是固定成本的一部分。目标收益定价法的缺陷在于忽略了市场的价格弹性与市场竞争。

目标收益定价法的基本计算公式为

$$P = \frac{\left(\dfrac{F_c + P_f}{Q}\right) + V_c}{1 - T_s}$$

以餐厅为例，若某餐厅根据经验确定扬州炒饭的理想盈利率为 40%。预期一个月卖出 200 份，总成本为 1000 元，且每份扬州炒饭的变动成本是 2 元，当前餐饮市场的营业税率为 10%，则按成本加成定价法有

$$P = \frac{\left(\dfrac{F_c}{Q} + V_c\right)(1 + R_p)}{1 - T_s} = \frac{\left(\dfrac{1000 - 200 \times 2}{200} + 2\right)(1 + 40\%)}{1 - 10\%} = 7.78(\text{元})$$

只有当扬州炒饭的单位价格达到 7.78 元时，该餐厅才能实现 40% 的目

1. Cost-plus pricing

Cost-plus pricing method counts all the expenses incurred to produce a product into the cost, calculates the variable cost of unit product with a reasonable allocation of the corresponding fixed costs, and determines the price through a certain target profit rate. The formula is as follows:

$$P = \frac{\left(\dfrac{F_c}{Q} + V_c\right)(1 + R_P)}{1 - T_s}$$

where P = unit tourism product price, Q = expected sales volume, F_c = fixed cost, V_c = unit variable cost, R_p = markup percentage (profit margin), and T_s = business tax rate.

Example A hotel has 600 rooms. The annual total fixed cost is 30 million yuan. The unit variable cost is 80 yuan per room per day. The expected annual occupancy rate is 70%. The profit margin is 30%. The rate of value-added tax (VAT) is 6%. Try to calculate the room rate.

Solution According to the given data and formula, the answer is calculated as follows:

$$P = \frac{\left(\dfrac{30000000}{600 \times 365 \times 70\%} + 80\right)(1 + 30\%)}{1 - 6\%} = \frac{358.4}{0.94} = 381.3 \text{(yuan per room per day)}$$

2. Target-return pricing

Target-return pricing, also known as rate of return pricing, is based on the total investment and the expected total sales to determine a target return as the pricing standard. Given that the target profit P_f is the part that "must be collected" by the company, it is part of the fixed cost. The flaw of the target-return pricing method is that it disregards the price elasticity and market competition.

The basic calculation formula of the target-return pricing method is

$$P = \frac{\left(\dfrac{F_c + P_f}{Q}\right) + V_c}{1 - T_s}$$

For example, a restaurant determines that the ideal profit margin for Yangzhou fried rice is 40% based on experience. The restaurant expects to sell 200 units in a month. The total cost is 1,000 yuan, and the unit price for Yangzhou fried rice is 2 yuan. The current business tax rate for the food and beverage sector is 10%.

Cost-plus pricing:

$$P = \frac{\left(\dfrac{F_c}{Q} + V_c\right)(1 + R_p)}{1 - T_s} = \frac{\left(\dfrac{1000 - 200 \times 2}{200} + 2\right)(1 + 40\%)}{1 - 10\%} = 7.78 \text{(yuan)}$$

Only when the unit price of Yangzhou fried rice reaches 7.78 yuan, the restaurant

标利润率。

而根据目标收益定价法,如果餐厅希望下月扬州炒饭能收益 800 元,则

$$F_c = 1000 - 200 \times 2 = 600（元）$$

$$P = \frac{\left(\dfrac{F_c + P_f}{Q} + V_c \right)}{1 - T_s} = \frac{\left(\dfrac{600 + 800}{200} + 2 \right)}{1 - 10\%} = 10（元）$$

只有当扬州炒饭的单位价格达到 10 元时,该餐厅下个月才能实现 800 元的目标收益。

3. 盈亏平衡定价法

盈亏平衡定价法是根据盈亏平衡点原理进行定价。盈亏平衡点又称保本点,是指在一定价格水平下,企业的销售收入刚好与同期发生的费用额相等,收支相抵、不盈不亏时的销售量,或在一定销售量前提下,使收支相抵的价格。

其计算公式为

$$P = \frac{\dfrac{F_c}{Q} + V_c}{1 - T_s}$$

例 某主题公园年度固定成本总额为 300 万元,接待每位游客的变动成本为 10 元,预计年平均游客数量为 87600 人次,增值税率为 6%,求该公园保本时的价格。

解 根据所给数据和公式,计算如下:

$$P = \frac{\dfrac{3000000}{87600} + 10}{1 - 6\%} = \frac{44.2}{0.94} = 47.0（元／人）$$

在以上餐厅的例子中,扬州炒饭的保本价应该为

$$P_{保本} = \frac{\left(\dfrac{F_c}{Q} + V_c \right)}{1 - T_s} = \frac{\left(\dfrac{1000 - 200 \times 2}{200} + 2 \right)}{1 - 10\%} = 5.56（元）$$

只有当扬州炒饭的单位价格达 5.56 元时,企业才能不亏损。

根据盈亏平衡定价法确定的旅游价格是旅游企业的保本价格。低于此价格旅游企业会亏损,高于此价格旅游企业则有盈利。实际售价高出保本价格越多,旅游企业盈利越大。因此,盈亏平衡定价法常用作对旅游企业各种定价方案进行比较和选择的依据。

could achieve the target profit margin of 40%.

Target-return pricing: If the restaurant hopes to achieve a profit of 800 yuan for Yangzhou fried rice in the next month, then

$$F_c = 1000 - 200 \times 2 = 600 \text{ (yuan)}$$

$$P = \frac{\left(\dfrac{F_c + P_f}{Q} + V_c\right)}{1 - T_s} = \frac{\left(\dfrac{600 + 800}{200} + 2\right)}{1 - 10\%} = 10 \text{(yuan)}$$

Only when the unit price of Yangzhou fried rice reaches 10 yuan, the restaurant can achieve the target profit of 800 yuan in the next month.

3. Breakeven pricing

Breakeven pricing is based on the principle of breakeven point. Breakeven point refers to the sales volume at which under a certain price level, the sales' revenue of a company is exactly the same as the cost; or the sales price at which under certain sales volume, the revenues and expenses are balanced off.

The calculation formula is

$$P = \frac{\dfrac{F_c}{Q} + V_c}{1 - T_s}$$

Example   The annual fixed cost of a certain theme park is 3 million yuan. The variable cost for receiving each visitor is 10 yuan. The estimated annual average number of visitors is 87,600. The VAT rate is 6%. Please solve the breakeven price of the theme park.

Solution   According to the given data and formula, the calculation is as follows:

$$P = \frac{\dfrac{3000000}{87600} + 10}{1 - 6\%} = \frac{44.2}{0.94} = 47.0 \text{(yuan per person)}$$

In the above example of the restaurant, the breakeven price for Yangzhou fried rice should be

$$P_{\text{breakeven}} = \frac{\left(\dfrac{F_c}{Q} + V_c\right)}{1 - T_s} = \frac{\left(\dfrac{1000 - 200 \times 2}{200} + 2\right)}{1 - 10\%} = 5.56 \text{(yuan)}$$

Only when the unit price for Yangzhou fried rice is 5.56 yuan can the company incur a loss.

The price determined by the breakeven pricing method is the breakeven price. Companies lose money when the price is lower than that price and gain when the price is higher than that price. The higher the actual price exceeds the breakeven price, the greater the profitability for tourism companies. Therefore, the breakeven pricing method is often used as a basis for tourism companies to compare and select from the various pricing options.

4. 千分之一法

千分之一法也是某些酒店定价的方法。他们以整个酒店造价的千分之一作为酒店的房价。这是因为酒店总投资中占绝大部分比例的是建筑投资,约占 70% 左右,因而造价应与房价相联系。如某酒店总造价 5000 万元,有客房 250 间,故每间客房价格为 200 元(即 250 间客房的总造价决定客房的销售价格)。

5. 赫伯特定价法

赫伯特定价法是以目标收益率为定价的出发点,在已确定计划期各项成本费用及酒店利润指标的前提下,通过计算客房部应承担的营业收入指标,进而确定房价的一种客房定价法(张燕,2007)。它以房价和客房出租率作为决定酒店收入和盈利能力的最主要因素,比千分之一法要合理得多。采取此方法的酒店在调整房价时,会将来自餐饮、会议设施和零售经营等其他利润中心的收入结合起来考虑。其他营业部门盈利高,房价则可降低;其他部门亏损,房价则上升。一般而言,新建酒店往往采用此种方法作为定价参考。

成本导向定价法的优点在于价格能补偿并满足利润的要求,计算简便,有利于核算。但成本导向定价法的明显缺陷是脱离实际的市场境况,市场适应性弱,灵活性较低。并且,它只考虑酒店的成本,忽略了供求关系、顾客需求及市场竞争状况等市场因素,对酒店自身的特点和优劣势的了解也不够清晰。当出现价格竞争时,企业很有可能陷入生存危机。

9.3.2　边际贡献定价法

边际贡献是指企业增加一个产品的销售所获得的收入减去增加的成本,是指这个增加的产品对企业的"固定成本和利润"的贡献。边际贡献定价法又称变动成本定价法,是旅游企业根据单位产品的变动成本来制定产品的价格。它有两种表现形式。一种是单位边际贡献,公式为

$$单位产品边际贡献 = 单位产品价格 - 单位产品变动成本$$

即

$$CM = P - V_c$$

4. The "rule of thumb method"

The "rule of thumb method" is a common pricing method for hotels. They take the one thousandth of hotel building cost as the room rate because the vast majority of the total investment for a hotel is construction cost, accounting for approximately 70%; therefore, the construction cost should be linked with the room rate. If the total building cost of a hotel is 50 million yuan and it has 250 rooms, then the room rate should be 200 yuan (i.e., the total building cost of 250 rooms decides the room rate).

5. Herbert pricing

Herbert pricing is a pricing method based on the target rate of return. This method sets the price by calculating the revenue target of the rooms department after confirming the target of every cost and hotel profits during the planning stage (Zhang, 2007). The room rate and occupancy are considered the most important factors to determine hotel revenues and profitability. This method is more reasonable than "the rule of thumb method." When using this approach to adjust the room rate, we should consider the incomes from restaurants, conference facilities, retail business, and other profit centers together. If the profitability of other business sectors is high, then the room rate can be decreased; if other departments lose money, then room rates can be increased. New hotels generally tend to use this method as a pricing reference.

The advantage of the cost-based pricing method is that price can compensate for and satisfy the requirements of profits, and the calculation is simple and conducive to accounting. However, an obvious drawback is that it is separated from the actual market situation, with low adaptability to the market and low flexibility. Moreover, this method considers only the hotel cost and ignores the relationship of supply and demand, the customer needs, market competition, and other market factors. This method does not fully determine the own characteristics, advantages, and disadvantages of the hotel. When a price competition occurs, companies are likely to fall into a crisis of survival.

9.3.2 Contribution margin pricing

CM refers to the amount of income increased by selling one product minus the increased cost, which is the contribution to the "fixed costs and profits" of a company from the increased product sale. In the CM-pricing method, also known as variable cost-pricing method, tourism companies set the product price according to the variable cost for unit product. This method has two forms. One is the unit product CM, which is formulated as

$$\text{Unit product} = \text{Unit product price} - \text{Unit product variable cost}$$

that is

$$CM = P - V_c$$

其中：CM 为单位产品边际贡献；P 为单位产品价格；V_c 为单位产品变动成本。

另一种是边际贡献总额，公式为

$$总边际贡献＝总销售收入－总变动成本$$

即

$$TCM = S - V_c = CM \times Q = (P - V_c) \times Q$$

其中：TCM 为单位产品边际贡献；S 为总销售收入；V_c 为总变动成本；Q 为销售数量。

此外，边际贡献率是指边际贡献总额占总销售收入的百分比，或单位边际贡献占销售单价的百分比，以百分数表示。公式表示为

$$CMR = \frac{TCM}{P \times Q} \times 100\% = \frac{(P - V_c)}{P} \times 100\%$$

从边际贡献的公式我们可以看出：

当 CM（TCM）＞0 时，增加的产品的边际贡献大于固定成本，不仅可补偿固定成本，超过的部分即为企业的盈利。

当 CM（TCM）≤0 时，边际贡献不能全部补偿固定成本，企业亏损。

对餐厅来说，菜品的边际贡献（CM）＝售价－单位食品变动成本，边际贡献用以支付固定成本和目标利润。菜品售价可用以下两个步骤来决定：

（1）每位客人的平均边际贡献＝（固定成本＋理想利润）÷期望的客人数量

（2）售价＝每位客人的平均边际贡献＋每份食品的变动成本

如果某家餐厅期望每个月服务 7000 位客人，每月该餐厅的红烧排骨的非食品固定成本是 50000 元，期望利润是 30000 元，那么每位客人的平均边际贡献：（50000 ＋ 30000）÷7000 ＝11.43（元）。若每份排骨的食品成本为 5 元，其红烧排骨的暂定售价则为 11.43＋5＝16.43（元）。要注意的是，边际贡献定价关注的是利润贡献水平而不是食品成本率。

当边际贡献等于或大于固定成本时，企业可以保本或盈利。当边际贡献小于固定成本时，企业有损失。但有时候在产品供过于求、竞争激烈的情况下，企业以低价保持市场，不计固定成本，以避免高价导致产品滞销积压，失去市场。此外，以下几种情况也可能允许边际贡献小于 0：（1）企业主要产品已分摊企业固定成本后的新增产品定价；（2）企业达到保本点后的产品定价；（3）企业开拓新地区市场的产品定价，即在现有市场的销售收入已能保本并有盈利的情况下，为拓展市场，可对新客户或新设网点的产品按变动成本定价；（4）企业经营淡季时的定价。

where CM = unit product, P = unit product price, and V_c = unit product variable cost.

The other one is the total CM, which is expressed as

$$\text{Total CM} = \text{Total sales-Total variable costs}$$

that is

$$\text{TCM} = S - V_c = \text{CM} \times Q = (P - V_c) \times Q$$

where TCM = total CM, S = total sales, V_c = total variable costs, and Q = quantity of sales.

CM rate (CMR) refers to the percentage of total CM to total sales or the percentage of unit CM to unit price. The formula is expressed as

$$\text{CMR} = \frac{\text{TCM}}{P \times Q} \times 100\% = \frac{(P - V_c)}{P} \times 100\%$$

When CM (TCM) > 0, the CM of the increased product sales is greater than the fixed cost and companies may achieve profits.

When CM (TCM)$\leqslant 0$, the CM cannot cover all fixed costs. The company will lose money.

For restaurants, the CM of a dish = price − unit variable cost for food. The CM is used to cover the fixed costs and target profits. Price can be determined by the following two steps:

(1) Average CM per customer = (Fixed cost + Target profit) ÷ Expected number of customers

(2) Price = Average CM per customer + Variable cost per serving

If a restaurant is expected to serve 7,000 customers a month, then the nonfood fixed costs of the restaurant for "braised pork ribs" is 50,000 yuan; the target profit is 30,000 yuan; the average contribution per customer is (50000 + 30000) ÷ 7000 = 11.43 (yuan). If the unit cost per serving is 5 yuan, then the provisional price for "braised pork ribs" is 11.43 + 5 = 16.43 (yuan). CM pricing concerns profit contribution levels rather than food cost percentage.

When the CM is equal to or greater than the fixed cost, companies can break even or make a profit. When the CM is less than the fixed cost, companies has a loss. However, sometimes, when oversupply of the product occurs, under fierce competition, companies will keep the market share via low prices, not considering the fixed costs, to avoid slow selling at high prices and the loss of market. The CM may be less than 0 under the following circumstances: (1) The price for new products after the major products of the company has already covered the fixed costs of the company. (2) The product price after the company reaches the breakeven point. (3) The product price for the company to develop new markets, that is, when sales in the existing market has already reached breakeven or even had profits, the company can set price at the variable cost for new customers or new distribution points to expand the market. (4) The price at off season.

9.3.3 需求导向定价法

需求导向定价法是指企业的定价不以成本为基础,而是根据市场需求状况和消费者对产品的感受价值为依据来定价的一种方法,又称顾客导向定价法或市场导向定价法。此方法灵活有效地运用价格差异,对平均成本相同的同一产品,随市场需求的变化相应地调整价格,不与成本因素发生直接关系。需求导向定价法可分为认知价值定价法、需求差异定价法和逆向定价法三种。

1. 认知价值定价法

认知价值定价法也称理解价值定价法,是指企业按照消费者主观上对该产品所理解的价值来定价,关注消费者对产品价值的感知。此方法认为,消费者对各种产品的价值都有心理定位,当他们选购某一产品时常会在多个同类产品间进行比较,权衡相对价值的高低而做出价格评判。产品的形象、性能、质量、服务、品牌、包装和价格等,都是影响消费者对产品的价值和价格认知的要素。以酒店客房为例,基于消费者认知价格的定价计算如下:

1000 元	竞争对手定价
100 元	更优越的地理位置
100 元	更好的硬件设施
200 元	更优质的服务
1400 元	体现酒店品质的一般定价
200 元	折扣
1200 元	最终价格

只有当产品价格水平与消费者对产品价值的理解至少趋于一致时,消费者才会接受该价格并购买,反之则不会购买。认知价值定价的关键在于企业如何比竞争对手提供更多的价值,并如何向潜在消费者证明这些价值,以及正确估计购买者所承认的价值。很多企业利用市场营销组合中的非价格变量,如消费环境和品牌形象等来影响购买者,在他们的头脑中形成认知价值,并据此定价。Adhikari、Basu 和 Raj(2013)对体验产品(如酒店客房、高级餐厅用餐体验等)定价进行研究,发现不同消费者对同一个体验产品都有不同的价值理解。因此,酒店或餐厅的管理层需要考虑设计不同的产品,以满足不同消费者的体验和价值需求。

9.3.3　Demand-based pricing

Demand-based pricing refers to the pricing method which is not based on cost, but the market demand and the perceived value of consumers about the product, also known as customer-oriented pricing or market-oriented pricing. This method flexibly and effectively utilizes the price differences. For the same product with the same average cost, the price is changed according to the fluctuation in market demand, instead of directly relating to cost factors. Demand-based pricing methods can be divided into perceived-value pricing, dynamic pricing, and bottom-up pricing.

1. Perceived value pricing

Perceived value pricing is that companies set the price according to the subjective understanding of consumers toward the product value, focusing on the consumer perception of product value. This method asserts that the consumer has target prices for different product types. When they purchase a product, they often compare among a number of similar products and make judgments of the price after weighing the relative value. Product image, performance, quality, service, brand, packaging, and pricing are the factors that influence the perceptions of consumers about value and price. The hotel room is taken as an example, and the pricing based on the perceived price of consumers can be calculated as follows:

1,000 yuan	Price by competitor
100 yuan	Better location
100 yuan	Better facilities
200 yuan	Better services
1,400 yuan	General price reflecting the hotel quality
200 yuan	Discounts
1,200 yuan	Final price

Only when the price level of the product tends to be the same as the understanding of consumers about the product value, consumers will accept the price and make a purchase; otherwise, they will not purchase. The key to perceived value pricing is how firms can provide more values than their competitors can, how to prove these values to potential consumers, and how to correctly estimate these values in a way that buyers will recognize. Many companies use the non-price variables in the marketing mix, such as consumption environment and brand image, to influence the buyers by forming perceived price in their mind and pricing accordingly. Adhikari, Basu, and Raj (2013) studied the pricing of experiential products (hotel rooms and dining experiences in fine dining restaurants) and found that different consumers have different perceived values for the same experience product. Therefore, the hotel or restaurant management may consider designing different products to satisfy the different needs of consumers for experiences and values.

2. 差异定价法

差异定价法根据需求的差异确定产品价格,强调适应消费者需求的不同特性,而将成本补偿放在次要的地位进行定价。它往往对同一产品制定两个或以上的价格,或使不同产品价格之间的差额大于其成本之间的差额。其好处是可以使企业定价最大限度地符合市场需求,促进产品销售,有利于企业获取最佳的经济效益。差异定价法的核心是价格歧视。价格歧视分为三个等级:一级价格歧视——企业根据顾客需求的强烈程度,向不同的客人收取不同的价格;二级价格歧视——购买量大的顾客能够获得较低的价格;三级价格歧视——企业向不同类别的顾客收取不同的价格。例如:

顾客细分市场——不同的顾客群体为同一项产品或服务支付不同的价格。例如,商务客人和休闲客人所支付的酒店房价不一样。

产品形态——同一项产品不同型号有不同的价格。例如,酒店豪华客房定价 800元/间·夜,而套房价格定价则是 2000 元/间·夜。

产品形象——基于不同的形象,企业对相同产品采取不同定价。例如,百事可乐在2016 年农历新年前发布全球限量版"乐猴王纪念罐",一套 6 罐价格高达 2016 元。

销售渠道——不同销售渠道的产品定价也存在差异。例如,消费者在西餐厅、快餐店和自动贩卖机所买到的可乐的价格并不相同。

地理位置——即使产品在不同的地理位置的成本是相同的,产品的价格也会存在差异。例如演唱会门票,越靠近舞台的门票价格越高。

时间差异——价格可能会随着季节、日期或小时而变化。例如,度假酒店周末的房价会较高,而工作日的房价会较低。

以市场为导向的定价目标通过价格变化平衡供求关系,寻求市场供需水平的匹配,从而保证在任何一个时点上生产资源和能力都能得到最优配置和利用。其中,收益管理导向下的客房定价或机票定价方法成为当前最受欢迎的定价方法。收益管理是指运用信息系统和定价策略,在合适的时间、合适的渠道、以合适的价格将合适的产品销售

2. Dynamic pricing

Dynamic pricing determines the product price according to the difference in demand levels, emphasizes the adaptation to the different characteristics of consumer needs, and sets the cost compensation to a secondary position when setting the price. This method tends to set two or more prices for the same product or to make the difference among the prices of different products greater than the difference among their costs. The advantage is that the price of the companies can be in line with market demand to the maximum, promotes product sales, and is conducive to obtaining the best possible economic benefits. The core of dynamic pricing is price discrimination. Price discrimination can be divided into three levels. First, the company charges different prices to different customers based on the desire level of consumers. Second, consumers with a larger amount of purchase can receive lower prices. Third, companies charge different prices to different categories of customers, such as follows:

Customer segments: Different customer segments pay different prices for the same product or service. For example, business and leisure guests pay different rates for their hotel rooms.

Product type: The same products with different models have different prices. For example, the price for a deluxe hotel room is 800 yuan/night, whereas the price for a suite is 2000 yuan/room/night.

Product image: Companies charge different prices for the same product based on different product images. For example, Pepsi released the global limited edition "Le Monkey King Memorial Can" before the 2016 Lunar New Year. The price for one pack with six cans is up to 2016 yuan.

Distribution channel: Price differences occur in different distribution channels. For example, the prices for coke in western restaurants, fast-food restaurants, and vending machines are not the same.

Geographic location: Even if the costs of products at different geographical locations are the same, the prices of the products can be different. For example, concert tickets closer to the stage have higher prices.

Time difference: Prices may vary by season, date, or hour. For example, the price of a resort hotel will be higher in the weekend but lower in the weekdays.

The market-oriented pricing objectives seek to match the supply and demand of the market by balancing the relationship between supply and demand through price changes to ensure optimal allocation and utilization of production resources and capacities at any point of time. The pricing method for rooms or air tickets under the revenue management approach becomes the most popular pricing method. Yield management or revenue management refers to the use of information systems and pricing strategies to sell the right product to the right customer at the right price through the right channel at the

给合适的顾客（Kimes，1989）。它将客房出租率和平均房价两个指标结合起来，形成平均每间房收益，追求整体收益最大化，而非削减成本。差异化定价是酒店收益管理以需求为导向的定价策略的集中体现。

酒店收益管理的有效运作建立在以下前提下：

（1）具体市场分析，预测长期与短期需求。商务客与休闲客在预订方式、价格敏感度、居住时段上都有明显的差别，因此在制定价格策略时可差别定价。会议策划者、公司差旅部人员、旅游批发商等的团购数量大，价格敏感，常提前预订且买卖关系长远且相对稳定；而散客要求即时入住，常发生短期购买行为，购买数量不大。因此，对散客的短期购买行为和团购客户的长期购买行为要有准确的预测和分析，平衡房价。Guo、Ling和 Yang 等(2013)对酒店的细分市场和动态定价进行了研究，结果表明酒店在市场分析中制定合适的市场细分，并根据不同细分市场的需求情况进行动态定价，能够提高酒店收入和利润。

（2）应有完整连续的预订数据统计资料，可掌握相应的预订特征数据，如预订但未到、取消预订、延期退房、提早退房的比例，从而科学预测需求量，制定特定夜晚、时段或特定房型接受的各类预订数量，并为超额预订提供依据，对需求进行管理。

（3）产品能进行灵活区分组合，根据各种产品满足客人的效用价值的异同差别定价，对产品进行管理。

（4）收益管理是一个复杂的系统。它一方面需要酒店内部长期的历史统计数据，如预订资料、客户档案资料等；另一方面需要外部市场环境的竞争数据，如当地重要的事件、政策导向、消费环境等。这些资料和信息都是支持收益管理所需的销售信息，以保证制定有效的价格策略，谋求收益最大化。

（5）酒店在进行收益管理的过程中同时需要对分销渠道进行分析和管理，例如分析不同分销渠道的收益、成本、顾客获取量等数据。单一分销渠道或是过多的分销渠道都不利于酒店的收入最大化。在线旅游分销商（OTA）是酒店在分销渠道中的一个主要的

right time (Kimes, 1989). This approach combines the occupancy rate and the average daily rate (ADR) to form the average revenue per available room (RevPAR), hence maximizing the overall returns rather than cutting costs. Dynamic pricing is an example of demand-based pricing strategy in hotel revenue management.

The effective operation of hotel revenue management is based on the following conditions:

(1) Specific market analysis is conducted by forecasting long-term and short-term demands. Business and leisure travelers have obvious differences in booking channel, price sensitivity, and time of stay, so the pricing strategy can be dynamic pricing. Meeting planners, corporate travel planning staff, and travel wholesalers are in large demand for group purchase and are price sensitive. They make advance booking, and they are in a long-term and relatively stable trading relationship. By contrast, frequent independent travelers (FITs) require immediate stay, exhibit short-term purchase behaviors, and need small quantities of purchase. Therefore, accurate forecasting and analysis of the short-term purchase behavior of FITs and the long-term purchase behavior of group-buying customers are significant to balance the price. Guo, Ling and Yang, et. al. (2013) studied hotel segmentation and dynamic pricing. The results showed that the hotel was able to develop appropriate market segments through market analysis and dynamically priced the products according to the demand of different market segments to increase hotel revenues and profits.

(2) Complete and continuous booking statistics is needed for understanding the corresponding booking patterns, such as the percentages of no-show (booked but show up), cancel, extent stay (late check-out), and early check-out, to scientifically predict the demand, to develop predetermined booking quotas for specific nights, time periods, or specific room types, and to provide basis for overbooking to manage the demand.

(3) Products can be flexibly distinguished or combined and managed through different prices based on the different utility values perceived by the guests.

(4) Revenue management is a complex system. On the one hand, this approach requires the long-term historical statistics from the hotel, such as booking information and customer profiles; on the other hand, it requires the competitive information from the external market environment, such as important local events, policy direction, and consumption environment. These data and information are the sales information needed to support revenue management to ensure that effective pricing strategies are in place to maximize revenues.

(5) Revenue management for hotels requires the analysis and management of distribution channels at the time, such as the data about revenues, costs, and number of customers acquired from different distribution channels. A single distribution channel or too many distribution channels are not conducive to hotel revenue maximization. Online travel agencies (OTA) are among the major partners in the distribution channel. The

合作对象,如何利用 OTA 将影响酒店的收益。研究发现,酒店和 OTA 之间签订合理的合作协议、依据酒店房价设定佣金比例等方法都能够有效提高酒店和 OTA 的收益(Guo、Ling 和 Dong 等,2013;Ling、Guo 和 Yang,2014)。

如果实施得当,收益管理会为酒店和客人创造一个双赢的局面。在高需求与低需求时期运用适当的战略,酒店的收入能最大化。能够接待必须在高需求的日子入住同时对价格不敏感的客人,客人的需求得到了更好的满足,而在低需求时期以较低房价入住也使对价格敏感的客人得到了更好的服务。成功的关键是早期准确的预测、适当的员工培训和奖励制度,以及灵活的定价。

3. 逆向定价法

逆向定价法是企业依据消费者能够接受的最终销售价格,逆向推算出中间商的批发价和生产企业的出厂价的定价方法。它的主要特点是:产品价格针对性强,反映市场需求情况,有利于加强与中间商的良好关系,保证中间商的正常利润,使产品迅速向市场渗透,并可根据市场供求情况及时调整,定价比较灵活。但同时也面临着产品的质量下降和客户的不满,并导致客源减少的危机。

在确定最终价格时,除了定价目标、需求、成本、竞争外,企业还需要考虑额外因素。例如定价对其他营销活动的影响,对企业内部的价格政策、风险控制和对其他利益相关群体的影响。最终价格必须将品牌形象、品牌质量和广告推广考虑在内。同时,价格要与企业内部的价格政策保持一致,必要时可以通过建立定价部门,如酒店行业中的收益管理部,来制定相关政策或批准定价决定。如果最终价格所带来的风险过高,如销量难以达到预期,或有损消费者的利益,消费者或分销商会拒绝购买或分销产品。因此,企业在确定最终定价前,需要考虑分销商、销售人员、供应商等利益相关群体的反应。另外,最终定价是否符合法律规定也是企业需要考虑的部分。

utilization of OTAs will affect hotel revenues. A study has found that the revenues are increased for hotels and OTAs through reasonable cooperation agreements and commission ratios based on the room rate (Guo, Ling & Dong, et. al. 2013; Ling, Guo & Yang, 2014).

If implemented properly, revenue management creates a win-win situation for both hotels and customers. If appropriate strategies are adopted during the high-demand and low-demand periods, then the hotel revenues can be maximized. The needs of the customers are better met with the ability to accommodate guests who must stay during high-demand periods while being price insensitive. The availability of lower prices during the low-demand periods also provides better services to price-sensitive customers. The key to success is accurate forecasting at the early stage, appropriate staff training and reward systems, and the pricing flexibility.

3. Bottom-up pricing

Bottom-up pricing is a pricing method to inversely calculate the wholesale price of the brokers and the ex-factory price of the manufactures based on the ending price that consumer can accept. Its main features are obvious targets for product price, reflection of the market demand, and strengthening the relationship with brokers to ensure their normal profits, so that the products can rapidly penetrate the market and adjust with the market supply and demand in a timely manner. The pricing is also highly flexible. However, this method is faced with decline of product quality and customer dissatisfaction, consequently leading to the crisis of decreasing customers.

When determining the final price, companies need to consider other factors in addition to pricing targets, demand, cost, and competition, such as the impact of pricing on other marketing activities, pricing policies within the firm, risk control, and other stakeholder groups. The final price must take the brand image, brand quality, and advertising into account. Prices should also be consistent with the pricing policies within the company. If necessary, the company can establish a pricing department to formulate relevant policies or approve pricing decisions, such as the revenue management department in the hotel industry. If the risk from the final price is too high, for example, the expected sales are difficult to achieve or detrimental to the interests of the consumers, then the consumers or distributors will refuse to purchase or distribute the product. Therefore, before determining the final price, companies need to consider the responses of distributors, sales staff, suppliers, and other stakeholders. Furthermore, the company needs to consider whether the final price is in line with legal requirements.

第 10 章 分销渠道

 本章要点

- 分销渠道的基本概念
- 旅游企业主要分销渠道
- 酒店分销体系
- 旅行社分销体系
- 分销渠道的选择标准和管理

对于企业来讲,创造价值和传递价值同等重要。营销人员越来越倾向于采用一种全方位的视角来看待企业的运营,不仅仅关注产品的销售,同时关注连接原材料、产品生产和销售的供应链。产品的生产者、销售渠道以及最终的使用者共同构成了企业的价值网络。价值网络利益的最大化成为营销人员关注的热点。旅游业产品的独特性使得旅游市场上的消费者只有亲临现场才能实现旅游产品的消费,这就使得在旅游业中分销渠道的选择格外重要。如果旅游者不知道如何到达目的地、如何购买机票、如何预订酒店,那么这些产品就会形同虚设。本章将涉及旅游业中的分销渠道的类型、特点、重要性,酒店的分销体系,旅行社的分销体系,以及分销渠道的选择和管理等内容。

10.1 分销渠道的基本概念

分销渠道是指一系列参与到企业生产产品或提供服务的过程中的独立机构(也称为中介)(Kotler 和 Keller,2009),其主要作用是在生产商与消费者之间建立路径,帮助消费者实现产品购买或使用。产品供应商、中间商、消费者三者构成了分销系统,而中间商由分销或营销渠道中位于产品供应商和最终消费者之间的一切企业或组织组成。旅游产品的生产消费同时性使得

Chapter 10　Distribution Channels

 Key points of the chapter

- ■ Basic concepts of distribution channels
- ■ Main distribution channels of tourism enterprises
- ■ Hotel distribution system
- ■ Distribution system of travel agencies
- ■ Selection criteria and management of distribution channels

Creating and delivering value are equally important for enterprises. An increasing number of marketers view their operations holistically. Rather than focusing only on selling products, marketers consider the supply chain from obtaining raw materials and manufacturing to selling. Manufacturers, distribution channels, and end users of products form the value network of enterprises. Marketers focus on maximizing interests in the value network. Given the unique feature of tourism, consumers can only consume tourism products on the spot, and, thus, selecting distribution channels is important. Tourism products become meaningless if tourists do not know how to reach the destinations, buy air tickets, or make hotel reservations. This chapter centers on the types, characteristics, and importance of distribution channels, hotel distribution system, and travel agency distribution system as well as the selection and management of distribution channels.

10.1　Basic Concepts of Distribution Channels

Distribution channels are series of independent institutions (i.e., intermediaries) involved in the production of goods or services (Kotler & Keller, 2009). They serve as an interface between manufacturers and consumers, allowing consumers to purchase and use products. Suppliers of products, intermediaries, and consumers constitute the distribution system; intermediaries are enterprises or entities between suppliers and end users in the distribution channel. Distribution channels must effectively convey compelling messages and deliver products and services to consumers appropriately given the simultaneous

分销渠道不仅需要能够有效传递有说服力的信息,还要能够把产品和服务按照消费者喜爱的地点、时间、方式传递给他们(Reid 和 Bojani,2006)。渠道的作用主要有以下几个方面:

- 收集有关潜在消费者、现有消费者、竞争对手以及其他影响营销环境的因素的信息。

- 建立并发布具有说服力的市场营销信息以刺激消费者进行购买。

- 企业与渠道中介,以及渠道中介之间在价格和相关条款方面达成协议,高效完成产品所有权的转换。

- 向生产商下达订单。

- 取得资金以便不同层级的渠道能够囤积一定的库存。

- 承担渠道运营过程中出现的风险。

- 实体货物存放和转移。

- 买家通过银行或其他金融机构完成支付。

- 监督实际的所有权转移。

渠道的重要性体现在,它能够将潜在消费者转化为实际消费者,渠道不仅服务市场,更重要的是能够制造市场(Kotler 和 Keller,2009)。除此以外,渠道选择与其他营销决策息息相关。企业的定价策略取决于它是通过在线旅游分销商销售还是通过销售代表;企业的销售和广告决策依赖于分销商需要什么程度的培训,以及分销商需要什么样的激励。另外,企业在渠道的决策也会影响企业实现对其他企业的商业承诺,以及相应的政策和程序。

渠道之间的物流和信息流在不同的渠道作用下有所不同。Kotler 和 Keller(2009)归纳了五种不同的渠道作用及其对应的物流及信息流,如图 10-1 所示。

分销体系的结构设计是营销策略的基础。不同的分销体系结构影响着旅游企业对分销体系的政策和管理手段。分销体系的长度、宽度和广度是所有企业设计分销体系结构时应考虑的三个关键要素。要素不同,分销渠道的分类也就不同。

production and consumption nature of tourism products (Reid & Bojani, 2006). Distribution channels perform the following functions:

- Collect information about potential consumers, existing consumers, competitors, and other factors affecting marketing environment.

- Create and publish compelling marketing messages to stimulate purchase.

- Effectively convert the product ownership between enterprises and channel intermediaries, or among channel intermediaries, regarding mutual agreement on price and related conditions.

- Place orders to manufacturers.

- Obtain funds for various channels to maintain certain amount of inventory.

- Undertake the risks arising from channel operation.

- Store and transfer physical goods.

- Ensure buyers settle payments through banks or other financial institutions.

- Monitor the actual transfer of ownership.

The importance of distribution channels is reflected in the ability to turn potential consumers into actual consumers. Channels not only serve markets; more importantly, they create markets (Kotler & Keller, 2009). Selecting channels is also closely related to other marketing decisions. A company's pricing strategy depends on whether it sells through an online travel agent (OTA) or through a sales representative. The company's sales and advertising decisions are determined by the degree of required training and the incentives provided to intermediaries. The company's selection of channels also affects its business commitment to other enterprises and the corresponding policies and procedures.

The logistics and information flow between the channels vary under different channels. Kotler and Keller (2009) summarize five channel functions and their corresponding logistics and information flows (Figure 10 - 1).

The structural design of distribution systems is the basis of marketing strategies. Various distribution system structures influence the policy and management means of the tourism enterprise to distribution systems. The length, width, and breadth of distribution systems are the three key determinants in designing distribution architecture. The classification of distribution channels responds differently to varying determinants.

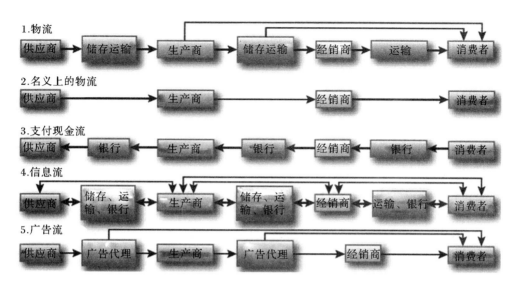

图 10-1 营销渠道中的物流、信息流及现金流
来源：Kotler，P.，Keller，K.（2009）. *Marketing Management*（13th ed.）.
Upper Saddle River，NJ：Pearson Prentice Hall.

1. 分销体系的长度

分销体系的长度是指旅游产品在分销体系的流通过程中，中间要经过的中介的层级。旅游分销体系可分为直接分销和间接分销两大类。直接分销简称直销，是指企业将旅游产品直接销售给最终顾客。由于没有中间商，也称零级分销。常见的直接分销形式有上门推销、直邮、在线直接预订、电话推销和零售点直销等。间接分销是指旅游企业经过若干层次的中间商，最终将其产品逐级转卖给顾客，包括一级分销体系：企业（指生产某项旅行产品的企业，如航空公司、酒店、目的地等）→某个中间商→顾客；二级分销体系：企业→批发商→零售商→顾客；三级分销体系：企业→总代理商→批发商→零售商→顾客。旅游企业依据分销体系的控制与资源运用的能力大小来选择长分销体系或短分销体系。

2. 分销体系的宽度

分销体系的宽度是指分销体系每一层级里中介的数量，如一级批发商或二级批发商各有多少等。根据分销体系的宽度，可将分销分为三种：密集型分销、选择型分销和专营型分销。（1）密集型分销渠道也称广泛型分销渠道，是指生产商在同一渠道层级上选用尽可能多的渠道中间商来经销自己的

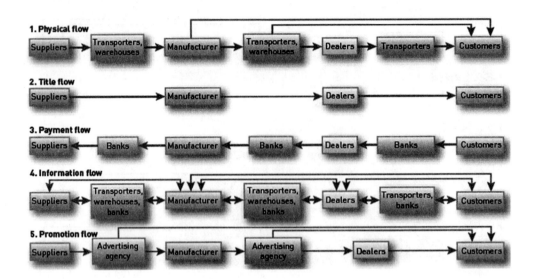

Figure 10 - 1　Logistics flow, information flow and capital flow in the marketing distributions

Source: Kotler, P., Keller, K. (2009). *Marketing Management* (13th ed.). Upper Saddle River, NJ: Pearson Prentice Hall.

1. The length of distribution system

The length of distribution system points to the intermediary levels throughout the distribution of tourism products. A tourism distribution system can be divided into two categories, namely, direct and indirect distribution. Direct distribution or zero-level distribution refers to direct marketing (DM). A company directly sells tourism products to customers without involving intermediaries. Door-to-door sales, direct mail, online direct booking, telephone sales, and retail outlets are common practices of direct distribution. Indirect distribution refers to tourism enterprises selling their products to customers through certain levels of intermediaries. This category includes the three following distribution systems. Primary distribution system: Companies producing tourism products (e.g., airline, hotel, and destinations) → intermediaries → customers; Secondary distribution system: Enterprises → wholesalers → retailers → customers; Tertiary distribution system: Enterprises → exclusive selling agent → wholesalers → retailers → customers. Tourism enterprises choose between a long and short distribution system on the basis of the control and capacity in utilizing resources in the distribution system.

2. The width of the distribution system

The width of the distribution system refers to the numbers of intermediaries in individual hierarchies within the distribution systems (e.g., the numbers of primary and secondary wholesalers). The width of the distribution system is divided into three means, namely, intensive, selective, and exclusive distribution. (1) Intensive distribution channel, also known as extensive distribution channel, refers to manufacturers utilizing as

产品。航空公司的分销战略多属此类。（2）选择型分销渠道是指在某一渠道层级上选择少量的渠道中间商来进行商品分销,使用较广泛。超豪华酒店和度假村如四季（Four Seasons）和悦榕庄（Banyan Tree）在选择分销渠道时常使用该战略。（3）专营型分销渠道是指在某一渠道层级上只选用唯一的中间商,即一个市场只有一个销售者。三种方式各具特点,表 10-1 是对这三种形式的简单概括。

表 10-1　三种分销体系的宽度上的方式特点

类型	特点	考虑要素
密集型分销	市场覆盖面广泛;中间商之间的竞争利于扩大销售量;分销越密集,销售的潜力越大;旅游企业对众多中间商控制力较弱	如何控制众多的分销商
选择型分销	市场覆盖面较大;企业对中间商的控制力较强;中间商之间的竞争程度较高	如何避免分销商资源的重复和浪费
专营型分销	中间商忠诚度高;企业对其控制力强;缺乏竞争,企业对中间商的依赖性较强	如何确定中间商区域重叠的程度

3. 分销体系的广度

分销体系的广度是指旅游企业采用分销类型的多少,即采用单一的直销制或某一种间接分销制,或是多种分销体系结合,如直销制与间接分销体系（一级分销制、二级分销制、三级分销制）中一种或多种结合分销的形式。从广度上分类,可将分销模式分为单一化模式和多种分销方式并用的多元化模式两种。单一型渠道是指企业只采用一种分销体系形式进行产品的分销,如餐厅不通过任何预订机构而只通过餐厅自有电话实现直接分销。多元化则指企业采用多种不同类型的分销形式进行分销,如酒店既通过官方网站直接预订,又通过与旅行社或其他中间商网络链接间接预订。这三个考虑因素划分出来的分销形式如表 10-2 所示。

many intermediaries at the same hierarchy in distributing their products. A typical example is the distribution strategy of airline companies. (2) Selective distribution channel, which is common in the business world, is selecting a small number of intermediaries for distributing products. High-end hotels and resorts, such as Four Seasons and Banyan Tree, adopt this strategy in selecting distribution channels. (3) Exclusive distribution channel is choosing a sole intermediary at each hierarchy, implying that the market has only one distributor. These three methods feature their own characteristics, and Table 10 – 1 summarizes them.

Table 10 – 1   The three types of distribution channels and corresponding characteristics

Type	Characteristics	Considerations
Intensive distribution channel	Broad market coverage; Competition among intermediaries is advantageous to expand the sales volume; The more intensive distribution, the greater sales potential; Tourism enterprises are weak inexerting control over intermediaries	How to control numerous distributors; How to avoid duplication and waste of distributor resources
Selective distribution channel	Broad market coverage; Strong control over intermediaries; High level of competition among intermediaries	How to determine the degree of overlap among intermediaries
Exclusive distribution channel	Highly loyal intermediaries; Tourism enterprises have strong control over intermediaries; lacking competition, resulting in strong dependence on intermediaries	How to avoid intermediaries in controlling the sales

3. The breadth of the distribution system

The breadth of the distribution system refers to the forms of distributors used by tourism enterprises. Enterprises may select from single direct selling system, indirect distribution system, or a combination of various distribution systems, such as direct and indirect distribution systems (primary, secondary, and territory distribution) in one or more combined forms. The breadth of distribution can be classified into single and multiple distribution models. Enterprises adopting a single model only rely on one form of distribution system for product distribution. For example, restaurants only allow reservation through direct telephone calls instead of any other reservation organization. Multiple distribution models refer to the use of different types of distributors. Examples include booking accommodations on the hotel official website and through travel agencies or other intermediaries. Table 10 – 2 lists the considerations in selecting distribution channels based on the three determinants.

表 10 - 2　旅游企业分销形式的划分标准

考虑要素	划分标准	划分结果
长度	分销渠道中间环节的多少	直接分销和间接分销
宽度	每级中间商数目的多少	密集型、选择型和专营型分销
广度	采用分销类型的多少	单一性渠道和多元化渠道

旅游产品的易逝性决定了分销强度在旅游业中的意义与制造业截然不同。服务企业有一定的实际接纳能力,当这个能力的使用率从经济角度来说没有达到可接受的标准时,就意味着该旅游企业不得不从市场中退出。因此,市场可以支撑的企业数量是有限的。在像快餐业这种以便利为导向的行业,密集型分销已成为一种惯例,所以大量快餐厅分布于同一城市,形成密集型分销。尽管方式各异,酒店、餐饮和其他旅游企业都在经历着日渐密集的分销。酒店通过不同的在线预订手段和传统的方法扩大酒店分销的覆盖面;餐厅通过增多零售店面抢占市场或利用第三方网站延长接触客户的触角;航空公司依靠全球分销系统广纳客源;旅行社则利用门市直销和电子商务分销的结合扩展客源市场。

10.2　旅游企业分销渠道

分销渠道是将产品或服务提供给消费者和商业客户过程中的各种独立组织的集合,主要是为了提供充分信息,使得适当的人、在适当的时间、在适当的地点做出购买决策,达成销售。换句话说,就是将消费者向产品移动。旅游营销渠道主要由旅游批发商、旅游零售商、专营机构、销售代表、政府旅游部门、旅游行业协会和电子商务预订系统(包括全球分销系统)构成。

旅游行业的分销渠道可以被分为四个阶段:全球分销系统(GDS)阶段,互联网阶段,社交、位置、移动(SoLoMo)阶段、渠道多元化阶段(Thakran 和 Verma,2013)。

1. 全球分销系统阶段

全球分销系统(GDS)阶段是旅游企业发展分销渠道的第一个重要阶段,行业依靠电话、电报,甚至是信件预订房间。在此阶段,飞机航班和酒店房间通过旅行社,利用全球分销系统实时出售。全球分销系统的出现和发展显著增加了酒店、航空公司、汽车租赁和邮轮公司跨国界的覆盖面,促进了全球旅游和旅游业的发展。旅游批发商、旅游零售商、专营机构、销售代表和全球分销系统都是这个阶段旅游行业分销链渠道上的重要组成部分。

Table 10 − 2   The classification standard of tourism enterprises' distribution system

Consideration	Classification standard	Outcome
Length	The intermediary levels throughout the distribution	Direct and indirect distribution
Width	The numbers of intermediaries in individual hierarchies within the distribution systems	Intensive, selective, and exclusive distribution
Breadth	The forms of distributors used	Single direct selling system, or a combination of various distribution systems

The perishability nature of tourism products determines the strength of distribution, which is highly different from that of the manufacturing industry. Service enterprises possess a certain degree of adaptability. From an economic perspective, service enterprises withdraw from the market if the use of the ability ratio has not reached acceptable standards because the market can only support a confined number of players. Intensive distribution is a common practice in the convenience-oriented industry, such as the fast food sector. Many fast-food restaurants are located in one city, forming an intensive distribution. Although they use different approaches, hotels, restaurants, and other tourism enterprises practice intensive distribution. Hotels expand their distribution coverage through various online booking and traditional methods. Restaurants gain access to customers by increasing retail outlets or using third-party websites. Airlines rely on global distribution system (GDS) to broaden their customer reach. Travel agencies pursue direct selling at retail outlets together with e-commerce distribution to expand source market.

10.2   Main Distribution Channels of Tourism Enterprises

Distribution channels are a collection of independent organizations that provide products or services to consumers and business customers. They primarily provide sufficient information to help the right people make appropriate purchase decisions. Distribution channels direct customers to products. Tourism marketing channels comprise tourism wholesalers, tourism retailers, franchisees, sales representatives, tourism bureaus, tourism industry associations, and e-commerce booking systems (including GDS).

Distribution channels for the travel industry can be divided into four stages, namely, the GDS stage; Internet stage; social, location, and mobile (SoLoMo) stage; and channel diversification stage (Thakran & Verma, 2013).

1. GDS stage

The GDS stage is the first yet important stage. Tourism businesses rely on telephone, telegraph, and mails to book rooms. At this stage, travel agencies sell flights and hotel rooms in real time via GDS. The emergence and growth of GDS has significantly increased the cross-border coverage of hotels, airlines, car leasing, and cruise lines, which contribute to the development of global travel and the tourism industry. Tourism wholesalers, travel retailers, franchisees, sales representatives, and GDS are important components of the distribution chain in the tourism industry at this stage.

（1）旅游批发商也叫批发旅游经营商,主要从事组织和批发包价旅游业务。他们与旅游产品生产商如酒店、车船、航空公司、旅游景点以及包价旅游中还涉及的其他企业签订协议,预先购买这些服务项目,然后根据旅游者的不同需求和消费水平,设计出各具特色的包价旅游产品,通过旅游零售商销售。批发商从批量购买中获取较大的折扣和优惠,通过组装,以较高价格出售给零售商或代理商,二者之间的差价即成为他们的主要商业利润。2004年,锦江国际集团与上海旅行社签署战略合作协议,进行资源整合,成为中国首个"旅游批发商"诞生的标志(新华社,2004)。目前中国的旅游批发商主要是大型的旅行社集团。中国国际旅行社、中国旅行社、中国青年旅行社、中国康辉旅行社、春秋旅行社、港中旅等大型旅行社集团就属此类。

（2）旅游零售商亦称零售旅行代理商,是旅游批发商和旅游者之间的联系纽带,它既包括旅游零售商也包括旅游代理商。他们主要代理批发商招徕和组织旅游者,并为旅游者提供接待服务。旅行代理主要有两种形式:一是旅游零售商从批发商处买下产品所有权,设定最后价格并销售给最终消费者——旅游者个人或团队。绝大部分酒店直接销售客房,属于零售商,也是分销渠道的成员。几乎所有餐厅都是直接为消费者提供餐饮产品和服务的,因此也是零售商中的一员。第二,部分旅游企业仅从事产品代理,不买下产品的所有权。它们通常不控制所代理产品的销售价格,而是根据所销售的产品多少提取佣金。旅行社一般都有从事代理的活动,他们主要代理酒店、航空公司、邮轮公司、汽车租赁公司和景点景区等其他旅游企业的产品,并根据销售额获得由旅游批发商支付的佣金。通过预订系统,旅行代理是旅游产品销售中一个很重要的分销渠道成员。

（3）专营机构是指那些专门经营某一旅游线路或某一项旅游产品的企业、专业的订房公司、商旅服务公司和票务和会展公司等,如旅行社的线路专营、航线买断、奖励旅游专营公司和会议会展专营商等。旅游线路专营就是旅行社通过买断自己开发的某条旅游线路中某些环节全部或某类产品和服务在某段时间内的使用权而形成的对某条线路的排他性经营(潘永涛,2004)。从 2014 年 12 月开始,中国旅游者只能通过新加坡中国大使馆指定的旅行社或机构办理新加坡旅游签证,这些旅行社或机构就是专营机构。

（4）销售代表一般包括酒店、餐厅、会议场所、航空公司等旅游企业指派的、与客人直接沟通的工作人员。他们一般为顾客提供售前咨询、预订服务、售中增值服务等。

（1）Tourism wholesalers or wholesale tourism operators engage in the organization and wholesale of tour packages business. They have agreements with tourism product manufacturers，such as hotels，travel agencies，airlines，tourist attractions，and other companies involved in packaged tours. Tourism wholesalers pre-purchase services from these manufacturers，design tour packages based on the demand and spending power of tourists，and sell the packages to travel retailers. Wholesalers enjoy economies of scale and discounts from bulk purchases and generate profit from the price difference after selling to retailers. In 2004，Jinjiang International Group and Shanghai Travel Service signed a strategic cooperation agreement on resource integration，which became the first "tourism wholesaler" in China（Xinhua News Agency，2004）. Tourism wholesalers in China are presently large-scale travel agencies(e.g.，China International Travel Service，China Travel Service，China Youth Travel Service，China Comfort Travel Agency，Spring Travel Agency，Hong Kong China Travel，and other large travel agencies).

（2）Travel retailers or retail travel agents are the middlemen between travel wholesalers，which include tourism retailers and travel agents，and tourists. They act on behalf of wholesalers and organized tourists and provide hospitality services for tourists. The two main types of travel agents are as follows. First，travel retailers buy the ownership of the product from the wholesaler and decide the final price for the end consumers，that is，individual tourists or tour groups. Most hotels，which act as both retailers and members of a distribution channel，sell rooms directly to customers. Nearly all restaurants directly provide consumers with food and beverage products and services. Therefore，they are members of retailers. Second，some tourism enterprises are only engaged in product agents without buying the product ownership. They usually do not control the sale price of the products and merely obtain commission from products sold. Travel agencies act as the agents of hotels，airlines，cruise companies，car rental companies，scenic spots，and other tourism products. They receive commissions from products sold. Through the reservation system，travel agents are crucial members of distribution channels for selling tourism products.

（3）Franchisees specialize in a particular tourist route or a tourism product，professional booking companies，business travel service companies，and ticketing and convention companies. Exclusive tourist routes are provided by travel agencies，airline buyouts，incentive travel franchisees，and exhibition franchisees. Tour franchisees are the exclusive operators of certain tourist routes or sole operators that offer products and services at certain routes in a designated period of time（Pan，2004）.Since December 2014，Chinese tourists can only apply for Singapore tourist visas through travel agencies designated by the Chinese Embassy in Singapore，which is an example of a franchisee.

（4）Sales representatives include hotels，restaurants，conference venues，airlines，and other tourism enterprises assigned to communicate directly with customers. They provide customers with pre-sale consultation services，booking services，and value-adding services.

（5）政府旅游部门向市场提供信息，在全国或更大范围内促销旅游业，同时也可以成为政府出游的安排中心，包括国家旅游局、各级省市级旅游局以及地方旅游局等。

（6）旅游行业协会进行旅游经济效益和服务质量等方面的调研工作，提供最新的行业信息或咨询服务。不同协会间的相互交流与合作利于开展整个行业的交叉营销，如旅游协会、旅行社协会、酒店业协会、旅游车船协会、旅游报刊协会等。

全球分销系统最早是依托航空公司的计算机票务预订系统，现已发展为同时向酒店、度假村、汽车租赁、铁路、邮轮等其他旅游相关行业提供预订和营销综合服务的销售系统。各 GDS 系统提供商均依托各自的计算机预订系统，通过国际航空运输协会的通信专网，将加入 GDS 的航空公司、酒店、汽车租赁公司等产品/服务的提供者（即卖方），和加入 GDS 的遍布全球的旅游代理人（即代理方），连成一个旅游专业网络系统，并通过后者实现对旅游者，即最终用户的销售（殷文，1998）。它通过庞大的计算机系统将航空、旅游产品与代理商连接起来，使代理商可以实时销售各类组合产品，从而使最终消费者（旅客）拥有最透明的信息、最广泛的选择范围、最强的议价能力和最低的购买成本。目前，北美的 Sabre 和 Worldspan、欧洲的 Amadeus 和 Cendant-Galileo 是世界上的 GDS 四巨头，可向全球分销 500 多家航空公司、6000 多家酒店、数百家租车公司和旅行社的产品。对于中国旅游分销体系来说，除了四大巨头的渗透之外，我国的中国民航订座系统中国航信（Travelsky）是唯一为国内全部航空公司、机场和国内外多家代理人提供服务的分销系统。

2. 互联网阶段

互联网阶段源自于互联网技术的飞速发展，为旅游企业和酒店供应商提供了具有显著成本效益的直接营销工具，其主要作用是消除了不同企业（无论是全球性品牌或者是地区性的独立品牌）在地理覆盖上的差异。在此阶段传统的分销模式被改变，旅游企业开始投资建设自己的品牌网站和预订引擎，而不是严重依赖于全球分销系统和旅行社。基于（移动）互联网技术的在线旅游平台逐渐成为占据主导地位的分销渠道，消费者能够通过在线旅游平台或搜索引擎直接接触产品信息，且平台提供实时的预订服务（例如 Google、

（5）Government tourism bureaus provide information to the market to promote tourism within or beyond a country. They also serve as the center for government travel arrangements. Examples include the National Tourism Administration, provincial and municipal tourism bureaus, and local tourism bureaus.

（6）Tourism industry associations study economic efficiency and service quality and offer the latest industry information or advisory services. Mutual communication and cooperation among associations are conducive to the cross-marketing of the entire industry, for example, tourism associations, travel agency associations, hotel industry associations, travel-related transportation associations, and travel press associations.

Global Distribution System （GDS） was first developed by an airline computer ticketing system. The use of the system is extended to provide reservation and marketing services to hotel, resort, car rental, rail, cruise, and other travel related industries. GDS system providers develop their own computer reservation systems. The International Air Transport Association creates a tourism professional network system, which links the GDS of the product or service providers, such as airlines, hotels, and car rental companies （i.e., sellers）, and the GDS of the global tourism agencies （i.e., agents）. The end users that the network system targets are the agents （Yin, 1998）. The system connects airlines, tourism products, and agents through a massive computer system that enables agents to sell different combinations of tourism products in real time. The final consumers （i.e., tourists） can obtain the most transparent information, the widest range of selections, and the strongest bargaining power at the lowest purchasing cost. Saber and Worldspan in North America along with Amadeus and Cendant-Galileo in Europe are the world's four giant systems. They distribute products and services to over 500 airlines, 6000 hotels, car rental companies, and travel agencies globally. These four giants also penetrate the tourism distribution system in China. Travelsky, the civil aviation distribution system in China, is the sole system that serves all airlines, airports, and agents overseas.

2. Internet stage

The Internet stage stems from the rapid advancement of Internet technology. It provides a highly cost-effective DM tool for tourism enterprises and hotel suppliers in eliminating the differences in geographical coverage among enterprises, which include international and regional independent brands. The conventional distribution model has changed at this stage. Tourism enterprises have begun to invest in building their own websites and booking engines instead of heavily relying on GDS and travel agencies. Online travel platforms, which are built on the mobile Internet technology, emerge as a dominant distribution channel. Consumers can directly access product information through online travel agencies or search engines that offer real-time reservation services （e. g., Google, Baidu, Expedia, Booking. com, and Ctrip）. Given the booming

百度、Expedia、Booking.com、携程等）。然而，在在线旅游平台和搜索引擎蓬勃发展的同时，酒店和旅行社逐渐失去了对直销渠道和价格的控制，导致利润减少（Thakran 和 Verma，2013）。

3. SoLoMo 阶段

移动技术和社交媒体的兴起让消费者处于一个掌上移动时代，旅游企业的分销渠道也随之向"社交、位置、移动"的方向发展。SoLoMo 体现的是移动时代的三大特点：So—Social，即社交化，社交媒体是互联网时代最具创新性的发展之一，旅游企业可以通过社交媒体直接与顾客进行交流，发展企业的忠诚顾客。Lo—Location，即地理位置技术，能方便顾客在社交媒体上发布自己所在的地点，而且能够为企业进行宣传。Mo—Mobile，即移动技术，智能手机的普遍应用让移动技术成为顾客生活中不可或缺的一部分，顾客借助移动技术在社交媒体上实时分享自身的体验，让好的产品得到快速推广（Thakran 和 Verma，2013）。很多国内外的旅游企业基于 SoLoMo 推出了自己的手机 App 或是对移动端网页进行定制化设计，例如喜达屋的 SPG App 以及基于其 App 的 Keyless 项目（利用手机 App 即可开启房门）。

4. 渠道多元化阶段

计算机、智能手机和平板电脑的普及和混合使用让消费者有更多不同的信息渠道。在渠道多元化阶段，消费者越来越依赖在线搜索，他们在一天的不同时间使用多个设备，搜索他们想要的供应商信息。在做出最终购买决定之前，消费者平均访问了近 20 个网站（Thakran 和 Verma，2013）。另一方面，旅游行业供应商正加大对直接分销渠道的投资，并试图向客户提供定制的、高品质的产品和服务体验。简而言之，旅游业正在慢慢地脱离对传统分销渠道中介的依赖。

从国内外的行业背景和投资主题来看，旅游行业的网络预订渠道可分为四种类型：（1）旅游供应商直销渠道。酒店、航空公司等供应商自设网络渠道以期直接获取客源，减少佣金并直接与顾客沟通。供应商网站主要有供应商官方网站，如上海迪斯尼乐园网站和凯悦酒店集团网站等，以及供应商官方 App，如喜达屋 SPG 和南方航空都推出了企业官方 App。（2）旅游中间商网络渠道，主要包括传统旅行社建立的商务网站或 App，如中青旅遨游网和

development of online travel agency and search engines, hotels and travel agencies are losing their place in direct sales and price control, which results in reduced profit margins (Thakran & Verma, 2013).

3. SoLoMo stage

The SoLoMo stage refers to the handheld mobile era that was induced by the rise of mobile technology and social media. The distribution channels of tourism enterprises target the SoLoMo direction. SoLoMo embodies three characteristics of the mobile age. So means social, that is, socialization. Social media is one of the most groundbreaking developments in the Internet age. Tourism companies can communicate directly with customers through social media and maintain a relationship with loyal customers. Lo refers to location, that is, the geographic location technology. Customers check-in on social media sites to indicate their geographical locations, which serve the promotion purpose of enterprises. Mo means mobile or mobile technology, which has become an integral part of customers' lives due to the universal application of smartphones. Customers share their real-time first-hand experiences on social media sites, enabling far-reaching promotion of quality products (Thakran & Verma, 2013). In the SoLoMo stage, many domestic and foreign tourism enterprises launch their own mobile apps or customized webpages, such as the Starwood's Starwood Preferred Guest(SPG) app and the Keyless project, which uses a mobile app to open doors.

4. Channel diversification stage

The channel diversification stage refers to the proliferation and mixed-use of computers, smartphones, and tablets, which allow consumers to access diverse information channels. Consumers increasingly rely on online information search in this stage. They search for information of suppliers several times daily using multiple devices. Consumers visit approximately 20 websites before making their final purchase decisions (Thakran & Verma, 2013). Suppliers in the travel industry increase their investment in direct distribution channels that offer customized and quality products and services to customers. In brief, the tourism industry is gradually detaching from the reliance on conventional distribution channels.

From the domestic and international industry background and investment environment, the tourism industry has four online booking channels. The first is the direct sales channels by tourism suppliers. Hotels, airlines, and other suppliers set up their own network channels for direct access to customers. Direct sales channels aim to pay less commission and have direct communication with customers. Supplier sites include official websites(e.g., Shanghai Disneyland and Hyatt Hotels) and official apps(e.g., Starwood SPG and China Southern Airlines).The second is network channels by tourism intermediaries, which include business sites or apps established by traditional travel

中国国旅 App。（3）由第三方运营商投资建立的大型专业预订网站，如携程网和阿里旅行等。它们的优势是资金、专业技术、广泛的代理网络和丰富的可选择产品。最后，旅游评论网站（也称为旅游 UGC 网站）也提供预订端口，如猫途鹰（TripAdvisor）和马蜂窝。

10.3　酒店分销体系

虽然分销的基本概念适用于旅游业的各个行业部门，但各旅游企业等所采取的分销体系也存有诸多差异。对于酒店来讲，分销体系的成形主要依托两种力量：第一种是自 20 世纪 50 年代在全球逐步发展起来的特许经营模式；第二种是基于互联网的在线分销系统。在线分销系统引起酒店分销的彻底变革，并与传统的销售渠道包括旅行社、订房中心、人员销售（特别是对政府和企业等大客户的销售）和线下直接预订等分销方式相抗衡。

10.3.1　特许经营

特许经营是指酒店集团将其拥有的具有知识产权性质的品牌，包括先进的预订网络和分销系统、成熟定型的酒店管理模式与服务标准等的使用权出售给酒店业主，由酒店业主依照品牌的质量标准与规范运营要求自主经营管理酒店（王德刚、孙万真、陈宝清，2007）。出让方一般是酒店管理集团，它们为接受酒店名称使用权的公司制定经营酒店的标准程序和方法，提供技术、市场营销、人员培训、物资采购、经营管理等方面的帮助，收取特许经营权使用费。这个费用可以是固定的，也可能与营业收入相关。受让方在酒店集团的监督与指导下，在产权和财务上保持独立，不受酒店集团的控制。自 20 世纪 50 年代假日集团开创现代酒店特许经营模式开始，许多国际知名酒店集团纷纷采用了特许经营模式。美国 *Hotels* 杂志 2015 年公布的最新数据表明，全球酒店集团的前十强几乎都运用了特许经营模式，精品国际的特许经营比例甚至已达到了 100%（见表 10-4）。资深特许经营咨询顾问 E. P. McGuite 指出：采取特许经营的最重要原因就是可以获得资金，同时也能够试图尽可能快地建立一种有效的分销渠道（Combs、Ketchen 和 Hoover，2004）。

agencies, such as CYTS travel network and the China International Travel app. The third is third-party operators, such as Ctrip and Ali travel, who invest in the establishment of large-scale professional booking sites. Their strengths include their capital, expertise, extensive agent network, and many alternative products. Finally, the travel review sites or travel UGC sites, such as TripAdvisor and Ants Cellular, provide reservation ports.

10.3   Hotel Distribution System

Although the basic concepts of distribution apply to all sectors in the tourism industry, the distribution systems adopted by tourism enterprises greatly vary. The formation of the distribution system for hotels include the franchise operation and the Internet-based online distribution system. The former has gradually developed since 1950s, whereas the latter has revolutionized the distribution of hotels and counters the conventional distribution channels, such as travel agencies, reservation centers, sales personnel (especially big customers, such as government and corporate), and offline direct bookings.

10.3.1   Franchising

Franchising means that a hotel group selling its branded intellectual property, including advanced booking network and distribution systems, well-established hotel management models, and service standards, to a hotel owner. The owner has full autonomy in managing the hotel in accordance with the quality standards and standardized operation requirements of the brand (Wang, Sun & Chen, 2007). The franchisors are hotel management groups that develop operation standards and methods for companies that adopt the brand name. They provide assistance in the areas of technology, marketing, personnel training, material procurement, and management and receive a royalty fee in return. The fee can be a fixed amount or calculated as a percentage of sales. The franchisee is independent in property and finance under the monitoring and supervision of hotel groups. The merchant is not controlled by the hotel group. Many international reputed hotel groups have begun to adopt the model since the Holiday Group introduced its modern franchising model in the 1950s. According to the American magazine *Hotels*, almost all of the top 10 hotel groups adopted the franchising model in 2015. Choice Hotels International completely adopted the franchising model (Table 10 – 4). Senior franchise consultant E. P. McGuite highlighted that the most important reason of adopting franchising is obtaining capital and the speedy development of effective distribution channels (Combs, Ketchen & Hoover, 2004).

表 10 - 4 国际著名酒店集团所属品牌及特许经营比例

酒店集团	主要品牌	酒店总数	特权经营店数	特许经营比例
精品国际 Choice	Comfort Inn、Comfort Suites、Quality、Clarion、Sleep Inn、Econo Lodge、Rodeway Inn、MainStay Suites	6300	6300	100%
温德姆 Wyndham	温德姆、华美达、戴斯、豪生、天天、速 8 等	7645	7585	99.2%
洲际 InterContinental	洲际、皇冠假日、假日、假日快捷、Staybridge Suites、Candlewood Suites、Hotel Indigo	4840	4096	84.6%
希尔顿 Hilton	希尔顿、Hilton、Scandic、Conrad 等	4322	3608	83.5%
万豪 Marriott	丽思卡尔顿、宝格丽、JW 万豪、万豪、万丽、万怡、万枫、Towne Place Suites、Residence Inn、Spring Hill Suites；Marriott Vacation Club International、Horizons、The Ritz-Carlton Club、Marriott Grand Residence Club；	4175	2882	69.0%
喜达屋 Starwood	瑞吉、豪华精选、W 酒店、威斯汀、喜来登、福朋、雅乐轩、源宿等	1222	588	48.1%
凯悦 Hyatt	凯悦、君悦、柏悦	587	248	42.2%
雅高 Accor	索菲特、美爵、诺富特、宜必思、佛缪勒第 1、汽车旅馆第 6	3717	1506	40.5%

资料来源：Hotels（2015）. *Hotels 325 Rank*. Retrieved June 21st，2016，from http：// www. marketingandtechnology. com/repository/webFeatures/HOTELS/h1507 _ Special _ Report.pdf.

随着市场份额的扩大,特许经营给特许方和受让方都带来了巨大发展,特别是在酒店规模扩张方面。对酒店集团来说,特许经营是一种有效的、低成本的集团扩张和品牌输出方式,它开发新业务快,能迅速提升品牌影响力。根据 Alon、Ni 和 Wang（2012）对美国 17 个酒店集团,117 个样本的研究,酒店集团在特许经营方面的管理经验（体现在实施特许经营的时长和特许经营酒店占集团酒店总数的比例两方面）越丰富,其在国际上的发展速度越快。

Table 10 - 4　Percentage of brand and franchise owned by World Famous Hotel Group

Hotel group	Major brands	Total numbers of properties	Numbers of franchise	Percentage of franchise
Choice	Comfort Inn，Comfort Suites，Quality，Clarion，Sleep Inn，Econo Lodge，Rodeway Inn，MainStay Suites	6,300	6,300	100%
Wyndham	Wyndham，Ramada，Days Inn，Howard Johnson，Super 8	7,645	7,585	99.2%
InterContinental	InterContinental，Holiday Inn，Holiday Inn Express，Staybridge Suites，Candlewood Suites，Hotel Indigo	4,840	4,096	84.6%
Hilton	Hilton，Hilton，Scandic，Conrad	4,322	3,608	83.5%
Marriott	Ritz-Carlton，Bulgari，JW Marriott，Marriott，Renaissance，Courtyard by Marriott，Fairfield by Marriott，Towne Place Suites，Residence Inn，Spring Hill Suites；Marriott Vacation Club International，Horizons，The Ritz-Carlton Club，Marriott Grand Residence Club；	4,175	2,882	69.0%
Starwood	Starwood，The Luxury Collection Hotels & Resorts，W Hotel，Westin，Sheraton，Four Points，Aloft，Element by Westin	1,222	588	48.1%
Hyatt	Hyatt，Grand Hyatt，Park Hyatt	587	248	42.2%
Accor	Sofitel，Grand Mercure，Novotel，ibis，Formule 1，Motel 6	3,717	1,506	40.5%

Source：*Hotels* (2015). *Hotels* 325 Rank. Retrieved June 21st，2016，from http：//www.marketingandtechnology.com/repository/webFeatures/HOTELS/h1507_Special_Report.pdf.

With the growth of market share，franchising has brought significant development to franchisors and franchisees in hotel scale expansion. A franchise is an effective yet low-cost method for group expansion and brand output for hotel groups. It enables the rapid development of new businesses and the brand influence. Alon，Ni，and Wang (2012) investigate 117 samples across 17 American hotel groups. The findings reveal that the more franchise experience hotel groups have，which is reflected in the seniority of adopting the franchise model and the proportion of franchising hotels to the total number of establishments in the groups，the faster the pace of development is in the international arena.

同时,特许经营模式也为大量的小型单体酒店打开了大门,为众多小型单体酒店的经营提供了良好的选择。因此,随着经营网络的拓展,特许经营系统成为当今酒店业最为重要的扩张方式(李金美、高鸿,2006)。

特许经营集团的运作需要有成熟的管理模式和经营体系为基础,以保证集团内的所有加盟成员的经营/管理/服务运作模式一致。酒店集团的特许经营体系中至少包含五项基本服务:统一的品牌标识和营销计划、预订系统、质量保证、采购团体化和培训项目。

1. 统一营销

品牌是获取顾客信任的关键。为了支持品牌和成员酒店,特许酒店集团集中广告费用以维持全国和区域广告及促销活动。集团还分发指南,让旅行者知道它在哪里有酒店,房价如何,有什么设施。关键城市的销售代表也是全国营销计划中的重要组成部分。专业销售点追求团体业务,区域办事处拜访当地的旅行大客户以销售其品牌。

2. 预订系统

全球分销系统和航空公司的中央预订系统在酒店业预订中发挥着越来越大的作用。但是,一个酒店集团从客人处获得的直接预订越多,它的预订成本就越低,因为它不用支付佣金。多数规模较大的酒店连锁运作自己的预订系统;而中小规模的连锁酒店一般和专门电话营销预订中心或预订中介公司签订合同。签约公司使用酒店名称和标识,为酒店体系提供预订服务,因此,客人甚至没有意识到他们是在和另一个机构打交道。

3. 质量保证

拥有大量下属酒店(有的下属酒店数超过了 7000 家)的大型酒店连锁体系要控制好所有酒店一致的服务质量不是件易事,但却是必须做的事。如何去控制受让方维持良好的品质,并使自己的商誉不断增值,这些成为目前保证特许经营长久生存的关键之一。特许经营的质量控制涉及多个方面:首先是受让酒店资格审查控制,尤其是硬件设施;其次,建立质量信息管理系统,对受让酒店在经营活动中所有的质量管理内容记录在案,并定期评估其质量管理工作。"观察员"制度、"客户热线"以及"博客"往往是很多大型酒店集团采取的质量评价的控制方法。

The franchise model opens the door for numerous small-scale independent hotels as good alternatives. The franchise system has become an important way for expansion in the hotel industry with the expansion of the business network (Li & Gao, 2006).

The operation of a franchise group needs a mature management model and an operating system as a basis to ensure consistent operation, management, and service across all members. The group's franchise system should include at least five basic services: unified brand identity and marketing plan, reservation system, quality assurance, and group procurement and training programs.

1. Unified marketing

Brand is the key to gain customer trust. Franchise hotel groups support their brands and member hotels by investing on advertising to maintain national and regional advertising and promotion. The system also distributes a guide to let travelers know about locations of hotels, room prices, and facilities. The regional office targets group businesses and visits local big clients to promote its brand.

2. Reservation System

The GDS and the airline's central reservation system play an increasingly important role in hotel bookings. However, the more direct bookings a hotel group receives from guests, the lower its booking costs because no commission is paid. Most large-scale hotels have chain booking systems, and small- to medium-scale hotels have agreements with specialized telephone booking centers or reservation intermediaries on the reservation arrangement. The contracted companies use hotel names and logos to provide booking services. Therefore, customers hardly recognize that they are dealing with other agencies while making reservations.

3. Quality assurance

Ensuring consistent service quality across many subordinate hotels (some with over 7,000 subordinate hotels) is a tough yet crucial task for large-scale hotel chains. Maintaining excellent quality and value-adding goodwill are key to long-term survival and success. Several aspects are involved in quality assurance. The first aspect is hotel audit (i.e., hardware facilities), which is followed by the establishment of quality management systems. Hotel audit documents quality management during business operations and periodically evaluates quality management. The "observer" mechanism, "customer hotline," and "blog" are typical measures adopted by large hotel groups in quality control.

4. 集团采购

特许经营的一个显著特点是 90% 以上的商品都由总部集中供货,出让方既可以利用大宗采购的优势使得受让方以较低的价格购买,同时又可以对加盟店的供货质量进行控制,不至于因为某个加盟店质量问题影响到整个特许体系的信誉,同时也可对加盟商的日常经营活动进行有效控制,保证加盟商权利金的提取。这是一个互利的模式。因此,如何对特许体系中的供应链进行管理,成为特许体系管理的一个很重要的内容。对于酒店来说,特许集团的采购团体化主要体现在酒店用品采购、信息系统和广告系统支持三个方面。中央预定系统为成员酒店提供信息的支持;统一的国际性、区域性或地区性广告则支持成员酒店的广告宣传。

5. 培训项目

培训系统是统一的特许经营体系下的一项重要内容,因为受让店的发展速度在很大程度上取决于培训系统的速度、效率和标准化。授权酒店把培训标准纳入整个体系,组织受让酒店的培训项目,如制作统一的培训录像和培训手册等。这些培训项目有助于服务质量标准化,也能在培训资料开发中节省成本。麦当劳的汉堡包大学就是为特许经营者、管理者和管理助理提供培训的主要模式。

20 世纪 50 年代酒店业特许经营早期,加盟者愿意接受特许酒店集团的所有规定和要求,双方之间的忠诚度很高,合作相对便利和容易。随着越来越多的酒店集团涉入特许经营领域,20 世纪 80 年代中期,单体酒店有了选择加盟品牌的权利。一个酒店可以从一个特许经营品牌变换到另一个特许经营品牌。到 90 年代初,酒店市场上出现严重的供过于求的状况,众多酒店开始在不同的品牌之间转换,引起了特许经营酒店集团之间争取成员酒店的竞争。特许方和受让方的角色也有所转移,特许集团一改曾经的准老板形象,变得更像服务提供者,特许经营加盟者变得更像顾客而不是从属者。成本是促使加盟者改变加盟酒店集团的一个主要考虑因素。一般来说,特许经营权使用费占酒店总收入的 4%～6%（Ross,1999）。为了争取更多的加盟者,众多特许经营集团采取了"折扣"等价格竞争策略。此外,顾客市场也是众多特许经营酒店集团之间竞争的重要原因。O'Neill、Dev 和 Yanagisawa (2013)对 52 个实施特许经营的国际酒店品牌进行研究,发现顾客满意度和知名度较高的品牌,能够获取更高比例的特许经营权使用费。

4. Group procurement

A distinctive feature of the franchise is that headquarters supply over 90% of goods. One advantage is bulk procurement in buying at a low price. Another merit is to ensure quality supply to a franchisee to avoid having a negative impact on the credibility of the franchise system, have effective control over the daily operation of the franchise, and ensure the extraction of royalty. This model is mutually beneficial. Therefore, managing the supply chain in the franchise system is very important for the franchise system management. For hotels, group procurement in the franchise system includes the procurement of hotel supplies, information systems, and advertising support. The centralized reservation system provides information support for member hotels. Unified international or regional advertising supports the promotion of member hotels.

5. Training programs

Training systems are important in a unified franchise system because the pace of development largely depends on the speed, efficiency, and standardization of training systems. Authorized hotels incorporate training standards into the system and develop training programs, such as developing consistent training videos and manuals. These training programs are conducive in standardizing service standards and save costs in the development of training materials. McDonald's University of Hamburg is the main mode of training for its franchisees, managers, and management assistants.

Franchisees were willing to accept all provisions and requirements stated by the franchising hotel groups in the 1950s, which is the early era of the franchise model. The franchise model ensures a high level of loyalty, which contributes to convenient and easy cooperation. Given the increasing number of hotel groups involved in the franchising model, independent hotels had the right to choose in joining the brand in the mid of 1980s. A hotel could switch from one franchised brand to another. The hotel market experienced a serious oversupply situation in the early 1990s. Many hotels switched franchised brands, which induced a competition of franchisees among hotel groups. The role of franchisees and franchisors has also changed. The franchising groups changed from a boss-like image into a service provider, which treat franchisees as customers rather than subordinates. Costs are a key consideration in forcing franchisees to change a franchise. Costs are a key consideration in changing franchises. The franchising royalty accounts for 4%~6% of the total revenue (Ross, 1999). Many franchising groups offer "discount" as price competition strategy to obtain more franchisees. Moreover, the customer market is an important reason that contributes to the competition among franchising hotel groups. O'Neill, Dev, and Yanagisawa (2013) investigated 52 franchised international hotel brands and found that brands with a high level of customer satisfaction and brand awareness were able to charge a high percentage of franchising royalty.

10.3.2　酒店业网络预订系统

酒店业利用现代信息技术进行营销的方式主要体现在两方面：以大型计算机数据库为核心、数据专网为纽带的专有集团封闭型分销模式——中央预定系统（CRS）；以互联网技术和多功能旅游产品数据库整合而成的全球开放性、综合性分销模式——全球分销系统（GDS）。此外，专业在线旅游分销商（OTA）和酒店网络营销联盟也是多元化的酒店在线分销系统的重要组成部分。

1. 中央预定系统

中央预定系统（CRS）主要是指集团酒店所采用的内部预订系统。它是一种封闭的、归属特定企业集团、由集团成员共享的预订网络，它具有排他性，较少对外开放，既是企业集团综合实力的体现，同时又是其垄断客源的一种途径。酒店集团通过其 CRS 对客源构成、流量及流向进行控制，并通过各种价位组合及调整实行收益管理，以实现集团利益的最大化（谷慧敏，1998）。同时，CRS 还具有集团内酒店信息共享、客户资源共享的联网销售优势。1965 年假日酒店集团建立的假日电讯网（Holidex）是最早的酒店中央预订系统。系统经过多次升级，目前客人通过系统已经可以预订假日酒店集团全球各地的酒店和度假村的不同等级的客房，并在几秒钟内得到确认。喜达屋酒店集团的 CRS 源自喜来登集团于 1970 年开通中央预订系统，其功能主要有：处理来自酒店、官方网站、官方 App、第三方（如 OTA，GDS）、电话预订服务中心的预订，并将预订准确传送至对应的酒店；在全球所有酒店内共享所有客人的信息、喜好、在同一集团其他酒店的入住历史等资料；与收益管理系统进行连接，实现实时收益管理。

2. 全球分销系统

全球酒店分销系统 EasyBooking 是中国航信以国外先进的旅行分销系统应用技术为基础，自行开发研制的新一代非航空产品，定位于国际酒店与汽车租赁信息的查询与预定操作的前端应用产品，为用户提供了一个直接参与酒店、租车产品分销的便利渠道。通过 EasyBooking 系统可以查询遍布全球 5 万多家酒店与近 50 家汽车租赁公司的客房和车辆信息，包括酒店地点、酒店服务设施、房间状态、客房价格以及与租车相关的各类信息，并可直接预订满足旅客需要的客房或车辆。

10.3.2　Hotel industry network reservation system

The hotel industry adopts the modern information technology to perform marketing activities in two aspects: the central reservation system (CRS), which is a closed distribution pattern that used a large-scale computer database as the core and data network as links, and GDS, which is a global open and integrated distribution model that integrates the Internet technology and multi-functional tourism product databases. Moreover, professional online tourism distributors and hotel network marketing alliance are important components of the diversified hotel online distribution system.

1. Central reservation system (CRS)

CRS refers to the internal reservation system adopted by hotel groups. It is owned by specific enterprise groups and shared by members of the booking network. It is also exclusive and seldom opens to the outsiders, which demonstrate the comprehensive strength of the enterprises and a way to monopolize the customer market. Hotel groups control the composition, flow, and direction of customers through the CRS, as well as maximizing the groups' interests through various price combinations and adjustments (Gu, 1998). The CRS also has the advantages of marketing in terms of internal information sharing and customer resources sharing network. The Holiday Inn Hotel Group established Holidex, which is the earliest hotel reservation system, in 1965. Customers can book any room types across the group's worldwide hotels and resorts and receive confirmation within seconds after multiple system upgrades. The CRS of Starwood Hotels and Resorts originated from the CRS that was first introduced by the Sheraton Group in 1970. The main functions are processing reservations from hotels, official websites, official App, third party distributors(such as OTA and GDS), and call centers and sending to corresponding hotels; sharing customers' information, preferences, and occupancy history with member hotels across global properties; and connecting real-time revenue management.

2. Global open and integrated distribution system (GDS)

GDS EasyBooking is a self-developed non-aviation products by China Hangxin. The system adopts the advanced application technology on the travel distribution system and serves the functions of international hotels and car rental information query and operation. It offers convenient distribution channels to directly involve users in hotel reservation and car rental. The EasyBooking system allows users to check room and vehicle information of over 50,000 hotels and nearly 50 car rental companies around the world, including hotel locations, hotel amenities, room status, room rates, and car rental-related information. Customers can book rooms and rent vehicles according to their travel needs.

GDS 具有系统开放、可进入性强以及组合分销产品的优势,全球主要酒店集团和单体酒店都已经由不同的途径建立了与 GDS 的系统连接,并通过GDS 渠道实现产品的全球分销。GDS 营销在酒店业中的作用主要体现在:(1) 全球覆盖性。酒店加入 GDS 系统后,可以通过其遍布全球的销售网络获得国际性的客源,实现酒店的跨国际、跨地区分销。(2) 细分市场多样性。其市场范围包括从豪华、高端、中端直至经济型等不同类型客源。(3) 间接销售性。GDS 将酒店产品存入数据库中,通过网络与安装有 GDS 终端的旅行社,实现面向酒店顾客的销售。而 GDS 公司以及旅行社都可被视为酒店与其顾客间的渠道。(4) 预订服务全面性。除了为酒店提供全球预订服务以实现客房销售收入外,各 GDS 系统还分别开发出网上服务的系列软件产品。酒店可以在网上多方位、形象直观地宣传自己的产品和服务,并在不同时期针对不同的目标市场制定不同的价格策略和促销活动。

3. 专业在线旅游分销商

专业在线旅游分销商(OTA)也是多元化的酒店在线分销的重要组成部分。酒店预订中介系统是指专门从事酒店营销的企业、协会或组织所建立的销售网络,它通过自己设立在世界或全国各地的销售点或终端接受客人委托预订,同时与入网酒店建立代理销售合同,通过佣金形式实现自己的利润。目前在国际上影响力较大的在线旅游分销商有 Expedia、Booking.com、Agoda 等。国内市场上,以携程、阿里旅游、同程等为首的综合性在线旅行服务平台,就属国内专业酒店在线预订中介行业的领导者。

4. 酒店网络营销联盟

酒店网络营销联盟也是极具潜力的互联网旅游分销渠道之一。在旅游电子商务营销中,仅靠单个酒店的力量可能难以形成市场影响,而一定数量的酒店联合起来,打破地域和行政条块的分割,形成网络营销联合体,有利于实现市场营销资源和旅游服务资源的整合,形成较强的集体竞争力。酒店网络营销联盟(也可是酒店、旅行社、餐饮、娱乐服务企业等结成的更广泛的旅游营销联盟)可以是由不同的旅游酒店的商务网站开展联合业务,也可是共同建立的新的电子商务系统。例如,为了平衡旅游预订中介销售量在总销售量中的比例,增加酒店直销的比例,五大酒店集团希尔顿(Hilton)、凯悦(Hyatt)、万豪(Marriott)、洲际(InterContinental)和喜达屋(Starwood)联合成立了 roomkey.com,提供各个酒店集团的最低在线房价。另外,喜达屋

GDS features advantages of openness, accessibility, and combined distribution. Major hotel groups and independent hotels worldwide have established system connections with the GDS through different channels and realized the global distribution of the products through GDS channels. The roles of GDS in the hotel industry are reflected in the following aspects: (1) Global coverage: Hotels that join the GDS can reach international customers and achieve international and regional distribution through the worldwide sales network. (2) Diversified segmentation: The range of markets includes luxury, high-end, mid-range, and economic types. (3) Indirect marketing: The GDS records the hotel products into the database by selling its products to customers through the network and travel agencies with the installation of the GDS terminal. Companies with the GDS and travel agencies can be seen as channels with hotels and its customers. (4) Booking comprehensiveness: The GDS offers global reservation service to obtain room sales revenue and develops a series of online-based software products. Hotels can go online using multi-faceted visual images to display their products and services. They can also tailor different pricing strategies and promotional activities at different times for different target markets.

3. Online travel distributors (OTA)

Online travel distributors (OTA) also take up important roles in online hotel distribution. The hotel booking intermediary system is specialized in hotel marketing enterprises, associations, or organizations to establish sales networks. The intermediary system establishes its point of sale or terminal across the globe or country, accepts booking from customers, and earns commissions by formulating sales contracts with hotels within the networks. The powerful worldwide online travel distributors are Expedia, Booking.com, and Agoda. Ctrip, Ali Tourism, and Tongcheng are industry leaders that offer integrated online travel service platform to the domestic market.

4. Hotel Internet marketing alliance

Hotel Internet marketing alliance is an online distribution channel with significant potential. The strength of a single hotel in tourism e-commerce marketing may not easily make an impact in the market. Multiple hotels bundle together to break geographic and administrative partitions and form an online sales entity. The combination of marketing and tourism service resources can be realized, which contribute to powerful collective competitiveness. Hotel Internet Marketing Alliance, which could include hotels, travel agencies, restaurants, and entertainment enterprises to form a broad tourism marketing alliance, can be joint businesses by establishing business websites among different tourism hotels or co-building a new e-commerce system. For instance, the world's top five hotel groups, Hilton, Hyatt, Marriott, InterContinental, and Starwood, jointly set up Roomkey.com to balance the proportion of direct booking and offer the best available rates. Moreover, the loyalty program of Starwood Hotel Group, SPG, works together

酒店集团的常客优惠计划"Starwood Preferred Guest"（SPG），现在与多家航空公司、零售店、网络租车企业和娱乐企业都有合作。因此，互联网不仅是新兴中介，而且是一个新的多层次、多方位的综合性中介系统。

5. 旅行社

旅行社一直以来都是酒店分销的重要渠道，即使在信息化时代，传统的旅行社在酒店分销系统中依然有着不可替代的作用。与旅行社的合作有助于增强酒店的知名度，旅行社也可扩大酒店的目标市场，扩大酒店的客源，带来更多的营业收入。酒店支付的成本是旅行社的佣金。

通过旅行代理销售的一个问题是代理的忠诚度和专一性。代理制中维系双方关系的是佣金，而代理商往往可以同时代理若干个不同品牌的产品，难以忠诚于某一家委托酒店，常常会为了追逐佣金收入而游离于各家酒店之间，从而酒店的产品难以从代理商代理的若干类似品牌中体现出自身的优势。当然，如果酒店采取某些特定的策略或政策与旅行代理合作，成为代理的唯一品牌则另当别论。成功的经验表明，酒店连锁对使用旅行代理的承诺必须始于高层管理者，且必须和所有层次的酒店员工沟通。当今，越来越多的酒店把对旅行代理商的培训纳入培训体系，目的在于提高旅行社对酒店产品的熟悉程度，体现出自身的特点。某些酒店就通过组织研讨会等使旅行社懂得如何组织会议和奖励活动。此外，酒店还应该保持与旅行社的沟通，及时提供有关特殊活动和大型活动的信息，尽早推广以便旅行社能够进行销售。希尔顿酒店设定了旅行社代理电话专线，且配备了经特别培训的代表辅助旅行社营销。此外，酒店还指派了有关行政人员与旅行代理一起组成了旅行代理咨询委员会，合作开展酒店的营销活动。例如凯悦培训员工不要当着客人的面批评旅行代理。万豪专为旅行代理开发的"酒店卓越"销售培训计划以及丽笙的"改进预订"项目都是酒店与旅行代理沟通协调的有效方式。

6. 酒店销售代理处

酒店销售代理处或酒店代理人员在特定市场代表了酒店。他们有自己的销售力量，通常有自己的预订中心。小型酒店的代表只在一个或一些市场运作，但是大型酒店/集团在全球范围内经营。

7. 奖励旅行服务公司

奖励旅行服务公司专门针对公司客户，为某些公司安排旅行组合作为其

with airlines, retail, online car rental companies, and entertainment enterprises. Therefore, the Internet is not only a new intermediary but also a new multi-level, multi-directional integrated intermediary system.

5. Travel agencies

Travel agencies have always been an important channel for hotel distribution. Traditional travel agencies play an irreplaceable role in the hotel distribution system even in the information age. Cooperation with travel agencies enhances hotel visibility. Travel agencies can expand the hotel's target market by expanding the customer source and bringing more revenue. Hotels pay the cost of a travel agency's commission.

Loyalty is a problem of sales through travel agents. Commission maintains the relationship between two parties under the agent system. Agents can act for a number of brands at the same time to have more commission. Thus, agents have difficulty being loyal to only one commissioned hotel. Thus, hotel products hardly stand out from other similar brands. However, hotels that adopt specific strategies or policies to work with a sole agent are exempted. Senior management learns to commit to travel agents and communicate with hotel staffs at all levels given successful experiences. Many hotels incorporate travel agent training into the training system, which enhances the familiarity with hotel products and highlight special features. For example, some hotels organize seminars to help travel agents understand how to organize meetings and incentives. Moreover, hotels should maintain communication with travel agencies and offer information on special events and large-scale activities in a timely manner. Travel agencies can engage with sales immediately. Hilton set up a hotline for travel agents that are equipped with trained assistants to help with marketing activities. Moreover, respective managerial staff assigned by hotels and travel agents forms a travel agent advisory committee to conduct marketing activities. For instance, Hyatt trained their staff not to criticize travel agents in the presence of guests. Marriott specially developed "Hotel Excellence" sales training program for travel agents and Radisson's "Better Booking" program are examples of effective communication and coordination between hotels and travel agents.

6. Hotel sales agents

Hotel sales agents or hotel agents represent hotels in specific markets. They have their own sales force and usually have their own booking center. Representatives of small hotels operate in only one or a few markets, and large hotels/groups operate on a global scale.

7. Incentive travel services companies

Incentive travel services companies are for corporate customers who arrange tours

对那些超过绩效目标或赢得销售竞赛的员工的奖励。奖励旅行通常是全包的，就是酒店、交通和其他的旅游产品所有都包含在由公司支付的包价旅游中。

　　分销渠道的多元化带来了酒店选择分销渠道的灵活性和多样性。传统的线下分销系统如旅行社门市部、酒店销售代表仍然发挥着销售作用的同时，依托互联网技术成形的各种在线预订模式在酒店分销方面凸显出巨大的影响力。图 10-2 所示是酒店电子商务分销系统的一个模型。酒店不仅可以选择全球分销系统和专业中介预订网站作为分销模式，同时也可以建立酒店的自有网站或与集团中央预定系统联网，甚至还可以与其他酒店联合成立分销联盟。

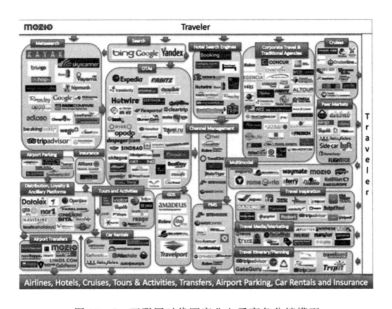

图 10-2　互联网时代酒店业电子商务分销模型

资料来源：Tnooz（2014）. Navigating the online travel landscape-a guide for startups. Retrieved Oct 10，2016，from https://www.tnooz.com/article/online-travel/

　　此外，酒店还通过网络直销模式直接面向消费者销售产品。网络直销包括酒店→酒店官方网站→顾客、酒店→CRS→酒店集团网站→顾客的方式，直销是各酒店或集团为了避免中介机构控制分销渠道所选的重要分销模式。为了防止中介机构控制分销渠道，酒店努力改善自身网站，争取把交易转移到自己的分销渠道上来。专门针对通过酒店网站预订的顾客提供最低房价（即通过中介预订则无法享有的价格）就是他们促进网络直销的策略之一。希尔顿酒店集团在 2016 年推出"Stop Clicking Around"活动，在酒店官方网站提供最优惠的价格，鼓励顾客通过希尔顿酒店官方网站或手机 App 进行预订。

for top performers or winners of sales competitions. Incentive travel is usually all-inclusive, which means that hotel, transportation, and other travel products included in the package are paid by companies.

The diversification of distribution channels has brought the flexibility and diversity of hotel distribution channels. Traditional offline distribution systems, such as travel agencies, retail outlets, and hotel sales representatives, play a role in sales, and various online booking models that rely on Internet technology creates enormous influence. Figure 10 – 2 is a model of a hotel e-commerce distribution system. Hotels can choose GDS and professional intermediary booking websites as the distribution model and build their own websites or the group's central reservation system. They can set up a distribution alliance with other hotels.

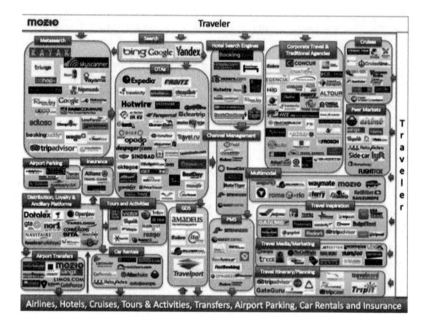

Figure 10 – 2　E-commerce distribution model for the hotel industry in the internet age
Source: Tnooz (2014). Navigating the online travel landscape—A guide for startups. Retrieved October 10, 2016, from https://www.tnooz.com/article/online-travel/

Hotels directly sell products to customers through an online direct model. Internet DM is as follows: hotel → hotel official website → customers, hotels → CRS → hotel group website → the way of customers. Direct sales are important distribution models of hotels or groups to prevent intermediaries from controlling the distribution channels. In doing so, hotels strive to improve their websites and drive transactions to their own distribution channels. Offering the best available room rate (i.e., the price that cannot enjoy when booking through intermediaries) is a strategy they use to drive direct sales to hotel websites. The Hilton Hotel Group launched the "Stop Clicking Around" event in 2016. The official hotel website offered the best rate. Customers were encouraged to make bookings via the hotel's official website or mobile App.

　　建设自身网站对小型的单体酒店的营销意义重大,它是酒店以较低的成本接触更广泛的客源的有效方式。但由于缺乏品牌知名度,小型酒店网站可以通过与有关旅游组织、旅游部门或协会等目的地营销组织的链接扩大网页点击量,提高知名度。《2015 中国酒店业务统计》显示,在 2014 年酒店订房渠道方面:五星酒店直接向酒店预订的量占 32.6%,四星酒店占 30.0%,三星酒店占 23.1%,经济型酒店占 51.3%。在通过连锁酒店总部网站预订方面,只有经济型酒店达到 34.7%,其他通过直销方式获得的预订渠道所占比例都低于 10%。通过分销商(旅行社、订房中心)的预订比例,除经济型酒店外,与酒店直销持平(浩华管理顾问公司,2015)。

10.4　旅行社分销体系

　　旅行社营销渠道是指旅行社通过各种直接或间接的方式,将旅游产品转移到最终消费者的途径(郑迎红、刘文军,2004)。分销体系策略是旅行社整个营销系统的重要组成部分,它可以解决旅行社产品上市初期渠道不畅、销售费用过大、启动市场难度大等困难;同时也可解决需要密集分销的旅游产品在市场网络建设中的不足等问题。所以分销体系策略的选择和执行对于旅行社的产品销售起着至关重要的作用。至今,在直销方式仍在旅行社业营销中扮演着重要角色的同时,旅行社的营销网络也在不断地拓展,特许经营方式已经渗入,而信息技术引起的电子商务分销方式也已经成了一种必然结果。

　　根据美国直销协会(ADMA)的定义,直复营销(DM)是一种为了在任何地方产生可度量的反应和达成交易而使用的一种或多种广告媒体相互作用的市场营销体系。旅行社直复营销是指旅行社不通过中间销售人员,直接采用邮件、电话、计算机网络以及报纸、杂志、广播等媒介,向旅游者宣传旅游产品,从而引发其购买欲望,使之最终通过邮寄、电话传真、网络等方式直接向旅行社购买旅游产品的一种销售方式(蒋丽娜、张树夫,2007)。直接邮件、电话或传真推销和电视营销都是旅行社直复营销的主要形式。此外,互联网在营销环境中,对于传递营销信息、沟通旅行社及旅游者需求来说是当前最为流行的中介技术。它不仅具备了其他直复营销形式的优点,而且还具有广域

Website construction is significant for small-scale independent hotels on sales. It allows hotels to reach a wide range of customers at low cost. Given the lack of brand recognition, websites of small-scale hotels can be linked with relevant tourism organizations, tourism departments, or associations, such as destination marketing organizations, to expand web traffic and improve visibility. The *2015 China Hotel Business Statistics* showed the hotel reservations channels in 2014 accounted 32.6% for the direct booking of five-star hotels, 30.0% for four-star hotels, 23.1% for three-star hotels, and 51.3% for budget hotels. Only budget hotels reached 34.7% in booking through the chain hotel websites. The percentage of obtaining booking through direct channels was less than 10%. The proportion of distributors (i.e., travel agencies and reservation centers) was the same as the direct sales of hotels (Crowe Horwath International, 2015).

10.4　Distribution system of travel agencies

The marketing channels of travel agencies refer to the direct and indirect ways of transferring tourism products to final customers (Zheng & Liu, 2004). The distribution system strategy is an important component of the entire marketing system of travel agencies. It offers the solution in the ineffective distribution and the early launch of tourism products, excessive sales costs, and difficulties in approaching the market. It also addresses the shortcoming induced by the intensive distribution of tourism products in the construction of market networks. Therefore, the selection and implementation of a distribution system strategy are vital for the product sales of travel agencies. DM continues to play an important role in marketing while the marketing network of travel agencies is constantly expanding. The franchise model has penetrated, and the e-commerce distribution induced by information technology has become a trend.

The American Direct Marketing Association (ADMA) defined direct marketing (DM) as the use of one or multiple advertising media to generate measurable responses and transactions anywhere. DM refers to the travel agencies that promote tourism products to travelers using direct mail, telephone, computer networks, newspapers, magazines, radio, and other media without the involvement of intermediaries. When the desire of buying has been triggered, customers directly buy tourism products from travel agencies through direct mail, fax, and websites (Jiang & Zhang, 2007). Direct mail, telephone, or fax and television marketing are the main forms of DM for travel agencies. In addition, the Internet is a popular intermediary technology in the marketing environment to convey sales information and communicate the needs of travel agencies and tourists. It has the advantages of other forms of DM and unique far-reach, real-time,

性、实时性、互动性及可扩展性等独特优势。旅行社自设网站内的"在线预订"就是网络直销方式的表现形式。西方旅行社的直销手段主要是体现在通信、电子和网络直销方面,而在国内旅游产品市场上,报纸、杂志和电视广告仍是主要渠道,另外还有一些传统的方式包括宣传册广告、直接邮寄和人员推销也被广泛应用。

作为一种现代营销方式,特许经营被认为是 21 世纪居于主导地位的商业模式,已在全球范围内得到了迅速的发展和普及。具体到旅游产业,它不仅在酒店业和餐饮业内被广泛应用,在旅行社业也日渐流行。旅行社行业的特许经营实质上是一种营销产品、服务和技术的体系,是旅游批发商(经营商)控制销售渠道的一种手段。它是靠既有的优势产品、商标或技术吸引并聚集众多的独立经济个体作为销售终端,通过构筑一个网络化的营销体系,在实现低成本、高效率的产品运营的同时,也通过品牌和销售渠道的独立性优势,强化了产品本身对于消费者的差异性与可识别性,从而实现特许双方共同利益的最大化(许静,2002)。

旅行社引入特许经营,是旅行社行业本身生存的必要,也是整体优化的理想选择。首先,从旅行社角度来说,无形的旅行社产品更多的是靠品牌、形象、信誉、人员、管理模式等智力资本参与竞争和实现发展的,特许经营使得出让方的核心资本得以输出。其次,旅游活动的移动性、分散性及服务提供的即时性,要求旅行社采用撒网式的经营方式——管理上的标准化、一体化和业务空间上的分散性,来降低跨区域经营带来的成本支出和可能产生的失控风险。第三,特许经营中难度最大的部分——配送体系可以被忽略。旅游产品生产和消费的同时性越过了可能扼制特许经营本身优势发挥的配送环节,使得构筑这条经营渠道的难度大大降低。此外,从特许经营的特点出发,特许经营是在各大小旅行社职能分解转型的基础之上,重构了企业价值链。上下游企业之间通过资源共享、职能分工来重构供应商价值链、企业价值链、销售渠道价值链和买方价值链,通过改变企业的成本结构来获得成本优势,部分地实现了企业之间互惠互利的"共生营销",走上了建立在专业化分工基础之上的联合道路。并且,特许经营对加入体系的单体企业要素的严格考核和系统管理,本身有利于旅行社作为单体经济要素的优化。

interactive, and expandable features. Travel agencies that set up "online booking" on their websites is a form of online DM. Travel agencies in Western countries mainly employ DM in telecommunications, e-commerce, and online marketing, whereas newspapers, magazines, and advertisements on television still dominate in the DM of domestic tourism markets. Some conventional methods, such as brochures, direct mail, and sales personnel, are commonly used.

Franchising is a modern marketing method and a dominant business model in the 21st century. It has a speedy development and is widespread on a global scale. Franchising is widely used in the hotel and catering industries and gains increasing popularity in the travel industry. Franchising in the travel agency industry, which is a system of marketing, service, and technology, allow wholesalers (operators) to control sales channels. It relies on quality products, trademarks, or technology to attract and gather many independent economic entities as a sales terminal. A franchise achieves low cost and efficient operations while building a network of marketing systems. The brand and independence of sales channels also strengthen the differentiation and awareness of the brand to maximize the common interests of franchisors and franchisees (Xu, 2002).

Travel agencies introduce franchising because it is necessary for survival and the ideal choice for optimization. First, intangible tourism products rely on brand, image, reputation, personnel, management, and other intellectual capital to compete and develop from a travel agency perspective. Franchising allows the core capital output of franchisees. Second, the mobility, geographic disparity, and provision of timely services of tourism activities require the use of a decentralized model of operation, standardized management, and the integration and dispersion of business space to reduce the cost of cross-regional business zones and potential yet uncontrollable risks. Third, the most difficult part of franchising is the ignorance of distribution system. The simultaneous production and consumption of tourism products may jeopardize the advantages of the distribution system in franchising, which reduces the difficulties in building business channels to a great extent. In addition, franchising reconstructs the value chain of enterprises based on the decomposition of functions among large- and scale-scale travel agencies. The upstream and downstream enterprises share resources and establish function division to reconstruct the supply chain of suppliers, enterprises, sales channels, and buyers. Cost advantage is obtained by changing the cost structure of enterprises. Enterprises are mutually beneficial by practicing "collaborate marketing" and embarking the journey of a specialized division of functions. Moreover, the franchise system requires strict examination and the system management of partaking independent enterprises. It is conducive to travel agencies as a single element of economic optimization.

特许经营模式在旅行社运行的成功,使其能够给参与运行的双方——出让方和受让方带来长期稳定的利益。对出让方来说,特许经营的主要意义体现在资金优势和规模扩张方面。他们可以不受资金的限制,迅速扩张规模,快捷高效地实现跨地区经营,利于旅行社网络化、集团化的发展,带来规模经济效益。随着特许加盟社的增多,出让方的议价能力得以提高,从而获取大批量采购的折扣和优惠,各种费用也可以分摊降低。受让方的收益主要来源于出让方提供的完善且先进的管理和经营模式上。首先,降低了创业风险,增加了成功机会。其次,享受低成本效应,包括系统的管理培训和指导、原料批量团购的优惠、节减广告宣传费和分享著名品牌与服务带来的无形资产。此外,受让方还可拥有更畅通、更广泛的信息渠道,扩大信息量。美国运通旅行社是采用特许经营制的典型代表,它特许经营了马来西亚"五月花"旅游公司、印度"马可波罗"旅行社等。它在为加盟旅行社提供强大的品牌支持的同时,还提供员工培训支持、定期的网络在线服务和相关的技术支持以及优秀的产品与服务。在国内旅行社业内,中国国旅是采用特许经营最早的旅行社之一,深圳国旅新景界是中国国旅在深圳的品牌特许经营旅行社,在港澳地区入境游、会议和奖励旅游方面有丰富的经验。

信息技术与互联网也给旅行社的经营方式带来一场深刻的革命。旅行社在兼顾传统的店面直营的同时,利用互联网进行产品推介、网上咨询,提供旅游服务预订、旅游线路编排等服务,以便将销售触角伸向每个潜在的旅游者。港中旅于 2006 年建立芒果网,利用网络开展预订及销售机票、酒店住宿及旅游相关产品、企业旅游管理服务等业务。经过十年发展,芒果网已成为国内领先的旅游度假综合服务商之一。

10.5　分销渠道的选择和管理

在进行分销渠道选择前,营销人员需要首先思考如何进行渠道设计,也即需要多少营销渠道,企业应该选择怎么样的渠道合作伙伴,怎样进行选择等。这些问题决定了不同营销渠道的作用。一般来讲,分销渠道的选择需要考虑三个方面的因素:第一,消费者的需求;第二,企业吸引渠道成员的能力;第三,衡量不同渠道成员的成本与收益,以及企业对成员的控制能力。

The successful operation of the franchise model brings stable profit to franchisors and franchisees. From a franchisor perspective, the main advantages are capital and scale expansion. They are free from the limitation of capital and enjoy the economies of scales through the rapid expansion and effective actualization of cross-regional operations that benefit the network of travel agencies and group development. The increase of franchisees can strengthen the bargaining power of the transferor when obtaining high-volume purchase discounts and concessions and reducing costs. The sound and advanced management and business model are the main benefits of franchisees. First, the risk of entrepreneurship is reduced, and the chance of success is increased. Second, another merit is the low-cost effect, which includes the systematic management of training and supervision, bulk purchase discounts of raw materials, reduced advertising costs, and the intangible assets brought by reputed brands and services. In addition, franchisees can enjoy smooth and extensive information channels to expand the amount of information. An American Express travel agency adopts the franchise system, which includes the franchise of Mayflower Travel Company in Malaysia and Marco Polo Travel Agency in India. It provides strong brand support for affiliated travel agencies and offers support on staff training, regular online services, technology, and excellent products and services. CITS is one of the earliest travel agencies that adopted the franchise system in China. CITS Shenzhen is the franchised travel agency of CITS, which has extensive experience in inbound tourism, conference, and incentive tours in Hong Kong and Macau.

Information technology and the Internet have brought a profound revolution to the operation mode of travel agencies. Travel agencies consider the traditional retail outlets and the use of the Internet for product promotion, online consultation, booking travel services, and itinerary planning to reach every potential tourist. Hong Kong China Travel Service established Mango Network in 2006. It began to use the Internet for booking and sales of air tickets, hotel accommodation, tourism related products, and corporate tourism management services. Mango Network has become a leading domestic tourism and leisure-integrated service provider after ten years of development.

10.5 *Distribution Channel Selection and Management*

Before choosing a distribution channel, marketers need to consider how to design the marketing channels, i.e., determining how many marketing channels there are and knowing how to select channel partners. These issues determine the roles of different marketing channels. Three factors determine the selection of distribution channels, namely, (1) the needs of consumers, (2) the ability of enterprises to attract channel members, and (3)the measurement of the costs and benefits of various channel members and the control exerted over members.

　　了解目标顾客群体的需求是分销渠道选择的基础。在设计营销渠道时，市场营销人员必须了解目标顾客群体的需求。不同的消费者有不同的服务需求，例如航空公司既提供头等舱服务，也提供廉价的有限服务，就是为了迎合不同消费者的不同需求。在选择分销渠道之前，营销人员除了需要了解市场对产品特性的需求之外，还需要了解：（1）一个普通消费者在某一特定渠道中一次购买的产品数量，例如酒店行业实行收益管理，会通过数据分析客人在什么时候通过什么渠道预订酒店产品，这些渠道占酒店总销售房晚数的比例。（2）等待交货时长，即消费者通过某个营销渠道购买产品或服务后，平均的等待交货时长。在航空业或酒店行业中，渠道分销商的订单平均处理时间是航空公司或酒店选择渠道合作伙伴的重要因素。（3）消费者通过特定渠道购买产品或服务的便利程度，例如猫途鹰（TripAdvisor）上现在已经提供即时预订服务，顾客可以在浏览评论后非常方便地立刻进行预订。（4）渠道提供的产品类别的广度，例如 OTA 上是否提供"机＋酒"或者"机＋接送"服务。（5）渠道提供的额外服务，如送货、安装、维修等。

　　不同发展阶段的企业对渠道的吸引能力存在差异。历史悠久的大型酒店集团相比新成立的规模较小的酒店拥有更强的议价能力。对于新的或者小型的酒店，应当尽量避免与多个分销商合作。

　　不同的分销渠道所需要的成本和带给企业的收益是不同的。渠道的成本有两类：直接成本和机会成本。例如，酒店通过旅行社或者协议公司可以提高入住率，但当市场需求提高时，使用旅行社或是协议公司就产生了机会成本。因此，企业应当定期评估其分销渠道的表现以避免机会成本的产生。

　　对所有经营者或服务供应商来说，加入市场营销渠道是一种权益平衡。他们享有成本、其他储备以及向参与各种业务的中介商分流责任的优势，同时也不可避免地失去对中间商所从事的业务部分的掌控。拿旅游地营销渠道网络来说，个体旅游业务供应商一旦成为目的地管理组织（DMOs）的成员，它们就要承担起广告宣传和推广该目的地的责任，这是销售渠道网络中市场营销活动的一种形式。当旅游业内的某些中小型企业为了减少昂贵的营销行动而不得不加入目的地管理组织时，它们也会因此失去对网络中的这些组成成分的掌控。旅游产品供应商要注重营销渠道网络系统内各成员之间实力与能力、规模与效益的平衡，避免大型的供应商为了自身利益凌驾于小型经营商之上从而操纵整个渠道，造成整个系统失衡。

　　有效分配和行使营销权力是有效管理整个分销渠道系统的出发点。营销

Understanding the needs of the target customer is the basis for distribution channel selection. When designing the marketing channels, marketers must understand the needs of the target customers. Different consumers have different service needs. For instance, airlines providing both first class and economic class with limited services are expected to cater the different needs of different customers. Before choosing a distribution channel, marketers need to understand the market demand for product features. Hence, marketers should have a thorough understanding of the following: (1) The number of products an average consumer buys in a particular channel: For example, hotels employ revenue management to analyze when and which channels customers make consumption, as well as the contribution of these channels to the total room nights sold. (2) Lead time: the average delivery time of products after consumers buy products or services through a parti cular channel. In the airline and hospitality industries, the processing time of distributors is an important factor for airlines or hotels to select channel partners. (3) The level of ease for consumers to buy products or services through certain channels: With real-time reservation services on TripAdvisor, customers can make instant reservation after reading the online reviews. (4) The breath of product offerings provided by channels: Examples are the availability of "flight tickets and hotel accommodations" and "flight tickets and airport transfer services" on OTA. (5) Additional services provided by channels, such as delivery, installation, and maintenance.

The attractiveness of channels varies for enterprises at different stages of development. Well-established and large-scale hotels have strong bargaining power over the newly established small-scale hotels. New or small-scale hotels should avoid utilizing multiple distributors.

The costs and benefits associated with respective distribution channels differ. Distribution channels can be classified to two types, namely, direct costs and opportunity costs. For example, hotels can increase occupancy rate with the help of travel agencies and contracted companies. The method creates opportunity costs when the market demand is high. Enterprises should, therefore, regularly evaluate the performance of their distribution channels so as to avoid opportunity costs.

From the perspective of operators and service providers, joining marketing channels is a balance of interests. They enjoy the benefits of sharing costs and reserves, as well as the division of responsibilities among intermediaries that are involved in various businesses. Inevitably, they lose control over the businesses taken care by intermediaries. The context of the distribution network of destination marketing is used to illustrate the aforementioned argument. Once individual tourism service providers become the members of destination management organizations (DMOs), they bear the responsibilities of advertising and promoting the destinations as forms of marketing campaign. Some small and medium-sized enterprises in the tourism industry join the DMOs in order to reduce cost in marketing activities. Consequently, they would lose control over the components in the network. Tourism suppliers should pay attention to the balance between the capabilities, scales, and efficiencies of members in the marketing distribution systems. It serves the purpose of avoiding large-scale suppliers to manipulate the entire channels for their own interests while jeopardizing their small-scale counterparts.

Effective distribution and exercising marketing power are the starting points for effective

渠道中的权力是指"某一特定渠道成员控制或影响另一个或几个成员的行为、说服他们做自身本不会去做的事情的能力"。奖赏权是营销渠道权力的一种,它可以被看作是某一渠道成员因为通过改变其行为来符合另一渠道成员的要求时而得到的作为补偿的利益或报酬,主要表现为经济利益上的满足,如提供适销对路的产品、推广支持、给予较大的价格上的折扣、独家经营权等。例如,航空公司根据旅行社销售机票的数量为旅行社提供特别的预订票价或其他奖励。与奖赏权对应的是强制权,它是对没有遵从意愿或执行责任的另一方进行惩罚的能力。一般来说,营销渠道协议中有真正的或可感知的丧失某种利益或奖赏的威胁。例如,企业 A 通过企业 B 发放宣传材料和促销广告,B 要求 A 提高会员订购费,若 A 不同意,会遭到 B 将其促销材料从展览窗口撤走的威胁。

营销渠道权力还可以是基于专长权。专长权来源于专业知识,它产生于一渠道成员在特定领域赋予另一个渠道成员的知识和有用的技能,如帮助渠道成员设计管理系统、进行人员的培训等。专长权是特许权授予者影响特许经营者行为的关键权力。例如,酒店特许经营集团通过向下属酒店持续提供管理支援、信息系统以及培训支持等帮助它们建立并维持运作,进而保持整个渠道的忠诚。这三种渠道权力是属于非正式权力,主要取决于渠道成员间的相互依赖性和回应性。从正式协议的角度来看,渠道权力可被称为"法制权力",即渠道成员借助正式的合同或协议对其他成员施加的影响,具体到指明谁能做、做什么、什么时候做以及怎样做等事项。例如,某些餐饮集团采取特许经营方式,通过与个体餐厅经营者签订特许合同,明确合同双方的权利和责任,获得渠道合法权。

渠道成员间分工明确,以协议的形式清晰地界定每个渠道成员的权力、职责、义务,以及应达成的销售业绩是有效解决冲突的方法。通过这种书面化的清晰表示,使渠道成员在日常分销工作中知道自己该做什么、该如何做、做到何种程度,以防由于职责不清而导致冲突的发生。此外,渠道成员之所以合作是因为合作能够创造出比独自经营更多的利益,能够实现各渠道成员长期利益最大化,因此利益分配机制合理与否对渠道成员十分重要。建立公平的利益共享机制不是件易事。尽管我们主张渠道各成员间的协作和权力平衡,但实际上为了达成共同的目标,总会有某个或几个成员扮演领袖的角色来领导其他成员。这些所谓的"渠道领袖"可能来源于营销渠道系统中的某个供应商股东,也可能是其中的某个中间商,但一般都是规模较大、比较固定且竞争优势较强的企业。生产商需要设计合理的利益分配与共享机制,综合考虑各种因素,使各渠道成员的应得利益得到保证,以防由此而引起渠道冲突或渠道瓦解。

management of the entire distribution channel system. The power in marketing channels is the ability of particular channel members to control or influence the behavior of another or a few members in persuading them to perform their unintended actions. Reward is a form of power in marketing channel. It can be regarded as compensation or remuneration that a channel member obtains because of its changing behavior in order to meet the requirements of other channel members. Financial reward is the main type of reward, such as offering larger discounts for marketable products and promotional support or the exclusive operation rights. For example, airline companies provide special booking fares or other incentives to travel agencies according to their tickets sold. Punishment is the opposite of reward, referring to penalties for parties who are unwilling or failed to comply with responsibilities. Generally speaking, a marketing channel agreement demonstrates real or perceivable threats of losing benefit or reward. For example, company A launches promotional materials and advertisements through company B, and company B requests for an increment in subscription fee. If company A refuses, then company B will threaten to remove its promotional materials from the window display.

Marketing channel power can also be based on the power of expertise. Expertise emanated from the knowledge and useful skills that a channel member endued with another channel member in a particular domain, such as helping channel members to design the management system and conducting personnel training. The power of expertise allows franchisor to exert significant influences on the behavior of franchisees. For example, the hotel franchising group maintains loyalty throughout the channel by assisting its franchisees with management support, information system, and training support to build and maintain operations. These three channel powers are informal power, depending on the interdependence and responsiveness among channel members. From a formal business agreement perspective, channel power can be labeled as "legal power." It enables channel members to exert influences on other members by specifying who can do, what to do, when to do, and how to do. For instance, some catering groups signed franchising contracts with individual restaurants, and the contracts clearly state mutual rights and responsibilities to obtain legal channel rights.

The clear division of works among channel members and the clarification of the rights, duties, obligations, rights, and sales performance of each channel member in the form of agreements are effective ways of resolving the conflict. With a clearly written document, channelmembers are aware of what they should do, how to do, and to what extent in the daily work distribution, thus preventing confusion due to role conflict. Besides, channel members cooperate because cooperation can create more profits than independent operation and maximize the long-term benefits of every channel member. A reasonable reward distribution mechanism is, therefore, very important. It is not easy to establish an equitable benefit-sharing mechanism. Despite the advocacy of coordination and balance of power among members, one or few members will always take up the role of leader to lead other members in reality. These so-called "channel leaders" can be the shareholders of suppliers or few intermediaries. They are generally large-scale, relatively established, and competitive enterprises. Manufacturers need to design a reasonable benefit-sharing mechanism, taking into account various factors, so as to guarantee the interests of members and prevent the resulting conflicts or collapse of channel.

第 11 章　营销传播

 本章要点

- 营销传播：概述
- 营销传播：战略
- 营销传播：广告
- 营销传播：公关关系和公众宣传
- 营销传播：销售推广
- 营销传播：人员推销
- 营销传播：网络传播

　　本章将介绍营销组合中最后一个要素——促销。企业不仅仅需要创造价值，还需要将其创造的价值以消费者愿意接受的方式，清晰地、有说服力地进行传递。在整合营销的框架下，促销是一组工具的组合。营销人员通过不同的组合方式，更加有效地吸引消费者的注意，构建关于与企业和产品的清晰、一致、有说服力的信息。本章将介绍不同的促销组合工具。

11.1　营销传播：概述

　　营销传播是企业直接或间接告知、说服和提醒消费者关于企业所销售的产品和品牌的方法。在某种程度上，营销传播代表了企业和品牌的"声音"，企业通过营销传播与消费者建立对话和关系。企业通过应用营销传播组合中的工具将旗下品牌和消费者、地点、时间、其他品牌、体验、感受和事物等因素联系起来，并促进产品的销售，甚至是影响利益相关者的价值（Luo 和 Donthu，2006）。营销传播组合主要包括广告、公共关系、销售推广、人员推销以及网络传播五大类，每一类包含特定的促销工具或形式。如广告包括电视广告、印刷品广告、手机广告、户外广告等形式；公共关系包括新闻发布会、

Chapter 11　Marketing Communications

 Key points of the chapter

- Marketing communications: Overview
- Marketing communications: Strategy
- Marketing communications: Advertising
- Marketing communications: Public relations and promotions
- Marketing communications: Sales promotion
- Marketing communications: Personnel marketing
- Marketing communications: Network communications

This chapter introduces the last element of the marketing mix: promotion. Enterprises should not only create value but also create value such that consumers become willing to accept and communicate with them in a clear and persuasive manner. In the integrated marketing framework, promotion is a combination of tools. Marketers use different combinations of promotions to effectively engage consumers and build a clear, consistent, and compelling message about their business and products. This chapter presents the different combinations of promotional tools.

11.1　Marketing Communications: Overview

Marketing communications refers to the direct or indirect way with which enterprises inform, persuade, and remind consumers about their products and brands. To a certain extent, marketing communications represent the "voice" of enterprises and their brands. Enterprises establish dialogue and relations with consumers through marketing communications. By using the tools in the marketing communication mix, enterprises can link their brands and consumers, locations, time, other brands, experiences, feelings, and things to promote the sales of products and even the value of stakeholders (Luo & Donthu, 2006). The marketing communication mix comprises five categories, namely, advertising, public relations, sales promotion, personnel marketing, and network communications. Each category involves specific promotional tools or forms. Advertising refers to television advertisements, printed advertisements, mobile advertisements, and outdoor advertisements. Public relations deal with press releases,

活动赞助、节事等形式;销售推广包括折扣、现金券、产品展示及试用等形式。

在传统营销时代,企业生产标准化的产品,营销传播也以大众媒体为主,通过电视、杂志、电台等媒体向数以万计的消费者传递企业的信息。而随着市场、营销战略、科学技术的发展及变化,传统的以大众传播为主的销售方式已逐渐淡出历史舞台。处在信息化时代的消费者拥有了更多的获取信息的渠道,因此不再依赖企业提供的信息。而随着互联网的不断发展和普及,消费者也逐渐参与到企业信息的创造中。在此背景之下,营销人员需要摒弃传统的营销方式,针对目标市场进行精准营销,通过向个体消费者传递独一无二的定制信息与其建立紧密的关系。虽然电视、杂志、电台等传统的大众媒体在营销传播中仍占据一席之地,但越来越多的营销人员开始使用新兴的媒体进行精准营销,如博客、电子邮件以及各种形式的社交媒体。与传统的大众媒体填鸭式的信息传播模式相比,新兴媒体能够以更加个性化的方式与消费者互动。

传统媒体与新媒体相结合的传播模式已成为市场趋势。韩国电视剧《来自星星的你》于 2013 年在国内众多在线视频网站热播,随后,2013 年到韩国旅游的中国游客共有 392 万人次,较 2012 年增加了 43.6%。中国赴韩游客呈年轻化、散客化特点,也与热播的韩国电视剧有关。与此同时,韩国政府部门也主动在中国推动影视旅游。首尔市政府在 2014 年 2 月宣布选定该市 120 处与韩剧、韩国音乐等相关的旅游景点,分为 4 种主题旅游和 7 大特色旅游圈,开发更多旅游资源,吸引年轻游客到来。市场的变化使得营销人员需要使用整合营销传播的思维模式进行营销传播。整合营销传播能够实现额外价值,评估不同传播渠道的战略作用,对这些传播渠道进行并用,且通过严谨地整合传播内容,提供清晰的、一致的、能够实现影响最大化的营销传播信息。实施整合营销传播需要多方合作,很少有企业能够单独完成整合营销传播,它们通常都需要传播渠道代理或传播渠道企业的帮忙。这些企业在传播渠道方面提供战略和实际操作的建议,帮助客户提高它们的整体渠道效率(Neuborne,2004)。例如,企业希望实现一站式购物,参与到这个过程中的渠

event sponsorships, and events. Sales promotion includes discounts, cash coupons, product coupons, product displays, and trials.

In the traditional marketing era, enterprises produce standardized products and use mass media as their main marketing communication tool. Thousands of consumers obtain business information through television programs, magazines, radios, and other media platforms. With the development and changes of markets, marketing strategies, and technologies, traditional mass-based marketing communications gradually faded out. In the information era, consumers possess broad access to information channels and do not rely on information provided by enterprises. With the continuous development and proliferation of the Internet, consumers gradually partake in the creation of enterprise information. In this situation, marketers need to eliminate traditional marketing methods. They should conduct precise marketing exercises to target markets by delivering unique and customized information for building close relationships. Although traditional mass media, such as television, magazine, and radio, are continuously utilized in marketing communications, an increasing number of marketers are using emerging media, such as blogs, emails, and social media, for specific marketing activities. Emerging media facilitates interaction with consumers in a more personalized way in comparison with traditional mass media, which employs a spoon-feeding style.

The integration of traditional media and emerging media has become a marketing trend. In 2013, the Korean drama *My Love from the Star* went viral on many domestic online video sites. Subsequently, Chinese outbound tourists to R.O. Korea reached 3.92 million, which represented a 43.6% increase from the previous percentage in 2012. Chinese tourists to R.O. Korea during this period were mainly young and independent travelers who were attracted to popular Korean dramas such as *My Love from the Star*. At the same time, the Korean government took initiatives to promote film tourism in China. In February 2014, the municipal government of Seoul selected 120 tourist attractions related to Korean drama and music and divided them into four thematic tours and seven special tourism zones geared at attracting young tourists. Changes in the market compel marketers to use an integrated communication mode to conduct marketing communication exercises. Integrated marketing communications enables additional value, involves assessing the strategic roles of different communication channels, and allows the simultaneous use of these channels. Through the rigorous integration of marketing information, integrated marketing communications enables the delivery of clear, consistent, and impact-maximizing marketing communications. Implementing integrated marketing communications requires multi-faceted collaboration. However, few enterprises are able to complete actions related to integrated marketing communications. The assistance of communication agencies is typically needed. These companies provide strategic and practical advice on implementation and contribute to the enhancement of the overall efficiency of channels (Neuborne, 2004). For example, enterprises want to

道代理包括推广代理、公共关系代理、包装设计咨询企业、网页创建人员以及邮寄代理。

整合营销传播能够提供更好的信息一致性，并帮助企业建立品牌资产，提高销售效果(Seric、Gil-Saura 和 Ruiz-Molina，2014)。整合营销传播促使管理层思考顾客如何接触企业、企业如何传播其定位、每个传播渠道的重要性以及时间范围等问题。主管营销的管理层现在多了一项责任，即如何统一企业形象和营销传播的内容。当企业能够真正实施整合营销管理时，企业能够将合适的营销信息，在合适的时间，通过合适的传播渠道，传递给合适的顾客(Schultz 和 Schultz，2003)。

整合营销传播要求营销人员不再像过去一样仅仅关注目标市场的即时反应，而是将营销传播视为一个管理顾客参与和顾客关系的长期持续工作。市场差异化的不断加剧使得营销人员不仅仅需要面向细分市场，有时甚至需要针对个体消费者进行品牌信息的传播，了解信息传播的过程因此至关重要。图 11-1 所示为信息传播的主要过程，包括九个要素。

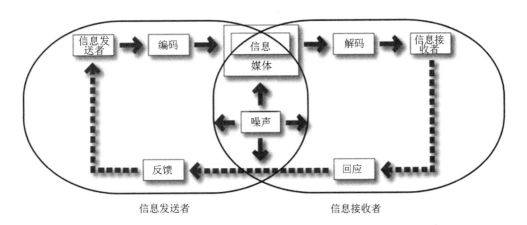

图 11-1 信息传播的要素
来源：Kotler，P. & Armstrong，G. (2014). *Principles of Marketing* (16th ed.). Boston：Pearson Education Limited.

(1) 信息发送者：将信息传递给另外一个群体的企业或组织。

(2) 编码：将营销目的具象化后放入传播载体的过程。例如香格里拉酒店集团的广告代理将设计好的词语、音乐等元素，加入到电视广告中，以传递

set up one-stop shopping platforms. Channel agencies, such as promotion agencies, public relations agencies, consulting firms providing packaging design, and web creators and mail agencies, should all participate in the process.

Integrated marketing communications can provide relevant and consistent information, thus helping enterprises to establish brand equity and increase sales (Seric, Gil-Saura & Ruiz-Molina, 2014). It encourages management to consider how customers reach out to businesses, how enterprises communicate their positioning, the importance of individual communication channels, and the scope of time. Managers who are in charge of marketing are now responsible for unifying the corporate image and marketing communication content. A true and successful implementation of integrated marketing communications means that enterprises can deliver the right marketing information at the right time through the right communication channels and to the right customers (Schultz & Schultz, 2003).

Integrated marketing communications require marketers to shift their focus from immediate responses of target markets to marketing communications as a long-term ongoing effort to manage customer engagement and customer relationships. Increasing market differentiation highlights the need for marketers to not only target market segments but also disseminate brand information to individual consumers. Understanding information dissemination is thus imperative. Figure 11-1 shows how information dissemination is carried out. The process includes the nine following elements.

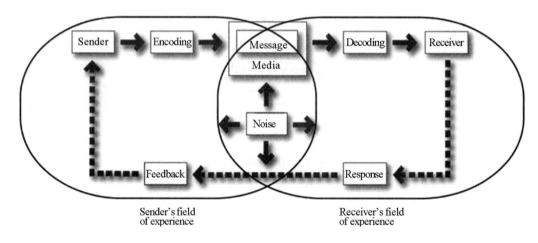

Figure 11 - 1　Elements of communication

Source: Kotler, P. & Armstrong, G. (2014). *Principles of Marketing* (16th ed.). Boston: Pearson Education Limited.

(1) Sender: An enterprise or organization that communicates information to other groups.

(2) Encoding: The process of visualizing the marketing objectives into a delivery form. For example, the advertising agency of the Shangri-La Hotel Group incorporates

营销信息,实现营销目的。

(3) 信息:信息传递者所传递的一组意象,例如香格里拉酒店集团的品牌广告。

(4) 媒体:营销信息从传递者送到接收者的过程中所使用的传播渠道。

(5) 解码:信息接收者解读营销信息所包含的意义的过程。例如,一个消费者看到了香格里拉酒店集团的广告,对广告中所包含的词语、图像进行解读。

(6) 信息接收者:接收另外一个群体(企业或组织)所传递的消息的个人或群体。

(7) 回应:信息接收者在解读营销信息后的反应。例如消费者在看到香格里拉酒店集团的广告后,更喜欢香格里拉品牌,或者更可能把香格里拉酒店作为下次入住的选择等。

(8) 反馈:信息接收者的回应送回信息发送者的过程。例如,香格里拉酒店集团的调查发现消费者对其品牌广告有深刻的印象。

(9) 噪声:信息传播过程中的信息扭曲或争论。例如,消费者在观看香格里拉酒店集团的品牌广告时注意力不集中,错过了关键信息。

Batra 和 Keller(2016)认为,整合营销包含两个方面的营销模型,一是匹配传播模型,另外一个是优化传播模型。匹配传播模型强调企业对消费者、语境和内容因素以及传播结果的理解,考虑消费者在决策过程中不同阶段的具体目标和期望结果以及不同媒体类型的特征,以推荐最佳匹配媒体和信息。优化传播模型则对所有传播选项的效度和效率进行评估,以确保营销活动能产生最大的集体效应(Batra 和 Keller,2016)。图 11-2 所示为整合营销传播的概念模型。

在实施整合营销的过程中,营销人员必须完全理解消费者的购买路径、被管理的品牌中消费者最感兴趣的特定产品类别以及消费者的决策影响因素。不是所有消费者都共享单一的购买路径,然而,营销人员在制定购买路径时,可以采用能够反映、解释更复杂和非线性的决策过程的模型,这些决策过程模型能够体现当今许多消费者的决策特征。

well-constructed words and music into their television advertisements to deliver marketing information that can actualize their marketing objectives.

（3）Message：A set of images conveyed by the message sender. An example is the branding advertisements of the Shangri-La Hotel Group.

（4）Media：The communication channel used to convey marketing messages from senders to recipients.

（5）Decoding：The process by which an information recipient interprets the meaning of a marketing message. For example, a consumer interprets the words and images in the advertisement of the Shangri-La Hotel Group.

（6）Receiver：An individual or group that receives messages from other groups （enterprise or organization）.

（7）Response：The response of the message recipient after reading the marketing message. For example, consumers become attracted to the Shangri-La Hotel brand or make Shangri-La Hotel their next choice of accommodation after watching the advertisement of the hotel group.

（8）Feedback：The process of the message recipient sending back his/her response to the sender. For example, the Shangri-La Hotels and Resorts survey reveals that consumers are impressed with their brand advertisement.

（9）Noise：Distortion or controversy in the dissemination of information. Consumers, for example, skip key messages when watching the brand advertisement of the Shangri-La Hotel Group.

Batra and Keller（2016）claim that integrated marketing communications incorporate two marketing models, namely, communication matching model and communication optimization model. The matching propagation model emphasizes the understanding of consumers, context, and content factors as well as the dissemination results. This model takes into account the specific goals and expectations of consumers at different stages during decision making. Consequently, the model recommends the best match of media and information to deliver. The communication optimization model evaluates the validity and efficiency of all communication options to ensure that marketing activities produce the greatest collective effect（Batra & Keller, 2016）. Figure 11 - 2 shows the conceptual model of integrated marketing communications.

In implementing integrated marketing communications, marketers must fully understand the buying patterns of consumers, the specific product categories in the managed brands that consumers are most interested in, and the determinants of consumer decision making. Not all consumers share a single buying pattern. When planning for purchase patterns, marketers can use models that reflect and interpret complex and non-linear decision-making processes. These decision-making models can reflect the decision-making features of consumers today.

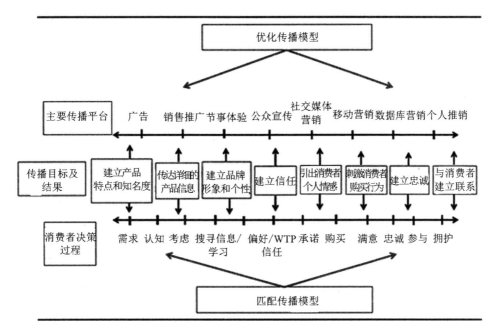

图 11 - 2　整合营销传播概念模型

来源：Batra，R. & Keller，K. L. (2016). Integrating marketing communications：New findings，new lessons，and new ideas. *Journal of Marketing*，80，122 - 145.

　　营销人员同时必须定期对任何传播项目进行审核，以评估其整合程度。整合营销传播模型的七个标准（消费者覆盖、成本、贡献、共性、互补性、交叉效应和一致性）可以为审核提供有用的依据。营销人员还必须对正在进行或已经执行的传播项目进行深入的评估。这种评估应尽可能对传播项目在品牌资产和销售方面的直接和间接影响进行分析，应用正确的测量模型至关重要。

11.2　营销传播：战略

　　有效的营销传播一般有六个步骤：识别目标群体、确定传播目标、制定营销传播战略、选择传播渠道、选择信息来源、制定传播预算。

1. 识别目标群体

　　在制定营销传播战略前，企业必须有一个清晰目标，这次营销传播的目标群体是企业产品的潜在顾客、现有顾客、购买决策者还是购买影响者？是针对个人、群体、特定群体还是普通大众？根据不同的目标人群，企业所制

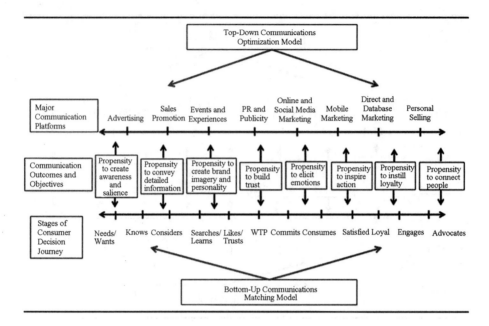

Figure 11 – 2 Conceptual model of integrated marketing communications

Source：Batra，R. & Keller，K. L.（2016）.Integrating marketing communications：New findings，new lessons，and new ldeas. *Journal of Marketing*，80，122 – 145.

Marketers must also periodically review any communication projects to assess their level of integration. The seven criteria of the integrated marketing communication model （consumer coverage，cost，contribution，commonality，complementarity，cross-effect，and consistency）can provide a useful basis for this audit. Marketers must also conduct in-depth evaluations of ongoing or implemented communication projects. As much as possible，this assessment should analyze the direct and indirect impacts of dissemination projects on brand equity and sales. The application of the appropriate measurement model is critical.

11.2　*Marketing Communications：Strategy*

Effective marketing communications generally involves six steps，namely，identify target groups，determine communication goals，develop marketing communication strategies，select communication channels，select information sources，and develop communication budget.

1. Identify target groups

Before developing marketing communication strategies，enterprises should establish a clear goal. Are potential customers，existing customers，purchase decision makers，or influencers the target audience of marketing communications? Is it for individuals，groups，particular public sectors，or the general public? According to different target groups，the

定的营销传播战略也有所不同。除此之外,企业也可以通过品牌形象分析,即根据对品牌的熟悉程度来选择目标群体。

2. 确定传播目标

一旦确定了目标群体,营销人员需要决定所期望的市场反应,也即营销传播希望达到的目标。对于所有企业和营销人员来讲,使得消费者产生购买行为,并成为终身客户是终极目标,但是对于消费者而言,在最终的购买行为产生前一般会经历一个较长的决策过程,因此,在不同的决策阶段,营销传播有不同的目标。营销人员在不同的阶段营销传播所要达到的目标可以总结为 AIDAA 模型,也即认知、兴趣、欲望、行动及支持。AIDAA 模型是从消费者心理的角度考虑传播从唤起认知到产生购买行为的心理模式,它反映的是消费者对企业所沟通的产品和服务的心理介入程度(见表 11-1)。如橘子精品酒店 2012 年在上海开业时,别出心裁地举行了主题为"女王的盛宴"的开幕典礼,让消费者认识到有"新酒店出现"。开业酬宾活动则主要为了激起公众对酒店提供的产品和服务的兴趣,引起购买该产品的欲望,并促使其做出购买或试买的决策。当顾客将意念中的购买付诸实施之时,也就是购买行为真正发生的过程。越来越多的企业在购买行为完成后会通过各种手段进行售后沟通,以获得消费者对企业或者品牌持续的支持并使其最终成为忠诚客户,这个完整的过程就是我们所提的 AIDAA 模型。

表 11-1 营销沟通的顾客反应层级:AIDAA 模型

字母	阶段	消费者反应
A	认知	我看到那里有新的……
I	兴趣	我在想是否……
D	欲望	我想试一下他们的……
A	行动	啊,终于来到这里了。
A	支持	嗯,一定要推荐给别人!

一般而言,企业可以从以下几个方面确定营销传播活动的目标(Rossiter 和 Percy,1987)。

(1)类别需求:企业通过建立必要的产品或服务类别,以去除或满足当前消费者的动机状态和所期望的情绪状态之间的感知差异。通常而言,企业在推出新产品前都会以建立类别需求作为营销传播的目标,例如特斯拉在推出电动汽车时,其宣传语是"特斯拉电动汽车在质量、安全和性能方面均达到

development of marketing communication strategies varies. In addition, enterprises can conduct image analyses on the basis of brand familiarity to select target groups.

2. Determine communication goals

After identifying target groups, marketers need to determine the desired market response, that is, the desired goals of marketing communications. For all enterprises and marketers, the ultimate goal is to make consumers purchase and become lifelong customers. However, consumers usually go through a long decision-making process before making their final buying decisions. Marketing communications therefore aim at different goals at different stages of decision making. The goal of marketers at different stages of marketing communications can be summed up in the AIDAA model (i.e., awareness, interest, desire, action, and advocacy). The AIDAA model is a psychological model of consumers from awareness to making purchasing behavior. It reflects the degree of psychological involvement of consumers in communicating products and services (Table 11 - 1). For example, the Orange Boutique Hotel was opened in Shanghai in 2012. The opening ceremony featured the theme "The feast of the queen,"which instilled the idea of "new hotel appears" among consumers. Aimed at arousing the interest of the public in the products and services provided by the hotel, the promotional activities induce among consumers a desire to buy products as well as make purchase or trial decisions. When customers actualize their perception and take action to buy, the real purchase behavior occurs. An increasing number of enterprises engage in after-sales communication with consumers through various means to obtain continuous support and eventually turn them into loyal customers. The entire process is described in the AIDAA model.

Table 11 - 1 Customer response levels for marketing communications: AIDAA model

Letter	Stage	Customer Response
A	Awareness	I see there is new…
I	Interest	I am thinking whether…
D	Desire	I want to try their …
A	Action	Finally I am here.
A	Advocacy	I have to recommend others!

Companies can determine the objectives of marketing communication activities in the following aspects (Rossiter & Percy, 1987).

(1) Category need: Enterprises remove or satisfy the perceived difference between consumers' current motivation and the desired emotional state by establishing the necessary product or service categories. In general, enterprises establish category need as a marketing communication target before the launch of a new product. For instance, Tesla introduced electric vehicles and featured the message, "Tesla electric vehicles

汽车行业最高标准,并提供融合最尖端技术的'空中升级'等服务方式和完备的充电解决方案,为人们带来了最极致的驾乘感受和最完备的拥有体验"(Tesla,2016)。

(2)品牌认知:消费者能够在产品类别中识别(辨认或回忆)品牌,并有足够详细的信息做出购买决策。品牌回忆在消费后较为重要,而品牌辨认在决策进行过程中较为重要。品牌认知是品牌资产的基础。在旅游和酒店行业的范畴内,品牌回忆是消费者在旅游决策阶段外对品牌的记忆或感知。例如,一位消费者向朋友介绍其在丽思卡尔顿酒店的入住体验;品牌辨认则是消费者在旅游决策过程中能够快速识别其喜爱的品牌,例如差旅客人在出发前需要预订酒店,他们会直接在喜爱的酒店官方网站进行预订,或者在 OTA 网站上快速找到他们想要预订的品牌酒店。

(3)品牌态度:通过评估品牌的感知功能以确定其能否满足相应的需求。相应品牌需求可能是消极导向的(如消除问题、避免问题、未被满足的需求、损耗等)或是积极导向的(如享乐、激发智慧或者社会认可)。一般而言,消费者对酒店品牌的需求都是积极导向的(享受、体验等),而酒店品牌也强调其相应的感知功能,例如丽思卡尔顿集团对使命的描述为"提供真诚的关怀以及卓越的产品和服务"。

(4)品牌购买意向:自主购买品牌产品或者进行与购买相关的活动。优惠券或买二送一的推广形式能鼓励消费者做出购买决策。但是,部分消费者没有明确的产品类别需求或者是并没有看到这些推广活动的广告,因而他们不会有购买产品的意向。例如,喜达屋集团每年夏季期间都会进行限时促销活动,折扣最高可达五折,其目的就是鼓励消费者预订酒店。

3. 制定营销传播战略

确定了营销传播目标后的下一步是制定营销传播战略。能够获得预期目标的营销传播战略需要解决两个方面的问题:说什么(信息战略)和怎么说(创意战略)。在制定传播战略时,管理层需要考虑传播方式、主题、创意等与品牌相关的问题,同时,这些问题有助于企业在营销传播的过程中建立与竞争对手之间的相同点或差异点。此外,上述需要考虑的问题可能与产品的表现直接相关(如品质或品牌价值),也可能影响外部因素(如品牌的形象是

achieve the highest standards in the automobile industry in terms of quality, safety and performance. The state-of-the-art technology offers a complete charging solution, presenting the ultimate driving and ownership experiences" (Tesla, 2016).

(2) Brand awareness: Consumers can identify (or recall) a brand in a product category and possess adequate detailed information to make a purchase decision. Brand recall is particularly important after consumption, and brand recognition is significant in the decision-making process. Brand awareness is the foundation of brand equity. In the context of the tourism and hospitality industry, brand recall is the memory or perception of the brand at the decision-making stage of consumers. An example of brand recall is when a consumer describes his or her experience in the Ritz-Carlton Hotel to a friend. Brand recognition is when consumers can quickly identify their favorite brands during the tourism decision-making process. Business travelers need to book hotel accommodations before their trips. They directly make reservations through the official websites of their favorite hotels or quickly find hotel brands from OTA websites.

(3) Brand attitude: Brand attitude involves assessing the perceived ability of a brand to determine whether it can satisfy a corresponding demand. The corresponding demand can be negative (e.g., eliminating problems, avoiding problems, unmet needs, and loss) or positive (e.g., pleasure, wisdom inspiration, or social recognition). In general, the demand of consumers for hotel brands is positively oriented (enjoyment and experience). Hotel brands also emphasize corresponding perceptual functions. For example, the Ritz-Carlton Group, states "a place where the genuine care and comfort of our guests is our highest mission."

(4) Brand purchase intention: The buying of branded products or engagement in purchase-related activities is self-initiated. Coupons or the buy-two-get-one-free promotional form can encourage consumers to make purchasing decisions. Some consumers do not intend to buy because they do not have a clear product category need or they have not seen any promotional advertisements. For instance, Starwood Group offers limited-time promotions in summer, including discounts of up to 50% off. The purpose of such promotions is to encourage consumers to book hotels.

3. Develop marketing communication strategies

Following the establishment of marketing communication objectives is the identification of marketing communication strategies. Marketing communication strategies that achieve the desired objectives should address two aspects, namely, what to say (message strategy) and how to say (creative strategy). In developing communication strategies, the management needs to consider several brand-related issues, such as communication methods, themes, and creativity. These issues can help companies to establish a point of parity and point of difference with competitors. Furthermore, the abovementioned considerations may be directly related to product performance (such as quality or brand value) and external factors (brand image

现代的、流行的或是传统的）。

营销传播是否有效取决于营销信息如何被表达以及信息内容。效度低的营销传播可能是选错了信息内容，也可能是好的信息内容通过不合理的方式进行表达。创意战略是指营销人员将希望传达的营销信息转化为特定的传播方式。创意战略一般分为信息法和转换法两种方式。信息法着重于对产品或服务的属性或好处进行详细说明。例如，运用信息法的广告分为解决问题式广告（如"Uber 解决出行问题"）、产品示范式广告（如"携程在手，说走就走"）、产品对比式广告（如"Trivago 帮助游客获取最低价"）。信息法认为消费者在接收营销传播的过程中都是非常理性的，因此，逻辑与合理是信息法的核心；转换法着重于强调与产品并非直接相关的好处或品牌形象。转换法的广告可能会描述哪一类人群会使用这个品牌（如文华东方的名人粉丝，包括杨紫琼、陈坤、摩根·费里曼、凯文·史派西等）或是使用这个品牌会得到什么样的体验（如香格里拉酒店集团的"至善盛情，源自天性"品牌广告）。转换法的关键是引起目标群体的情感，从而鼓励其进行购买。

4. 选择传播渠道

传播渠道日益多元化使得营销人员在传播渠道的选择上面临更大的挑战。例如，酒店行业现有的营销传播渠道包括杂志广告、电子邮件推广、小册子、搜索引擎、OTA 竞价排名、赞助演唱会、智能手机 App 等。传播渠道分为个人式传播渠道和非个人传播渠道。

个人传播是指让两个或更多的人通过面对面、演讲、电话或电子邮件进行交流。即时信息和利用网页收集消费者的评价也是个人传播的渠道。个人传播的营销在两个情境下会产生重大的影响。一是当产品是昂贵的、有风险的或者消费者并非经常购买的；二是产品能够反映消费者的地位或者品味。个人传播的效度源于个人化的展示和反馈。通常而言，个人传播有三种模式，即鼓动模式、专家模式和社交模式。鼓动模式是由企业的销售人员在目标群体中联系买家；专家模式是指企业外的独立专家向买家介绍和推荐产品；社交模式是指买家的家庭成员、邻居、朋友、同事与买家进行交谈。根据

perceived to be modern, popular, or traditional).

The effectiveness of marketing communications depends on the way marketing messages are expressed and on the content of the messages. Ineffective marketing communications may deliver the wrong message or express a good message in an unreasonable way. Creative strategies involve conveying marketing information via a specific mode of transmission. These strategies can be informational and transformational. The former focuses on the attributes or benefits of products or services. Informational advertisements are classified into problem solving (as "Uber for travel problems"), product demonstration (as "Ctrip on hand for making instant travel arrangements"), and product comparison (as "Trivago helping visitors to obtain the lowest prices for accommodations"). The informational approach regards consumers as highly rational when receiving marketing information. Logic and rationality is the core of the informational approach. The transformational approach emphasizes the benefits or brand images that are indirectly associated with products. Its advertisements describe the type of people using the brands (such as the celebrity fans of Mandarin Oriental, including Michelle Yeoh, Chen Kun, Morgan Freeman, and Kevin Spacey) or the experiences of using the brands (for example, Shangri-La launched a new global brand campaign called "It's In Our Nature"). The objective of the transformational strategy is to arouse the emotions of target groups and encourage them to make purchases.

4. Select communication channels

The increasing diversification of markets poses a significant challenge to marketers in terms of channel selection. For instance, the existing marketing communication channels of the hotel industry include magazines, email promotions, brochures, search engines, the ranking bids of OTA, sponsored concerts, and smart phone applications. Communication channels can be divided into personal communication channels and non-personal communication channels.

Personal communication refers to the communication between two or more people through face-to-face settings, speaking, telephone, or e-mail. Instant messaging and the use of web pages to collect consumer evaluation is also a channel of personal communication. Marketing via personal communication creates significant impact under two conditions. First, the product is expensive, risky, or not frequently purchased by consumers; second, the product reflects the status or taste of consumers. The effectiveness of personal communication comes from personal display and feedback. In general, personal communication comes in three types: advocate channels, expert channels, and social channels. Advocate channels allow marketers to contact buyers from target groups. Expert channels allow independents and external experts to introduce and recommend products to buyers. Social channels allow buyers to engage in conversations with their family members, neighbors, friends, and colleagues. According to Hon and

Hon 和 Grunig（1999）的研究，一个人对产品的评价通常会影响另外两个人对产品的购买态度。而在互联网环境下，口碑的影响人数会增加至八人，这使得社交模式的个人传播日益重要，而这一渠道又恰恰是超出企业掌控范围的。认识到用户产生信息的重要性，澳大利亚旅游局鼓励曾经到澳大利亚旅游的游客在 Nothing Like Australia 网站上共享他们旅行住宿和游玩经历。接近 3 万个故事和图片被上传至 www.nothinglikeaustralia.com 网站，之后，澳洲旅游局让所有参与者共建一个互动电子旅行地图，这项活动吸引了超过百万的游客每月点击 www.nothinglikeaustralia.com 网站。另一方面，关于酒店的网络差评同样会对酒店品牌的形象产生巨大影响。喜达屋酒店集团旗下某家 W 酒店曾经发生客人意外触电事件，事件当事人在网络平台上公布此事并给予了 W 酒店差评。事件发生后，酒店承担客人在医院的检查与治疗费用，并免除了客人的入住费用。同时，酒店的公关部门在网络平台和社交媒体上及时发布事件的跟进信息、酒店的道歉信以及未来的整改措施，挽回酒店的形象与声誉。

非个人传播是指传播过程中不涉及人际交往和沟通的传播渠道。非个人传播渠道包括媒体、节事以及氛围。媒体包括纸质媒体（报纸、杂志）、广播媒体（电台与电视）、网络媒体（电话、电报、卫星通信、无线网络）、电子媒体（录音带、录像带、录像机、CD、网页）以及陈列媒体（广告牌、路标、海报）。大部分的非个人传播内容来自付费媒体。节事包括体育、艺术、娱乐等活动，以及能够与顾客建立新的品牌互动的非正式互动，例如酒店的开业仪式就是一种节事。氛围通过对环境的营造和创造提升消费者对产品的好感度并向消费者传递品牌信息。如安缦酒店在设计上体现本地文化特色，同时营造与酒店特色相适应的氛围。杭州法云安缦位于杭州灵隐寺旁的法云古村，设计师保留原有房屋的外表，以佛教和中国明代建筑风格为主题，将房屋内部改造为体现明清文人隐士文化的客房。如今，大部分的非个人传播渠道增长都来自于节事和体验。企业可以通过创办或赞助节事活动来推广品牌。以往偏好体育节事的节事营销人员现在偏好利用艺术博物馆、动物园或者冰雪表演来娱乐客户和员工。另一方面，企业正在寻找更好的方法来计算赞助一个节

Grunig (1999), a person's WOM promotion of a product affects the buying attitude of another two buyers on average. In the context of the Internet, the impact of word of mouth increases and spreads to up to eight people. This situation makes the social model of personal communication increasingly important, especially with this channel being outside the control of enterprises. Recognizing the importance of the information generated by users, Tourism Australian encouraged visitors who have traveled to Australia to share their travel and entertainment experiences on the Nothing Like Australia website. Nearly 30,000 stories and pictures were uploaded to www.nothinglikeaustralia.com. Thereafter, Tourism Australia invited all participants to build an interactive e-travel map, consequently attracting over a million clicks on the afore mentioned website every month. Negative comments on hotel websites exert a significant impact on brand image. The W Hotel, one of the subsidiaries of the Starwood Hotels Group, dealt with an electric shock accident. The involved customers posted a negative comment on the online platform. After the incident, the hotel assumed financial responsibility by paying for the hospital charges and waiving the hotel room fees of the affected customers. At the same time, the public relations department of the hotel promptly released an apology letter and follow-up information on future rectification measures on the online platform and social media so as to restore the hotel's image and reputation.

Non-personal communication refers to the process of communication without the involvement of interpersonal interaction and communication in communication channels. Non-personal communication channels include media, festivals, and atmospheres. The media incorporates print media (newspapers and magazines), broadcast media (radio and television), network media (telephones, telegrams, satellite communications, wireless networks), electronic media (tapes, videos, video cassette recorders, CDs, web pages), and display media (billboard, sign, poster). Most non-personal communication comes from paid media. Festivals include sports, art, entertainment, and informal interaction with customers to create new brands, such as the opening ceremonies of hotels. Atmosphere is achieved through the construction and creation of a physical environment so as to enhance consumer desirability and convey brand information. The Aman Hotel features local cultural characteristics in their design while creating an atmosphere that suits the hotel features. Amanfayun, a hotel located in Hangzhou, resides in the Fayun Village near the Lingyin Temple. The designer retained the original appearance of the house. With the theme of Buddhism and the architecture style of the Ming Dynasty, the interior design of the rooms reflects the literati and hermit culture of the Ming and Qing Dynasties. Today, the growth of most non-personal communication channels is based on festivals and experiences. Enterprises can promote their brands by creating or sponsoring festive events. Marketers who used to favor sports-related festivals are inclined to entertain customers and employees with art museums, zoos, or ice shows. Enterprises also search for reasonable alternatives to calculate the benefits of sponsoring festive events or making event owners or organizers take up additional marketing responsibilities.

事的收益,或是让节事的所有者或组织者承担更大的营销责任。

不同的传播渠道有不同的营销效果,如表 11-2 所示。数字营销传播渠道(社交媒体、搜索引擎、移动端)在建立产品特性和知名度方面有较为显著的效果,而传统营销传播渠道中只有电视和广告牌有同样的效果。网站、直销和推销能够更详细地向消费者传达产品的信息,而社交媒体和电视更适用于建立品牌形象和个性。在建立信任方面,公共宣传、社交媒体和推销都是较好的传播渠道。电视、节事、公共宣传和社交媒体在唤起消费者个人情感方面能获得较好的结果。适当的推广、搜索引擎结果、移动端营销传播、直销和推销都能较好地刺激消费者的购买行为。社交媒体、网站和移动端的营销传播能帮助企业与消费者建立联系。然而,所有的传播渠道在建立消费者忠诚方面都不甚理想。

表 11-2 传播渠道营销效果差异

传播结果	传播渠道选择										
	电视	推广	节事	公共宣传	社交媒体	网站	搜索引擎	广告牌	移动端	直销	推销
建立产品特点和知名度	+++	++	++	++	+++	++	+++	+++	+++	++	+
建立品牌形象和个性	+	+	+	+	++	+++	+	+	++	+++	+++
传达详细的产品信息	+++	++	++	++	+++	++	+	+	++	+	+
建立信任	+	+	+	+++	+++	+	+	++		+	+++
唤起消费者个人情感	+++	++	+++	+++	+++	+	+	++	+		+
刺激消费者购买行为	+	+++	+	+	+	++	+++	++	+++	+++	+++
建立忠诚	++	+	+	+	++	++	+	+	++	++	++
与消费者建立联系	+	+	++	+	+++	+++	+	+	+++	+	+

注:+++ = 影响较大;++ = 影响中等;+ = 影响较小

来源:Batra,R. & Keller,K. L. (2016). Integrating marketing communications:New findings,new lessons,and new ideas. *Journal of Marketing*,80,122-145.

Different communication channels exert different marketing effects, as shown in Table 11 - 2. Digital marketing communication channels (e.g., social media, search engine, mobile terminal) exert a significant effect in the establishment of product features and visibility. Only television and display panels yield equivalent effects among all traditional marketing communication channels. Websites, direct sales, and marketing can convey detailed information to consumers, whereas social media and television are appropriate for building brand images and personalities. Publicity, social media, and marketing are good channels for building trust. TV, festivals, publicity, and social media are effective in arousing consumers' personal feelings. Appropriate promotion, search engine results, marketing communications in mobile terminals, direct marketing, and promotion can stimulate the buying behaviors of consumers. Social media, websites, and mobile terminals can help enterprises build relationships with consumers. Not all communication channels, however, are ideal for building consumer loyalty.

Table 11 - 2　Effectiveness of various marketing communication channels

Marketing communication channels											
Outcome	TV	Promotion	Festivals	Publicity	Social media	Website	Search engine	Display panels	Mobile terminals	Direct sales	Marketing
Building product features and visibility	+++	++	++	++	+++	++	+++	+++	+++	++	+
Building brand images and personalities	+	+	+	+	++	+++	+	+	++	+++	+++
Conveying detailed information	+++	++	++	++	+++	++	+	+	++	+	+
Building trust	+	+	+	+++	+++	+	+	+	++	+	+++
Arousing personal feelings	+++	++	+++	+++	+++	++	+	+	++	+	+
Stimulating buying behaviors	+	+++	+	+	+	++	+++	++	+++	+++	+++
Building loyalty	++	+	+	+	++	++	+	+	++	++	++
Building relationship	+	+	++	+	+++	+++	+	+	+++	+	+

Note: + + + = Greater impact; + + = Moderately affected; + = Less affected

Source: Batra, R. & Keller, K. L. (2016). Integrating marketing communications: New findings, new lessons, and new ideas. *Journal of Marketing*, 80, 122 - 145.

5.选择信息来源

无论是个人传播还是非个人传播,信息传播者的选择都会影响目标市场的感知。许多营销传播活动的信息来源都是企业本身,或者是邀请名人作为代言人。通过有吸引力或者知名的信息源来传达信息内容有助于吸引目标群体的注意,甚至容易引起他们的品牌回忆(Kotler 和 Keller,2009)。最可信的信息源会在三个方面有很好的表现——专业知识、信任和吸引力(Kelman 和 Hovland,1953)。专业知识是指传播发起人所拥有的用于支持营销传播活动的专业知识;信任与信息来源的客观性和诚实相关;吸引力则是信息源在多大程度上能够吸引目标群体。

6.制定传播预算

营销传播战略的最后一步是决定预算总额以及用在不同组合元素上的比例。制定传播预算一般有四种方法:支付能力法、销售比例法、竞争应对法和目标任务法。(1)支付能力法是指根据企业管理层所认为的企业支付能力制定营销传播预算的方法。这种方法忽略了营销传播推广在投资方面的作用,以及对销售量的影响。这导致每年的传播预算都处于不稳定的状态,使得企业进行长期营销计划出现困难。(2)销售比例法是指企业将特定比例的销售额(现有销售额或预测销售额)设定为用于营销传播的费用。销售比例法的好处在于:1)营销传播的费用在企业的支付能力范围内变动;2)鼓励管理层思考推广费用、销售价格和单位利润之间的关系;3)在竞争对手设定大致相同比例的营销传播费用时,销售比例法有助于企业保持稳定的推广支出。然而,销售比例法将销售额作为决定营销传播预算的因素,而非结果。另一方面,销售比例法并不鼓励企业为单独的产品或地理区域设定独立的营销推广预算。(3)竞争应对法是指企业的营销传播预算根据竞争对手的市场份额和营销传播预算来制定。这些企业认为竞争对手在推广上的花费体现了整个行业的经验,与竞争对手保持平等能够避免价格战。然而,这种想法并不成立,因为竞争对手的花费并不能反映全行业的经验,同时价格战与营销推广的费用并没有直接的关系。(4)目标任务法需要市场营销

5. Choose information sources

Selecting information communicators influences the perception of the target market regardless of the communication channel used. The information sources of many marketing communication activities originate from enterprises themselves or from celebrities invited as spokespersons. Communicating information through appealing and well-known information sources helps arouse the interests of target groups or even facilitate brand recall (Kotler & Keller, 2009). The most credible information source performs well in three areas, namely, expertise, trustworthiness, and likability (Kelman & Hovland, 1953). Expertise is the professional knowledge that advocators use to support marketing communication activities. Trustworthiness is associated with the objectivity and honesty of information sources. Likability is the extent of attractiveness of information sources for luring target groups.

6. Develop communication budget

The final step in a marketing communication strategy is to determine the total budget and proportion used in different combinations of elements. The four ways of developing a communication budget are as follows: affordable method, percentage-of-sales method, competitive parity method, and objective-and-task method. (1) The affordable method is a budgeting method based on enterprise managements' perceived ability to pay for marketing communications. This approach ignores the role of marketing communications in investment and the impact on sales. It results in an unstable annual budget and creates difficulties in conducting marketing communication plans in the long run. (2) The percentage-of-sales method is about setting a specific percentage of sales (current sales or forecast sales) for the budget of marketing communications. The advantages of this method are three-fold. 1) The expenses of marketing communications fluctuate within the capacity of the enterprises to pay. 2) The management is encouraged to consider the relationship between promotional costs, sales prices, and unit profits. 3) When competitors set roughly the same proportion of marketing communication expenses, the method helps to maintain a stable promotional expense. In this method, sales rather than outcomes are the determinants of the budget for marketing communications. The method discourages enterprises from setting separate marketing budgets for specific products or geographical regions. (3) The competitive parity method is when enterprises set their budgets on the basis of the market share and marking budgets of their competitors. These enterprises believe that the marketing dollars of competitors reflect the experience of the entire industry. Maintaining equality with competitors avoids a price war. This mindset is inappropriate because the expenses of competitors do not reflect industry-wide experiences. Furthermore, no direct relationship exists between price war and marketing expenses. (4) The objective-and-task method requires marketers to identify specific marketing communications goals, tasks, and estimated costs to

人员通过确定具体的营销传播目标、任务以及预估完成这些目标和任务所需要的成本,来制定营销传播所需的费用。目标任务法能让管理层发掘费用、产品曝光率、试用率和经常性购买之间的关系。

11.3 营销传播:广告

广告是指一切付费的非个人传播渠道。广告花费是企业营销预算中重要的组成部分。营销人员在制定广告时需要考虑四个重要因素:设定广告目标、制定广告预算、信息及渠道选择以及广告效果衡量。

11.3.1 设定广告目标

广告的目标通常与企业和产品/品牌的发展目标相一致,和产品/品牌的生命周期相配合,可以说广告目标是企业目标和产品生命周期的外在表现。按照最终目的,广告可被划分为产品销售广告、企业形象广告和企业理念广告三种。

1. 产品销售广告

产品销售广告是最常见的销售推广形式,其以销售产品为目的,从中直接获取经济利益。产品销售广告主要告知消费者新产品的上市,或特别时段提供的特殊产品,促进及时的销售。产品销售广告一般包括产品品牌、活动名称、时间和期限、方式和方法等信息。它时效性强,属短期目标。旅游企业销售推广方式多样,包括折扣、优惠券、积分、抽奖、"多买多得"等(后面将有详细阐述)。

2. 企业形象广告

企业形象广告不直接介绍产品和宣传产品的优点,而是宣传企业的宗旨和信誉、企业的历史与成就、经营与管理情况,目的是为了建立商业信誉,加强企业自身形象,沟通企业与消费者的公共关系,从而达成产品销售。形象广告通过视觉、听觉等诠释品牌的内在价值,旨在塑造和维持品牌/产品形象,提升和强化品牌的品质与价值。它承载和表现品牌的核心理念和价值,不仅体现出品牌本身的特性,更体现了品牌对顾客做出的服务承诺。香格里拉酒店在 2010 年推出品牌广告"至善盛情,源自天性",正体现了香格里拉品

achieve these goals and tasks for the sake of determining the budgets. This method allows the management to explore the relationship among expenses, product exposure, rate of trial, and recurring purchases.

11.3　Marketing Communications：Advertising

Advertising is a paid, non-personal communication channel. Advertising spending is an important component of the marketing budget of enterprises. Marketers should consider four important factors when planning advertising efforts. These factors are setting advertising goals, establishing budgets, selecting information and channels, and evaluating advertising effectiveness.

11.3.1　Setting advertising goals

The goals of advertising are usually consistent with the development goals of enterprises and their products/brands. Advertising goals are external reflections of the product/brand lifecycle. According to the final aims of advertising, it is divided into product sales advertising, corporate image advertising, and corporate concept advertising.

1. Product sales advertising

As the most common form of sales advertising, product sales advertising is aimed at selling products and directly obtaining financial benefits. The advertisements inform consumers about new product launches or specific products offered at particular times so as to encourage timely sales. It generally covers product brands, names of events, time and duration, and formats and methods. It is time sensitive and is regarded as a short-term goal. Tourism enterprises employ a wide variety of advertising mechanisms, such as discounts, coupons, points, sweepstakes, and buy-more-get-more (detailed discussions are presented in the following section).

2. Corporate image advertising

Corporate image advertising does not directly introduce the advantages of products or promotional products. Instead, it promotes the principles and credibility of enterprises, the history and achievements of establishments, and the operation and management conditions. The purposes are to establish reputations, strengthen images, and establish communications between enterprises and consumers, all of which lead to product sales. Corporate image advertising interprets the intrinsic values of brands through visual and auditory senses and shapes, upholds brand/product images, and enhances and strengthens the quality and value of brands. It carries and demonstrates the core concepts and values, reflecting not only the characteristics of the brand itself but also the service pledge to customers. In 2010, Shangri-La launched the "It's In Our Nature" brand campaign, which reflected the service pledge of the brand as "To delight

牌"发自内心的待客之道"的服务承诺。

3. 企业理念广告

企业理念广告是指建立或改变消费者对企业或某一产品在他们心目中的形象,从而建立或改变一种消费习惯或消费观念的广告。"晚1点"是国内新兴的网上餐饮品牌,主打海鲜,定位中高端网络外卖。其品牌理念就是要打造"外卖中的海底捞",除了食材高端以外,贴心有温度的服务也改变了消费者对餐饮外卖的观念。

广告目标不仅是企业制定广告活动的主要依据,也是具体的广告创作的指引。明确性、可衡量性和可实现性是衡量广告目标的三个基本标准。一个合理的广告目标应该符合以下要求。

(1)明确性。目标的明确性直接影响到广告活动效果的衡量。广告目标是一系列广告决策的准则、评测广告效果的依据,也是广告主同广告公司中间商以及企业广告部人员之间相互协调的宗旨,所以广告目标必须清楚明确。

(2)可衡量性。广告目标的定量化是明确性的主要表现,因为它为广告效果的衡量制订了可比较的标准。如某酒店的广告目标为,支持夏季的销售推广活动,使7月和8月的平均房客入住人次比去年同期上升10%。

(3)可实现性。广告目标虽然主要由广告主来确定,但是因为广告活动是集团与个人相互协调的产物,所以这就要求广告目标必须切实可行、符合实际。也只有切实可行、符合实际的广告目标,才能保证广告活动的顺利进行。

11.3.2　制定广告预算

制定广告预算的主要方法前文已有提及,除了上述四种方法之外,在制定广告预算时还需要考虑产品所处的生命周期和产品的独特性。一般而言,新品牌进入市场时需要相对较多的广告预算来建立品牌的知名度,鼓励消费者试用产品,以获取相应的市场份额。当品牌进入成熟阶段后,市场份额较为稳定,企业通常是基于销售额制定一个合适的比例作为广告预算。与品牌新进入市场时相比,成熟时期的广告预算会有所下降。

如果品牌是处于一个高度竞争、品牌之间差异并不突出的市场,市场环境中存在大量其他品牌的信息或争论,企业就需要通过大量的广告使得自身

our guests every time by creating engaging experiences straight from our heart."

3. Corporate concept advertising

Corporate concept advertising is to build or change customer-perceived images of enterprises or products so as to establish or change buying habits or consumption. "Wan1dian" is an emerging online food and beverage brand that features seafood and high-end delivery services. Its brand concept is to become the "Take-away Haidilao." Its high-quality food and detail-oriented service have changed consumers' perception of take-away food and beverage outlets.

Advertising objectives are not the only basis for the development of advertising activities for they also serve as guidelines of advertisement creation. Clarity, measurability, and achievability are the three basic criteria for evaluating advertising goals. A reasonable advertising goal should meet the following requirements.

(1) Clarity: The clarity of the goal directly affects the measurement of the effectiveness of a campaign. Advertising objectives are a set of criteria for advertising decisions, the basis for evaluating the effectiveness of advertising, and the principles for the coordination between marketing intermediaries and the advertising departments of enterprises. Advertising goals should thus be clear.

(2) Measurability: To quantify advertising objectives is a key reflection of clarity because it offers a comparable standard for measuring the effectiveness of advertising. Take for example the advertising goal of a hotel to support the summer sales promotional activities, which increased the average occupancy for the months of July and August by 10% relative to the occupancy in the same period last year.

(3) Achievability: Although advertising goals are mainly determined by advertisers, goals should remain practical and realistic because they represent the product of coordination between groups and individuals. Only practical and realistic advertising objectives can ensure the smooth progress of advertising campaigns.

11.3.2　Establishing budgets

The main methods for establishing budgets for marketing communications are stated in the previous section. Apart from the four methods, product lifecycle and its uniqueness should be considered when developing budgets. In general, a new brand, in comparison with an established product, requires relatively more advertising budget to build brand awareness and encourage trial so as to obtain an appropriate market share. When the brand becomes mature and maintains a stable market share, enterprises generally allocate an advertising budget on the basis of a suitable ratio of sales. Over time, advertising budgets decline relative to the budgets for new brands entering the market.

If the brand is in a highly competitive market, in which the difference between brands is not prominent and voluminous yet controversial information about brands is widely available, then enterprises need to exert significant advertising efforts to make

产品能够脱颖而出。而特色十分明显的品牌只需要较少的广告预算,就能向消费者突出自身特点,获得更多的市场份额。

11.3.3 广告信息设计及渠道选择

Rosser Reeves(1961)在 20 世纪 60 年代提出了广告中的"产品的核心价值理念",并沿用至今。顾客购买产品的主要理由来自于产品能提供的价值和利益,因此有效的核心价值理念应该是产品提供的价值和利益的综合。它的基本要点是:(1)广告须以产品的核心价值作为主要理念,明确购买该产品可以获得的价值和利益。(2)核心价值应具独特性和新颖性,具有竞争对手所做不到的或者无法提供的价值。(3)所强调的理念必须真实、可靠,聚焦于某个点或面来刺激消费者的购买欲望。产品的核心价值应是广告的主题,也是能否吸引消费者的关键。

广告需要传递的信息内容可以通过不同形式的风格、语气、格式等实现。常用的信息风格有以下类别。

(1)日常生活:此类广告信息风格呈现的是普通人在普通的情境下使用产品,日常用品较多使用这种风格。

(2)生活方式:此类风格主要体现产品是如何创造或符合某种生活方式的。例如洲际酒店邀请吴尊拍摄其新的品牌广告"知停而行",强调"停下脚步,享受幸福"的生活方式。

(3)梦幻:此类风格主要是为品牌或产品创造一种梦幻的氛围,Dior J'adore 的广告强调的是其梦幻的气质,即能提升女性的自信和魅力。

(4)音乐性:此类广告风格由人物或卡通形象以歌曲或音乐的形式突出品牌的特质,例如麦当劳电视广告的结尾都会有一句"I'm love'in it"的歌曲。

(5)性格象征:信息传递者通过创造一个形象来表现产品,例如麦当劳叔叔。

在信息渠道多元化、信息内容碎片化的时代,消费者已不再被动地接受广告信息,这就使得营销人员必须更好地设计具有想象力、娱乐性、参与性的信息以获得消费者的情感认同。广告和娱乐相结合是在此背景下产生的一种广告信息设计趋势。其包括两个主要方式。第一是广告娱乐化,即增添广告的娱乐性,如桔子酒店的十二星座广告。2011 年春季到秋季的大半年时间,桔子酒店十二星座广告的播放量已达 4000 万次。酒店微电影团队挑选

their products stand out. Brands with specific characteristics only require minimal advertising budget because consumers can easily notice these brands, resulting in a high market share.

11.3.3 Selecting advertising information design and channels

In the 1960s, Reeves (1961) proposed the unique selling proposition in advertising, and since then, it has been widely used. Customers buy products mainly because of the values and benefits provided by these products. Effective core values should therefore integrate the values and benefits of products. Three fundamental essences must be taken into account. (1) The center of advertising should be the core value of products and specify the values and benefits obtained after buying the products. (2) Core values should be unique and novel that competitors cannot perform and provide these values. (3) The claims must be true, reliable, and specific to stimulate consumers' desires to buy. The core values of products are the theme of advertising, and they are the key to attracting consumers.

The content that advertisements convey is presented through different forms of style, tone, and format. Commonly used information styles fall into the following categories:

(1) Slice of life: This style of advertising information features ordinary people in daily situations. Daily commodities often adopt this style in advertising.

(2) Lifestyle: This style is about how products create and conform to certain lifestyles. For example, Intercontinental Hotels invited Wu Zun to shoot their new advertisements "Pause for a Greater", emphasizing the "Pause in the pursuit of happiness" lifestyle.

(3) Fantasy: This style creates a fantasy-driven atmosphere for brands or products. The advertisement of Dior J'adore emphasizes its dreamy temperament, which can enhance women's self-confidence and charm.

(4) Musicality: This style of advertising features characters or cartoon characters that highlight brand features in the form of songs or music. For example, "I'm Lovin'It" is a song at the end of McDonald's television advertisements.

(5) Personality symbol: The message conveyer creates an image to represent products (e.g., Uncle McDonald).

In the era of diversified information channels with fragmented information content, consumers no longer passively accept advertising information. Thus, marketers should effectively design imaginative, entertaining, and participatory information to obtain the affective commitment of consumers. The combination of advertising and entertainment is a trend in advertising information design under this context; it includes two main approaches. The first is advertisement, which means to make advertisements highly entertaining. The 12 constellations advertisement of the Crystal Orange Hotel is an example. From spring to fall in 2011, this advertisement recorded 40 million views. The microfilm team of the hotel selected constellation and love themes that are popular

了年轻人热衷的星座、爱情话题拍摄了系列广告。而且将星座电影的播出时间固定化，提前公布出每部微电影的播出时间（每周一上午十点），让观众看到预告后产生一种期待心理，尤其是对自己感兴趣的星座微电影。同时桔子水晶酒店还鼓励网友转发、评论，并设置相应的问题与网友互动。除了桔子酒店以外，澳洲旅游局曾邀请台湾地区明星罗志祥和杨丞琳拍摄微电影《再一次心跳》，推广澳洲旅游目的地塔斯马尼亚。第二种方式是品牌化娱乐，也即将品牌作为娱乐产品中的一部分，最常见的是植入式广告。影视旅游是品牌化娱乐的一种，如电影《非诚勿扰》的拍摄地就是位于海南的石梅湾艾美酒店。香港洲际酒店也将自身植入到电影《港囧》中，并随后推出《港囧》专题套房。

当然，不管广告的形式有多么新颖别致，别具一格，最关键的一个因素还是具体、真实的广告内容。广告传递的信息建立起消费者的期望值，实际行为也必须与广告中的承诺一致。如果传递的信息与实际行为不一致，即使吸引来了再多客人的首次购买，这种被顾客认为"欺骗行为的广告"最终只会造成巨大的顾客流动和资金损失。所以，企业与广告代理商进行沟通以确保广告的真实性也是必不可少的。

对旅游业来说，传统的媒体如印刷类的报纸、手册和杂志，电子类的电视、电台，户外墙体广告等仍然是进行信息沟通的主要媒体形式。但新出现的精准媒体也已经被越来越多地应用于旅游广告，造成了多种媒体并存的格局。旅游业常用的广告媒体有以下几种。

1. 印刷媒体

报纸是餐厅和旅行社最广泛使用的印刷媒体。旅游企业投放的报纸广告以销售推广类为主。旅行社的广告是推出新的旅游线路。航空公司或酒店新的优惠活动或餐厅派发的优惠券都是销售推广广告的内容。杂志广告也被广泛应用于旅游企业，如飞机上的各类航空杂志以及酒店、餐厅和会议中心的宣传册子，把广告的艺术性、故事性及可读性集于一体，以鲜明的个性主张和悦目的色彩吸引乘客的注意力。

2. 电子媒体

电视和电台目前仍是中国最普遍、最主流的媒体。对旅游企业来说，电视媒体往往是树立品牌、制造知名度或推行新理念的主要方式。"明星效应"

among youngsters for their series of advertisements. The broadcast of every constellation microfilm at a fixed schedule and broadcasting time（every Monday at 10 am）was announced in advance. The audience developed a psychological expectation after watching the trailers, especially those related to their favorite constellations. At the same time, the Crystal Orange Hotel encouraged netizens to share, comment, and set appropriate questions for interaction. Tourism Australia invited Taiwanese stars Show Lo and Rainie Yang for the *Heartbeat Love* microfilm shooting to promote Tasmania as a tourism destination. The second approach is branded entertainment, which enables brands to become part of entertainment products. The most common branded entertainment includes implantable advertising and film tourism. The movie *If You Are the One* was filmed at the Le Méridien Shimei Bay Beach Resort & Spa, Hainan. After InterContinental Hong Kong was featured in the movie *Lost in Hong Kong*, the hotel launched suites designed according to the movie's theme.

Regardless of the approach to innovation or the chic or unique advertisement features, the most critical factor is the specific and real advertising content. The message that the advertisement delivers sets consumer expectations, and actual performance must be consistent with promises stated in the advertisement. Inconsistency of message and actual performance may attract many first-time purchases, but this deceptive advertising will eventually result in huge customer flow and financial loss. Therefore, enterprises and advertising agencies must communicate and ensure the authenticity of advertisements.

For the tourism industry, traditional media, such as printed newspapers, manuals and magazines, electronic television, radio, and billboard, remain the main form of communication. The emergence of precision marketing has increasingly been used in tourism advertising, resulting in a coexistence of multiple media. The media commonly used for tourism advertising include the following:

1. Print media

Newspapers are the most widely used print media in restaurants and travel agencies. The advertisement in newspapers is mainly for promotion purposes. Travel agencies introduce a new tour route, airlines or hotels have new promotions, and restaurants distribute coupons for promotions. Magazine advertising is widely adopted in tourism enterprises. For example, in-flight magazines, as well as brochures of hotels, restaurants, and conference, blend arts, storytelling, and readability with pleasing colors to draw attention of passengers with distinctive personalities.

2. Electronic media

TV and radio are currently the most popular and mainstream media in China. For tourism enterprises, television media is for brand building, creating awareness, and launching new concepts. The celebrity effect is one way to enhance the effectiveness of

就是增强广告效果的方式之一。由 Rain 出演的"KOREA，Sparkling"广告自 2007 年下半年开始向全世界宣传韩国旅游的魅力。

3. 户外媒体

凡是能在露天或公共场合通过广告表现形式同时向许多消费者进行宣传，能达到推销产品目的的物质都可称为户外广告媒体。户外广告可分为平面和立体两大类：平面的有路牌广告、招贴广告、壁墙广告、海报、条幅等；立体广告分为霓虹灯、广告柱以及广告塔灯箱等。

4. 网络媒体

当今的网络广告媒体主要表现在：（1）最基本的网幅广告，包括在网页上显示一幅固定的广告图片的静态网幅广告和把一连串图像连贯起来形成动画的动态网幅广告。（2）电邮广告，即把一段广告性的文字放置在新闻邮件或经许可的电子邮件中间，也可以设置一个网址，链接到广告主公司的主页或提供产品或服务的特定页面。电邮广告一般包括企业的即时资讯、公司特殊事件、销售推广信息如特价机票、品酒聚会等。（3）搜索引擎广告是指当用户利用某一关键词进行检索时，在检索结果页面会出现与该关键词相关的广告内容。由于关键词广告具有较强的针对性，其效果比一般网络广告形式要好，因而获得快速发展。Google 的关键词广告 AdWords 是最有影响力的付费搜索引擎营销方法之一。（4）博客广告，即利用博客平台为企业推销产品和服务、塑造品牌、树立形象。博客广告分三种：利用第三方博客平台的博客文章发布功能开展网络营销活动，如"企博网"；企业募集专业写作者撰写博客日志，企业提供的内容由专业博客网站负责发布；"个人博客广告"。（5）窄告，即将企业的广告不仅直接投放到与之内容相关的网络媒体上的文章周围，还会根据浏览者的偏好、使用习性、地理位置、访问历史等信息，有针对性地将广告投放到真正感兴趣的浏览者面前。酒店、航空公司、景区、餐饮企业将窄告投放在票务预订、景点介绍、旅游新闻、游记等文章的周围，人们在阅读相关内容时，更容易注意到这些旅游广告并受到购买刺激。如餐饮业新闻旁边，出现的是餐厅的销售推广信息；或游客的游历文章周围，读者更多看到的是旅行社广告。（6）内文广告，它是互联网最新的以关键字链接和鼠标移动触发方式实现广告曝光效果的智能化广告模式。它准确地将广告、内

advertising. For instance, the touristic promotional video *KOREA*, *Sparkling* with Rain publicized the charm of Korean tourism to the world as early as the second half of 2007.

3. Outdoor media

The methods that address demands to many consumers and achieve the purpose of marketing in open air or public places are regarded as outdoor advertising media. The two major types of outdoor advertising are flat and dimensional. Flat advertising includes signs, posters, walls, and banners. Dimensional advertising use neon lights, advertising columns, and light boxes.

4. Internet media

Present online advertising media mainly use the following methods: (1) The basic banner includes static banner advertisement display on webpages or dynamic banner advertisements that combine a series of images. (2) Email advertising places advertising text in the middle of a newsletter or licensed emails, connecting the site with the URL of the advertiser homepage or specific webpage to promote products or services. Email advertisement generally includes real-time information, special events, and sales promotion information, such as special fares or wine tasting events. (3) Search engine advertising refers to the search results page where keywords related advertising content appear when users perform keyword search. As keyword advertising demonstrates higher relevance, the effectiveness is better than the general form of online advertising. This result explains why search engine advertisement is rapidly developing. Adwords, which is the keyword advertising of Google, is one of the most influential paid search engine marketing methods. (4) Blog advertising is the use of blog platforms for enterprises to sell products and services, as well as brand and image building. Blog advertising is divided into three kinds. Blog publishing functions of third-party blog platform are used to conduct online marketing activities, such as Bokee. net. Then, enterprises recruit professional writers to write blogs. The content is provided by enterprises and the professional blog site is responsible for publishing. In addition, advertising is done on personal blogs. (5) Narrowcasting directly places advertisements around the articles on online media and performs targeted advertising to bring the advertisements to really interested viewers based on their preferences, habits, geographical location, and browsing history. Hotels, airlines, scenic sports, catering enterprises place narrowcasting advertisements on ticket booking, attraction introduction, travel news, and other articles. When reading relevant content, people are more likely to notice these tourism advertisements, which stimulate the purchase. For example, the sales promotion information of restaurants appears in the news of food and beverage industry, and readers can easily see advertisements of travel agencies when reading travel articles. (6) Text advertisement is an intelligent advertising platform that displays advertisements on the latest Internet keyword links that are triggered by mouse

容、浏览者三者紧密结合在一起,是一种崭新、温和,完全由消费者触发的广告形式。内文广告将纯文字式、图片式、动画式、影音视频式等广告"根植于"文章内容的某些相关性关键词,当鼠标移到关键词上时,广告就自动展示出来,无须开启新的广告页面。

另外,酒店和旅游地网页成为提供信息和吸引客人的主要载体。网页图文并茂,包括服务内容、产品介绍、图片展览、交通指南以及相关旅游信息等。顾客可以在公司网站预订客房、餐饮、会议、机票、文娱或体育类门票等。有的网页甚至有视频供虚拟参观,顾客只要点击鼠标便可了解酒店内况。

辅助材料广告也是旅游企业常用的广告形式。辅助材料上印有鲜明的企业标识和名称,包括企业的宣传手册、说明书、图片、销售材料、礼品或纪念品等。如旅行社将广告印制在旅行袋、旅行帽、徽章、纪念品上。

表 11-3 对旅游业常用的几类广告媒体进行了概括,并简要归纳了各类媒体的优、缺点。

表 11-3　媒体类型和各自的优缺点

类型		优势	劣势
印刷媒体	报纸	及时性强; 阅读人群广泛、覆盖面大; 地理针对性强; 易于传阅和保存; 优惠券兑换率较高。	印刷质量较低,产品质量或价值体现性不高; 受众针对性有限; 设计比较简单。
	杂志	受众针对性强; 可保存,有效时间长; 发行量大、面广,部分可全国甚至全世界发行; 编辑精美,印刷精美,形象表现产品的色彩、质感等; 二次流通量大。	出版周期长,时效性不强; 专业杂志的专业性在一定程度上限制了读者人数; 成本高于报纸。
电子媒体	电视	到达率高; 图像、动作和声音的结合; 吸引观众的注意力; 利用有线电视和卫星电视提高受众针对性。	总成本高; 广告丛林造成信息超负荷; 频道转换率高,浪费严重。
	电台	受众针对性强; 成本低于电视; 更易于被旅游者接触。	仅仅依靠声效; 吸引力不够全面和强烈。
户外媒体	平面立体	对地区和消费者的选择性强; 抓住受众的空白心理,被注意率高,易被接受; 强迫诉求性质强,可多次重复记忆; 内容精简,易记; 广告费用较低。	信息容纳量极其有限; 移动性差; 受众相对有限; 效果难以测评。

movement. Text advertising precisely brings the advertisement, content, and viewers together, as a new, gentle, and completely consumer-driven form of advertising. Text advertisement roots plain text, image, flash, or video advertisements in the content of relevant keywords. When the mouse moves to the keywords, the advertisement will automatically show up without opening a new advertising page.

In addition, the hotel and tourist websites become the main vehicle for providing information and attracting guests. The webpage illustrates service contents, product introductions, photo exhibitions, transportation guides, and related tourist information. Customers can book rooms, restaurants, conferences, airline, entertainment, or sports tickets on the company website. Several pages even have video for a virtual tour. Customers can then understand the hotel interiors by clicking the mouse.

Tourism enterprises are using collateral material as a form of advertising. Collateral materials are printed with a distinctive corporate logo and name, including corporate brochures, manuals, photographs, sales materials, gifts, and souvenirs. For example, travel agencies will print the advertisements on their travel bags, caps, badges, and souvenirs.

Table 11-3 presents the common types of advertising media in tourism and briefly summarizes their advantages and disadvantages.

Table 11-3 Types of media and corresponding advantages and disadvantages

Types		Advantages	Disadvantages
Print media	Newspapers	Timely; Large number of readers, broad coverage; Geographically targeted; Easy to circulate and keep; Higher coupon exchange rate.	Poor printing quality, product quality and value; Limited target audience; Relatively simple design.
Print media	Magazines	High reach of target audience; Can be kept for long time; Large circulation with broad coverage (some magazines can be issued through the nation or worldwide); Finely edited and printed, which shows color and texture of products; Large-scale secondary circulation.	Long publication cycle, untimely; Professionalism of professional magazines limits the number of readers to a certain extent; Higher cost compared with newspaper.
Electronic media	TV	High reach; Combination of images, movements, and sound; Attract the attention of the audience; Cable television and satellite television can reach more target audience.	High total cost; Information overload due to massive advertisements; High level of channel conversion resulting in a big waste.
Electronic media	Radio station	High reach of target audience; Lower cost than TV; More easily accessible to tourists.	Rely on sound effects only; Attractiveness is not comprehensive and strong.
Outdoor media	Flat Dimensional	Highly selective of regions and consumers; Easy to capture attention and be accepted by audience; Compulsive nature reinforces memories of audiences; Content is compact and easy to remember; advertising costs are low.	Information capacity is extremely limited; Poor mobility; limited audience; Effect is difficult to evaluate.

续　表

类型		优势	劣势
网络媒体	网幅	静态网幅广告制作简单； 动态网幅广告的动画元素传递更多信息，且加深印象； 交互式广告形式多样，内容丰富，表现力强，且参与性较强。	静态的网幅广告表现较呆板和枯燥； 动态和交互式广告的效果受站点的服务器端设置和访问者的浏览器的双重影响。
	电邮	针对性强、成本低，可接触大量的潜在顾客； 广告内容全面、灵活，不受限制； 个人针对性强，易于统计。	某些系统的互不兼容可能导致 html 格式的广告无法完整读出； 带有强迫性，易被当成垃圾邮件，命中率较低。
网络媒体	博客	针对性强，有效到达率高； 口碑式营销，信任度高； 名人博客的意见领袖效应； 商业性最弱，受众参与性和互动性更强。	大多专注于某一专题或领域，受众面窄； 需不断更新内容； 费时间和精力。
	窄播	P4P（Pay for performance）：按广告投放后带来的实际效果付费，节约费用； 网络传播覆盖范围广泛（＞4000 家主流合作媒体）； 节省费用与时间的支出； 受众针对性极强。	关键词与广告的匹配程度不高造成"窄播不窄"； 模式单一。
	内文	精准命中目标群体，针对性强； 温和投放，提升网民浏览网页的舒适度； 一触即现，主动出击：实现信息的快速传播。	
辅助媒体	手册	内容专业，全面； 受众针对性强； 制作精美，印刷质量高。	一般时效性短，容易过时； 用过后成为垃圾，不环保。
	物品	消费者回忆率高； 相对比较便宜。	

选择好适当的媒体之后，媒体策划人员就要决定广告在什么时间投放、投放时间长短和频率等方面的问题，也就是我们所说的"广告排期"。最常见的广告排期法有三种。（1）持续式排期：在整个活动期间匀速地投放广告，没有什么变动。广告持续出现，不间断地累积效果，维持广告记忆度，持续刺激消费动机，行程涵盖整个购买周期。该方法一般适用于季节性和时间性不明显的产品。（2）起伏式排期：将大量投放广告与全部停止广告交替进行，适用于一年中需求波动较大的产品和服务。它灵活性强，广告强度根据市场

Continued

	Types	Advantages	Disadvantages
Internet media	Banner	Simple production of web banner; Animated elements of the dynamic web banner deliver more information and deepen the impression; Interactive advertising in various forms, rich in content, strong performance, and highly participative.	Static banner is dull and boring. Effect of dynamic and interactive advertising is affected by the server-side settings of the site and the browser of visitors.
	E-mail	High reach of target audience and low cost that can reach a large number of potential customers; Advertising content is comprehensive, flexible, and unrestricted. High reach of individual audience, easy for statistics.	Several systems are not compatible with each other and result in incomplete presentation of html-format advertisements; Compulsive, easily be treated as span and low hit rate.
	Blog	High and effective reach of target audience; WOM marketing, high degree of trustworthiness; Opinion leaders' effect of celebrity blogs; Least commercial, high level of participation and interaction with audience.	Mostly focused on a particular topic or area, narrow audience; Need to update the content constantly; Time and effort consuming.
	Narrowcasting	P4P (Pay for performance): Pay according to the actual effect of advertising to save costs; Extensive network coverage (> 4, 000 mainstream media); Save costs and time consumed; High reach of target audience.	The match between keywords and advertisements is low which cause "Narrowcasting is not narrow"; Single model.
	Content	Accurately hits the target audience, high reach in targets; Mild delivery to make browsers comfort; Appears in one touch, takes initiatives, realizes rapid dissemination of information	
Auxiliary media	Manual	Professional and comprehensive content; High reach in target audience; Fine production and high-quality printing.	Untimely, easily outdated; Becomes garbage after use, not environmentally friendly.
	Article	High level of consumers recall; Relatively cheap	

After selecting the appropriate media, media planners have to decide when, where, and how frequent to run the advertisements. This process is known as advertisement scheduling. Three common scheduling methods are continuing, flighting, and pulsing. (1) Continuing refers to broadcasting the advertisements throughout the entire event without any change. The continuous emergence of advertisements benefits from the repeating accumulation effect by maintaining the memory and stimulating the buying motives of consumers. The effect covers the entire buying cycle. This method is suitable for products with inconspicuous seasonality and timeliness. (2) Flighting refers to taking turns at massive advertising or no advertising. This method is applicable to products and services with fluctuated demand in a year. Flighting is highly flexible and adjusts the

上的实际需求进行调整,利用最有利的暴露时机,获得最高的有效到达率。但其不足在于广告空档期间可能使广告记忆度下降,增加再认知难度,并且有其他竞争品牌切入广告空档的威胁。旅游产品的季节性明显,一般根据淡季和旺季调节广告投放量,较多采用这种排期。(3)脉冲式排期,即将持续性排期和起伏式排期结合的方式。广告主全年都维持较低的广告水平,但针对销售高峰期采用急剧性脉冲效果。产品或服务的购买周期越长,越适合采用脉冲式排期。其优点在于持续累积广告效果,并根据品牌需要强化重点期间的暴露度。但费用较高。像快餐食品和饮料等,虽然一年四季都有广告,但在夏季或冬季推出新产品时广告量猛增。

广告重复能提高并加强品牌的知名度。事实上,绝大多数的知名品牌或企业所以知名,和广告重复的频率是分不开的。无论国际知名品牌如麦当劳、可口可乐、希尔顿酒店,还是国内品牌如如家酒店、小肥羊火锅等,消费者都反复在电视或其他媒体上看到或听过。有调查研究显示,被消费者看或听到三次或以上的产品广告,其再认知度明显高于接触不到三次的产品广告。除了能提高知名度,广告重复还能促进对广告内容的理解和记忆,实现广告的说服目的。

11.3.4　广告效果衡量

广告效果主要通过两个维度进行衡量,即传播效果和销售业绩。

1. 传播效果

传播效果主要衡量广告和媒体是否有效地传播营销信息。企业可以在播放前和播放后衡量广告的传播效果。在广告投放前,企业对消费者进行调查,了解消费者对品牌的态度、认知、品牌回忆水平等因素。在广告投放后,除了消费者对品牌的态度、认知、品牌回忆水平外,企业还可以调查消费者是否喜欢广告、对广告内容的回忆水平、对品牌或产品的偏好等要素。

2. 销售业绩

相对于传播效果,广告对销售业绩的影响较难被测量,因为除了广告以外,其他因素也会影响品牌或产品的销售业绩,例如目标消费者群体的消费

intensity of advertising based on actual demand. The advantage of determining the best timing in exposure can maximize the reach to customers. One problem, however, is that the memory of advertisements declines during the interval, which poses difficulties of reintroduction and threats of the competing brands cutting in. Tourism products are highly seasonal. The number of advertisements depends on the low or high seasons and is likely to adopt flighting. (3) In addition, many advertisements apply the combination of continuing and flighting schedules, which is known as pulsing. Advertisers maintain a low level of advertising throughout the year, but apply a sharp pulse for peak sales. The longer the product or service purchasing cycle is, the more suitable is the use of pulsing scheduling. The advantage is the continued accumulation of advertising effect, which strengthens the exposure period based on the needs of the brands. Cost is a disadvantage. For instance, fast food and beverage have advertisements throughout the year, but advertising booms when introducing new products during summer or winter.

Repeated advertising can increase and enhance brand awareness. In fact, the vast majority of well-known brands or enterprises becoming reputable are inseparable with the frequency of advertising. Consumers have repeatedly seen and heard about the advertisements of international brands, such as McDonald's, Coca-Cola, Hilton Hotel, and domestic brands, namely, Home Inns and Little Sheep Hotpot, on televisions or other media. Consumers who watch or hear an advertisement three times or more exhibit higher re-recognition than watching less than three times. Apart from increasing awareness, repeated advertisements promote understanding of the content and memory to achieve the persuading purpose of advertising.

11.3.4　Evaluating advertising effectiveness

Advertising effectiveness is measured in two dimensions, namely, advertising effect and sales performance.

1. Advertising effect

This communication effect measures the effectiveness of disseminating the marketing message through advertising and media. Enterprises can measure advertising effect before and after broadcasting the advertisements. Before placing advertisements, enterprises research on the attitudes, recognition, and recall of brands of consumers. After placing advertisements, enterprises can further study whether consumers favor, recall, and prefer brands or products.

2. Sales performance

The impact of advertising on sales performance is more difficult to measure compared with advertising effect. Many factors could affect the sales performance of brands or products in addition to the advertisements. Changing consumption levels of

水平变化、产品特征偏好变化、社会事件等都会对销售产生影响。研究方法中的实验法可以作为一种衡量广告对销售业绩影响的工具,例如企业可以在不同地区投放不同的广告预算,以此衡量不同销售业绩的差异。

11.4 营销传播:公共关系和公众宣传

公共关系是营销传播的一种形式,是面向现有购买者、潜在购买者或其他相关利益群体,向他们传递产品或服务的价值,并影响他们对企业的产品或服务的感受、观点和信心的各种活动(Bennett,1995)。公众宣传则被认为是在各种印刷品和广播媒体上获得免费或相对不付费的报道版面,由媒体对某项产品、服务或某个人进行非商业性报道或评论。公共关系和公众宣传的目的不同,但成功的公共关系活动随之而来的是媒体赞美性的报道,并且积极的宣传效果又有利于公共关系更加顺利地开展。

公共关系活动主要是企业为了维持与特殊公众和普通大众的关系而举行的若干活动的总和。特殊公众是那些与企业有直接利益关系的群体,如消费者、雇员、供应商、中间商和股东。这些群体对企业的利益要求都有所不同。其他特殊公众还包括政治和法规部门工作人员以及那些社区的意见领袖,如教师或一些事业和商业组织的关键人物等。普通公众则包括企业所在地区的所有人,甚至对一些连锁经营的组织来说,可能是整个地区或国家的人们。

公共关系活动把企业定位成一个有责任心的商务公民,并把这个形象推广给目标公众。公共关系活动的关键是把理解公众的兴趣作为开发运营政策和程序的依据。也就是说,企业必须是一个负责任的、诚实的好公民。但企业好的表现还必须得到公众的感知和认可。

公众宣传不是企业自身所执行的,而是由持中立立场的第三方发表的。它最主要的优点是易于建立良好的可信度,对企业具有重大的营销沟通意义。新闻是企业进行公众宣传的最主要形式。一篇新闻,即使是企业新闻发布会的报道,读者也会认为是比较客观、符合事实的。

非商业性的媒体报道为企业带来的广告效应比商业性的广告效应实际上更有说服力。在广告费用不断上升的情况下,借鉴媒体报道发布信息可大量节约成本,产生成本效益。仅仅新建的一个昂贵的宴会厅可能不足以成为媒体新闻,但如果能以某名人命名或请名人出席开业剪彩的话,其具有的新闻价值足以引起媒体和业界的广泛关注。当然,宴会厅可以通过广告的形式

target groups, preferences of product characteristics, and social events can affect the sales of products. Experimental method, as one of the research methods, can measure the impact of advertising on sales performance. For instance, enterprises can allocate different advertising budget in different regions to measure the sales differences.

11.4   Marketing Communications: Public Relations and Publicity

Public relations is a form of marketing communications facing existing and potential buyers, as well as other related stakeholders that aims to communicate the values of products and services, as well as influence their feelings, views, and trust towards products or services (Bennett, 1995). Publicityis considered as free, relatively unpaid, coverage on various print or broadcast media that the media express non-commercial reports or comments about certain products, services, or persons. Public relations and public information are different, but the success of public relations is followed by complimentary reports of media. Aggressive promotional effect contributes to the smooth development of public relation.

Public relation activities are primarily the sum of activities undertaken by an enterprise to maintain its relationship with the special and general public. Special public refers to groups that have a direct interest in the enterprises, such as consumers, employees, suppliers, intermediaries, and shareholders. These groups have different requirements on the interests of enterprises. Other special public groups include people working in the political and regulatory sectors as well as opinion leaders in the communities, namely teachers or key figures in several business and business organizations. The general public groups include everyone in the area where the enterprise is located. To several chained organizations, the public can be the people in the entire country or region.

Public relations activities position the enterprise as responsible business citizens, and promote the image to the appropriate public. The key of public relations activities is to understand public interest as the basis for developing operational policies and procedures. In other words, enterprises must be responsible, honest, and responsible citizens. The good performance of enterprises, however, has to be perceived and recognized by public.

Publicity is not performed by the enterprise itself, but by a neutral third party. The main advantage is the ease of establishing good credibility, which has significant impact on the marketing communications of enterprises. News is the main form of corporate public promotion. A news report, even just a report of the corporate press conference, is perceived by readers as objective and in line with facts.

Non-commercial media coverage is more persuasive than commercial advertising effect. Under the situation of rising advertising costs, releasing information through media can save substantial costs, which can result in cost effectiveness. A new expensive banquet hall may not be enough to become news. If the hall is named after a celebrity or celebrities attend the ribbon-cutting ceremony, then the event will be good enough to

对目标受众提供信息，但也可以通过媒体报道或通过某部电影、电视剧的播放传递出这个宴会厅的特点、造价，后者则更像是免费的广告。这也就是为什么很多企业通过赞助电影或电视以及重大赛事活动打开市场的主要原因。

公正、客观的第三方媒体是宣传的主要优点，但同时也是风险的来源。企业可以严格审核和掌控广告的内容，但对大众宣传内容却无能为力，因为那是由媒体的编辑人员决定的。媒体发布的信息可能会比较模糊，无法把企业想要传递的信息全面而准确地传递给受众，这样会在某种程度上造成顾客的困惑，从而因为信息不全而无法产生购买行为。更糟糕的是，媒体的新闻有正面和负面之分，编辑人员既不会放过正面新闻，也不会刻意去掉对企业有负面影响的新闻。如果播出负面报道，对企业的不利影响也是巨大的。

如上所述，新闻因为高可信度的特点而成为开展公共关系的最主要工具。此外，演说、记者招待会或新闻发布会也能提高企业和产品的知名度。特别是会上圆满地回答媒体或公众问题的环节为企业更深入彻底地向目标受众传达企业或产品信息提供了条件。另一种较为普遍的公共关系工具是特殊事件，其内容从隆重的开幕典礼、演唱会、教育活动到重大节庆活动等都是为接触目标大众和激发他们的兴趣而设计的。公共关系人员在策划这些活动时还要准备充分的书面材料，以接触和影响目标市场，这些材料包括带有企业标识的说明书、照片、视听材料、小册子和杂志等。照片能使读者更易识别企业，而视听材料包括影片、HTML5、虚拟现实（VR）等也是有效的沟通工具。另外，企业网站也是很好的公共关系途径之一，它接触范围广泛且可达性高。利用企业网站，顾客和其他公众能不受时间和地域限制地了解企业和产品信息，而且有的企业网站还提供娱乐项目以吸引顾客的点击率。

积极的宣传活动还可以与企业所有者或经营者以及内部工作人员联系起来。企业获取的特殊成就、积极的评价甚至是经营者或员工爱好等都能用来吸引公众。名人的到访容易引起公众的关注，而企业善于抓住这一机会扩大宣传则会收益颇丰，即使企业专门为此配备一名摄影师也是非常值得的。如果这个名人的影响力够大，媒体预先知晓其到访的话，电视台可能会专派摄影组过来。当然，不管媒体提供什么样的报道，都需要经过名人的同意。

attract widespread concern of the media. The banquet hall can provide information to target audience through advertising. However, the advertising can be free if media reports, movies, or soap operas convey the characteristics and costs of the banquet hall. This reason is why many enterprises sponsor movies, television programs, or major events to open the market.

Fairness and objectivity are the main advantages of publicity through the third parties, but are sources of risk as well. Enterprises can strictly audit and control the advertising content, but cannot do anything on publicity. These strategies are purely based on the decision of the editors of media. The information released by the media can be vague and unable to convey comprehensive and accurate information to the public, resulting in confusion to customers and no purchase due to incomplete information. To make matters worse is that media news has positive and negative views. Editors will not let go of the positive news, but will not deliberately remove the news posing negative impact to enterprises. The adverse effect on the enterprises is enormous after broadcasting the negative news.

As mentioned above, news becomes the most important public relation tool because of its high level of credibility. Second, speeches, press conferences, or news conferences can improve the visibility of businesses and products. In particular, a successful response in the question and answer section to media or public offers opportunities for enterprises to communicate their businesses or products to target audience in a greater depth. Another popular public relation tool is the special event, which ranges from grand opening ceremonies, concerts, and educational events to major festivals, designed to reach the target audience and spark their interest. Public relations officers prepare sufficient written materials to reach and influence target markets when planning these activities. These materials cover manuals, photographs, audiovisual materials, brochures, and magazines with corporate identity. Photos can enhance the recognition of readers, and audio-visual materials, including video, HTML5, and virtual reality. In addition, the corporate website is a very good way of public relations due to its far reach and highly accessible nature. Customers and other publics can understand the business and product information without time and geographical constraints. Several corporate websites may provide entertainment to attract click-through rate of customers.

Aggressive campaigns can also connect business owners, operators, and internal staff. Special achievements, positive evaluations, and even hobbies of operator or employee are useful to attract the public. Celebrity visits attract public attention, and enterprises that are good at seizing the opportunity to expand their publicity yield significant profits. An investment specifically for an in-house photographer is worth the resources. If the influence of a celebrity is big enough and the media is aware of his/her visit in advance, then the television station may dedicate professional crewmembers to cover the visit. Regardless of the kinds of reports provided by media, the consent of celebrity is necessary.

参与慈善事业或公益活动也成为企业建立信誉的一种工具,这就是我们所说的公益营销。所谓公益营销,就是通过赞助、捐赠等公益手段对企业社会公众形象进行商业推广的营销方式(曾朝晖,2005)。企业公益活动的主题有教育、环保、体育、健康事业等,其效果亲切自然,易于被接受。它实质上是一种商业性及功利性不明显的软广告,并且沟通对象量大面广、有针对性。虽然不能直接带来产品的销售,但长远地看,它会改变人们对企业的看法,间接地提升品牌的声誉、形象以及销售量等(袁桂芳,2004)。不仅大型企业的公益活动能产生良好的社会效应,如深圳华侨城欢乐海岸与世界自然基金会(WWF)共同组织了一次大型公益环保活动"2014 欢乐海岸中国自然使者行动",获得了王石、李云迪、萨顶顶、蒋方舟等知名人士的支持。即便是小型企业也能通过慈善或公益活动在当地产生重大影响。有的小型企业通过支持当地学校的运动会或学生会活动来提高公众知晓度。另外,企业也可以参与当地的节庆活动、体育比赛、社区事务或捐款活动等作为慈善营销的手段。大型的集团或企业可能会有一个专门的公关负责人,而小型的企业则通常靠一个其他部门的经理兼管公关事务,或从广告代理商那里得到协助。

在向社会公众宣传企业的正面业绩和经营表现的同时,旅游企业也不得不面对经营过程中的负面性新闻,包括质量投诉、操作事故、员工暴动、食物中毒、违规行为或其他问题等。企业如果能未雨绸缪,事先做好防备措施防止此类事件的发生,是最明智的。如果不得不面对的话,则应该用缜密的计划和积极的行动来处理这些负面新闻,减少不良影响。危机管理应该始于危机的预防,也就是在危机真正发生之前,而不应是事故发生之后被动地应对。企业不仅要制定缜密的危机管理的政策和措施,而且要考虑到公众的利益。这不仅是企业尽责的表现,而且也能减少归责与企业疏忽的概率。应变计划是另一个危机发生前企业要做的事。企业要预测企业的潜在危机以及潜在危机发生后的应对措施。危机具有不可控制性以及信息多变性,因此,应变计划不应一成不变,而应是灵活的。

发言人是危机管理的必要条件。他应该是一个决策者,具有调查事情真相的权力。在企业内部,应该有可遵循的处理危机的沟通程序,以便于及时处理紧急情况。对于某些不能及时解决的危机,发言人应该积极收集信息,告知有关人士解决的进度并给出明确时间界定的信息。同时,企业也应该有

Participation in charity or charity activities has become a tool for enterprises to establish credibility. Charity marketing is a form of marketing via sponsorship, donation, and other public means to promote corporate social image (Zeng, 2005). The themes of corporate social activities are education, environmental protection, sports, and health, which are easy to be accepted. Inherently, charity marketing is soft advertising featuring commercial and subtle utilitarian concepts, with a wide range of specific communication objects. Although this marketing strategy cannot directly lead to product sales, perception can change on enterprises in the long run and indirectly enhance the reputation, image, and sales of brands (Yuan, 2004). Public welfare activities of large enterprises can produce good social effects, such as Shenzhen OCT Harbor, which co-organized a large-scale public environmental activity "2014 Action of China Nature Envoy" with World Wildlife Fund, with the support of many celebrities, namely Wang Shi, Li Yundi, Sa Dingding, and Jiang Fangzhou. Even small businesses can have significant local impact through charitable or charitable activities. Several small-scale enterprises support the sports gala or student union activities of local schools to raise public awareness. In addition, enterprises can participate in local festivals, sports competitions, community affairs, or donation activities as a means of charitable marketing. Large-scale groups or enterprises may have a dedicated public relation chief, while small businesses typically rely on a manager in another department to manage the public relation affairs or obtain the help from advertising agencies.

While demonstrating positive performance and operations to public, tourism enterprises have to manage negatives news, including complaints about inferior quality, operation accidents, employee insurrection, food poisoning, irregularities, or other problems. The most sensible strategy occurs when companies can take precautionary measures in advance to prevent the occurrence of such incidents. Sophisticated planning and constructive actions are necessary to deal with the negative news to reduce adverse effects if issues are unavoidable. Crisis management should start with the prevention of crises, in which being proactive is preferred over being reactive after the occurrence of accident. Enterprises require developing sophisticated crisis management policies and measures, and consider the interests of the public. This practice is a demonstration of corporate social responsibility, as well as reducing the risk of imputation and corporate negligence. Contingency planning is necessary before the occurrence of crisis, and prediction of potential risks and corresponding measures of crisis. Crises are uncontrollable and volatile, and thus, contingency plans should not be static, but flexible.

A spokesperson is a necessary condition for crisis management, and should be a decision-maker and possesses the right to investigate the truth of the matter. Within the enterprise, communication procedures must be present to deal with crisis to ensure timely treatment in emergencies. For the crisis that cannot be resolved in a timely manner, the spokesperson should actively collect information and inform concerned parties about progress and specify timely information. Meanwhile, enterprises should have a clear channel to release information to the

清晰的渠道向内部员工发布有关信息,这不仅对保持员工的士气非常重要,而且不管是在职的或离职的员工都与公众有接触,公众会认为他们仍然是企业的代表,他们的评价也会在社会上引起很大的反响,因此他们也需要知道真相。"保持沉默"或"不发表任何评论"都不是应对公众提出的问题的最佳措施。

由于商业广告价格昂贵且费时,公共关系和宣传的使用率越来越高。虽说公共关系和宣传并不是免费的,准备新闻稿、照片和新闻发布会都会产生成本,但花费的金钱和时间与购买同等广告版面相比均低得多。尽管公共关系和宣传活动中不包含具体的销售信息,但是公共关系和宣传活动由于其较高的可信度,效果还是会比相同版面或时间的广告更好。

11.5　营销传播：销售推广

销售推广是指企业通过媒介或非媒介的营销方式在有限的时间里推出某一种或几种产品/服务,刺激消费者试买或更频繁地重复购买,鼓励他们升级购买产品/服务或与竞争者的营销活动相抗衡的营销行为（Bennett,1995）。与为了在一段时间内影响消费者态度的广告不同的是,销售推广活动更倾向于用经济方面的激励来达成即时销售量的增加。同时,理想的销售推广行为还是支持企业形象的方式。企业举行销售推广活动的原因很多,表 11－4 进行了部分列举。

表 11－4　利用销售推广的原因

● 鼓励试用型购买	● 推广新产品
● 刺激重复购买	● 与其他经营者竞争
● 通过奖赏建立顾客忠诚	● 利用特殊的事件或潮流
● 在特别时期增加销售额	● 增加顾客的兴奋度
● 增加顾客消费或延长逗留时间	● 激励雇员

同其他沟通元素一样,销售推广也有特定的受众,如家庭、青少年或商务旅行者等。企业尤其是大企业的销售推广活动事先都会做详细的计划;评估销售推广效果的方法就是计划的内容之一。旅游业的惯常销售推广评估法是将销售推广前、销售推广中和销售推广后的业绩进行比较;有时也会比较之前年份的同期业绩。但企业实施销售推广活动期间的业绩会因为某些大型的特殊事件(大型音乐会、足球赛、演唱会等)而受到重大影响。所以企业在进行评估的时候需要据此做出相应的调整。

最常见的销售推广形式有优惠券、现金折扣、实物赠品、奖品(游戏、抽奖、

internal staff. Maintaining staff morale is important. Current and former employees are both incontact with public, and the public perceives that employees are representatives of the enterprises. The employees have to know the truth given that their evaluation will create significant impact in the community. Remaining silent or having no comments is not the best response to public inquiry.

The use of public relations and promotions is increasing due to expensive and time-consuming commercials. Public relations and advocacy are not free of charge, and preparing press releases, photos, and press conferences generate costs. The cost and time spent are, however, lower than buying the same advertising space. Despite public relations and promotions not having specific sales information, these strategies are more effective and credible than the advertisements with the same layout or time.

11.5 *Marketing Communications*: *Sales Promotion*

Sales promotion refers to the promotion of a certain product or service in a limited time by means of media or non-media marketing. This strategy encourages consumers to try out or buy more frequently, to encourage them to upgrade their products or services, or to counter marketing activities of competitors (Bennett, 1995). Unlike advertisements that affect consumer attitudes over time, sales promotions tend to use economic incentives to achieve immediate sales increases. At the same time, the ideal sales promotion behavior supports corporate image. Enterprises have several reasons for having sales promotion activities. Table 11 - 4 lists several of these reasons.

Table 11 - 4   Reasons for sales promotion

● Encourage trial purchase	● Promote new products
● Stimulate repeat purchase	● Compete with other operators
● Build customer loyalty through rewards	● Use special events or trends
● Increase sales in special times	● Increase customer excitement
● Increase customer spending or extend their length of stay	● Motivate employees

Similar to other communication elements, sales promotions have specific audiences, such as family, youth, or business travelers. Enterprises, especially large-scale enterprises, conduct detailed planning before carrying out sales promotion activities. An assessment of the promotion effect is one of the contents of the plan. A common practice for tourism enterprises is to compare the performance before, during, and after sales promotion. Comparison of the performance at the same period of the previous year is common practice. However, the performances of launching sales promotion will be significantly affected due to certain large-scale special events (large concerts, football competitions, and music concerts). Enterprises should therefore make appropriate adjustments timely.

The most common forms of sales promotion are coupons, cash discounts, in-kind

竞赛）、售点销售推广、捆绑销售和免费样品。

1. 优惠券

优惠券是一种凭证,顾客可以在购买特定的产品/服务时用于抵消本应支付的价格的部分或全部,一般不能兑换现金。优惠券可邮寄、附于其他产品之内,也可刊登在报纸、杂志上。优惠券一般有有效期,以鼓励即时购买。许多企业还通过企业官方或其他相关网站及 App 派送电子优惠券,方便顾客下载。快餐业最频繁使用优惠券,酒店也会通过邮件或杂志分发优惠券,用以提高周末或淡季的生意,或鼓励延长入住时间、扩大顾客群等。回购优惠券是在顾客此次消费结束时送出供下次使用的一种优惠券,主要用以鼓励顾客重复购买。例如,必胜客的外卖盒子上贴有供下次使用的优惠券。回购优惠券因为无需分发的费用,成本较低,也能适用于小型商家。

优惠券是现在旅游行业常用的一种销售推广形式,OTA 使用较多的是新型的回购优惠券,即返现,消费者在 OTA 上预订了酒店的客房,可在 OTA 的账户上获得返现,用于下次预订。Guo、Zheng 和 Li,等(2014)的研究发现,OTA 的返现金额取决于 OTA 所能获得的利润率,而利润率与 OTA 和酒店之间的竞争与合作有关,OTA 可以通过基于收入分成的折扣合同与酒店协调竞争与合作的关系。

2. 折扣或特卖

折扣或特卖是另一种销售推广形式,常用于淡季。折扣可用于"新品优惠",但"推广价"有一定的期限。此外,"满额即有折扣"也是折扣销售推广的最常见方式,即消费每达一定的数目即可获取对应的折扣率,消费数目越大,折扣率越高。例如,满 1000 元有 8 折优惠;2000 元则 7 折优惠。另外,将折扣产品与不享有折扣的产品一起销售也是折扣的形式,如餐厅的全价菜品与半价冰冻饮料的套餐。

3. 赠品

赠品是指顾客在购买某一特定产品/服务的同时,获得旅游企业以较低价格或免费提供的同一或另一产品/服务。餐厅顾客用餐时的免费饮料、酒

gifts, prizes (games, sweepstakes, and contests), point-of-sale promotions, bundle selling, and free samples.

1. Coupon

The coupon is a voucher that allows customers to buy particular products or services to offset part or the entire price, and generally, a coupon cannot be exchanged for cash. Coupons can be mailed, attached to other products, or published in newspapers or magazines. Coupons usually have a valid period to encourage immediate purchase. Many enterprises distribute electronic coupons through official or other related websites and applications to facilitate customer download at ease. The most frequent use of coupons is in the fast-food industry. Hotels distribute coupons through courier or magazines to improve business during weekends or low season, or to encourage extended stay or enlarge customer base. A bounce-back coupon is given to customers at the end of their current consumption for the next purchase, which aims to encourage repeat purchase. For example, the takeaway box of Pizza Hut attaches a coupon for the next purchase. Bounce-back coupon is free from distribution fee, resulting in lower cost and suitable for small-scale businesses.

Coupons are commonly used in the tourism industry as a form of sales promotion. OTA usually utilize the new form of buy-back coupons, namely cash-back. Consumers who make hotel rooms reservations on OTA can obtain cash-back for their next booking. Guo, Zheng & Lin, et al. (2014) found that the amount of cash-back depends on the profit rate obtained by OTA, which is related to the competition and cooperation between OTA and hotels. OTA can manage the competing and cooperating relationship with hotels based on the revenue-shared discounts.

2. Discount

The discount is another form of sales promotion that is commonly used during low season. Discounts can be used for new offers, but promotional price is only available within a limited timeframe. In addition, another popular form of discount sales promotion is the price-break discount , which allows customers a corresponding discount if their consumption exceeds a threshold amount. The more they buy, the higher the discount rate. For example, 20% off when spending over RMB 1,000, or 30% off when spending over RMB 2,000. Besides, the sales of discounted products with non-discounted products comprise other forms of discounts, such as a combo of full-price meals with half-price cold drinks at restaurants.

3. Premiums

Premiums refer to customers obtaining the same or another product or service at a lower price or free-of-charge while buying a particular product or service. Restaurant

店客人入住时的免费纪念品等都是赠品的形式。旅行包、帽子、雨伞、T恤、茶杯、电话卡、笔、记事本、日历等都可以被旅游企业用来作为消费赠品。还有部分旅游企业采取"累积式赠品"的形式鼓励消费者的多次光顾。只有顾客消费累计一定次数之后才可获得相对单次消费赠品折扣更高或价值更大的免费赠品。

4. 奖品

奖品是鼓励消费者参与某种活动并赢取奖品的形式。活动一般包括游戏、抽奖和比赛；奖品一般有现金、实物、机票、免费住宿等，这种机会可能全凭运气或需要付出额外的努力。(1)游戏，既可是现场的猜谜、拼图或纸牌游戏，也可以是在购买商品、货品和其他物品时积累的刮奖卡。其主要目的是刺激顾客想要中奖的欲望从而频繁购买产品/服务。(2)抽奖券，则是企业从顾客填写的抽奖表中随机抽取获胜者。它也是一种收集顾客信息的有效方式。(3)比赛不以购买为条件，让消费者应募参加竞赛或比赛。比赛既可是体育类，也可是娱乐或技能类，如绘画、书法、唱歌、跳舞、产品命名比赛等。

5. 售点销售

售点销售是在售点展示产品或在消费现场示范使用方法的活动。此销售方式主要是借助商品或推广材料进行推广——包括餐单、饮料单、送餐服务单、昭示海报等。酒店和餐厅以及旅行社都广泛采用这种销售推广方式，因为旅游服务产品只能通过销售推广材料将无形产品有形化，增加客人对服务质量的信心。常见的有橱柜菜品实物展示、厨艺演示、客房迷你吧或模拟客房展示等。(1)组合销售主要是成品经营商与原料供应商联合销售推广，一般由供应商免费或低价提供销售推广产品，经营商则负责销售推广活动的开展和组织。餐厅常与相关食品、饮料供应商一起联合销售推广。品酒宴就是联合销售推广的例子。供酒商免费或低价赞助供应酒，并提供小册子、说明书或海报类的销售推广材料；餐厅则负责举办品酒活动并提供餐点，吸引顾客参与。酒店常常将餐饮与客房结合起来销售推广，其中包括景点门票或围绕体育或娱乐性事件票类的套餐。(2)免费样品是派送给消费者以供其试用的产品。虽然旅游产品不能像其他有形产品那样让顾客试用之后再购买，但有的经营者提供免费食用的食物或酒店康乐设施让顾客进行事先体验。例如酒店邀请旅行社提前参观就是展示酒店样品的一种手段。并且酒

customers get free drinks when dining and hotel guests get free souvenirs are examples of premiums. Travel bags, caps, umbrellas, t-shirts, teacups, phone cards, pens, notepads, and calendars can be used as premiums for tourism enterprises. Tourism enterprises offer cumulative premiums to encourage repeat patronage. Customers who accumulate certain consumption can receive more valuable premiums in comparison with single purchases.

4. Prizes

Prizes are rewards that consumers win from participating in certain activities. Activities include games, sweepstakes, and competitions, and prizes are cash, products, air tickets, or free accommodation. Such opportunities may simply rely on luck or need to pay extra effort. (1) Games can be riddle teasers, puzzles, or card games, as well as the accumulation of scratch cards in the purchase of goods, items, and other parts. The main purpose of games is to stimulate the frequent purchase due to the desirability of customers to win. (2) In the sweepstakes, enterprises randomly select winners from those customers who filled in the lottery tickets. This promotion strategy is an effective way of collecting customer information. (3) Contests are about customers participating in races or competitions regardless of purchase as a condition. Contests can be related to sports, entertainment events, or skills, such as painting, calligraphy, singing, dancing, or product-naming competition.

5. Merchandizing

Merchandizing is a non-site demonstration of the use of the product at the point of sale. This method involves conducting sales promotions through commodities or promotional materials, including menus, beverage lists, menu delivery, or posters. Hotels, restaurants, and travel agencies widely use such methods because these ways make intangible tourism products tangible, and consequently enhance customer confidence in service quality. Kitchen cabinet displays, cooking demonstration, minibar in guestrooms, and simulated guestroom displays are common examples. (1) Packaging is a joint sales promotion by the finished product operators and raw material suppliers. Overall, suppliers provide free or low-cost promotional products, and finished product operators are responsible for the organization and implementation of sales promotion activities. Restaurants often have joint promotions with relevant food and beverage suppliers. Wine tasting is an example of a joint sales promotion. Wine suppliers offer free or sponsor wine at a lower price, brochures, manuals, or posters as promotional materials. Restaurants are in-charge of organizing wine-tasting events and offering refreshments to attract customers. Hotels often combine rooms and meals as joint promotions, and the combination can include tickets for attractions, sports, and entertainment packages. (2) In addition, sampling includes products offered to consumers for trial. Unlike tangible products, tourism products cannot be sampled before purchase. Several operators offer free food or hotel recreational facilities to give

店客房的免费或优惠升级也让顾客有机会体验不同的房型,为其下次升级消费做准备。

　　这里需要指出一些销售推广中需要注意的问题。首先,销售推广为许多经营者提供了快速解决"销售额下降"的方法,但有时忽略了"查明销售额下降的真正原因"的重要性。不仅如此,销售推广吸引来的顾客有很大部分不是出于对企业的忠诚。他们购买行为的产生是由于企业提供的优惠条件的刺激。当销售推广活动结束的时候,他们的惠顾可能也就结束了。甚至有的消费者还会对销售推广期间的产品和服务的质量产生怀疑,觉得它们可能不如非销售推广期间的质量。此外,已经真正具有忠诚度的现有顾客并不会在销售推广期间真正增加购买额,他们的购买实际上与销售推广和非销售推广没有太大的关系。最后,销售推广若使用不当还可能会影响企业的形象。

11.6　营销传播:人员推销

　　人员推销是指企业派出的销售人员,运用营销知识和技能向顾客直接传播信息以赢得顾客的信任和好感,达到扩大销售目的的一种销售推广方式(徐青,2001)。旅游企业的销售并不仅仅是营销部人员的工作,实际上是全体员工共同努力的结果,尤其是那些与顾客接触的一线员工或那些"营销大使",比如酒店前台接待、旅行社导游和餐厅服务员等。人员推销是一种非常昂贵的营销方式,成本包括销售人员的工资、培训费、差旅费、娱乐费以及办公设备费等。往往长时间的准备工作就是为了短短几十分钟的真正"推销"时间,即与顾客面对面交流的时间相对较少,而大部分时间都用来做准备工作及跟进工作。因此,这就更显示出了那部分真正与顾客接触的时间的"昂贵"了。日常经营活动中对现有客人进行推销虽说在酒店比较常见,但很多旅游企业更倾向于将人员推销用于能产生大量销售额的团体销售,如酒店针对会议团体、旅行社、航空公司等进行的推销或旅行社针对企业进行的奖励销售。人员推销也是餐饮承包公司获取新客户的主要方式。但这里我们主要以酒店为例子讨论人员销售。

　　推销的过程可以说是一个开放式的过程,它始于销售洽谈,但没有限定的终结点,因为长期保留现有顾客是每个销售代表必须承担的责任。推销的主要活动包括搜寻潜在顾客、策划销售内容、销售洽谈现场(电话、面对面等)、达成销售以及销售跟进几个步骤。

customers a prior experience. For example, hotels invite travel agencies for site visits in advance, as the display of samples. Free rooms or upgrades to customers allow them to experience different room types, as a preparation for the next upgrade or consumption.

Special points-to-note should be considered for sales promotion. First, sales promotion provides many operators with a quick solution to the decline in sales. Sometimes, sales promotions neglect the true reasons of the decline in sales. Sale promotions attract a large number of customers because of the incentives, rather than loyalty to the enterprises. When sales promotion is over, their patronage may be over. Several consumers would even question the quality of products and services they bought during the promotion period. Moreover, other consumers perceive that the product quality is inferior compared to the non-sales promotion period. Besides, existing customers who are truly loyal do not actually increase their purchases during sales promotion. Their actual purchases are unrelated to sales and non-sales promotion. Finally, the inappropriate use of sales promotion may affect the image of the enterprises.

11.6 *Marketing Communications: Personnel Marketing*

Personnel marketing refers to the sales personnel dispatched by enterprises, who use their marketing knowledge and skills to disseminate information directly to customers to win the trust and goodwill of customers, and consequently achieve the purpose of sales promotion (Xu, 2001). The sales task of tourism enterprises is the work of the marketing department and the outcome of the joint efforts of all the staff. In particular, frontline employees are in touch with customers, or are marketing ambassadors, such as front desk receptionists, tour guides, and restaurant waiters. Personnel marketing is a very expensive marketing method. The cost includes the salaries of sales staff, training, business travel, entertainment, and office equipment. Long preparation time is required for just a few dozen minutes of the actual marketing time. Face-to-face communication with customers is relatively limited, and most of the time is used to prepare and follow-up. Therefore, this strategy shows that particular part of the real contact time with customers is expensive. Although the hotel industry commonly sells products to existing customers, many tourism enterprises tend to utilize sales personnel for groups sales that generate large sales volume. Hotel selling conference groups, travel agencies and airlines, as well as travel agencies selling enterprises for business incentives, are examples. Personnel selling is the main way for catering contractors to acquire new customers. The focus of this section is, however, about hotels.

The marketing process is as an open process. The process begins with sales negotiations, and has no definite end. The long-term retention of existing customers is the responsibility of every sales representative. The main activities of the sales include searching for potential customers and planning sales content as well as negotiating (telephone and face-to-face), achieving, and following-up sales.

11.6.1 搜寻潜在顾客

所谓潜在顾客是与现实顾客相对应的,是指有购买兴趣、购买需求,或有购买欲望、购买能力,但尚未与企业或组织发生交易关系的个人或组织。他们是有意向并且有能力(包括经济能力和身体能力)使用企业提供的产品和服务的那部分群体。企业不仅要识别出哪些群体是购买产品和服务的对象,还要确定他们是否有能力消费此类产品和服务。因此,搜寻潜在顾客包括开发销售线索并从线索中确定潜在顾客两个部分。

1. 开发销售线索

开车绕城区而行或访问当地的商务部门都是获取销售线索的机会。周围的新建筑物意味着新的商业活动和商业机构出现。通过政府或民间商务部门一般可获取即将开张的公司名单,以及公司的性质、大小等方面的信息。浏览黄页分类信息有助于发现需要客房或会议空间的企业客户。同时,当地某些协会组织及其成员名单指南则是寻找组织内销售对象的依据和借鉴。浏览竞争者张贴或发布出来的日常会议名单也是很常用并且有效的方式。社区中的朋友和现有顾客也是销售线索的来源之一。在收集销售线索阶段,我们可能会说"多多益善",但在确定潜在客户阶段,企业要从这些线索中找出真正有可能转化为企业现有顾客的群体,更在乎的是质量。

2. 挑选合格的潜在顾客

合格的潜在顾客对旅游企业提供的产品或服务有需求,能为企业带来收入,并能弥补人员推销所产生的费用。他们一般包括那些预订相当数量的客房、餐饮或其他设施和服务如会议室、宴会厅、旅游用车等的顾客,或是某个有购买决策权的个人。因此,潜在顾客可以包括秘书、办公室助理、差旅负责人、销售或培训经理以及其他管理层人员。旅游企业的销售代表应该弄清楚谁是与公司的差旅、会议事务有直接关系或有购买决策权的负责人,并适时与之沟通、交流。秘书通常是一个组织中重要的"看门人",他们通常控制了通向组织决策者的路径。他们自己本身也会做出决策,比如给访客选择入住

11.6.1　Searching for potential customers

The so-called potential customer can correspond to the actual customer and refer to individuals or groups who are interested in buying, purchasing needs, or desire to buy or exercise purchasing power, but not transacting with the enterprises. Potential groups are people who have the intention and ability (including financial and physical abilities) to use the products and services provided by the enterprises. Businesses need to identify the groups that are the targets of purchasing the goods and services, and to confirm whether they have the ability to consume such products and services. Therefore, searching for potential customers is two-fold, such as developing sales leads and identifying potential customers from the leads.

1. Develop sales leads

Driving around cities or visiting local commerce departments are the opportunities to get leads. The new buildings around the corners mean new business activities and establishments. The lists of companies to be opened, nature of companies, size, and other aspects of information, can be obtained through the government or the civil commerce sector. Browsing the classified information in Yellow Pages is conducive to identify business customers who need guestrooms or meeting spaces. At the same time, local associations and their member lists are the basis and reference points to find sales targets within the organizations. Browsing the list of daily meetings posted or published by competitors is a very common and effective way of identifying potential customers. Friends in the community and existing customers are sources of generating sales leads. In the lead-gathering phase, quantity is important. In the stage of determining potential customers, enterprises care more about product quality such that finding clues to convert potential into real is important.

2. Select qualified potential customers

Qualified potential customers need products or services provided by tourism enterprises, and they generate revenues and compensate for the costs of personnel marketing. These customers book a significant number of guestrooms, meals, and other facilities, such as conference rooms, banquet halls, and coaches, or the decision makers with buying power. As a result, potential customers can be secretaries, office assistants, travel executives, sales or training managers, and other managerial staff. Sales representatives of tourism enterprises should be clear who has direct relationship with the travel and conference businesses of companies, or make timely communication and information exchange with the decision makers. Secretaries are usually important gatekeepers in an organization, as they usually control the path to the decision makers of organizations. These decision makers inherently decide on matters, such as choosing

酒店等。因此,许多酒店为他们成立了专门的"秘书俱乐部",还定期举办宴请活动以增进交流和信任,获取客源。

虽说旅游企业的销售人员把主要精力集中于合格的潜在顾客身上,但也应该花时间在发掘新的销售机会上。销售人员在空闲的时间里也会通过"突访"获取可能的销售机会,发掘新的客户。突访是指事先没有与受话方预约,而是通过从公用电话本或其他渠道得到的电话号码与之进行电话联系,与对方结识并推销产品的行为。这种推销在很多情况下都是在不了解客人的基础上首次进行联系。比如企业的市场人员在某行业会展后,将会展上收集到的1000多张客户名片进行过滤,找到可能的潜在用户,然后把这些人的名字交给销售人员,销售人员逐个打电话或亲自拜访,寻找潜在的销售机会。

"突访"是"地毯式推销"常用的一种手段。地毯式推销是指推销人员在不熟悉或不太熟悉顾客的情况下,直接访问某一特定地区或某一特定行业的所有用户和经营单位或个人,从中寻找目标购买者的产品推销方法。几个销售员有组织、全面地对某一个特定地区的所有写字楼里的商户展开电话或面对面联络,采用的就是"地毯式突访"方式。这种地毯式推销大多都是针对某特定的区域,也可能是针对某一类型的组织,如某城市中所有的大学和大专院校。而且推销一般都是由企业的销售人员来完成,但运营部门的工作人员有时也会加入他们的推销队伍。

11.6.2 策划销售洽谈

任何成功的销售都离不开周密的计划。销售洽谈的策划是建立在营销人员已经确认了合格的潜在顾客之后,因此,销售对象具有明确针对性。销售员对推销对象的了解越深,制订的销售计划就越有效。销售对象的组织信息和个人背景信息在策划过程中起着很重要的作用。组织信息包括整个组织或企业的大小和经营性质、使用酒店和会议设备的历史以及其对产品和服务的偏好。个人信息可能包括兴趣、爱好、俱乐部或社团关系和社会地位等。首先,礼貌和专业是销售洽谈的首要要求。接触顾客不是件易事,因为难以获取客户初次的信任。一些小型对话就可以成为获取个人信息的机会,但尊重对方的隐私是最起码的行为。此外,预约是销售人员对已经确认的潜在顾客进行推销时体现专业化和正式化的关键,包括电话预约或邮件预约。电子邮件预约最好有电话的跟进确认。一旦预约确定之后,就要开始做进一步的准备和计划工作了。

hotels for visitors to stay. Therefore, many hotels set up a special secretarial club and organize regular banquets to enhance communication and trust to obtain sales.

Although the sales personnel of tourism enterprises focus on qualified potential customers, they should spend time on exploring new sales opportunities. Salespeople, in their free time, use cold calls to capture potential sales opportunities and discover new customers. A cold call uses telephone communication without prior appointment. A caller obtains numbers from public telephone books or other channels to know and promote products to another party. In most cases, this kind of marketing is the first communication without knowing the customers. For example, in an industry exhibition, marketers filter the 1,000 name cards collected and identify potential customers. The names of these customers are passed on to the sales personnel. The sales personnel conduct phone calls one-by-one or visit the customers in person to search for potential sales opportunities.

A cold call is a typical means of blanketing marketing. Blanketing marketing is a sales method that sales personnel are unfamiliar with customers and directly visit all the users, business units, or individuals with a particular area or industry for the sake of finding targeted buyers. Using the blanketing approach, several salespersons have telephones or face-to-face contacts in an organized and comprehensive manner. This approach is mostly for a particular region, or for a certain type of organization, such as all universities and colleges in a city. The sales personnel of enterprise generally perform sales, but staff in the operation department occasionally joins the marketing team.

11.6.2 Planning sales negotiations

Any successful sales are inseparable from careful planning. Negotiating sales plans following the marketers has confirmed the qualified potential customers. Thus, the sales targets undergo clear specifications. The deeper the salesperson's understanding of the sales targets, the more effective the sales plan will be. Organizational and personal background information of the sales targets plays a crucial role in the planning process. Organizational information includes the size and nature of the organization or business as a whole, the history of using hotels and conference facilities, and their preferences for products and services. Personal information may include interests, hobbies, clubs or social relations, and social status. First, courtesy and professionalism are the primary requirements for sales negotiations. Accessing customers is difficult because obtaining the initial trust from customers is difficult. Some small conversations can be an opportunity to obtain personal information; however, maintaining a respectful attitude toward the privacy of customers is the most basic. Furthermore, making appointments is the key for salespersons to demonstrate professionalization and formalization toward prospective customers, including telephone reservations or mail appointments. E-mail reservation is best with telephone follow-up confirmation. Once the appointment is established, further preparations and planning begin.

　　其次,明确的目标也是策划销售洽谈的关键。这个明确的目标包括充分了解推销的产品和服务的特征、最能引起潜在顾客强烈共鸣的沟通方式、产品信息的轻重把握以及介绍的逻辑顺序。根据顾客的特点"对症下药"才是销售人员取得成功的重点所在,所以,销售人员必须识别潜在顾客的具体需求,并有针对性地展示能满足他们的具体需求的方法和能力。销售沟通的过程必须有逻辑顺序,销售洽谈应条理清晰,内容包含必要的信息以及凸显吸引点。简单有序的销售沟通方式有利于建立良好的第一印象并长期保持下去。所以,只要能成功地吸引潜在顾客的注意力和兴趣就是推销成功的第一步,为紧接而来的销售洽谈做好了铺垫。礼貌且得体的自我介绍以及更重要的用来吸引顾客的兴趣和注意力的沟通都必须显示出训练有素,真实诚恳。

　　顾客最关注的是能从购买中获得何种价值,因此消费利益法,即明确告知顾客他们能获取的利益或价值是进行推销的有效方式。对于不同的销售对象,销售人员传递的消费利益和价值可能是不同的。首先,当我们需要获得秘书的推荐时,借助秘书俱乐部的销售洽谈是一种有效的方法。邀请他们参与秘书俱乐部,并阐明参与俱乐部的利益和价值是重要的。而对公司会议负责人则可以展示酒店所能提供的有关会议的价值和利益,酒店的一些显著特征也是推销的基础,如价格的可协调性和特殊优惠性。展示与众不同的价值特征是销售人员打开沟通之门的有效手段。邀请顾客亲临酒店参观是获取顾客信任的最好方式。特别是当业务销售量大、消费水平高时,邀请顾客一起用餐,早、中商务餐或晚餐是一种好的选择。

　　推荐在店顾客购买其他服务项目也属于针对潜在顾客销售的一种,因为此时向他们销售的实际上也是新的产品或服务。利用他们住店期间展开销售,酒店员工可以向顾客推荐酒店的餐厅、特色菜品、水疗等服务。我们还可以把酒店的关键人物介绍给潜在顾客,比如行政总厨和行政管家,他们对达成销售是很有影响力的。另外,让操作层面的员工知道他们对达成销售有帮助能够增强他们与销售团队的关系。

11.6.3　销售洽谈现场

　　销售洽谈的方式很多,可以是电话洽谈、产品演示,也可以是面对面的对话。产品演示是一种比较正式的现场演示,可以使产品更加具体、生动,形象更加突出。它可以借助视听资料如录像或幻灯片作为视觉上的补充,用情况

Second, a clear goal is key to planning the negotiations. The clear objective comprises understanding the characteristics of the products and services, the means of communication mostly resonating with potential customers, the level of importance regarding the product information, and the logical order of presentation. The key to success is focusing on the characteristics of customers. Sales personnel should therefore identify the specific requirements of potential customers and demonstrate the methods and capability to satisfy their specific needs. The process of sales communication must have logic and order, the negotiations require clarity, and the content should contain the necessary information and highlight the selling points. Simple and orderly sales communication is conducive to establishing a convincing first impression and long-term relationship. Therefore, successfully attracting the attention and interest of potential customers is the first step to succeed and to set up the consequent negotiations. Courtesy and decent self-introduction and more importantly, communication to attract customers' interest and attention must demonstrate superior training and sincerity.

The customer is most concerned on the value possibly derived from the purchase. Consumer interest, which clearly informs customers regarding the benefits or values, is an effective method to sell. Sales personnel should convey different consumer interests and values for different sales targets. First, obtaining recommendations from secretaries is necessary, given that negotiation with the secretary club is an effective method. Inviting them to join the club and illustrating the benefits or values of joining the club are important. Showcasing the values and benefits of the values and benefits of hosting conferences in hotels is an approach to sell the corporate meeting leaders. Some features of hotels are also a basis for sales, such as the price adjustment and special offers. Presenting the distinctive values is an effective approach to open up conversation, while inviting customers to visit the hotels is the best strategy to obtain their trust. Inviting customers for breakfast, luncheon, or dinner together is a good choice, particularly for those big spenders bringing huge sales volume.

Recommending in-store customers to buy other services is a form of sales targeting potential customers as well, because that moment introduces new products or services to them. During their stay, the hotel staff can recommend the hotel's restaurant, signature dishes, spa, and other services. Introducing the key people in hotels to potential customers, such as executive chef and executive housekeeper, is highly influential to achieve sales. Furthermore, informing the operational staff that they play a role in achieving sales can enhance their relationship with the sales team.

11.6.3　Negotiation onsite sales

Sales negotiations can occur in several forms, namely, telephone negotiations, product demonstrations, or a face-to-face dialogue. Product demonstration adds formality to the on-the-spot demonstration, specifying and enhancing the vividness of the product with a more

说明书或图片介绍酒店的业务组合等。销售演示也可以是销售代表和买方人员之间的小型会面。随意性的对话和交流有利于拉近与顾客之间的距离。不管何种形式,出色的销售代表能通过洽谈让顾客建立起对销售本人以及他们代表的企业的信任,甚至达到让客户当场实现销售的目标。

虽说不存在可以让销售人员每次都达成销售的完美剧本,但如果销售人员能参考以下基本准则,至少可以获取更大的成功可能。

(1) 实事求是:既将企业的特点公布于众,又不能承诺企业做不到的事情。虚张声势的宣言无法取得顾客的信任,向顾客承诺企业能实现的事情才是取得信任和认可的关键。

(2) 表现积极:千万不要攻击自己的组织、上司、竞争对手或销售同行。如果必须做出一些负面的评价,那也要强调一下事情的积极面,做到具体问题具体分析。

(3) 产品或服务介绍:我们不能假设每个人对酒店的服务都了然于心。让企业的产品和服务在潜在顾客中留下好的印象非常重要,尤其是对那些从未使用过酒店的某些服务的客人。以故事的方式传递企业价值是一种策略,这样更能吸引听众的兴趣,如酒店的某项设施经营的成功案例,或获得一个特别忠诚顾客的重复光顾的事例等。

(4) 顾客推荐:口头宣传很多时候比商业性宣传更有说服力,因此,有过消费经历的顾客的评价对潜在顾客的影响不容忽视。企业可以利用顾客的推荐词感动潜在顾客,获取信任。让潜在顾客与酒店常客沟通是其中的一种方式,当然事先要得到常客的同意。事实上,并不是所有人都会真正打电话询问常客,但至少从中能体现出销售代表对酒店的信心。一些销售代表还会随身携带一些顾客的亲笔感谢信。

(5) 友好的交流和倾听:尽管销售代表不能表现得像是潜在顾客的老朋友一样,但是销售洽谈中应该保持友好,不仅当一个口才好的演说家,还应该是一个愉悦的听众。如果一直是销售代表在讲话,不仅显得在向对方加压,而且也听不到顾客的真实想法。积极的倾听包括眼神交流以及观察对方的肢体语言。同时,销售代表也要使用自己的面部表情和身体语言来表达我们的兴趣和投入。

(6) 适当询问:当对方的回应不是很积极时,销售人员也可以采取问问

prominent image. It can utilize audio-visual materials, such as video or slides as a visual supplement, with the situational description or picture describing the hotel's business portfolio. Furthermore, a sales presentation can manifest as a small meeting between sales representatives and representatives of buyers. Casual dialogue and communication conducively narrow down the distance with customers. Regardless of forms, an excellent sales representative can build customers' trust in the enterprises and products on his/her behalf through negotiations. Target customers may even reach instant deals.

Attaining a perfect situation of reaching instant deals is impossible. If sales personnel can refer to the following basic rules in sales negotiation, then the chances of obtaining the business may increase.

(1) Seek truth from facts: Publicly announcing the feature of enterprises without promising the potential performance of enterprises is a bluff, such claim cannot win public trust. Promising customers regarding the enterprises' possible achievement is the key to obtain trust and recognition.

(2) Be proactive: Do not attack the organization, supervisors, competitors, or sales peers. If making negative evaluation is inevitable, then the positive aspects should receive equal focus to allow specific analysis for specific issues.

(3) Provide product or service description: We cannot assume that everyone has a clear understanding of the hotel services. Winning the potential customers' positive impression of the company's products and services is important, especially for those without any experiences utilizing some services of the hotels. Storytelling in delivering corporate values is a strategy drawing the interest of audience, such as a successful operation of hotel facilities or a repeat visit of extremely loyal customers.

(4) Encourage WOM: Verbal communication is frequently more persuasive than commercial advertising. Thus, the influence of a customer's evaluations on the potential customers is inevitable. Enterprises can use the customer's words to convince the potential customers and gain their trust. Communication between potential customers and regular customers is one of the strategies; of course, prior consent from regular customers is required. In fact, not everyone will call and ask a regular customer; nevertheless, this act demonstrates the confidence of sales representative toward the hotels. Some sales representatives will even receive a handwritten thank-you note from some customers.

(5) Practice friendly communication and listening: Although sales representatives cannot treat potential customers similar to old friends, they require friendliness not only as an effective orator but as a pleasant listener as well. If a sales representative dominates the conversation, then the pressure seemingly lies on the counterparts and cannot manifest the genuine thoughts of the customers. Active listening includes eye contact and observation of the body language. Simultaneously, sales representatives further utilize their facial expressions and body language to express their interest and commitment.

(6) Make appropriate inquiries: When the response is not highly positive, sales

题的方式帮助其加入交流中来。他们说话的语气和内容可以显示他们的信任或疑惑,销售人员可以由此判断自己的表现。

(7)善待竞争:在了解竞争对手的基础上合情合理地进行分析,说服顾客。

(8)处理抱怨和异议:以积极的心态面对顾客的投诉和异议,识别工作中的不足和失误,适当的解决方法还可能将不满转为感动,获取更多的肯定和信任。

11.6.4　达成销售

没有一个销售代表能保证每次都能达成销售。但销售洽谈结束的时刻就是显示销售成功与否的关键,也是所有销售代表一直致力达到的目标。然而,也许是因为害怕失败,抑或是出于礼貌因素的考虑,很多销售代表对直接询问顾客是否在此刻做出下订单的决定会犹豫不决。也有些销售代表对自己的销售演示效果很自信,充分相信已经说服潜在顾客产生订货的打算从而认为没必要询问。不管上述这些理由是否合理,只要达成销售是销售洽谈的目的,销售代表就应采取某种方法明确得知顾客是否做了下订单的决定。

1. 假定成交法

假定成交法也称假设成交法,是指推销人员假定顾客已经接受推销建议而直接要求顾客购买推销产品的一种成交技术。销售代表可以在销售洽谈结束的时候假定销售达成,并询问对方关于订单的问题,如"我们什么时候能够知道你们的订房清单?""你现在就订下菜单,还是等你跟贵公司的其他人商量了之后再说?"使用电话也是销售人员表示认定成交达成的方式,如"我现在就可以打电话回公司帮您预留位置。"

2. 订购紧张激将法

当销售人员觉得在本应该达成销售的时刻却仍不能确定销售是否达成时,我们可以利用"订购紧张"的理由刺激对方当场进行预订。因为"订购紧张"的事实会增加顾客的紧迫感,促使他们快速做出决定。但"订购紧张"的理由必须建立在真实的基础之上,不能夸大其词、言不符实。顾客终究会知道真相,而过分夸大只会让潜在顾客失去对企业的信任,损害酒店的声誉。

personnel can ask questions to assist them in joining the conversation. Their tone of voice and content can illustrate the trust or doubt of counterparts and thus demonstrate the performance of the sales personnel.

（7）Be constructively competitive: Analyze and persuade customers based on the sensible analysis of competitors.

（8）Handle complaints and objections: A positive attitude toward customer complaints and objections, identification of shortcomings and mistakes at work, and appropriate solutions may convert dissatisfaction to satisfaction, as well as gaining an increased affirmation and trust.

11.6.4 Achieving sales

No sales representative can guarantee sales each time. The closing of sales negotiations is key to prove the success of the sale, which has been a committed goal of sales representatives. However, probably due to fear of failure or courtesy, many sales representatives hesitate to ask customers directly if they have the ordering decision at this moment. Some sales representatives are confident in their sales presentation and believe that they have convinced potential customers to order without having to ask. Whether these reasons are justified, a sales representative should take a certain approach to clarify whether the customer has placed an order, as long as reaching a deal is the goal of the negotiation.

1. Assumptive Close

Also known as the presumptive close, this approach refers to a technique in making a deal by which the sales personnel assume that the customer has accepted the recommendation and thus directly ask customers to buy products. Sales representative can assume sales at the end of the sales negotiations and ask questions regarding the order, such as "When will we be able to know your booking list?" or "Would you like to book the menu or after discussing with the staff in your company?" Utilizing telephone calls is a method to indicate making the deal as well, such as "I will call the company to reserve a place for you."

2. Pressure close

When sales personnel perceive that the required sales has yet to be reached, turning up the pressure, such as stock out soon, can stimulate on-the-spot booking. The stock out soon claim increases the sense of urgency to customers, prompting them to make a quick decision. The claims should base on the actual situation rather than overstatement or the making of false claims. Customers will eventually know the truth, and excessive exaggeration will only allow potential customers to lose trust and creat damage to the reputation of hotels.

3. 试销订单法

如果潜在顾客没有表现出购买的意愿,销售人员也可以说服其下一个试销订单,购买少量产品试用。有的销售员会说"我们希望有一次向你们证明的机会",或向对方承诺举办一个小型活动作为试用订单。如果销售员不能得到一个明确的订单,则应试着取得对方暂时的承诺,并让其告知方便的时间以便电话确认。其实最关键的还是不管怎么样都尽量争取到销售洽谈的某种或几种积极的解决办法。就算当时没有达成销售,从销售线索变成潜在顾客的转变也可以促成未来达成大量的销售。

11.6.5　销售跟进

销售洽谈的结束并不是销售行为的结束,接下来的跟进工作对全面实现销售的意义也不容忽视。即便对方没有下订单,一封感谢信或其他传递我们真诚意愿的沟通方法也是必要的。推销员应该把推销对象的资料以及他们不下订单的原因记录在案以做参考。另外,跟进电话确认顾客将来可能会有的住宿、会议、餐饮或旅游服务的需求也不能少。此外,长期性的电话或邮件跟进是保留客户的有效方法。

同样,销售达成的整个过程中相应的跟进服务也非常重要。在销售达成之前,销售代表应该帮助客户做好使用各项功能应有的准备工作;在购买过程中,负责此次业务的销售代表应该协助顾客审核产品和服务并确保各项功能运作正常。当出现问题时,销售代表比顾客更适合向有关负责人提出意见,因为销售代表比顾客更了解企业的工作人员。但此时销售代表应该处理得当,不然极有可能使得其他部门人员有被指挥的感觉,从而致使两部门之间产生摩擦。售后的跟进工作同样必不可少。顾客或其他相关人员对购买的产品或服务的评价将成为以后开展销售的有效参考依据。如果是负面的评价,销售人员需要适时地进行修正,改进不足。如果是积极的反馈,我们就应该抓住机会建立顾客的忠诚度,为其他业务的顺利开展奠定基础。

其次,跟进工作有助于阻止其他竞争者的介入。之前我们提到过,销售线索可以通过阅读竞争酒店大厅里的功能列表得到,竞争者也可以如此。他们可能从中发现销售线索,并对我们的现有客户展开销售。如果我们能跟现有客户保持积极的联系,增强顾客的忠诚度,竞争者将很难抢走我们的客户。售后的跟进电话只是为了与顾客保持联系、传递最新资讯和获取顾客的信息反馈,所以要控制得当,一般应比较简短,且频率不要太高,因为电话太多会

3. Trial Order

If the prospect fails to show a willingness to buy, then salespersons can alternately persuade his next trial order or buy a small amount as a product trial. Some salespeople say, "we want to have a chance to prove to you" or promise to hold a small event as a trial order. If a clear order fails, then a temporary commitment is an alternative asking the available time for telephone confirmation. Obtaining certain or multiple solutions for sales negotiations is critical. Even in failing to reach the sales, a possibility in the sales leads occurs converting potential customers into big spenders.

11.6.5　Following-up sales

Closing sales negotiations is not the end of sales. Follow-up actions fully realizing the significance of sales require attention. Even if the prospects have not placed an order, a thank-you note or other tools communicating the sincere intentions is necessary. Salespersons should document the information regarding the prospective consumers and the reasons for not placing an order. In addition, follow-up calls should be made to confirm that the customer may have accommodation, meeting, catering, or travel service needs. Maintaining telephone or mail follow ups is an effective technique to retain customers.

Similarly, sales follow-up services throughout the process are equally important. Before completing sales, sales representatives should be well prepared to enable customers' understanding of all features; during the purchasing process, sales representatives are responsible for assisting customers in reviewing the products and services and ensuring the proper operations of all functions. When problems arise, sales representatives are in a better position to advise the person in charge than the customers because the sales representative has better familiarity of the workforce in the company. Sales representatives should cautiously handle the staff in other departments who may negatively respond to commands or orders, thereby resulting in conflicts between departments. After-sales follow-up work is essential as well. Customers or other relevant personnel purchasing the products or services will affect references for future sales. Sales representatives should conduct timely rectification to improve deficiencies if the evaluation is negative. As for positive feedback, sales representatives should seize the opportunity to build customer loyalty and lay the foundation for the smooth development of other businesses.

Second, follow-up task can aid in preventing the involvement of other competitors. As aforementioned, reading the list of features in the lobby of competing hotels can obtain sales leads. Competitors can do the same. They may find leads and sell to our existing customers. If a positive relationship with existing customers can be maintained and their loyalty can be enhanced, then taking away customers will be difficult for competitors. After-sales follow-up phone aims to maintain contact with customers, convey the latest information, and gain access

引起顾客的厌烦情绪。当然,我们也要意识到不是每次的努力都能得到预想的回报的。甚至有时拒绝率远远大于接受率。我们虽说不能奢望 100% 的成功率,但完全可以用击棒球理论做个类比:没人可以达到 100% 的成功率,那些有 30% 的击中率的已经是英雄了。

11.7　营销传播:网络传播

广告、公共关系、促销推广和人员销售都是大众营销时代的营销传播工具,他们的共性在于信息的标准性和目标的广泛性。而时代的发展使得越来越多的企业开始采用网络直接营销的方式,与目标顾客进行互动,获取即时的反馈并建立持久的关系。2014 年,国内五星级酒店的在线预订量占所有预订的 8%(浩华管理顾问公司,2015)。网络直接营销包括在线营销、搜索引擎营销、移动营销以及社交媒体营销。

11.7.1　在线营销

1. 网站

企业网站一般分为两种类型,即营销网站和品牌社区网站。营销网站的主要功能是与消费者进行互动,鼓励消费者在网站上直接进行购买或者进一步提高他们对品牌的认知,例如各大国际酒店集团的官方网站;品牌社区网站则是展示品牌内容,强调品牌与消费者之间的互动。品牌社区网站一般向消费者提供丰富的品牌信息、视频、博客、活动等内容,与消费者建立更为紧密的关系。利用网站进行在线营销的关键是吸引消费者访问网站,企业可以通过线下印刷品宣传或者广告引导客人访问网站。

2. 在线广告

随着人们使用互联网的时间越来越长,在线广告成了一种重要的信息传播媒介。其主要形式是展示性广告(display ads)和搜索相关广告(search-related ads)。展示性广告可以在任何时候出现在互联网使用者正在浏览的网页上,并且与互联网使用者正在浏览的信息相关。例如消费者在浏览携程网站时,会出现各种关于酒店、机票的广告;搜索相关广告是在线广告的主要形式,占据超过一半的在线广告份额(Kotler 和 Armstrong,2014)。搜索广告主要是企业向搜索网站购买搜索短语,并根据点击数量支付费用。文字或图像广告是搜索广告主要的表现形式,通常出现在搜索网站的顶部或左右两侧。

to customer feedback. Such method requires proper control. Short and non-frequent calls are sufficient because frequent phone calls will induce negative reactions. Of course, not every effort pays off, and rejection rate is occasionally far greater than the acceptance rate. Despite the impossibility of a 100% success rate, a baseball theory can be an analogy: no one can achieve a 100% complete success; thus, those who have a 30% hit rate are already a hero.

11.7　Marketing Communications: Online Communication

Advertising, public relations, promotion, and personnel marketing are communication tools in the era of mass marketing. Their commonality lies in the standardization and broad coverage of information. As times progress, increasing the number of enterprises adopts online direct marketing, obtains real-time feedback, and builds a continuous relationship. In 2014, the online direct booking of five-star hotels in China accounted for 8% of all bookings (Crowe Horwath International, 2015). Online direct marketing comprises online, search engine, mobile, and social media marketing.

11.7.1　Online marketing

1. Website

Enterprise website is two-fold, namely, marketing website and brand community website. The marketing website mainly aims to interact with consumers, encourage consumers to buy directly on the site, or further enhance their awareness of the brand, such as the official websites of major international hotel groups. Brand community website is displaying the brand content and thus focusing on the interaction with customers. Brand community sites generally provide consumers with a wealth of brand information, video, blog, activities, and other content, to establish a closer relationship with customers. The key to using websites for online direct marketing is to attract consumers to visit the site. Enterprises can drive traffic through offline print advertising or advertisements.

2. Online advertisement

As people spend extra time on the Internet, online advertisements have become an important information media. The two main forms are display advertisements and search-related advertisements. The display advertisement may appear at any time on the website when users are viewing relevant information. For example, when consumers visit the Ctrip website, various advertisements on hotels and air tickets are available. Search-related advertisements are the main forms of online advertising, accounting for over half of the online advertising share (Kotler & Armstrong, 2014). Such advertisements include the following process: enterprises buy search phrase form search engines and the cost depends on the numbers of clicks. Text or image advertisements are the primary forms of search advertising, usually appearing at the top or left and right sides of the search sites.

3. 电子邮件

电子邮件依然是在线营销的一个重要工具,特别是在智能手机逐渐成熟的今天,电子邮件收发不再局限于电脑,更有利于电子邮件营销的进一步发展。电子邮件是一种直接的营销媒介,企业可以通过发送有明确目标、个性化、能与消费者建立关系的电子邮件来传递企业的营销信息。然而,消费者日益重视个人隐私,不愿意收到大量的商业电子邮件。因此,现阶段更为合理、合法的电子邮件营销方式是授权式电子邮件营销,即企业在发送电子邮件广告前已经获得消费者同意。

4. 在线视频

随着视频网站的兴起和发展,在线视频也成为一种营销的载体。企业一般会在品牌网站、在线视频网站或者社交网站发布视频(如微博、微信、优酷、爱奇艺,国外的 Facebook、YouTube 等)。好的视频能够吸引到数以万计的消费者。例如百事可乐在 2016 年春节前发布的品牌视频《把乐带回家之猴王世家》,在腾讯视频这一平台上就已经获得超过 10 万次的播放量。由于在线视频具有快速传播、高点击率的特征,因此也经常被企业作为进行病毒营销的载体。病毒营销是一种基于网络的口碑营销,企业通过视频、在线广告或其他营销载体传播经过精心设计的营销内容,利用视频和在线广告内容丰富、快速传播的特征,吸引消费者观看广告并分享给朋友,从而使营销内容像病毒一样能够快速扩散,形成热点话题。

5. 博客及论坛

博客和论坛都是人们或企业对一个明确的话题发表意见的载体。不少企业通过发布与品牌有关的博客,与消费者群体建立联系。例如迪士尼主题公园有自己专门的博客,介绍迪士尼员工的日常工作、培训等内容。除了自己的博客以外,企业也会通过第三方的博客来推广自身的品牌。例如新西兰旅游局曾邀请意见领袖洪晃多次赴新旅游并在其博客上撰文宣传新西兰旅游。

11.7.2　搜索引擎营销

搜索引擎营销(SEM)是一种以通过增加搜索引擎结果页能被搜索引擎使用者看见的频率,或是通过搜索引擎的内容来推销网站的网络营销模式。对于搜索引擎营销专业机构的整理显示,目前主流的 SEM 包含搜索引擎优

3. E-mail

E-mail remains an important tool in online marketing. In particular, checking e-mails is no longer confined to computers, given the mature development of smart phones. Such technological progress offers a beneficial condition for further development of e-mail marketing. E-mail is a direct marketing medium. Enterprises can send a personalized marketing message to specific targets that build relationship by conveying business marketing information. Consumers are increasingly concerned of personal privacy and are unwilling to receive numerous commercial e-mails. At this stage, performing permission-based e-mail marketing is more reasonable and legitimate. That is, enterprises obtain consents from consumers before performing e-mail marketing.

4. Online video

With the emergence and development of video sites, online video has become a carrier of marketing. Enterprises put videos on brand website, online video sites, or social networking sites (e.g., Weibo, WeChat, Youku, iQIYI, and foreign sites, namely, Facebook and YouTube). Compelling videos can attract thousands of consumers, such as Pepsi broadcasting the brand video *Bring Happiness Home : The Monkey King Family* before the Chinese New Year in 2016. It recorded 100,000 views on the Tencent video sites. The widespread and high click-through rate features of online videos invite its frequent use as a carrier of viral marketing. Viral marketing is a digital version of worol-of-mouth (WOM) marketing, where enterprises deliver well-designed marketing contents through video, online advertisements, or other marketing vehicles. This marketing vehicle maximizes the rich content and widespread nature of video marketing, attracting consumers to watch and share with friends. Akin to virus, it spreads rapidly and creates a hot topic.

5. Blogs and forums

Blogs and forums are the platforms where people or enterprises express their views on a clear topic. Many enterprises release the brand-related blogs to establish contacts with consumer groups. For example, the Disney theme park has its own blog dedicated to introduce the daily work of Disney employees and training. Apart from their own blog, enterprises further promote their own brands through the third-party blog. For example, Tourism New Zealand has invited the opinion leader Hong Huang to play repeat visits to New Zealand and write on her blog to promote tourism destination.

11.7.2 Search engine marketing

Search engine marketing (SEM) is a technique to increase the search engine results page to enhance the viewing frequency of search engine users or an online marketing model promoting a

化（SEO）和关键字点击广告（PPC）（Search Engine Land，2007）。

搜索引擎优化是一种通过了解搜索引擎的运作规则来调整网站，以及提高目的网站在相关搜索引擎内排名的方式。由于搜索引擎的用户往往只会留意搜索结果最前面的几个条目，所以不少网站都希望通过各种形式来影响搜索引擎的排序，让自己的网站可以有优秀的搜索排名。搜索引擎优化中最常用的方法是关键字研究和分析，这个过程涉及两个步骤：首先相关营销人员要确保网站可以在搜索引擎中编入索引，为网站及其产品找到最相关和最受欢迎的关键字，并在网站上使用这些关键字引导搜索引擎使用者点击企业网站。然后，营销人员需要了解搜索感知影响。搜索感知影响是指品牌的搜索结果对消费者感知的识别影响，其中包括网站标题、元标记、网站索引和重点关键字。由于在线搜索通常是潜在消费者/客户行动的第一步，因此搜索感知影响会影响每个人对品牌的印象。营销人员需要通过这两个步骤对企业品牌和产品进行关键字优化，实现搜索引擎营销。搜索引擎营销对旅游目的地来说非常重要，根据 Pan（2015）的研究，出现在搜索引擎结果页面前列的旅游目的地网站能够获得更多的点击率，而点击率随着搜索引擎结果排名的下降而急剧下降。同时，此结果适用于网页搜索和移动端搜索。

关键字点击广告是一种网络广告的收费计算形式，广泛应用在搜索引擎、广告网络以及网站或博客等网络广告平台。规则是当使用者实际上点击广告以拜访广告主的网站时，广告主需要向点击广告服务商支付费用。广告主可以对企业潜在顾客可能会在搜寻时输入的关键字进行竞标。当使用者键入关键字查询与广告主的列表匹配或者检视某相关内容的网页时，该广告主投放的广告就会显示在网页上。该联结被称为"赞助联结"或者"赞助广告"。它通常出现于自然或者随机结果页的侧栏（有时位于其上）或者网管或博客主决定放于内容页的任何地方。

11.7.3　移动营销

移动营销是指企业通过移动智能设备，将营销信息、推广或其他营销内容推送给消费者（Kotler 和 Armstrong，2014）。移动智能设备和移动互联网的发展与成熟使得移动营销成为大部分企业需要重视的营销方式。根据 Expedia 对全球 1 万名旅游者的调查，旅游者在旅途中最爱携带的物件首选

website via the content of search engines. Professional search engine marketing organizations sorted out the mainstream of current SEM. It contains search engine optimization (SEO) and pay-per-click advertising (PPC) (*Search Engine Land*, 2007).

SEO is a technique of adjusting the website by understanding the operation rules of the search engine to improve the ranking of the destination sites in the search engine. Search engine users tend to focus on the first few search results. Many sites therefore want to affect the search engine orders through various means, thereby enabling excellent search ranking of their own sites. The most common approach in search engine optimization is keyword research and analysis. The process involves two steps. Relevant marketers must ensure that the site can put indexes in the search engine. It can ensure identifying the more relevant and popular keywords of the site and the products, consequently guiding the search engine users to click on the corporate website. Marketers must then understand the search perception impact. Search perception impact is the impact of a brand's search on consumer perception, including site title, meta tag, site index, and key keywords. Given that online search is frequently the first step of potential consumers, search perception impact would affect the brand impression of individuals. Marketers must go through these two steps on the corporate brand and product keyword optimization while performing search engine marketing. Search engine marketing is extremely important for tourism destinations. Pan (2015) demonstrates that destination websites appearing in the forefront of search engine results obtain substantial click-through rates. A sharp decline of the click-through rates for those destination websites came last. The findings applied to both web search and mobile search.

PPC is a form of online advertising charges widely used in search engines, advertising networks, web sites or blogs, and other online advertising platforms. The rule is that when a user actually clicks on an advertisement to visit an advertiser's website, the advertiser must pay the clicks to the advertiser. Advertisers may bid on keywords potential business customers may enter during the search. When a user types a keyword query matching the list of advertisers or views a page of relevant content, the advertiser's advertisement will appear on the page. This link calls a sponsored link or sponsored advertisement commonly appearing in the sidebar (sometimes on it) of a natural or random results page, or anywhere the webmaster or blog master decides to put it on the content page.

11.7.3　Mobile marketing

Mobile marketing refers to the delivery of marketing messages, promotions, or other marketing content to consumers through mobile smart devices (Kotler & Armstrong, 2014). Mobile smart devices, as well as the mature development of mobile internet, enable mobile marketing to become an important marketing method drawing the attention of enterprises. According to the survey of Expedia with 10,000 travelers,

是移动设备（76%）；最受旅游者欢迎的 App 前三名分别是社交媒体类（40%）、地图类（35%）、旅游类（33%）；37% 的受访者表示移动设备是出门在外获取信息的重要来源；42% 的人曾使用智能手机预订酒店；52% 的受访者表示智能手机使他们更容易冲动地做决定（品橙旅游，2016）。这些数据体现了移动设备对其旅游行为和购买决策行为的影响，因为移动设备能够在旅途中为消费者提供产品信息、价格对比、其他顾客评论、电子优惠券、即时预订等功能。

通过移动营销，企业能够实现许多营销目的，比如鼓励实时购买或预订、提供更为方便的购买体验、提高消费者对品牌的体验等。在消费者的购买过程中，移动营销能提供品牌或产品信息、奖励或其他更好的产品选择。因此，企业要重视在移动营销方面的投入。根据普华永道（PwC）发布的《2016 年至 2020 年全球娱乐及传媒展望报告》，2015 年中国互联网广告收入为 232 亿美元，仅次于美国。但其中的移动终端广告收入仅占中国互联网广告总收入的 10.6%，显著低于全球平均水平（26.0%）（财新网，2016）。

11.7.4　社交媒体营销

社交媒体是一个独立的或商业性的在线社区，人们可以聚集在一起社交，相互交流看法和信息（Kotler 和 Armstrong，2014）。如国内的微博、微信、人人网，国外的 Facebook、Google＋、Twitter、Instagram 等都是社交媒体。接近 90% 的美国企业都在使用社交媒体作为它们营销组合的一部分（Kotler 和 Armstrong，2014）。

1. 使用社交媒体

市场营销人员可以从两个方面利用社交媒体，即在现有的社交媒体上建立企业或品牌的账号或者建立自己特有的社交媒体。在现有的社交媒体上建立企业或品牌账号是较为普遍的做法，因为现有社交媒体都已经有一定数量的用户。微博 2015 年的月度活跃用户数量为 23600 万（微博，2016），微信 2015 年的月度活跃用户数量为 69700 万（腾讯，2016）。大量的社交媒体用户能够让企业从中挑选潜在顾客，企业通过在社交媒体上发送合适的营销信息，吸引这些潜在顾客关注企业，并与企业建立联系。万豪、希尔顿、洲际等知名国际酒店集团都在微博上建立了集团或品牌账号。

the top item of travelers to carry with is the mobile device (76%). The top three most popular applications are social media (40%), map (35%), and tourism (33%). 37% of respondents expressed that mobile devices were an important source of information when travelling; 42% used smartphones to book hotel accommodations; 52% signified that smartphones easily compelled them to make impulsive decisions (Orange Travel, 2016). These findings reflect the influence of mobile devices on travelers' and purchase behaviors because mobile devices provide consumers with on-the-go product information, price comparisons, other customer reviews, electronic coupons, instant subscriptions, and more.

Through mobile marketing, enterprises can achieve many marketing purposes. Encouraging real-time purchase or booking, providing a convenient purchase experience, and improving the consumer experience of the brand are examples. During purchase, mobile marketing can provide brand or product information, incentives, or other better product selection. Therefore, enterprises should focus on investing in mobile marketing. According to *The Global Entertainment and Media Outlook 2016—2020* launched by PricewaterhouseCoopers, the Internet advertising revenue in China was USD23.2 billion in 2015 as the first-runner up after the United States. However, the revenue of mobile advertising only accounted for 10.6% of the country's total Internet advertising revenue, which was significantly lower than the global average (26.0%) (CaiXin, 2016).

11.7.4　Social media marketing

Social media pertain to an independent or commercial online community where people socialize and exchange ideas and information (Kotler & Armstrong, 2014). The domestic sites, namely, Weibo, WeChat, and Renren, as well as foreign sites, such as Facebook, Google+, Twitter, and Instagram are examples of social media sites. Nearly 90% of the US businesses are using social media as part of their marketing mix (Kotler & Armstrong, 2014).

1. Using social media

Marketers can maximize social media through two methods, namely, building an account for a business or brand on an existing social media or building their own unique social media account. Establishing a business or brand account on an existing social media is a relatively common practice, given that existing social media previously owns a certain number of users. In 2015, Weibo recorded 236 million monthly active users (Weibo, 2016). As for WeChat, the number of monthly active users was 697 million (Tencent, 2016). Massive numbers of social media users enable enterprises to select potential customers. Enterprises send appropriate marketing information to attract potential customers and establish contact with them on social media. Marriott, Hilton, Intercontinental, and other well-known international hotel groups own group or brand

除了在现有社交媒体建立账号,也有企业建立了自己特有的社交媒体。针对越来越多的社交媒体用户都喜欢跑步这一特点,耐克(Nike)建立了自己的跑步喜爱者社交媒体 Nike＋。Nike＋有 2000 万的用户,每月跑步距离超过 10 亿英里(1 英里＝1.609 公里)。由于 Nike＋在跑步爱好者中取得了成功,耐克将这个社交媒体应用至篮球方面(Nike,2013)。

2. 社交媒体的营销作用

社交媒体在营销方面的积极作用主要有四个方面:(1) 分享与联系,这是社交媒体最大的优点,企业能够利用社交媒体与潜在顾客进行沟通交流,从而建立联系,让潜在顾客能够了解更多的品牌知识。(2) 互动,企业通过制造话题与顾客交流,并了解顾客对品牌或产品的反馈。(3) 即时性与及时信息,社交媒体的不断发展使得企业能够与消费者在一定情况下进行实时的互动,例如企业在举办活动时,以及活动结束后向社交媒体的用户发布与活动相关的营销内容。(4) 高成本效益,企业在社交媒体上发布的内容和消息可以由内部市场营销人员进行设计,也可以外包给营销代理进行管理,企业能够根据自己的预算自由选择。此外,当社交媒体上的营销内容被大量转发,形成热点话题时,企业的品牌知名度会得到大幅提高,其销售额也会得到相应的增加,企业在社交媒体上的投资将获得很高的回报率。

除了积极作用外,营销人员也应该了解社交媒体在营销方面的缺点。首先,许多企业其实并不具备利用社交媒体的知识、技能或人力资源,此时企业在社交媒体方面的投资将不能发挥最大的效果。其次,社交媒体的主导权在用户而非企业,因此市场营销人员不能只是简单地将品牌或产品推给社交媒体用户,而要通过有效的方式让企业的品牌或产品成为他们日常在社交媒体中互动的话题。

3. 整合社交媒体营销

利用社交媒体进行营销并不只是发布品牌或产品信息,企业需要根据自身的营销战略,选择合适的策略和其他要素,将社交媒体打造为实现营销战略的重要部分。成功利用社交媒体的企业会同时利用社交媒体和其他媒体(如传统媒体、在线营销媒介等),在互联网上创造一个与品牌相关的,可以进行分享、互动的顾客社区。

整合社交媒体营销的一个关键是管理社交媒体账号,这也是工作量最大

accounts on Weibo.

Apart from owning an account on existing social media, some enterprises establish their own unique social media account. As an increasing number of millennial social media users develop interest in running, Nike builds their own runners social media Nike + . Nike + has 20 million users, running over billion miles per month. As Nike + gained success among running enthusiasts, Nike expands this social media account to basketball (Nike, 2013).

2. Marketing role of social media

Social media in marketing take up the proactive role in the four following main aspects: (1) Sharing and contact: These aspects are the biggest advantages of social media. Enterprises can utilize social media to communicate with potential customers to establish contact. Potential customers can understand other brand knowledge. (2) Interaction: Enterprises create topics to communicate with customers and obtain their feedback to the brand or products. (3) Real-time and timely information: The continuous development of social media allows enterprises and consumers to establish real-time interactions under certain circumstances, such as posing marketing-related activities during and after events on social media. (4) Cost effectiveness: The content and messages posted on social media can be designed by internal marketers or outsourced to marketing agencies. Enterprises are free to choose, depending on the budgets. In addition, brand awareness has substantially increased when the marketing content on social media has been significantly shared. The sales manifest a corresponding increase, and the investment on social media yields a high return of investment.

Apart from the positive effects, marketers should also understand the marketing shortcomings of social media. First, many enterprises do not have the knowledge, skills, or human resources to utilize social media. Investment in social media cannot achieve maximum effect. Second, the leading power on social media lies on the hand of users rather than the enterprises. Marketers cannot simply present the brands or products to users. Instead, they should utilize effective strategies in establishing their brands or products to users as interactive topics on social media.

3. Integration of social media marketing

Using social media marketing not only aims to release brand or product information. Enterprises must elect the appropriate strategies and other essential elements according to their marketing strategy, aiding in making social media an important part of the marketing strategy. Enterprises successfully employing social media will further utilize the social media and other media (e.g., traditional media and online marketing media) to create a brand-related, shareable, and interactive customer community on the Internet.

A key to integrate social media marketing is managing the social media accounts,

的一部分。一般而言,国际酒店集团在集团层面上都会有一位数字营销副总裁(总监)为集团旗下所有品牌和酒店制定数字营销战略,而酒店层面的社交媒体则由数字营销经理专门进行管理。一般来说,数字营销经理需要同时管理一个微信公众号、三个与酒店相关的微博(酒店、餐厅、水疗或健身中心)、酒店官网、OTA 上的评论、猫途鹰(TripAdvisor)、优酷等 8 个网站和社交媒体上的内容。如果酒店也在国外的社交媒体上开通了酒店的账号,需要管理的网站和社交媒体会增加至 18～20 个。与此同时,市场营销人员还要针对这些网站和社交媒体上用户的特征,设计不同的营销内容和传播风格,并决定将主要的浏览量引导至哪个网站或社交媒体上。因此,整合社交媒体营销需要企业管理层重点关注。

到访洛杉矶的中国游客数量从 2005 年以来增长了 523%,其中一个重要的原因是洛杉矶旅游局利用整合社交媒体营销对洛杉矶旅游进行了宣传。2014 年,洛杉矶旅游局借助"市长中国行"活动,全程引入社交媒体营销手段,有效唤起读者对"发现洛杉矶"的主动诉求,从而对"发现洛杉矶"旅游主题实现更深一层的营销和推广,取得了显著的效果(品橙旅游,2015)。

洛杉矶市长在中国摒弃了以往以新闻通稿形式见诸媒体的做法,取而代之的是利用实时、高效、互动的新媒体将活动展现在公众面前。从 2014 年 11 月 14 日开始,洛杉矶旅游局就通过官方微信发布了"洛杉矶市长将展开为期 8 天的中国之行"的消息,作为活动的预热。在随后的行程中,一方面通过官方微信直播市长每天的行程,植入目的地资讯,一方面通过极富吸引力的抽奖活动,吸引粉丝的持续关注、参与和传播,建立内在的情感联系,充分发挥微信、微博等平台各自的媒体属性和优势,有效对接了作为中国新游客主力军的 80、90 后群体,实现了营销效果的最大化。从量化角度分析,在 2016 年 11 月 15—23 日的 8 天直播期间,洛杉矶旅游局的微信官方账号累计发送 13 条视频和图文信息,其微博账号新增粉丝 440 人。

除此以外,洛杉矶市长在访华期间,曾携手优酷土豆集团董事长兼 CEO 古永锵录制《老友记》特别节目,截至 2017 年 1 月 9 日,相关视频的点击量已经超过 30 万。而在线下,洛杉矶旅游局以市长访华为契机,联合蚂蜂窝和国贸商城,推出了"来国贸,看世界之洛杉矶"的主题宣传月活动,现代与传统并行,对洛杉矶目的地品牌形象的树立和品牌影响的持续发酵产生了积极的推动作用。

which is the biggest part of the workload. In general, the international hotel groups assign a digital marketing vice president (director) at the group level to develop digital marketing strategy for all brands and hotels. At hotel-level, the digital marketing managers especially manage social media. Generally speaking, digital marketing managers must simultaneously manage the contents on eight social media sites, including the public account of WeChat, three hotel-related Weibo (hotel, restaurants, spa, or fitness center), official website of hotel, OTA comments, TripAdvisor, and Youku. If hotels have accounts on foreign social media sites, then the number of social media requiring management may increase to 18 ~ 20. Marketers must design different marketing contents and communication styles for the features of users on these social media accounts. Furthermore, they must decide in directing the main views to preferred sites or social media accounts. Integrating social media marketing is therefore a focus on business management.

The number of Chinese tourists visiting Los Angeles has increased by 523% since 2005. One of the important reasons is that Los Angeles Tourism Bureau used the integrated social media marketing to promote tourism in the city. In 2014, the Los Angeles Tourism Board fully introduced social media marketing with the "Mayor's visit to China"; the activity effectively aroused the interests of the readers of "Discover Los Angeles". The tourism theme "Discover Los Angeles" achieved a deeper marketing and promotion as well as yielded remarkable results (Orange Tourism, 2015).

During the visit in China, the Mayor of Los Angeles abandoned the form of news release for media. Instead, a real-time, effective, and interactive new media showing to the public replaced the original form. Since 14 November 2014, the Los Angeles Tourism Board released the "Los Angeles Mayor starting an eight-day trip to China" as warm-up activities through the official WeChat account. In the subsequent itinerary, the official WeChat account live-broadcasted the daily itinerary, implanted the destination information, and attracted continuous attention, participation, and dissemination of fans through highly attractive sweepstakes. These broadcasted activities established emotional links and maximized the use of WeChat and Weibo. Thus, this broadcasting format was effective in maximizing the marketing effect to the main tourist groups in China, the Post-80s and Post-90s. From a quantitative perspective, during the eight-day live broadcast from 15—23 November, the official WeChat account of Los Angeles Tourism & Convention Board sent 13 videos and graphic information. A total of 440 fans were added to the Weibo account.

In addition, the visit of the mayor of Los Angeles featured Gu Yongqiang, the Chairman and CEO of Youku Tudou during the special program of *Friends*. The video has reached 300, 000 views since January 9 as of this year. The Los Angeles Tourism & Convention Board captured the mayor's visit as an opportunity, jointly operating a thematic publicity activity "Going to China World Mall for the World's Los Angeles" with Mafengwo and China World Mall. The publicity advocates the co-existence of both the traditional and modern forms,

2015 年 5 月份洛杉矶旅游局携手李健通过优酷平台制作并播出了《电影带你去旅行》的 6 集系列宣传片,截至 2015 年 8 月,6 集视频总播放量接近 1400 万次,单集播放量都超过 300 万次,让中国消费者通过李健在洛杉矶的体验和视角从各方面深入了解这座天使之城。这在目的地营销上又是一个创新和突破。

enabling the impetus and brand image of Los Angeles as a tourism destination.

In May 2015, the Los Angeles Tourism & Convention Board, together with Li Jian, produced and broadcasted a series of six promotional videos titled, *Travel with Movies* on the Youku platform. As of August 2015, the six videos reached approximately 14 million views. The views of a single video exceeded 300 million. Chinese consumers gained an in-depth understanding of the City of Angels from the experience and lens of Li Jian. Such phenomenon was an innovation and breakthrough in destination marketing.

第 12 章　营销规划及营销绩效评估

 **本章要点**

- 战略营销规划
- 战术营销规划
- 营销绩效评估

市场营销规划是对市场营销活动的一个整体规划,用于指导和协调市场营销活动,并作为最终评估的依据,是市场营销中的核心部分。市场需求和竞争环境的持续变化使得企业每年都需要为下一年制订营销规划。市场营销规划分为两个层次,即战略营销规划和战术营销规划。战略营销规划关注对市场机会的分析,并根据目标市场的特征设定企业所提供的能满足顾客感知价值的产品。战术营销规划用于确定市场营销的策略,包括产品特征、推广与产品销售、价格、销售渠道以及服务。

12.1　战略营销规划

一般而言,企业按年度制订整体的营销规划。年度营销规划必须体现企业的战略方向,同时为企业其他具体的运营计划提供参考。

营销规划一般包括以下内容:执行摘要、企业内部关系协调、定位说明、内外部环境分析及预测、市场细分和目标确定、营销战略制定及预算、行动计划、资源分配、实施与控制。

1. 执行摘要

执行摘要是对营销目的、市场分析、营销战略、营销成果的简要概括,方便高层管理人员对营销规划有整体的了解。执行摘要的撰写应该:

Chapter 12   Marketing Planning and Marketing Performance Evaluation

 ## Key points of the chapter

- ■ Strategic marketing planning
- ■ Tactical marketing planning
- ■ Marketing performance evaluation

Marketing planning is the integral planning of marketing activities; it guides and coordinates the activities. Marketing planning serves as the basis of the final evaluation and the core part of marketing. Market demand, along with the changing competitive environment, drive companies to develop marketing plans for the following year. Marketing planning features two levels, namely, strategic and tactical marketing planning. Strategic marketing planning concerns the analysis of opportunities in the market and the design of products that can meet the perceived values of target customers. Tactical marketing planning determines the marketing strategy, including product characteristics, promotion and product sales, pricing, sales channels, and services.

12.1 *Strategic Marketing Planning*

Enterprises develop marketing plan on annual basis. The marketing plan must reflect the strategic direction of enterprises and provide references for other specific business plans.

Marketing planning involves the following steps: drafting of executive summary, internal coordination of enterprise; positioning, analysis and forecasting of internal and external environments, market segmentation and goal determination, formulation and budgeting of strategic marketing planning, action plan; resource allocation, implementation and control.

1. Drafting of executive summary

Executive summary is a brief summary of marketing objectives, market analysis, marketing strategies, and marketing targets to facilitate the understanding of senior management about the marketing plan. The executive summary should

- ● be concise;

- 简洁明了；

- 使用短句和短的段落；

- 使用数字呈现下一年的营销目标,简要介绍营销战略以及各季度目标；

- 介绍营销活动所需要的成本。

2. 企业内部关系协调

营销规划并不是一个单独实施的战略工具,成功的营销规划能够支持企业其他的战略决策,包括企业的利润目标、增长目标、期望达到的市场份额、企业或产品线的定位、纵向或横向合并、战略联盟、产品线的广度和深度、和顾客关系管理。因此,企业在制订营销规划时,需要充分考虑营销规划与其他部门之间的联系,以及如何将其与企业的战略目标相结合。管理层可以邀请不同部门的管理者参与营销规划的制订,增加相关部门间的了解,减少营销规划在执行过程中的摩擦和冲突。一般而言,运营和财务是两个与营销有密切关系的部门。

3. 定位说明

营销规划需要对企业进行定位说明,阐述企业的目标市场,以及企业如何在市场中脱颖而出,其作用是为营销规划中的其他内容奠定方向。例如,一家小型度假酒店的定位说明是"为个人、情侣和家庭提供个性化的度假服务",而大型度假酒店则是在上述的基础上增加企业会议、奖励旅游等范畴。

4. 内外部环境分析及预测

外部环境主要包括宏观环境的分析和市场环境分析。市场环境分析主要是对相关的市场数据(销售收入、成本、市场情况、竞争对手及其他相关因素)进行解读。SWOT 分析是企业进行市场环境分析的主要工具之一,分析重点主要集中在企业所面对的外部机会与威胁,以及内部的优势和劣势。SWOT 分析的结果是企业确定进入哪个目标市场、采用哪种产品、经营何种业务的一种依据。市场环境的信息内容包括:(1) 整体市场情况(如市场整体客房供给、市场整体入住率、游客接待数量等);(2) 行业信息(行业发展分析报告、旅游景区接待人数统计、旅游业收入等);(3) 企业所在地区市场信息(就业率、新企业数量、在建工程数量、交通设施等);(4) 企业所在社区信息(当地历史、文化传统、政治环境、人口统计等)(徐惠群,2009)。

- use short sentences and short paragraphs;
- present the marketing objectives of the following year in numeric formats, with a brief overview of the marketing strategies and quarterly goals; and
- describe the cost of marketing activities.

2. Internal coordination of enterprise

Marketing planning is not an independent strategic tool. A successful marketing planning should support other strategic decisions of an enterprise, including profit targets, growth targets, targeted market share, enterprise or product line positioning, vertical or horizontal integration, strategic alliance, product line breadth and depth, and customer relationship management. Enterprises, therefore, must fully consider the connection between marketing plans and other departments, as well as the integration of the organizational strategic goals, when developing the marketing plan. Management can invite various department heads to partake in marketing planning to enhance understanding between relevant departments and reduce the friction and conflict during implementation. Operations and finance departments are closely related to the marketing department.

3. Positioning

Marketing planning should clearly illustrate the position of the company by elaborating the target market and the manner in which companies can stand out in the market. Positioning determines the direction of the remaining content in the marketing plan. For instance, the positioning of a small-scale resort hotel is to provide individuals, couples, and families with personalized vacation services, whereas a large-scale resort hotel also offer corporate meetings and incentive travel.

4. Analysis and forecasting of internal and external environments

The external environment involves macro and market environment analyses. Market environment analysis is the interpretation of market data (sales revenue, cost, market conditions, competitors, and other related factors). SWOT analysis is one of the main tools used by enterprises to conduct market environment analysis. The analysis focuses on the external opportunities and threats faced by enterprises as along with internal advantages and disadvantages. The outcomes of SWOT analysis inform the entry to particular target markets and the types of products and businesses. Information on the market environment includes (1) overall market condition (e.g., room supply, occupancy rate, and visitor arrivals), (2) industry information (analysis report on industry development, visitor arrivals at attractions, and number of visitors), (3) local market information (employment rate, number of new establishments, number of projects under construction, and transportation facilities), and (4) community information (local history, cultural traditions, political environment, and demographic profiles) (Hsu, 2009).

除了整体市场环境外,消费者群体也是企业需要关注的市场环境因素,企业必须清楚现有消费者群体的来源、人口统计特征(心理统计特征或行为统计特征)、产品和服务需求、期望价值等影响企业营销决策的要素。另外,企业的产品和服务也受到消费者的使用状态(如购买时机、频率、目的等)影响。竞争对手情况是企业进行市场环境分析时不能忽略的一个关键因素。竞争对手一般分为直接和间接竞争者。直接竞争者是指与企业有相同目标市场,并提供相同或相似产品或服务的企业;间接竞争者是指其产品或服务能够对企业现有的产品有替代作用的其他企业(徐惠群,2009)。企业在对竞争对手进行分析时,需要列出直接竞争者和间接竞争者,并对直接竞争者进行详细的描述,包括其竞争优势、劣势、市场份额、市场营销策略等。企业内其他职能部门会影响企业营销战略的实施和效果。因此,在制定营销战略时,需要对企业内部所有职能部门的角色、工作内容、表现等方面的优势和劣势进行分析和评估。

企业内部各职能部门的优势和劣势对于企业的营销目标有着不同的影响,因而有着不同的重要性。另外,企业难以同时增强所有的优势,也难以一次性改进所有劣势,所以也需要对优势和劣势进行重要性排序。重要性—绩效分析就是帮助企业进行优势和劣势重要性排序的一种工具(如图 12-1 所示)。

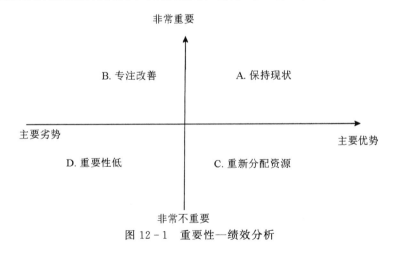

图 12-1　重要性—绩效分析

5. 市场细分和目标确定

分析可进入的细分市场和选择合适的目标顾客群体是营销计划中的核心。细分市场的选择受三大因素影响:(1) 企业的现状及愿景;(2) 市场分析;

In addition to overall market environment, enterprises should pay attention to consumer group. Companies must understand several determinants of marketing decision, such as the source of existing consumer sources, demographic characteristics (psychological or behavioral characteristics), product and service requirements, and expected value. The products and services of companies are also affected by consumer status (such as the timing, frequency, and purposes of consumption). Enterprises should not overlook the competitor situation when conducting market environment analysis. Competitors are divided into direct and indirect. Direct competitors refer to enterprises sharing the same target market and providing the same or similar products or services; indirect competitors are other enterprises whose products or services are substitutes of the existing products of enterprises (Hus, 2009). In analyzing competitors, enterprises should list both direct and indirect competitors. Detailed descriptions of direct competitors is also necessary; their competitive advantages, disadvantages, market share, and marketing strategy should be noted. Other departments within enterprises affect the implementation and effectiveness of corporate marketing strategies. The advantages and disadvantages of respective departmental roles, work content, and performance should be evaluated during the development of marketing strategies.

The advantages and disadvantages of various departments within the enterprise exert different effects on the marketing objectives of enterprises, and thus bear varying importance levels. In addition, enterprises can hardly enhance all advantages and improve all disadvantages at the same time. The importance level of advantages and disadvantages must be ranked. Importance-performance analysis is one of the tools that help companies prioritize their strengths andweaknesses(Figure 12 - 1).

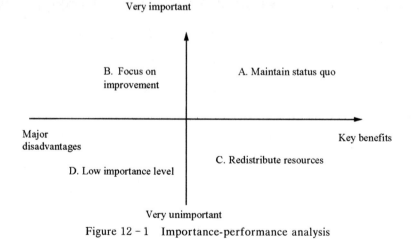

Figure 12 - 1　Importance-performance analysis

5. Market segmentation and goal determination

Analyzing the market segments that can be entered and selecting the right target audience are at the core of the marketing plan. Selecting market segment is influenced by three factors, that is, (1) the current situation and vision of the enterprise, (2) market

（3）企业是否有足够的能力和资源进入相应的细分市场。选择不合适的细分市场会浪费企业资源，影响企业的收入和增长，进而影响企业的长期发展。

在选择细分市场后，企业需要选择细分市场中合适的顾客群体作为目标顾客。企业习惯根据过往经验来选择目标顾客群体。然而，不同目标顾客群体的重要性会随着市场的变化而发生改变。一些顾客群体会逐渐消失，而一些新的顾客群体会开始出现，甚至是成为非常重要的生意来源。因此，企业需要利用所拥有的信息，重新审视目标顾客群体，调整企业的发展方向和业务范围。

营销计划目标与企业愿景相比更为具体，一般而言，营销计划的目标主要涉及企业的增长率、利润率以及其他主要运营数据（比如入住率、平均房价等）。企业可以通过 SMART 法则制定一个清晰的营销目标。

- S——明确的；
- M——可衡量的；
- A——可实现的；
- R——与企业战略相关的；
- T——时限性。

6. 营销战略的制定及预算

营销战略是实现营销计划目标的工具，其内容包括：广告与推广、销售与分销、产品与定价。内容中的每一部分都需要体现企业的营销目标，符合企业的实际需求。盲目跟随或采用行业平均数据并不能满足企业在营销方面的需要。

（1）广告与推广战略：在理想的情况下，在制定广告与推广战略时应该由企业的管理层与外部专业人士一同研究企业的营销规划目标，通过讨论的方式得出最符合企业预算和时间安排的策略。随后，企业营销人员根据策略，选择最适合的广告与推广组合。例如，是选择平面广告、电视广告，还是在线广告；是企业自己单独进行推广，还是联合其他企业一起进行推广（如喜达屋与优步的联合营销）。

（2）销售与分销战略：销售战略着重于体现企业向哪个目标销售群体进行销售，并通过何种方式实现企业的营销目标。例如，酒店的销售部门每年都会分析明年的重点协议客户的销售情况（房晚数、宴会举办次数、总收入等），评估其在未来的增长情况，有什么样的措施可以保持与这些客户的关系。

analysis, and (3) the capacity and resources to enter the corresponding market segments. Selecting inappropriate market segments will waste business resources and affect business income and growth, thereby disrupting the long-term development of enterprises.

After choosing market segments, companies should select appropriate market segments as target customers. Enterprises are accustomed to selecting target customers based on past experience, but the importance level of different target customer groups changes with the market. Some customer groups gradually disappear, and new customer groups emerge or even become important sources of business. Enterprises, therefore, should use the marketing information to re-examine target customer groups and adjust the direction and scope of businesses.

The goal of the marketing plan is more specific than the corporate vision. The goal primarily concerns the growth rate, profit rate, and other key operational data (e.g., occupancy and average room rates). Companies can develop a clear marketing goal through the SMART rule.

- Specific
- Measurable
- Attainable
- Relevant
- Time-based

6. Formulation and budgeting of marketing strategy

Marketing strategy is a tool for achieving the goals of a marketing plan. It includes advertising and promotion, sales and distribution, product and pricing strategies. Each component must be in line with the marketing objective and actual needs of enterprises. Being a blind follower or using industry average data cannot cater the needs of enterprises in marketing.

(1) Advertising and promotion strategies: Ideally, to formulate advertising and promotion strategies, the management of enterprises and external professionals should study the enterprise's marketing planning objectives as well as discuss the formula that best suits the budget and schedule of the company. Subsequently, corporate marketing staff selects the most suitable combination of advertising and promotion based on the marketing strategy, such as the printed advertisements, advertisements on televisions, or online advertising. Another consideration is conducting the promotion alone or in conjunction with other enterprises for promotional activities (e.g., the joint marketing effort by Starwood and Uber).

(2) Sales and distribution strategies: Sales strategy focuses on which target sales groups and in what ways to achieve the marketing objectives of enterprises. For example, the sales department in hotels analyzes the sales condition of key accounts in the following years (room nights, number of events, and total revenue) and evaluates the

同时,酒店也会了解未来有哪些新的客户可以挖掘,用什么样的方式能够争取这些客户到酒店进行消费。分销战略则是如何选择合适的分销渠道,使得企业能够以最合理的分销成本获得最大的收益。例如,酒店未来的分销渠道份额怎么进行分配,是增加自有渠道的销售比例,还是维持现状。

（3）产品策略:产品策略主要与市场环境和企业的营销目标相关,市场营销人员需要根据市场变化决定如何进行产品改进或创造新产品,比如现在许多酒店推出的亲子客房。能满足市场需求的产品能够显著地帮助企业获得额外的收入。因此,企业在制定产品策略时,需要首先了解自身有多少不同的产品种类,这些产品种类对应的是何种市场需求。随后,企业再针对细分市场或者目标顾客群体中出现的新的需求,决定是否提供新的产品种类。

（4）定价策略:定价策略同样也是企业营销规划中的一个重要部分,价格的高低会影响企业的收入、产品的销售和推广。在酒店行业中,大部分国际酒店管理集团已经将定价的工作分配到收益管理部门,销售经理或者市场营销经理在制定营销策划或者进行产品推广时,都需要与收益管理部门进行沟通。

制定营销战略以后,企业需要对营销战略进行评估,预算就是评估的其中一个标准。制定预算需要遵循以下的原则:

- 预算必须基于企业下一年度（季度）的目标;
- 预算必须是部门和员工个人都要达成的收入预算;
- 预算是可实现的;
- 预算需要细分,比如说每个销售人员每周需要完成的业务量;
- 预算能够被理解,而且是可衡量的。

7. 行动计划

对各种营销策略的实施制定详细的行动方案,即阐述以下问题:

- 将做什么
- 何时开始
- 何时完成
- 谁来做
- 成本是多少

整个行动计划必须具体、明确、可衡量、可实现。制订行动计划应该以结

future growth and measures in maintaining relationship with these customers. Hotels also explore potential new customers in the future and how to attract them to their services. The distribution strategy pertains to choosing the right distribution channels, thus allowing enterprises to maximize the profits with the most reasonable distribution costs. For example, the allocation of shares among future distribution channels of hotels can increase the channel sales ratio or maintain the status quo.

(3) Product strategies: Product strategies are related to the market environment and sales targets of enterprises. Markets must improve existing products or create new products depending on the market changes, such as the family rooms offered by hotels. Products that meet the needs of the market can significantly help companies to obtain additional revenue. When planning for product strategies, enterprises need to first understand the different types of products and their corresponding market demands. Subsequently, enterprises should consider the new demands of segments or target customer groups to determine the provision of a new product category.

(4) Pricing strategies: Pricing strategies are also important to marketing planning. Price level affects the profits, product sales, and promotion of enterprises. In the hotel industry, the majority of the international hotel management groups assigns the pricing work to the revenue management department (i.e., yield management department). Sales or marketing managers are required to communicate with the yield management department when developing marketing strategies or promoting products.

After developing marketing strategies, companies should evaluate them. Budget is one of the assessment criteria. The following principles apply to budgeting:

- The budget must be based on the objectives of the enterprise in the following year (quarter).
- Performance targets for individual departments and employees are detailed.
- The budget should be feasible.
- The budget must be broken down, e.g., the amount of business that each salesperson needs to complete each week.
- The budget should be clear and measurable.

7. Action plan

Action plan details the implementation of various marketing strategies. It describes the following issues:

- What will be done
- When to start
- When to complete
- Who does it
- What is the cost

The entire action plan must be specific, measurable, and attainable. The action plan

果为导向,各项活动都要有明确的起止时间,市场营销人员可以通过列表加以说明,表中具体说明每一时期应执行和完成的活动时间安排、任务要求和费用开支等,使整个营销战略落实于行动,并能循序渐进地贯彻执行。

8. 资源分配

财务资源分配包括销售预测、费用预测和收支平衡分析。在销售预测部分,需要进行每月整体销售预测和产品类别销售预测;在费用预测部分,需要对营销活动的成本做出分析,并将成本细分至相应的产品类别。收支平衡分析主要确定企业每月需要达到多少的销售量才能抵消固定成本和相应的变动成本。另外,人力也是营销活动中的重要资源。因此,营销人员在制订营销规划时,需要慎重考虑整个规划实施过程中所需要的人员数量,是否需要进行培训,以及与招聘及培训相关的成本。

9. 实施与控制

在实施与控制部分,产品或服务负责人需要明确营销规划的实施过程,包括每个月或每个季度所要达到的目标和相应的财务预算。除此以外,在营销规划实施的过程中,企业营销人员需要根据企业现状、市场环境等因素,每个月或每个季度对销售额和成本进行预测,并将实际结果、预测、预算三者进行对比。在此基础上,管理层可以监测每个时间段的成果,并在必要时对规划或实施过程进行调整。一些企业还会制订应急计划,以应对特定的环境变化,如价格战或罢工等。

12.2　战术营销规划

战术营销规划是指企业在决定了目标市场、市场定位后,对企业可以控制的营销手段进行的组合或策划。即企业在确定做什么的情况下,决定如何做的问题,其中包括产品、价格、销售渠道等要素。战术营销规划是战略营销规划的具体化,企业会针对不同的产品和细分市场,制定相应的战术营销规划。4P 理论(产品、价格、促销推广、渠道)(McCarthy,1975)是企业常用的战术营销规划。

12.2.1　产品策划

企业要靠产品去满足消费者和用户的需要和欲望,占领市场。产品是企业市场营销组合中最重要的一种手段,是企业决定其价格、分销和促销手段

should be result-oriented, with the starting and ending times of all activities clearly indicated. Marketers should tabulate the timetables, mission requirements, and expenses of activities at different phases. Action plan facilitates the step-by-step implementation of all marketing strategies.

8. Resource allocation

The allocation of financial resources includes sales forecasting, cost forecasting, and breakeven analysis. Monthly and product category sales forecasts are required in sales forecasting. The cost of the marketing campaign should be analyzed for cost forecasting. The breakdown of costs into corresponding product categories is needed in breakeven analysis. Breakeven analysis primarily determines how much sales a company needs to meet each month to offset fixed costs and the corresponding variable costs. Manpower is also an important resource in marketing activities. Therefore, marketers must carefully consider the number of people required in implementing the program, the need for training, and the costs associated with hiring and training.

9. Implementation and control

In implementation and control, the person responsible for the product or service should clarify the implementation of the marketing plan. This part includes the monthly and quarterly goals and corresponding financial budgets. During the implementation of marketing plan, marketers must forecast the monthly and quarterly sales and costs on the basis of business conditions and market environments. The actual results, forecasts, and budget should be compared. Using the comparison as basis, management can monitor the periodic results and, if necessary, adjust the planning or implementation. Some enterprises also develop contingency plans to respond to the specific environmental changes, such as price wars or strikes.

12.2 Tactical Marketing Planning

In tactical marketing planning, enterprises control the combination and planning of marketing strategies after determining the target markets and positioning. Enterprises determine what to do and how, including the elements of product, price, and distribution channels. Tactical marketing planning is the embodiment of strategic marketing planning. Enterprises establish corresponding tactical marketing plans for different products and market segments. The commonly used tactical business plan for enterprises is 4P theory (product, price, promotion, and place) (McCarthy, 1975).

12.2.1 Product planning

Enterprises rely on products to meet the needs and desires of consumers and users to capture the market. Products are the most important means of an enterprise's marketing

的基础。战术营销规划中的产品策划是基于战略营销规划中产品策略而来的,着重于如何实现产品策略。产品策划是指企业从产品开发、上市、销售至报废的全过程的活动及方案。产品策划也可称为商品企划。产品策划从类型上说,包括新产品开发、旧产品的改良和新用途的拓展等三方面的内容;从现代营销观点上说,其过程和内容应包括产品创意、可行性评价、产品开发设计、产品营销设计、产品目标等方面的策划。

12.2.2　价格策划

价格是市场营销组合中最重要的因素之一,是企业完成其市场营销目标的有效工具。价格策划就是企业产品在进入市场过程中如何利用价格因素来争取进入目标市场,进而渗透甚至占领目标市场,以及为达到营销目标而制定相应的价格策略的一系列活动及方案、措施。企业在产品进入阶段、渗透阶段和占领阶段应采用不同的价格策略。企业能否正确地运用价格杠杆策划与实施有效的价格策略,关系到企业营销的成败及其经济效益。

12.2.3　促销推广策划

促销推广策划主要是指如何对产品进行营销传播,包括广告、公关、直销和促销活动。在进行促销推广策划时,营销人员需要确定促销推广使用的信息策略、媒体策略和媒体传播频率。信息策略即传播什么样的产品信息;媒体策略是指企业选择什么样的媒体,如何接触目标顾客群体;媒体传播频率指企业多长时间传播一次产品信息。

12.2.4　分销渠道策划

产品要经过一定的方式、方法和路线才能进入消费者和用户手中,分销便是企业使其产品由生产地点向销售地点运动的过程。在这个过程中,企业要进行一系列活动策划。产品的进入期、渗透期和占有期有不同特点,企划策略也有所差别。在进入阶段的分销渠道策划中,企业首先选择某一细分市场,如以某一地区市场作为突破口,选择特定的经销商,在地区市场分销渠道的基础上进一步渗透到其他地区市场。在渗透阶段的分销渠道策划中,随着

mix and the basis for the enterprise to determine price, distribution, and promotion. Product planning is based on the product strategy derived from strategic marketing planning, and it focuses on how to achieve product strategy. Product planning refers to all activities and programs ranging from product development, marketing, and sales to disposal. Also known as commodity planning, product planning includes the development of new products, improvement of old products, and development of new functions. From a modern marketing perspective, the process and content should incorporate the planning aspects, such as product innovation, feasibility study, product development and design, product marketing design, and product targets.

12.2.2　Price planning

Price is one of the most important factors in marketing mix, and it is an effective tool for the enterprise to fulfill its marketing objectives. Price planning determines how to use the price factor for products to enter the target markets and, consequently, penetrate and even dominate these markets. This type of planning involves a series of activities, programs, and measures to develop the corresponding pricing strategy for achieving marketing objectives. Enterprises adopt different pricing strategies at the product entry, penetration, and domination stages. The appropriate use of prices in leveraging the planning and implementation of effective pricing strategies is related to the success and economic benefits of enterprise marketing.

12.2.3　Promotional planning

Promotional planning mainly refers to the marketing communications of products, including advertising, public relations, direct marketing, and promotional activities. During the emergence of promotion, marketers must determine the use of information strategy, media strategy, and media transmission frequency. Information strategy concerns the types of product information for dissemination. Media strategy refers to the selection of the types of media and the means to reach target customer groups. Media transmission frequency pertains to how frequent enterprises spread product information.

12.2.4　Distribution channel planning

Products must pass through certain methods and routes before reaching consumers and users. Distribution is moving products from production sites to sales locations. In this process, enterprises should conduct a series of planned activities. The entry, penetration, and domination periods have their own features, resulting in varying planning strategies. In the distribution channel planning at the entry stage, enterprises select particular market segments, such as a regional market, as a breakthrough point. Selecting a specific distributor follows on the basis of further penetration to other regional markets. In the distribution channel planning at the penetration stage, enterprises will lose control over

市场渗透程度的加深,如果完全依赖中间商就无法控制其销售业务,因此建立自己的营销组织和分销网络就势在必行。

12.2.5　服务营销策划

由于科学技术的进步和社会生产力的显著提高,产业升级和生产的专业化发展日益加速。一方面使产品的服务含量,即产品的服务密集度日益增大;另一方面,随着劳动生产率的提高,市场转向买方市场,消费者随着收入水平提高,消费需求也逐渐发生变化,需求层次也相应提高,并向多样化方向拓展。在此基础上,服务也成了战术营销规划中的重要组成部分。

服务营销是一种通过关注顾客,进而提供服务,最终实现有利的交换的营销手段。实施服务营销首先必须明确服务对象,即"谁是顾客"。服务营销策划需要关注消费者在购买产品中的全过程,并在过程中的每个阶段提供相应的服务,注重消费者在购买过程中的感受,从而提高顾客满意度和建立顾客忠诚度。例如,高端酒店会为酒店会员提供针对性的服务和区别于一般顾客的礼遇,这实际上就是服务营销的一种表现。

12.3　营销绩效评估

营销绩效涉及多个方面,因此需要通过不同的绩效进行评估。市场营销的主要目标是通过发掘、维持并提高现有盈利顾客的价值,实现企业收入的增长(Kotler,1999)。根据此观点,营销绩效必须与发掘顾客(获取消费者)、维持顾客(保有消费者)和提高顾客价值(价值货币化)相关。因此,营销绩效可以分为三个维度:活动绩效、会计(运营)绩效和成果绩效。活动绩效包括顾客投诉量、销售、员工总数、顾客人数、订单数量、新增职位等可被计算的内部或外部项目。本节将详细介绍会计(运营)绩效及成果绩效。

12.3.1　会计(运营)绩效

一般而言,会计绩效有两种较为普遍的计算方式:一是投资回报率(ROI)和资产回报率(ROA);二是项目净现值(NPV)。

business sales if they rely entirely on the distributors with intensive market penetration. Enterprises should, thus, establish their own marketing organizations and distribution networks.

12.2.5 Service marketing planning

The professional development of industry upgrade and production is accelerating because of the advancement of technology and social productivity. On one hand, the service content of products, that is, the service provision intensifies. On the other hand, the markets shift to buyer markets along with the improvement of labor productivity. As the income level increases, the consumption demand gradually changes. The demand level increases and becomes more diversified. On this basis, service has become an imperative component of tactical marketing planning.

Service marketing is a marketing tool centering on customers and then providing services to them to achieve a favorable exchange. The implementation of service marketing must begin with determining the service target, that is, "who the customer is." Service marketing planning requires the attention to the entire consumption of customers and the provision of corresponding services at every stage of the process. Enterprises also need to pay attention to the feelings of customers to enhance customer satisfaction and build customer loyalty. For instance, high-end hotels provide hotel members with specific services that differ from services for general customer. The special services serve as a demonstration of service marketing.

12.3 Marketing Performance Evaluation

Marketing performance involves many aspects and, therefore, should be assessed through different performance evaluations. The primary goal of marketing is to achieve revenue growth by discovering, maintaining, and enhancing the value of existing profitable customers (Kotler, 1999). Based on this objective, marketing performance is related to the development of customer acquisition, customer retention, and monetization. Marketing performance can be divided into three dimensions, namely, activity, accounting-based (operational), and outcome metrics. Activity metrics are measurable internal or external projects including the amount of customer complaints, sales, total number of employees, number of customers, number of orders, and new positions. This section details the accounting-based (operational) and outcome metrics.

12.3.1 Accounting-based(operational) metrics

Accounting-based (operation) metrics can be calculated using two indicators, that is, return on investment (ROI) and return on assets (ROA), and net present value (NPV).

1. 投资回报率和资产回报率

投资回报率通常用于计算特定活动或项目在特定时间点所带来的收益，其公式为

$$投资回报率(\mathrm{ROI}\%) = \frac{税前净收入}{投资额} \times 100\%$$

资产回报率则是考虑整个企业利用资产获得收益的效率，其公式为

$$资产回报率(\mathrm{ROA}\%) = \frac{税前净收入}{资产总额} \times 100\%$$

投资回报率和资产回报率两个主要的缺陷是（Kotler 和 Keller，2009）：（1）资金成本并没有被考虑在内，企业需要根据投资资金成本设定一个标准；（2）投资回报率和资产回报率只关注营销计划在财务方面是否达成目标，但忽略了营销计划对于品牌的影响，而品牌影响的是企业未来的财务表现。

2. 项目净现值

净现值对项目的现金流进行评估，以确定项目未来所带来的现金流对企业的价值，其公式为

$$\sum_{t=0}^{n} \frac{C_t}{(1+i)^t}$$

其中：t 为现金流的时间段；n 为项目总时间；i 为折现率；C_t 为某个时间段的净现金流。

与投资回报率或资产回报率相比，净现值法体现了企业的资金成本（折现率）。在计算项目净现值的过程中，项目在未来所实现的现金流是企业未来财务表现的一部分，因而此方法也能计算营销计划对企业未来财务表现的影响。

12.3.2　成果绩效

营销组合分析是评估营销成果绩效的一种工具。通过分析不同来源的数据，营销组合分析能够更清晰地指出不同营销活动的效度（Tellis，2006）。除此之外，市场营销者可以利用多元分析明确不同的营销元素对营销成果的影响。

成果绩效可以从四个方面进行评估：股权价值、顾客终身价值、品牌资产和平衡计分卡。

1. 股权价值

企业的股权价值除了用于衡量股东的股权在公司或业务单位的价值，也

1. ROI and ROA

ROI is typically used to calculate the benefits of a particular activity or project at a particular point in time, and the formula is as follows:

$$\text{ROI}\% = \frac{\text{Net income before tax}}{\text{Investment}} \times 100\%$$

ROA considers the efficiency of the entire enterprise to use assets for obtaining benefits. The formula is as follows:

$$\text{ROA}\% = \frac{\text{Net income before tax}}{\text{Investment}} \times 100\%$$

ROI and ROA bear two shortcomings (Kotler & Keller, 2009). (1) The cost of capital is overlooked. Enterprises should set a standard based on the cost of investment capital.(2) ROI and ROA merely focus on whether the financial targets in the marketing plans have been reached. The effect of marketing plan on the brand has been discounted, although it affects the future financial performance of enterprises.

2. NPV

NPV assesses the cash flow of projects to confirm the cash flow brought by future projects on the value of enterprises. The formula is as follows:

$$\sum_{t=0}^{n} \frac{C_t}{(1+i)^t}$$

Where t = the time of cash flow, n = the total time of the project, i = the discount rate, C_t = the net cash flow for a period.

Compared to ROI and ROA, the method of NPV reflects the capital costs (discount rate) of the enterprises. In calculating NPV, the cash flow is realized by the future projects as a reflection of the future financial performance. This method, therefore, indicates the influence of marketing plan on the future financial performance of the enterprises.

12.3.2 Outcome Metrics

Marketing mix model is a tool for evaluating marketing outcomes. By analyzing the data from different sources, marketing mix analysis clearly indicates the effectiveness of the different marketing activities (Tellis, 2006). Marketers can also use multivariate analysis to determine the effect of various marketing elements on marketing outcomes.

The results of performance can be evaluated in four aspects, namely, equity value, customer lifetime value (CLV), brand equity, and balanced scorecard.

1. Equity value

The equity value of an enterprise can be used to evaluate marketing decisions in

可以用于评估市场营销决策(Cooper 和 Davies，2004)。股权价值从五个方面影响营销绩效(Lukas、Whitwell 和 Doyle，2005)。

(1) 营销决策对股权价值的影响促使管理层明确营销决策的目标；

(2) 采用股权价值对营销决策进行评估有利于将营销与企业内其他部门进行整合；

(3) 股权价值有利于证明营销资产(如品牌)的重要性；

(4) 采用股权价值对营销决策进行评估有利于防止企业为了实现利润最大化，而不合理地削减营销预算；

(5) 股权价值评估将营销放在了企业制定战略过程中的关键位置。

2. 顾客终身价值

顾客终身价值(CLV)是指企业通过合适的营销方法长期从顾客群体中实现盈利最大化(Gupta 等，2006)。实现顾客终身价值强调企业能够通过顾客关系管理，获取、保有并提高"正确"的顾客的价值(Venkatesan 和 Kumar，2004)。企业可以通过计算一位顾客在一段较长时期(一般为五年)内所带来的现金流的净现值，来确定某位顾客的终身价值是多少(Chenhall 和 Langfield-Smith，2007)，其公式为

$$\mathrm{CLV} = \sum_{t=0}^{T} \frac{(P_t - C_t)}{(1+i)^t} - \mathrm{AC}$$

其中：P_t 为顾客在 t 时间内所支付的价格；C_t 为在 t 时间内服务该顾客的直接成本；i 为折现率；t 为该顾客使用企业产品或服务的期望时间长度；AC 为获得该顾客的成本。

通过计算顾客终身价值，并对比不同类型的顾客、服务或产品，企业可以发掘能够给企业带来最大盈利的顾客群体，同时获得关于该顾客群体的相关信息，并将其进一步发展为顾客资产。顾客资产是指企业现有和未来顾客总共的终身价值(Gupta 和 Zeithaml，2006)。

3. 品牌资产

Kotler 和 Keller(2009)对品牌资产的定义为"品牌赋予产品或服务的额外价值"。这种额外价值能体现顾客在看到品牌时的想法、感受和行动。品牌资产主要体现在两个方面：一是财务上的产出；二是基于消费者对企业的认知。品牌的影响力依赖于消费者通过体验产品或服务，进而学习、思考、感受、观察和听取有关品牌的知识(Keller，2003)。

addition to the value of a shareholder's equity in a company or business unit (Cooper & Davies, 2004). Equity value affects marketing performance in five aspects (Lukas, Whitwell, & Doyle, 2005).

(1) The influence of marketing decisions on equity value drives the management to clarify the goals of marketing decision.

(2) Using equity value on assessing marketing decision making is conducive to the integration of marketing and other departments within enterprises.

(3) Equity value helps to justify the importance of marketing assets, such as brands.

(4) Using equity value in assessing marketing decision making prevents enterprises from unreasonably reducing marketing budgets to maximize profits.

(5) Equity valuation places marketing at the heart of the strategic planning of enterprises.

2. CLV

CLV is the maximization of profitability from customer groups in the long run through appropriate marketing methods (Gupta, et al., 2006). Achieving CLV emphasizes the ability of enterprises to manage, acquire, retain, and improve the value of the "right" customers via customer relationship management (Venkatesan & Kumar, 2004). Enterprises can determine CLV by calculating the NPV of cash flow brought by a customer over a long period (typically five years) (Chenhall & Langfield-Smith, 2007). The formula is as follows:

$$\text{CLV} = \sum_{t=0}^{T} \frac{(P_t - C_t)}{(1+i)^t} - \text{AC}$$

Where P_t = the price paid by the customer over a period (t), C_t = the direct cost of serving the customer over time (t), i = discount rate, t = the expected length of time the customer uses the enterprises' product or service, AC = acquisition cost.

By calculating CLV and comparing the different types of customers, services, or products, enterprises can identify the customer groups that yield the maximized profits and gain relevant information about the customer group. It can further develop into customer equity (CE), which is the total lifetime value of existing and future customers (Gupta & Zeithaml, 2006).

3. Brand equity

Kotler and Keller (2009) define brand equity as "the added value of a brand to products or services". This extra value reflects the customers' thoughts, feelings, and actions when they see the brand. Brand assets are reflected in two main aspects, namely, financial output and consumer perception of an enterprise. The influence of brand depends on how the consumers learn, think, feel, observe, and listen to the brand knowledge when experiencing a product or service (Keller, 2003).

The perception-based brand asset measurement is divided into direct and indirect

基于消费者认知的品牌资产测量一般分为直接法和间接法。直接法是以对比的方式体现品牌资产。营销研究人员设计一个实验,分为实验组和参照组。实验组内的消费者会看到与品牌相关的营销计划元素(如名字、标志、广告语等);参照组内的消费者会看到与实验组相同的元素,但消费者并不知道这些元素属于哪个品牌,或被告知这些元素是属于一个虚构的品牌。营销研究人员分别记录并比较两组消费者的反馈以鉴定品牌资产。盲测就是直接法的一种(H. Kim、W. Kim 和 An,2003)。间接法则是通过识别和追踪消费者的品牌知识结构,测量品牌资产潜在的来源。例如企业通过问卷调查,了解消费者的品牌回忆、熟悉程度、喜好的品牌形象和品牌信任评价等因素。

4. 平衡计分卡

平衡计分卡(如图 12-2 所示)是由 Robert Kaplan 和 David Norton 于 1992 年提出的。平衡计分卡是一个结合了财务和非财务的业绩考核的工具,能够帮助企业追踪营销活动是否符合其战略。

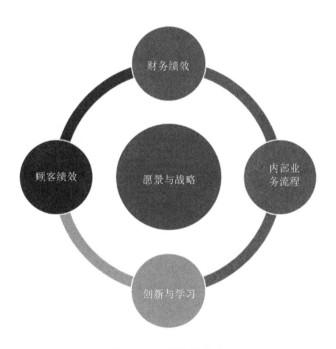

图 12-2　平衡计分卡

来源:Kaplan,R. S. & Norton,D. P. (1992). The balanced scorecard—Measures that drive performance. *Harvard Business Review*,70(1),70-79.

methods. Direct method reflects the brand equity through comparison. Marketing researchers design an experiment and divide participants into experimental and reference groups. Consumers in the experiment group see branding-related marketing plan elements (e.g., names, logos, and slogans); consumers in the reference group see the same elements as the experimental group. Consumers in the latter group, however, are unaware of the belongingness of these elements to particular brands or are told that these elements are of a fictional brand. Marketing researchers record and compare the feedback from the consumers in the two groups to identify brand equity. Blind test is one of the direct methods (Kim, Kim & An, 2003). The indirect method measures the potential source of the brand equity by identifying and tracking the brand knowledge structure of consumers. For example, enterprises understand the consumer brand recall, familiarity, preferable brand image, and trust toward a brand through questionnaires.

4. Balanced scorecard

This tool was introduced by Robert Kaplan and David Norton in 1992. Balanced scorecard (Figure 12 - 2) combines financial and non-financial performance measures to help companies to track the alignment of marketing campaigns and their marketing strategies.

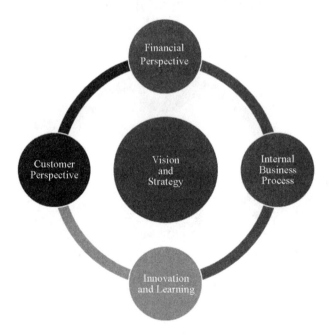

Figure 12 - 2　Balanced Scorecard

Source: Adapted from Kaplan, R. S. & Norton, D. P. (1992). The balanced scorecard—Measures that drive performance. *Harvard Business Review*, 70(1), 70 - 79.

通常而言,平衡计分卡主要测量四个方面的业绩(Voelpel、Leibold 和 Eckhoff,2006).

(1) 财务绩效:用于评估企业短期的财务表现,包括投资回报率(ROI)、现金流、资产回报率(ROA)等数据。

(2) 顾客绩效:用于评估目标市场的顾客满意度,包括送货满意度、顾客满意率和顾客保持率等数据。

(3) 内部业务流程:用于评估企业内部价值链,以及开发新产品或服务的流程的表现,包括机遇成功率、缺陷率等。

(4) 创新与学习:强调人力资源方面的影响和企业内学习支持系统的有效程度,包括病假率、内部提升比例、员工流失率等。

Balanced scorecard measures the four following aspects of performance（Voelpel, Leibold & Eckhoff，2006）.

（1）Financial perspective: The short-term financial performance of an organization, including ROI, cash flow, and ROA, is assessed.

（2）Customer perspective: Customer satisfaction in the target markets, including delivery satisfaction, customer satisfaction, and customer retention, is assessed.

（3）Internal business process: The internal value chain of enterprises is assessed along with the performance of new product and service development.

（4）Innovation and learning: The influence of human resources is emphasized along with the effectiveness of learning support systems within enterprises, including illness rate, internal promotions, and turnover.

参考文献
References

References of Chapter 1

AMA，2013. Definition of marketing. Retrieved Jan 17，2017，from https://www.ama.org/AboutAMA/Pages/Definition-of-Marketing.aspx.

Bartels R，1983. Is marketing defaulting its responsibilities? *Journal of Marketing*，47（4）:32－35.

Drucker P F，1974. *Management：Tasks，responsibilities，practices*（1st ed.）. New York：Harper & Row.

Gronroos C，1990. Relationship approach to marketing in service contexts：The marketing and organizational behavior interface. *Journal of Business Research*，20（1）:3－11.

Institute of Statistical Science，National Bureau of Statistics of the People's Republic of China，2014. 我国经济增长动力及其转换. Retrieved Apr 26，2016，from http://www.stats.gov.cn/tjzs/tjsj/tjcb/dysj/201412/t20141231_662243.html.

Kotler P，Bowen J T，Makens J C，2010. *Marketing for Hospitality and Tourism*（5th ed.）. Upper Saddle River，NJ：Pearson Prentice Hall.

Kotler P，Bowen J T，Makens J C，2014. *Marketing for Hospitality and Tourism*（6th ed.）. Upper Saddle River，NJ：Pearson Education.

Kotler P，Keller K L，2007. *A Framework for Marketing Management*（3th ed.）. Upper Saddle River，NJ：Prentice Hall.

Kotler P，Keller K L，2016. *Marketing Management*（15th ed.）. Boston：Pearson.

Ries A，Trout J，1972. The positioning era cometh. *Advertising Age*，24(4)：35－38.

STR，2016. About History. Retrieved Apr 26，2016，from http://www.str.com/about.

Webster F，Lusch R，2013. Elevating marketing：Marketing is dead! Long live marketing！. *Journal of the Academy of Marketing Science*，41（4）：389 – 399.

References of Chapter 2

Ansoff H I，1957. Strategies for diversification. *Harvard Business Review*，35（5）：113 – 124.

BTG，2016. 组织结构. Retrieved Apr 26，2016，from http://www.btg.com.cn/about/about.asp？tid＝8.

Butler Service，2016. 如何在丽江开精品客栈？看看"花间堂"怎么做. Retrieved Apr 26，2016，from http://mp.weixin.qq.com/s？ __biz＝MjM5Nzc5ODI5Mg

＝＝&mid＝200775503&idx＝4&sn＝2f006526a731816e735810e43e65f52e&scene＝2&from＝timeline&isappinstalled＝0♯wechat_redirect.

China Business Network，2016. 雅高与华住交叉持股完成交割. Retrieved Apr 29，2016，from http://m.yicai.com/news/4745223.html.

Crouch G，Ritchie J，1999. Tourism，competitiveness，and societal prosperity. *Journal of Business Research*，44（3）：137 – 152.

Diebold W，Scott B，Lodge G，1985. U.S. competitiveness in the world economy. *Foreign Affairs*，63（4）：916.

Enright M，Newton J，2004. Tourism destination competitiveness：a quantitative approach. *Tourism Management*，25（6）：777 – 788.

Gronroos C，1984. A service quality model and its marketing implications. *European Journal of Marketing*，18（4）：36 – 44.

Gruen T W，Osmonbekov T，Czaplewski A J，2006. eWOM：The impact of customer-to-customer online know-how exchange on customer value and loyalty. *Journal of Business Research*，59：449 – 456.

HHtravel，2016. 品牌理念. Retrieved Apr 26，2016，from http://pages.hhtravel.com/event/standard980w/standard_cn.html.

Hjalager A – M，2009. Innovations in travel medicine and the progress of tourism — Selected narratives. *Technovation*，29（9）：596 – 601.

Hotel Internal Reference. （2016）. 机器人酒店来袭,酒店人会失业?. Retrieved Apr 28，2016，from http://mp.weixin.qq.com/s？ __biz＝MzA5NDM5NDcwMQ

＝＝&mid＝402148195&idx＝1&sn＝e26d45e1d1659948e5d13a64ce94a1d5&scene＝5&srcid＝0427zQGdl3TRdYSDTyOiQgcE♯rd.

Hsu C H C，2009. 旅游营销.北京:中国人民大学出版社.

Hurun Report,2015. 中国奢华旅游白皮书. Retrieved Apr 27，2016，from http：//183.91.33.14/cache/up.hurun.net/Hufiles/201506/20150617153558265.pdf？ich_args = e90292e67bd2fdf6c9e32fbac81a2adc _ 1 _ 0 _ 0 _ 10 _ 8d7cf57c05d87d6c6a1c04ca37786f99c46ea405c5307e2d429158fe59371094 613cf31258d213ec1665ea7f9e9cfc8e_1_0&ich_ip＝33－6.

Ji M，Li M，King B，2016. Incremental effects of the Shanghai Free-trade Zone — An internet informed assessment of hong kong's tourism competitiveness. *Journal of China Tourism Research*. doi：10.1080/19388160.2015.1137851.

Kotler P，Bowen J T，Makens J C，2010. *Marketing for Hospitality and Tourism* (5th ed.). Upper Saddle River，NJ：Pearson Prentice Hall.

Kotler P，Jain D C，Maesincee S，2002. *Marketing Moves ：A New Approach to Profits，Growth，and Renewal*. Boston，Mass：Harvard Business School Press.

Kotler P，Keller K，Brady M，2009. *Marketing Management* (13th ed.). Upper Saddle River，NJ：Pearson Prentice Hall

Porter M E，1985. *Competitive Advantage ：Creating and Sustaining Superior Performance*. New York；London：Free Press ；Collier Macmillan.

Porter M E，1990. *The competitive advantage of nations*. New York：Free Press.

Prahalad C K，Hamel G，1990. The core competence of the corporation. *Harvard Business Review*，May-Jun：79－91.

World Economic Forum，2015. *The Travel & Tourism Competitiveness Report 2015*. World Economic Forum 2015.

References of Chapter 3

Choi H J，Kim Y，2012. Work-family conflict，work-family facilitation，and job outcomes in the Korean hotel industry. *International Journal of Contemporary Hospitality Management*，24(7)：1011－1028.

Fielding M，2006. Global insights：Synovate's Chedore discusses MR trends. *Marketing News*，15 May：41－42.

Han X J，2002. *A Study on Outsourcing in Shanghai Hotel Industry*. (M. Sc.)，The Hong Kong Polytechnic University. (b16431248)

Hsu C H C，2009. 旅游营销.北京：中国人民大学出版社.

Kotler P，Keller K，Brady M，2009. *Marketing Management* (13 ed.). Upper Saddle River，NJ：Pearson Prentice Hall

Kotler P，Keller K L，2007. *A Framework for Marketing Management*（3th ed.）. Upper Saddle River，NJ：Prentice Hall.

Li X，Harrill R，Uysal M，et al.，2010. Estimating the size of the Chinese outbound travel market：A demand-side approach. *Tourism Management*，31(2)：250 - 259.

Little C J D C，1979. Decision support systems for marketing managers. *Journal of Marketing*，Summer：11.

Mattila A S，2004. The impact of service failures on customer loyalty：The moderating role of affective commitment. *International Journal of Service Industry Management*，15(2)：134 - 149.

McManus J，2004. Stumbling into intelligence. *American Demographics*，April：22 - 26.

Tellis G J，2004. Modeling marketing mix. In Grover R，Vriens M（Eds.）. *Handbook of Marketing Research*. Thousand Oaks，CA：Sage.

Tischler L，2004. Every move you make. *Fast Company*，April：73 - 77.

References of Chapter 4

Benson M，2011. *The British in rural France：Lifestyle migration and the ongoing quest for a better way of life*. Manchester：Manchester University Press.

Benson M，O'Reilly K，2009）*Lifestyle migration：Expectations，aspirations and experiences*. Aldershot：Ashgate.

Berelson B，Steiner G A，1964. *Human Behavior：An Inventory of Scientific Findings*. New York：Harcourt Brace Jovanovich.

Britton S，1991. Tourism，capital and place：Towards a critical geography of tourism. *Society and Space*，9(4)：451 - 478.

Correia A，Kozak M，2012. Exploring prestige and status on domestic destinations：The case of Algarve. *Annals of Tourism Research*，39(4)：1951 - 1967

Chinese Culture Connection，1987. Chinese values and the search for culture-free dimensions of culture. *Journal of Cross-cultural Psychology*，18(2)：143 - 164.

Dann G M S，1977. Anomie，ego-enhancement and tourism. *Annals of Tourism Research*，4(4)：184 - 194.

Dann G M S，1981. Tourist motivation an appraisal. *Annals of Tourism Research*，8(2)：187 - 219.

Fan Y，2000. A classification of Chinese culture. *Cross Cultural Management：An International Journal*，7(2)：3 - 10.

Freud S，1899. *Die Traumdeutung*. Leipzig und Wien：Franz Deuticke.

Hall C M，Müller D，2004. *Tourism，Mobility，and Second Homes：Between Elite Landscape and Common Ground*. Clevedon：Cromwell Press.

Herzberg F. 1966. *Work and the Nature of Man*. Cleveland，OH：William Collins.

Hiltunen M J，2007. Environmental impacts of rural second home tourism：Case Lake district in Finland. *Scandinavian Journal of Hospitality and Tourism*，7(3)：243 - 265.

Howard D R，Madrigal R，1990. Who makes the decision：The parent or child? The perceived influence of parents or children on the purchase of recreation services. *Journal of Leisure Research*，22(3)：244 - 258.

Hsu C H C，2009. 旅游营销.北京：中国人民大学出版社.

Hsu C H C，Kang S K，Lam T，2006. Reference group influences among Chinese travelers. *Journal of Travel Research*，44：474 - 484.

Hsu C H C，Huang SS，2016. Reconfiguring Chinese cultural values and their tourism implications. *Tourism Management*，54：230 - 242.

Iso-Ahola S E，1982. Toward a social psychological theory of tourism motivation：A rejoinder. *Annals of Tourism Research*，9(2)：256 - 262.

Jamal T，Lee J H，2003. Integrating micro and macro approaches to tourist motivations：Toward an interdisciplinary theory. *Tourism Analysis*，8：47 - 59.

Jauhari V，2013. Building employability in hospitality industry；Insights from IIMT Gurgaon—Oxford Brookes University collaborative effort. *Worldwide Hospitality and Tourism Themes*，5(3)：268 - 276.

Kim J-H，Ritchie J R B，McCormick B，2012. Development of a scale to measure memorable tourism experiences. *Journal of Travel Research*，51(1)：12 - 25.

Kotler P，Keller K，Brady M，2009. *Marketing Management*（13th ed.）. Upper Saddle River，NJ：Pearson Prentice Hall

Li M，Cai L，2012. The effects of values on travel motivation and behavioral intention. *Journal of Travel Research*，51(4)：473 - 487.

Li M，Zhang H，Cai L，2016. A sub-cultural analysis of tourism motivations. *Journal of Hospitality and Tourism Research*，40(1)：85 - 113.

Maslow A H，1943. A theory of human motivation. *Psychological Review*，50(4)：370 - 396.

MaslowA H，1954. *Motivation and Personality*. New York：Harper and Row.

McWatters M R，2009. *Residential tourism：（De）Constructing paradise*. Bristol：

Channel View Publications.

Mottiar Z, Quinn D, 2004. Couple dynamics in household tourism decision making: Women as the gatekeepers? *Journal of Vacation Marketing*, 10(2): 149 – 160.

O'Reilly K, 2007. Intra-European migration and the mobility-enclosure dialectic. *Sociology*, 41(2): 277 – 293.

Palan K M, Wilkes R E, 1997. Adolescent – parent interaction in family decision making. *Journal of Consumer Research*, 24: 159 – 169.

Pappas N, 2014. The effect of distance, expenditure and culture on the expression of social status through tourism. *Tourism Planning & Development*, 6 (February): 1 – 18

Pearce P, Caltabiano M, 1983. Inferring travel motivation from travelers' experiences. *Journal of Travel Research*, 22(2): 16.

Pearce P, Kim U, 2005. Developing the travel career approach to tourist motivation. *Journal of Travel Research*, 43(3): 226 – 237.

Peter J P, Olson J C, 1996. *Consumer Behaviour and Marketing Strategy* (4th ed.). Chicago: Irwin.

Rojek C, 1995. *Decentring Leisure: Rethinking Leisure Theory*. London: Sage.

Rokeach M, 1968. The role of values in public opinion research. *The Public Opinion Quarterly*, 32(4): 547 – 559.

Rokeach M, 1971. Long-range experimental modification of values, attitudes, and behavior. *American Psychologist*, 26(5): 453 – 459.

Russo J E, Meloy M G, Medvec V H, 1998. The distortion of product information during brand choice. *Journal of Marketing Research*, 35(November): 438 – 452.

Ryan C, Glendon I, 1998. Application of leisure motivation scale to tourism. *Annals of Tourism Research*, 25(1): 169 – 184.

Sato M, 2001. *Farewell to Nippon: Japanese lifestyle migrants in Australia*. Melbourne: Trans Pacific Press.

Schiffman L G, Kanuk L L, 2004. *Consumer Behavior* (8th ed.). Upper Saddle River, NJ: Pearson Prentice Hall.

Simonson I, Carmon Z, Dhar R, et al., 2001. Consumer research: In search of identity. *Annual Review of Psychology*, 52: 249 – 275.

Sirgy M J, 1982. Self concept in consumer behavior: A critical review. *Journal of Consumer Research*, 9(December): 298 – 300.

Tomas M, 2006. Inquiring into residential tourism: The Costa Blanca case.

Tourism & Hospitality Planning and Development，3(2)：89 - 97.

Wang N，2000. *Tourism and Modernity：A Sociological Analysis*. Oxford：Pergamon.

Watson G，Kopachevsky J，1994. Interpretation of tourism as commodity. *Annals of Tourism Research*，21(3)：643 - 660.

Wyer Jr R S，Srull T K，1989. Person memory and judgment. *Psychological Review*，96：58 - 83.

Zheng W，2015. "私人订制"的中老年旅游产品或能成为新增长点. Retrieved May 11，2016，from http://biz.zjol.com.cn/system/2015/10/19/020877292.shtml.

References of Chapter 5

Bunn M D，1993. Taxonomy of buying decision approaches. *Journal of Marketing*，57(January)：38 - 56.

Buvik A，John G，2000. When does vertical coordination improve industrial purchasing relationships? *Journal of Marketing*，64(October)：52 - 64.

Cannon J P，Perreault Jr W D，1999. Buyer-seller relationships in business markets. *Journal of Marketing，Research*，36(November)：439 - 460.

Donath B，2005. Customer knowledge takes priority in study. *Marketing News*，15 (December)：7.

Dyer J H，1997. Effective interfirm collaboration：how firms minimize transaction costs and maximize transaction value. *Strategic Management Journal*，18 (5)：535 - 556.

Elston K，Draper J，2012. A review of meeting planner site selection criteria research. *Journal of Convention & Event Tourism*，13：203 - 220.

Giddens A，1990. *The Consequences of Modernity*. Stanford，CA：Stanford University Press.

Jarillo J C，1988. On strategic networks. *Strategic Management Journal*，9：31 - 41.

Kotler P，Keller K，Brady M，2009. *Marketing Management* (13th ed.). Upper Saddle River，NJ：Pearson Prentice Hall

LeFlanchec A，2004. How to reduce uncertainty in a context of innovation：the case of IBM's negotiation of its European Works Council. *International Negotiation*，9(2)：271 - 289.

Lundgren A，1993. Technological innovation and the emergence and evolution of industrial networks: The case of digital image technology in Sweden. *Advances in International Marketing*, 5: 145 – 170.

Mair J, 2015. Incentive travel: A theoretical perspective. *Event Management*, 19 (4): 543 – 552.

Narayandas D, Rangan V K, 2004. Building and sustaining buyer – seller relationships in mature industrial markets. *Journal of Marketing*, 68(July): 63 – 77.

Ozanne U B, Churchill Jr G A, 1971. Five dimensions of the industrial adoption process. *Journal of Marketing Research*, August: 322 – 328.

Pinchain Travel, 2016. 中国商旅市场总量 2015 年超过 1 万 5 千亿元人民币. retrieved from http://mp.weixin.qq.com/s/X0QZ_TcNjl15s0IWoZSdzWw.

Rinehart L M, Eckert J A, Handfield R B, et al., 2004. An assessment of buyer – seller relationships. *Journal of Business Logistics*, 25(1): 25 – 62.

Ritter T, 1999. The networking company: antecedents for coping with relationships and networks effectively. *Industrial Marketing Management*, 28(5): 467 – 479.

Robinson P J, Faris C W, Wind Y, 1967. *Industrial Buying and Creative Marketing*. Boston, MA: Allyn & Bacon.

Rogers T, 2013. *Conferences and Conventions—A Global Industry*. Abingdon, Oxon: Routledge.

Rokkan A I, Heide J B, Wathne K W, 2003. Specific investment in marketing relationships: expropriation and bonding effects. *Journal of Marketing Research*, 40 (May): 210 – 224.

Sanders K, 2011. The true value of the United States meeting and events industry. retrieved May 9, 2014, from http://planyourmeetings.com/2011/03/25/the-true
-valueof-the-u-s-meetings-and-events-industry/.

Society of Incentive Travel Executives, 2014. Purchasing Motivational Travel-Revisited (May 2014). retrived from http://www.siteglobal.com/page/research.

Todd P M, Gigerenzer G, 2003. Bounded rationality to the world. *Journal of Economic Psychology*, 24(2), 143 – 165.

Trottman M, 2003. First class at coach prices. *Wall Street Journal*, 17 (December): D1.

Ward S, WebsterJr F E, 1991. Organizational buying behavior. In Robertson T, Kassarjian H, (Eds). *Handbook of Consumer Behavior*. Upper Saddle River, NJ: Prentice Hall.

WebsterJr F E，Wind Y，1972. *Organizational Buying Behavior*. Upper Saddle River，NJ：Prentice Hall.

References of Chapter 6

Anderson J C，Narus J A，1995. Capturing the value of supplementary service. *Harvard Business Review*，(January-February)：75 – 83.

Best R J，2005. *Market-based Management* (4th ed.). Upper Saddle River，NJ：Prentice Hall.

Blattberg R，Deighton J，1991. Interactive marketing：Exploiting the age of addressability. *Sloan Management Review*，33(1)：5 – 14.

Bonoma T V，Shapiro B P，1983. *Segmenting the Industrial Market*. Lexington MA：Lexington Books.

Brown G H，1953. Brand loyalty：fact or fiction? *Advertising Age*，(June 1952 – January 1953)：a series.

Cai L，Li M，2009. Distance-segmented rural tourists. *Journal of Travel & Tourism Marketing*，26(8)：751 – 761.

Cao S X，Lai J F，Qiu B X，2006.国际观光旅馆市场区隔之研究:服务认知价值变数.餐旅及家政学刊,3(3):309 – 328.

Cunningham J，Roberts P，2006. What woman want. *Brand Strategy*，(December – January)：40 – 41.

Kotler P，Keller K，Brady M，2009. *Marketing Management* (13th ed.). Upper Saddle River，NJ：Pearson Prentice Hall

Leiper N，1979. The framework of tourism. *Annals of Tourism Research*，6(4)：390 – 407.

National Tourism Administration，2016. 四川：以乡村旅游持续助力精准扶贫. retrieved May 16，2016，from http://www.cnta.gov.cn/ztwz/lyfp/zyhd/201603/t20160311_763147.shtml

Peppers D，Rogers M，2001. *One to One B2B：Customer Development Strategies for the Business-to-Business World*. New York：Doubleday.

SBI International，2015. The proven segmentation system. retrieved Dec 20，2016，from http://www.strategicbusinessinsights.com/vals/ustypes.shtml.

Sleight P，2004. *Targeting Customers：How to Use Geodemographics：Lifestyle Data in Your Business* (3th ed.). Henley-on-Thames，England：WARC (World

Advertising Research Centre).

van Hoffman C, 2006. For some marketers, low income is hot. *Brandweek*, 11 (September): 6.

White G L, Leung S, 2002. Middle market shrinks as americans migrate toward the higher end. *Wall Street Journal*, 29 (March): A1, A8.

Wu Y, 2005. 关于中国消费者分群范式的研究. 南开管理评论, 8(2):9-15.

References of Chapter 7

Aaker D A, 1991. *Managing Brand Equity*. New York: Free Press.

Bagley C E, 2005. *Managers and the Legal Environment: Strategies for the 21st Century* (3th ed.). Cincinnati, OH: Southwestern College/West Publishing.

Coop W, 2005. A question of identity. *MFSA Journal of Marketing*, 11(1):36-37.

DeChernatony L, Drury S, Segal-Horn S, 2003. Building a services brand: Stages, people and orientations. *The Service Industries Journal*, 23(3): 1-21.

DeChernatony L, Segal-Horn S, 2001. Building on services' characteristics to develop successful services brands. *Journal of Marketing Management*, 17(7-8): 645-669.

Erdem T, 1998a. Brand equity as a signaling phenomenon. *Journal of Consumer Psychology*, 7(2): 131-157.

Erdem T, 1998b. An empirical analysis of umbrella branding. *Journal of Marketing Research*, 35(3): 339-351.

Heskett J L, Sasser Jr W E, Hart C W L, 1990. Service breakthroughs: Changing the rules of the game. *Human Resource Management*, 33(1): 169-172.

Hong Kong Tourism Board, 2015. Annual Report 2014/2015, retrieved on 30th December, 2016 from http://www.discoverhongkong.com/china/about

-hktb/annual-report/annual-report-20142015/strategic-focus/marketing

-initatives/.

Hong Kong Tourism Board, 2016. Our Brand. retrieved from http://www.discoverhongkong.com/eng/about-hktb/our-brand.jsp.

Hsu C H C, Oh H, Assaf A G, 2012. A customer-based brand equity model for upscale hotels. *Journal of Travel Research*, 51(1): 81-93.

Interbrand, 2016. Brand Definition. retrieved from http://interbrand.com/services/brand-definition/.

Keller K L, 2000. The brand report card. *Harvard Business Review*, (January -

February)：147 - 157.

Keller K L，Lehmann D，2006. Brand and branding：Research findings and future priorities. *Marketing Science*，25(6)：740 - 759.

Klein N，2000. *No Logo：Taking Aim at the Brand Bullies*. New York：Picador.

Kotler P，Keller K，Brady M，2009. *Marketing Management* (13th ed.). Upper Saddle River，NJ：Pearson Prentice Hall

Li T Y，2007. 旅游目的地定位研究中的几个理论问题. 旅游科学，21(4)：1 - 7.

Morrison S，Crane F G，2007. Building the service brand by creating and managing an emotional brand experience. *Journal of Brand Management*，14(5)：410 - 422.

Ryan R，2015. Tourism Australia launches "GIGA Selfie"，the world's biggest selfie for Japanese tourists. retrieved Mar 27，2016，from http://www.news.com.au/travel/tourism-australia-launches-giga-selfie-the-worlds-biggest-selfie-for-japanese-tourists/news-story/88043b298d4a1cf673b3a422777b016f

Suri R，Monroe K B，2003. The effects of time pressure on consumers' judgments of prices and products. *Journal of Consumer Research*，30(1)：92 - 104.

VonKunde J，Cunningham B J，2002. *Corporate Religion*. Harlow，England：Financial Times Prentice Hall.

Wong T，Wickham M，2015. An examination of Marriott's entry into the Chinese hospitality industry：A Brand Equity perspective. *Tourism Management*，48：439 - 454.

Zhang Y，2003. 旅游目的地品牌化及其品牌杠杆力探析. 重庆师范大学学报(自然科学版)，20(4)：76 - 78.

References of Chapter 8

Butler R W，1980. The concept of a tourist area life cycle of evolution：Implications for management of resources. *The Canadian Geographer*，24(1)：5 - 12.

Day G S，Shocker A D，Srivastava R K，1979. Identifying competitive product markets：A review of customer-oriented approaches. *Journal of Marketing*，43(Fall)：8 - 19.

Dong E，Morais D B，Dowler L，2003. *Ethnic tourism development in Yunnan，China：Revisiting Butler's Tourist Area Lifecycle*. Paper presented at the Northeastern Recreation Research Symposium，Bolton Landing，NY.

Harrigan K R，1980. The effect of exit barriers upon strategic flexibility. *Strategic Management Journal*，1：165 - 176.

Harrison D，1995. Development of tourism in Swaziland. *Annals of Tourism*

Research，22(1)：135 – 156.

Host W J，2004. The changing face of package travel. in Dickinson B，Vladimir A (Eds.). *The Complete 21ˢᵗ Century Travel & Hospitality Marketing Handbook*. Upper Saddle River，NJ：Pearson Prentice Hall.

iResearch，2015. 2015 年中国在线旅游度假行业研究报告. retrieved Oct 29，2016，from http://www.iresearch.com.cn/report/2318.html.

Kotler P，1965. Phasing out weak products. *Harvard Business Review*，(March-April)：107 – 118.

Kotler P，Armstrong G，Brown L，et al.，1998. *Marketing*. Sydney：Prentice Hall.

Kotler P，Keller K，Brady M，2009. *Marketing Management* (13th ed.). Upper Saddle River，NJ：Pearson Prentice Hall.

Kotler P，Keller K L，2012. *Marketing Management* (14th ed.). Upper Saddle River，NJ：Prentice Hall.

McKercher B，2016. Towards a taxonomy of tourism products. *Tourism Management*，54：196 – 208.

Middleton V T C，Clarke J，2001. *Marketing in Travel and Tourism* (3th ed.). Oxford；Boston：Butterworth-Heinemann.

The United Nations World Tourism Organization，2008. UNWTO Annual Report 2007. reetrieved from http://media.unwto.org/publications.

Urban G L，Hauser J R，1993. *Design and marketing of new products* (2th ed.). Upper Saddle River，NJ：Prentice Hall.

Vernon R，1966. International investment and international trade in the product cycle. *The Quarterly Journal of Economics*，80(2)：190 – 207.

References of Chapter 9

Adhikaria A，Basu A，Raj S P，2013. Pricing of experience products under consumer heterogeneity. *International Journal of Hospitality Management*，33：6 – 18.

Ailawadi K L，Lehmann D R，Neslin S A，2001. Market response to a major policy change in the marketing mix：Learning from Procter & Gamble's value pricing strategy. *Journal of Marketing*，65(1)：44 – 61.

Anderson E T，Simester D，2003. Effects of $ 19 price endings on retail sales：evidence from field experiments. *Quantitative Marketing and Economics*，1(1)：93 – 110.

Chen B C，2003. 浅论旅游产品定价策略. 价格理论与实践，(4)：49 – 50.

Cui Z J，2004. 需求价格弹性分析. 经济与管理，(11)：84 - 86.

Guo X，Ling L，Dong Y，Liang L，2013. Cooperation contract in tourism supply chains：The optimal pricing strategy of hotels for cooperative third party strategic websites. *Annals of Tourism Research*，41：20 - 41.

Guo X，Ling L，Yang C，Li Z，et al.，2013. Optimal pricing strategy based on market segmentation for service products using online reservation systems：An application to hotel rooms. *International Journal of Hospitality Management*，35：274 - 281.

Howard D J，Kerin R A，2006. Broadening the scope of reference-price advertising research：a field study of consumer shopping involvement. *Journal of Marketing*，70(October)：185 - 204.

Kimes S E，1989. Yield management：A tool for capacity-considered service firms. *Journal of Operations Management*，8(4)：348 - 368.

Kotler P，Keller K，Brady M，2009. *Marketing Management*（13th ed.）. Upper Saddle River，NJ：Pearson Prentice Hall.

Liao S C，2002. 浅议旅游产品的整合定价. 渝西学院学报：自然科学版，1(3)：74 - 77.

Ling L，Guo X，Yang C，2014. Opening the online marketplace：An examination of hotel pricing and travel agency on-line distribution of rooms. *Tourism Management*，45：234 - 243

Noone B M，McGuire K A，2013. Pricing in a social world：The influence of non-price information on hotel choice. *Journal of Revenue and Pricing Management*，12(5)：385 - 401

Ofir C，Winer R S，2002. Pricing：economic and behavioral models. in Weitz B，Wensley R（Eds.）. *Handbook of Marketing*. London：Sage.

Silverstein M，Fiske N，2003a. Luxury for the masses. *Harvard Business Review*，81(4)：48 - 57.

Silverstein M，Fiske N，2003b. *Trading Up：The New American Luxury*. New York：Portfolio.

Sivy M，1991. Japan's smart secret weapon. *Fortune*，12(August)：75.

Dai B，2007. 当前饭店产业环境与政府管制体系的调整. retrieve from http://ihfo. com/news_view.asp? id＝633.

Veblen T，1899. *The Theory of the Leisure Class*. Boston：Houghton Mifflin.

Wang X X，2001. 价格敏感商品浅析. 上海商业，2001(5)：59 - 60.

Winer R S，1988. Behavioral perspectives on pricing：buyers' subjective perceptions of price revisited. in Devinney T（Ed.）. *Issues in Pricing*：*Theory and Research*. Lexington，MA：Lexington Books.

Yang Y，Mueller N J，Croes R R，2016. Market accessibility and hotel prices in the Caribbean：The moderating effect of quality-signaling factors. *Tourism Management*，56：40 - 51.

Zhang Y，2007. 酒店业的品牌创新必须融入人文关怀. 上海商业，(9)：78 - 80.

References of Chapter 10

Alon I，Ni L，Wang Y，2012. Examining the determinants of hotel chain expansion through international franchising. *International Journal of Hospitality Management*，31(2)：379 - 386.

CroweHorwath International，2015. *Hotel yearbook* 2014：*China*. Fuzhou，China.

Combs J G，Ketchen D J，Hoover V L，2004. A strategic groups approach to the franchising-performance relationship. *Journal of Business Venturing*，19(6)：877 - 897.

Gu H，1998. CRS and the marketing of Chinese hotels，*Tourism Tribune*，5：23 - 26.

Hotels，2015. Hotels 325 Rank. retrieved June 21，2016，from http://www. marketingandtechnology. com/repository/webFeatures/HOTELS/h1507 _ Special _ Report.pdf.

Jiang L N，Zhang S F，2007. Scenic area water district tourism resources development's innovation research，*Special Zone Economy*，10：186 - 188.

Kotler P，Keller K，Brady M，2009）*Marketing Management*（13th ed.）. Upper Saddle River，NJ：Pearson Prentice Hall

Li J，Gao H，2006. Application of Franchising Model in the development of hotel group. *Journal of Shaoyang Teachers College*，5(5)：41 - 44.

O'Neill J W，Dev C S，Yanagisawa H，2013. Hotel assets：An analysis of brand attributes，franchise fees，hotel age and performance. *International Journal of Built Environment and Asset Management*，1(2)：139 - 164.

Pan Y，2004. A study of monopoly of tourist route. *Social Scientist*，1：96 - 97.

Thakran K，Verma R，2013. The emergence of hybrid online distribution channels in travel，tourism and hospitality. *Cornell Hospitality Quarterly*，54(3)：240 - 247

Tnooz，2014. Navigating the online travel landscape — a guide for startups. retrieved at Oct 10，2016，from https://www.tnooz.com/article/online-travel/.

Wang D G，Sun W Z，Cheng B G，2007. An analysis of the application of franchising to Chinese hotel industry. *Commercial Research*，2：186 – 189.

Xu J，2002. Franchise — a fresh Idea for the development of the travel service industry. *Journal of Guilin Institute of Tourism*，13(2)：49 – 53.

Yin W，1998. The new marketing channels of hotels：Global distribution system. *China Computer & Communication*，5：19 – 21.

Zheng Y，Liu W，2004. A comparative study on the development of sales channels of Chinese and Western travel agencies. *Economy and Management*，5：63 – 65.

References of Chapter 11

Batra R，Keller K L，2016. Integrating marketing communications：New findings，new lessons，and new ideas. *Journal of Marketing*，80：122 – 145.

Bennett P D，1995. *Dictionary of Marketing*. Chicago：American Marketing Association.

Cai X，2016. Revenue of China mobile advertising：Big but not big enough. retrieved June 28，2016 from http://datanews.caixin.com/2016 – 06 – 27/100959180.html.

CroweHorwath International，2015. *Hotel Yearbook* 2014：*China*. Fuzhou，China.

Guo X，Zheng X，Ling L，et al.，2014.Online cooperation between hotels and online travel agencies：From the perspective of cash back after stay. *Tourism Management Perspectives*，12：104 – 122.

Hon L C，Grunig J E，1999.Guidelines for Measuring Relationships in Public Relations. reetrieved May 19，2016，from http://www.instituteforpr.org/wp
-content/uploads/Guidelines_Measuring_Relationships.pdf.

Hsu C，2009) *Tourism Marketing*. Beijing：China Renmin University Press.

Kelman H C，Hovland C I，1953. Reinstatement of the communication in delayed measurement of opinion change. *Journal of Abnormal and Social Psychology*，48：327 – 335.

Kotler P，Armstrong G，2016. *Principles of Marketing*（16th ed.）. Boston：Pearson Education Limited.

Kotler P，Keller K L，2009.*Marketing Management*（13th ed.）. Upper Saddle River，NJ：Pearson Prentice Hall

Luo X，Donthu N，2006. Marketing's credibility：A longtitudinal investigation of marketing communication productivity and shareholder value. *Journal of Marketing*，

70：70 – 91.

Neuborne E，2004. Ads that actually sell stuff. *Business* 2.0，（June）：78.

Nike，2013. Nike＋ Coach Feature Motivates Runners with Customized Training Plans. retrieved June 26，2016，from http://news.nike.com/news/nike-coach-feature-motivates-runners-with-customized-training-plans.

Orange Travel，2015. Interpretation：Discovery of the innovation trilogy of Los Angeles destination marketing. retrieved November 29，2016，from http://www.pinchain.com/article/24247.

Orange Travel，2016. Investigation：Only smart phones cannot live up to. retrieved June 12，2016，from http://mp. weixin. qq. com/s? ＿ ＿ biz ＝ MzA3MDEzOTMwMw ＝ ＝ &mid ＝ 2658721899&idx ＝ 6&sn ＝ daa1358e7d787f7b9686e2349e99e9d4&scene＝1&srcid＝0617hSIEyh95z2woG4UZgDcC ＃wechat_redirect.

Pan B，2015. The power of search engine ranking for tourist destinations. *Tourism Management*，47：79 – 87.

Reeves R，1961.*Reality in Advertising*. New York：Knopf 1990.

Rossiter J R，Percy L，1997. *Advertising and Promotion Management*（2th ed.）. New York：McGraw-Hill.

Šerić M，Gil-Saura I，Ruiz-Molina M E，2014. How can integrated marketing communications and advanced technology influence the creation of customer-based brand equity? Evidence from the hospitality industry. *International Journal of Hospitality Management*，39：144 – 156.

Search Engine Land，（2007. The state of search engine marketing. retrieved Oct 16，2016，from http://searchengineland. com/the-state-of-search-engine-marketing-2006 – 10474.

Schultz D E，Schultz H，2003. *IMC，The Next Generation：Five Steps for Delivergin Value and Measuring Financial Returns*. New York：McGraw-Hill.

Tesla，2016. About Tesla. retrieved May 18，2016，from https://www.tesla.cn/about.

Xu Q，2001. A preliminary study on the development strategy of new Mongolian medicine market. *Scientific China*，2：38 – 39.

Yuan G F，2004. Brand mergers and acquisition，flowers or traps? Reflections on L'Oreal acquisition of Mininurse. *Brand Truth*，31：32 – 35.

Zeng C Z, 2005. Brand diagnostic workshop — Zeng Zhaohui answer: SME brand and financing. *China Quality and Brand*, 1: 34 – 37.

References of Chapter 12

Chenhall R H, Langfield-Smith K, 2007. Multiple perspectives of performance measures. *European Management Journal*, 25(4): 266 – 282.

Cooper S, Davies M, 2004. Measuring shareholder value: The metrics maximising shareholder value achieving clarity in Decision-making. *CIMA Technical Report*, London: The Chartered Institute of Management Accountants.

Gupta S, Hanssens D, Hardie B, et al., 2006. Modeling customer lifetime value. *Journal of Service Research*, 19(2): 139 – 155.

Gupta S, Zeithaml V, 2006. Customer metrics and their impact on financial performance. *Marketing Science*, 25(6): 718 – 739.

Kaplan R S, Norton D P, 1992. The balanced scorecard — measures that drive performance. *Harvard Business Review*, 70(1):70 – 79.

Keller K L, 2003. *Strategic Brand Management: Building, Measuring and Managing Brand Equity* (2th ed.). Englewood Cliffs, NJ: Prentice-Hall.

Kim H-b, Kim W G, An J A, 2003. The effect of consumer-based brand equity on firms' financial performance. *Journal of Consumer Marketing*, 20(4): 335 – 351.

Kotler P, 1999. *Kotler on Marketing: How to Create, Win, and Dominate Markets*. New York: Free Press.

Kotler P, Keller K, Brady M, 2009) *Marketing Management* (13th ed.). Upper Saddle River, NJ: Pearson Prentice Hall

Lukas B A, Whitwell G J, Doyle P, 2005. How can a shareholder value approach improve marketing's strategic influence? *Journal of Business Research*, 58(4): 414 – 422.

McCarthy E J, 1975. *Basic Marketing : A Managerial Approach* (5th ed). Homewood, Ill : R. D. Irwin.

Tellis G J, 2006. Modeling marketing mix. in Grover R, Vriens M (Eds.). *Handbook of Marketing Research*. Thousand Oaks, CA: Sage.

Venkatesan R, Kumar V, 2004. A customer lifetime value framework for customer selection and resource allocation strategy. *Journal of Marketing*, 68: 106 – 125.

Voelpel S C, Leibold M, Eckhoff R A, 2006. The tyranny of the balanced scorecard in the innovation economy. *Journal of Intellectual Capital*, 7(1): 43 – 60.